Proceedings of COOP 2010

Myriam Lewkowicz • Parina Hassanaly
Markus Rohde • Volker Wulf
Editors

Proceedings of COOP 2010

Proceedings of the 9th International
Conference on Designing Cooperative
Systems, May, 18–21, 2010, Aix-en-Provence

 Springer

Editors

Myriam Lewkowicz
Troyes University of Technology (UTT)
ICD/Tech-CICO
12 rue marie curie – BP2060
10010 Troyes Cedex – France
Myriam.Lewkowicz@utt.fr

Parina Hassanaly
IEP, 25 rue Gaston de Saporta
13625 Aix-en-Provence
cedex 1
France
parina.hassanaly@univ-cezanne.fr

Markus Rohde
Information Systems and New Media
University of Siegen
Hölderlin Str. 3, 57076, Siegen
Germany
International Institute for Socio-Informatics
(IISI), Bonn, Germany
markus.rohde@iisi.de

Volker Wulf
Information Systems and New Media
University of Siegen
Hölderlin Str. 3, 57076
Siegen, Germany
Fraunhofer-Institute FIT, Sankt Augustin,
Germany
volker.wulf@fit.fraunhofer.de

ISBN 978-1-4471-6227-8   ISBN 978-1-84996-211-7 (eBook)
DOI 10.1007/978-1-84996-211-7
Springer London Dordrecht Heidelberg New York

Preface

The ninth edition of the International Conference on Designing Cooperative Systems (COOP'2010) provides a forum for researchers who contribute to the analysis and design of cooperative systems and their integration in organizations, communities, and other social settings, as well as their implications for policy and decision-making.

The COOP conferences suggest that cooperative systems design requires deep understanding of collective activities, involving both artifacts and social practices. Contributions are solicited from a wide range of domains contributing to the fields of cooperative systems design and evaluation such as Computer Supported Cooperative Work, Human Computer Interaction, Participatory Design, Information Systems, Knowledge Management, Ethnography, Organizational and Management Sciences, Sociology, Psychology, and Linguistics.

COOP has been created by the COOP French group, now replaced by the COOP steering committee for its management. The current composition of the steering committee is as follows Liam Bannon, Françoise Darses, Gorgio De Michelis, Alain Giboin, Parina Hassanaly, Thomas Herrmann, Pascal Salembier, Kjeld Schmidt, Carla Simone, Wolfgang Prinz, Volker Wulf, and Manuel Zacklad. During the past 18 years, COOP underwent a thematic development and understands itself nowadays to be the second European conference on Computer Supported Cooperative Work. The COOP conference series is supported by the European Society of Socially Embedded Technologies (EUSSET) and is held every second year alternately with then European Conference on Computer Supported Cooperative Work (ECSCW), usually at the French Riviera.

In these proceedings, we document the selected full and short papers. We received this year 49 submissions and we were able to accept 17 papers at unacceptance rate of 35%.

Full and short papers were chosen in a severe and quality oriented selection process in which each contribution was evaluated by at least three reviewers. After the completion of the reviews the scientific chairs spent 3 days to carefully evaluate the reviews and make final decisions on acceptance. We paid specific attention to the scientific value of the contribution, the methods applied, and the societal relevance of its findings. We hope that this quality-oriented selection process will contribute the international positioning of COOP in the field of Computer Supported Cooperative Work.

We are grateful to the distinguished members of our program committee:

Gabriela Avram, Ireland
Mark Ackermann, USA
Michael Baker, France
Liam Bannon, Ireland
Suzanne Bodker, Denmark
Jean-Francois Boujut, France
Béatrice Cahour, France
Bruno Carron, France
Peter Carstensen, Denmark
Luigina Ciolfi, Ireland
Graham Connor, Australia
Franzeska Costabile, Italy
Françoise Darses, France
Antonella De Angeli, UK
Francoise Decortis, Belgium
Giorgio De Michelis, Italy
Boris De Ruyter, Netherlands
Cleidson De Souza, Brazil
Francoise Detienne, France
Yvonne Dittrich, Denmark
Monica Divitini, Norway
Julie Dugdale, France
Myriam Frejus, France
Alain Giboin, France
Tom Gross, Germany
Richard Harper, UK
Thomas Herrmann, Germany
Giulio Jacucci, Finland
Marina Jirotka , UK
Aditya Johri, USA
Andrea Kienle, Germany
Catherine Letondal, France
Christian Licoppe, France
Jan Ljundberg, Sweden
Paul Luff, UK
Gloria Mark, USA
David Martin, France
Anders Morch, Norway
Keiichi Nakata, Japan
Bernhard Nett, Germany
Laurence Nigay, France

Jackie O'Neill, France
Bernard Pavard, France
Volkmar Pipek, Germany
Wolfgang Prinz, Germany
Dave Randall, UK
Markus Rohde, Germany
Mark Rouncefield, UK
Pascal Salembier, France
Kjeld Schmidt, Denmark
Carla Simone, Italy
Gunnar Stevens, Germany
Hilda Tellioglu , Austria
Manuel Zacklad, France

The program of COOP 2010 will be complemented by workshops and a doctoral colloquium taking place the day before the conference. The conference will start with an invited talk by Gary M. Olson on "Trends in Scholarly Collaboration" and will close with a panel on the future of CSCW.

Organizing an international conference requires team efforts over a considerable period of time. We would like to thank Markus Rohde for the proceedings, Gunnar Stevens for the workshops, and Mark Ackerman and Kjeld Schmidt for the Doctoral Colloquium. Mary-Ann Sprenger and Martin Stein have supported us in maintaining the www-site and formatting the proceedings. We are deeply indebted to their high engagement. Finally, the conference can take place thanks to the IEP (Institut d'Etudes Politiques) in Aix which is welcoming us and its Research Department which organized our venue. We are grateful to Parina Hassanaly and Athissingh Ramrajsingh who ran this organization.

December 2009   Troyes and Siegen

Myriam Lewkowicz and Volker Wulf
Scientific Chairs

Contents

Trends in Scholarly Collaboration 1
Gary M. Olson

**Distributed Design and Distributed Social Awareness:
Exploring Inter-subjective Dimensions of Roles** 3
Flore Barcellini, Françoise Détienne, and Jean-Marie Burkhardt

**Faithful to the Earth: Reporting Experiences of Artifact-Centered
Design in Healthcare** 25
Federico Cabitza

**A Reformulation of the Semantic Gap Problem in Content-Based
Image Retrieval Scenarios** 45
Tommaso Colombino, Dave Martin, Antonietta Grasso,
and Luca Marchesotti

**Design of a Collaborative Disaster Response Process
Management System** 57
Jörn Franke and François Charoy

**Supporting Collaborative Workflows of Digital
Multimedia Annotation** 79
Cristian Hofmann and Dieter W. Fellner

Change Awareness for Collaborative Video Annotation 101
Cristian Hofmann, Uwe Boettcher, and Dieter W. Fellner

Rethinking Laboratory Notebooks 119
Clemens Nylandsted Klokmose and Pär-Ola Zander

**Supporting Reflection in Software Development with Everyday
Working Tools** 141
Birgit Krogstie and Monica Divitini

Collocated Social Practices Surrounding Photo
Usage in Archaeology.. 163
Marco P. Locatelli, Carla Simone, and Viviana Ardesia

Direct Deliberative Governance and the Web: The Collaborative
Work of Democratic Decision-Making Mediated by an Online
Social Environment... 183
Rean van der Merwe and Anthony Meehan

How Creative Groups Structure Tasks Through
Negotiating Resources.. 203
Christopher Paul Middup, Tim Coughlan, and Peter Johnson

The Role of Social Capital and Cooperation Infrastructures
Within Microfinance... 223
Simon Plogmann, Muhammad Adeel, Bernhard Nett, and Volker Wulf

Computer Enabled Social Movements? Usage of a Collaborative
Web Platform within the European Social Forum....................................... 245
Saqib Saeed and Markus Rohde

'Keep Up the Good Work!': The Concept of 'Work' in CSCW 265
Kjeld Schmidt

Appropriation of the Eclipse Ecosystem: Local Integration
of Global Network Production 287
Gunnar Stevens and Sebastian Draxler

Practices Analysis and Digital Platform Design:
An Interdisciplinary Study of Social Support... 309
Matthieu Tixier, Myriam Lewkowicz, Michel Marcoccia, Hassan Atifi,
Aurélien Bénel, Gérald Gaglio, and Nadia Gauducheau

Creative Collective Efficacy in Scientific Communities.............................. 331
Jing Wang, Umer Farooq, and John M. Carroll

Contributors

Adeel Muhammad
Information Systems and New Media, University of Siegen, Hölderlin Str. 3,
57076 Siegen, Germany
muhammad.adeel@uni-siegen.de

Ardesia Viviana
Department of Archaeology, University of Bologna, Via Zamboni 33, 40126
Bologna, Italy
viviana.ardesia@disco.unimib.it

Atifi Hassan
Troyes University of Technology (UTT), ICD/Tech-CICO, 12 rue marie curie,
BP2060, 10010 Troyes Cedex, France
Hassan.Atifi@utt.fr

Barcellini Flore
Ergonomics Lab, Research Center on Work and Development,
Cnam, 41 rue Gay-Lussac, 75005, Paris, France
flore.barcellini@cnam.fr

Bénel Aurélien
Troyes University of Technology (UTT), ICD/Tech-CICO,
12 rue marie curie, BP2060, 10010 Troyes Cedex, France
Aurélien.Bénel@utt.fr

Boettcher Uwe
Technische Universtät Darmstadt, Interactive Graphics Systems Group,
Darmstadt, Germany
boettcher@gris.informatik.tu-darmstadt.de

Burkhardt Jean-Marie
Ergonomics-Behavior-Interaction Lab, Paris Descartes University,
45 rue des Saints-Pères, 75006, Paris, France
jean-marie.burkhardt@parisdescartes.fr

Cabitza Federico
Universita degli Studi di Milano Bicocca, via Bicocca degli Arcimboldi 8, 20126
Milano, Italy
cabitza@disco.unimib.it

Carroll John M.
College of Information Sciences and Technology, The Pennsylvania State
University, University Park, PA, USA
jcarroll@ist.psu.edu

Charoy François
LORIA-INRIA, Nancy-Université, BP 239-54506,
Vandoeuvre-lès-Nancy Cedex, France
charoy@loria.fr

Colombino Tommaso
Xerox Research Centre Europe, 6, chemin de Maupertuis, 38240 Meylan, France
Tommaso.Colombino@xerox.com

Coughlan Tim
Department of Computer Science, HCI Group, University of Bath,
Bath BA2 7AY, UK
t.coughlan@bath.ac.uk

Détienne Françoise
LTCI- UMR 5141 - CNRS - Telecom Paris Tech/Département SES - Bureau B,
421/46 rue Barrault, 75634 Cedex 13/INRIA, Paris, France
Francoise.detienne@telecom-paristech.fr

Divitini Monica
Norwegian University of Science and Technology, Sem Sælands vei 7-9,
NO-7491 Trondheim, Norway
divitini@idi.ntnu.no

Draxler Sebastian
Information Systems and New Media, University of Siegen,
Hölderlin Str. 3, 57076 Siegen, Germany
sebastian.draxler@uni-siegen.de

Farooq Umer
Microsoft Corporation, One Microsoft Way, Redmond, WA 98052, USA
umfarooq@microsoft.com

Fellner Dieter W
Fraunhofer Institute for Computer Graphics Research Darmstadt,
Darmstadt, Germany
Technische Universtät Darmstadt, Interactive Graphics Systems Group,
Fraunhoferstr. 5, 64283, Darmstadt, Germany
d.fellner@igd.fraunhofer.de

Franke Jörn
Public Security, SAP Research Center (SRC) Sophia Antipolis, 805,
Avenue du Docteur Maurice Donat, BP1216-06254 Mougins, France
joern.franke@sap.com

Gaglio Gérald
Troyes University of Technology (UTT), ICD/Tech-CICO,
12 rue marie curie, BP2060, 10010 Troyes Cedex, France
Gérald.Gaglio@utt.fr

Gauducheau Nadia
Troyes University of Technology (UTT), ICD/Tech-CICO,
12 rue marie curie, BP2060, 10010 Troyes Cedex, France
Nadia.Gauducheau@utt.fr

Grasso Antonietta
Xerox Research Centre Europe, 6, chemin de Maupertuis, 38240 Meylan, France
Antonietta.Grasso@xerox.com

Hassanaly Parina
IEP, 25 rue Gaston de Saporta, 13, 625 Aix-en-Provence cedex 1, France
parina.hassanaly@univ-cezanne.fr

Hofmann Cristian
Fraunhofer Institute for Computer Graphics Research Darmstadt Fraunhoferstr. 5,
64283 Darmstadt, Germany
Technische Universtät Darmstadt, Interactive Graphics Systems Group,
Darmstadt, Germany
cristian.hofmann@igd.fraunhofer.de

Johnson Peter
Department of Computer Science, HCI Group, University of Bath,
Bath BA2 7AY, UK
p.johnson@bath.ac.uk

Klokmose Clemens Nylandsted
Department of Computer Science, Aarhus University, Aabogade 34, 8240,
Aarhus N
Laboratorie de Recherche en Informatique, Univ. Paris-Sud, Bâtiment 490
F-91405, Orsay, France
clemens@lri.fr

Krogstie Birgit
Norwegian University of Science and Technology, Sem Sælands vei 7-9,
NO-7491 Trondheim, Norway
birgitkr@idi.ntnu.no

Lewkowicz Myriam
Troyes University of Technology (UTT), ICD/Tech-CICO,
12 rue marie curie, BP2060, 10010 Troyes Cedex, France
Myriam.Lewkowicz@utt.fr

Locatelli Marco P
Department of Informatics, Systems and Communication, University of Milano
Bicocca, viale Sarca 336, U14 building, 20126 Milano, Italy
flocatelli@disco.unimib.it

Marchesotti Luca
Xerox Research Centre Europe, 6, chemin de Maupertuis, 38240 Meylan, France
Luca.Marchesotti@xerox.com

Marcoccia Michel
Troyes University of Technology (UTT), ICD/Tech-CICO, 12 rue marie curie,
BP2060, 10010 Troyes Cedex, France
Michel.Marcoccia@utt.fr

Martin Dave
Xerox Research Centre Europe, 6, chemin de Maupertuis, 38240 Meylan, France
David.Martin@xerox.com

Meehan Anthony
Center for Research in Computing, The Open University,
Walton Hall, Milton Keynes, MK7 6AA, UK
a.s.meehan@open.ac.uk

Rean van der Merwe
Centre for Research in Computing, The Open University, Walton Hall, Milton
Keynes, MK7 6AA, UK
r.vandermerwe@open.ac.uk

Middup Christopher Paul
Department of Computer Science, HCI Group, University of Bath,
Bath BA2 7AY, UK
c.p.middup@bath.ac.uk

Nett Bernhard
Information Systems and New Media, University of Siegen,
Hölderlin Str. 3, 57076 Siegen, Germany
bernhard.nett@uni-siegen.de

Olson Gary M.
Donald Bren Chair of Information and Computer Sciences Department
of Informatics Bren School of Information and Computer Sciences,
University of California, Irvine, DBH 5202, Irvine, CA 92697-3440, USA
gary.olson@uci.edu

Plogmann Simon
Information Systems and New Media, University of Siegen,
Hölderlin Str. 3, 57076 Siegen, Germany
simonplogmann@gmx.de

Rohde Markus
Information Systems and New Media, University of Siegen,
Hölderlin Str. 3, 57076 Siegen, Germany
markus.rohde@uni-siegen.de

Saeed Saqib
Information Systems and New Media, University of Siegen,
Hölderlin Str. 3, 57076 Siegen, Germany
saqib.saeed@uni-siegen.de

Schmidt Kjeld
Department of Organization, Copenhagen Business School, Denmark
schmidt@cscw.dk

Simone Carla
Department of Informatics, Systems and Communication,
University of Milano Bicocca, viale Sarca 336, U14 building, 20126 Milano, Italy
simoneg@disco.unimib.it

Stevens Gunnar
Information Systems and New Media, University of Siegen,
Hölderlin Str. 3, 57076 Siegen, Germany
gunnar.stevens@uni-siegen.de

Tixier Matthieu
Troyes University of Technology (UTT), ICD/Tech-CICO,
12 rue marie curie, BP2060, 10010 Troyes Cedex, France
Matthieu.Tixier@utt.fr

Wang Jing
College of Information Sciences and Technology, The Pennsylvania State
University, University Park, PA, USA
jzw143@ist.psu.edu

Wulf Volker
Information Systems and New Media, University of Siegen,
Hölderlin Str. 3, 57076 Siegen, Germany
volker.wulf@uni-siegen.de

Zander Pär-Ola
Department of Computer Science, Aarhus University,
Aabogade 34, 8200 Aarhus N
poz@cs.au.dk

Trends in Scholarly Collaboration

Gary M. Olson

Abstract Researchers in science and engineering have a long tradition of collaboration, and increasingly carry out these collaborations across geographical distance. Similar trends exist in industry, where virtual teams are increasing in frequency. While we know that such dispersed collaborations are difficult, there is growing evidence of success. The physical and biological sciences have led the way, though more recently social and behavioral scientists have also adopted these new modes of working. Most recently of all, there is growing evidence of collaborative scholarship in the humanities, including some of it carried out under conditions of geographical dispersion. I will review these trends, and in particular comment on whether the factors that distinguish success from failure in such collaborations are the same across these diverse domains.

G.M. Olson (✉)
Donald Bren Chair of Information and Computer Sciences, Department of Informatics Bren School of Information and Computer Sciences, University of California, Irvine DBH, 5202 Irvine, CA
e-mail: gary.olson@uci.edu

M. Lewkowicz et al. (eds.), *Proceedings of COOP 2010*,
DOI 10.1007/978-1-84996-211-7_1, © Springer-Verlag London Limited 2010

Distributed Design and Distributed Social Awareness: Exploring Inter-subjective Dimensions of Roles

Flore Barcellini, Françoise Détienne, and Jean-Marie Burkhardt

Abstract This research deals with the investigation of inter-subjective dimensions of roles and participation in distributed design processes (DDP), as linked to group or social awareness. It is focused on an open-source software community – the Python programming language community – as a model of DDP. On the basis of semi-structured interviews, we show that participants agree upon a typology of roles based on evident activities and experiences of participants, and that this knowledge guides their strategic use of archives for maintaining situation awareness. Contextualized interviews on a specific design process helps in understanding how this typology of roles is instantiated in a design situation and how social awareness is distributed among participants.

Introduction

Distributed design processes do not require that everyone within the project has a perfect and complete understanding of who is involved, for what tasks, with what experience or expertise at any time of the design process. It is also not required that

F. Barcellini (✉)
Ergonomics Lab, Research Center on Work and Development, Cnam, 41 rue Gay-Lussac, 75005, Paris, France
e-mail: flore.barcellini@cnam.fr

F. Détienne
Département SES – Bureau B 421, LTCI- UMR 5141 – CNRS – Telecom Paris Tech, 46 rue Barrault, 75634, Paris, Cedex 13, France
and
INRIA, Paris, France
e-mail: Francoise.detienne@telecom-paristech.fr

J.-M. Burkhardt
Ergonomics-Behavior-Interaction Lab, Paris Descartes University, 45 rue des Saints-Pères, 75006, Paris, France
e-mail: jean-marie.burkhardt@parisdescartes.fr

M. Lewkowicz et al. (eds.), *Proceedings of COOP 2010*,
DOI 10.1007/978-1-84996-211-7_2, © Springer-Verlag London Limited 2010

among all the participants, one of them, e.g. the coordinator or project manager, has such knowledge available to support design problem solving and coordination decision. In fact, some minimal knowledge about the social community of participants could be enough, as far as this knowledge can support localization or mobilization of relevant agents at any step of the design process. An issue is to investigate content, forms, and ways of distribution of such knowledge among participants in a distributed design community.

The issue related to understanding how knowledge about participants in a distributed design community is constructed, distributed and mobilized as a resource for design, has been addressed under the heading of several theoretical frameworks in the literature. We will consider specifically the following concepts and their associated frameworks: social awareness [35] or group awareness [17] and team mental model [24]. Transversal to these theories is the (often ill-defined) notion of role, usually mobilized in other contexts of collective practices. It is consequently important to review these approaches in order to clarify both conceptual and methodological aspects relevant to investigate the issue of social awareness in the field of real distributed design communities. As emphasized by Prasolova-Forland and Diviniti [27], such knowledge can be considered as twofold: as a description of roles and participants within a community "in a general social situation", or as specifically contextualized knowledge related to specific events.

Our objective is to understand social awareness, and the mechanisms underlying the distribution of such social knowledge within participants in an Open Source Software (OSS) design community. OSS is probably one of the most representative cases of distributed design today. Although understanding how OSS communities are organized has been investigated recently through various approaches (e.g. [5,11–13,20, 21, 28, 29]), only very few studies have focused on group or social awareness in OSS (but see e.g. [17]). However, this issue has been recently recognized as most important for understanding the success of OSS.

In this paper, we focus on the Python OSS community dedicated to the design and use of the Python programming language, and on a specific design process in this community. After a review of the theoretical framework, we will present our research questions and methodological approach. Then, we will present the results and discuss the perspectives of this research.

Theoretical Framework

Distributed Knowledge Across Distributed Design Communities: Theoretical Approaches

Several theoretical approaches have addressed the issue of knowledge about participants in groups, such as teams, or in more distributed collective activities as found in online epistemic communities [10]. Whereas teams are composed of stable members, often with identified statuses, online design communities such as OSS communities are composed of a large and unstable number of participants whose statuses and roles are constructed throughout interactions.

One theoretical approach is embraced by the notions of team mental model or shared mental model, both referring to an organized understanding of relevant knowledge that is shared by team members [24]. A team mental model is defined as team members' shared, organized understanding and mental representations of knowledge about key elements of the team's relevant environment, amongst which knowledge about roles and statutes.

Mostly applied to very minimal teams, sometimes reduced to dyads (e.g. [23]), this approach has several limits which have been emphasized in the literature. Firstly, the team mental model literature has overemphasized the overlapping perspective of sharing knowledge (knowledge common to all members) leaving aside more complementary or distributed perspectives [24]. Indeed, in a more distributed perspective, which may be more relevant for design online communities, members may be supposed to gain distinct knowledge depending on their activity. Furthermore this distribution of knowledge may be considered in a complementary perspective, as in the theory of transactive memory. According to this latter approach, the individual memories of group members are supplemented by shared knowledge of who knows what. Secondly, and in a related manner, the shared mental models approach leaves aside the social, cultural, and physical contexts within which mental structures are embedded [9]. It leaves aside norms, values, rewarding systems constructed and adopted in a social group. Finally, this approach is mostly static and de-contextualised from action.

The literature on awareness, and more particularly social awareness or group awareness, also addresses these questions of group knowledge related to roles with a more contextualised, socially and technically embedded perspective. Social awareness or group awareness is a lateral dimension of situation awareness [19], referring to practices through which participants regulate their activities to adapt to discrepancies and tasks interdependencies [19,20]. Social awareness is awareness of the social situation in a group or community in a shared environment, which can be physical, virtual or both.

Social awareness encompasses awareness of social situation in general and social situation at a certain moment. Prasolova-Forland and Diviniti [27] distinguish these two conceptions of social awareness in the literature, depending on the emphasis made on concrete events or on general concepts. According to the former approach (see e.g. [35]) social awareness is defined as awareness about the social situation of other people, i.e. what they are doing, whether they are engaged in a conversation and can be disturbed or not, and of who is around and what is up, at a certain moment of time. According to the latter approach, social awareness is considered in a broader context. An example is group-structural awareness (see e.g. [16]) as knowledge about people's roles, positions, status, responsibilities and group processes.

Prasolova-Forland and Diviniti's definition embeds both approaches considering awareness of social situation in general and social situation at a certain moment: people's roles, activities, positions, status, responsibilities, social connections and group processes.

Based on these various models, two main focuses seem to be as particularly relevant for exploring social awareness in distributed design communities: its distributed characteristic and its strong link with activity. Firstly, the distributed perspective could be explored in relationship with the distinction between general and specific social awareness. Secondly, the emphasis put on activity as an input and a main component of social awareness could also be approached through the notion of role, distinguishing one's own role and other participants' roles in a community. Our definition of role refers to effective and emerging behaviour of participants that appears and differentiates through interactions [1–3]. In online communities [22] and more specifically in OSS [17], the importance of constructing knowledge of other participants' roles has been stressed as required for getting involved in and participating in online interactions. We develop this notion of role in the following section.

Multiple Dimensions of Roles and Participation Profiles Essential for the Design Process

The role of a participant can be characterized by some degree of regularity in his/her activity in interaction with the group and technological artefacts [2,3]. Three types of roles are usually distinguished to characterize profiles of participation:

- *Interactive roles* identified through structural analyses of communication, e.g. level of participation and place in a network of communication.
- *Task-oriented roles* associated with both production and coordination activities: cognitive roles are oriented toward generation or evaluation of ideas; epistemic roles are oriented toward knowledge sharing activities [2]; coordination roles are oriented toward definition and reformulation of group objectives, or synthesis activities. These roles also refer to activities analyzed in previous studies of collaborative design (e.g. [6,11,25,26]).
- *Socio-relational* roles associated to activities whose objective is to facilitate interpersonal relationships, i.e. reducing conflict, harmonizing and researching consensus. They concern the creation of a free, expressive and participative context of work.

Thus the notion of role may be viewed and analyzed along several combined dimensions. For example, the epistemic dimension refers to the type of knowledge brought by participants; the interactive dimension refers to the activities of interaction management, e.g. opening of topics in discussions. Analyses along these primary dimensions allow a second-level analysis, where their combination allows participation profiles to be revealed (cf. [2]).

Up to now, two participation profiles have been identified in the literature as important for the performance of the design process:

- *Boundary spanners* who compensate for communications deficit between different groups [19,29,30,33]. They are literally persons who span the gap between their organization and external ones [29,33]. Their activity is characterized by communication or behaviour between two or more networks or groups. They move across different teams transferring and translating information about the state of the project. This profile combines a task-oriented role focused on coordination and knowledge sharing with a socio-relational role focused on group support. This profile remains often invisible from the participants' perspective [15].

- *Leaders* who are persons recognized for their competences and to whom power is accorded. They have not forcedly the status of manager. They have a central interactive role characterized by high participation and highly quoted interventions. Their socio-relational role is oriented toward the creation of an harmonious work setting. Their task-oriented role is dominated by coordination activities.

Previous Studies on OSS Communities: From Trace-Based Analyses of Roles to Social Awareness

In OSS communities, roles and participation profiles have been mostly approached via traces-based analyses of interaction in three interaction spaces [6,29]: a discussion space (mailing lists, forums, chat), a documentation space (project web site, related websites, blog, wiki, online documentation), and an implementation space (source code and its development history). Several research works have aimed to identify roles which emerge in online communities (in particular, [4,18,34] for OSS; [14] for wikipedia and usenet). They have been mostly developed on the basis of analyses of traces oriented by researchers pre-categories. Their more or less explicit twofold objective is to understand the collective dynamics and to specify/ construct external representations for supporting situation and social awareness in these communities.

Two types of analyses are usually conducted, structural analyses and social network analysis (SNA) (e.g. [20]), or, more rarely, content analyses based on more qualitative analyses of the content (e.g. [28]). Based on both types of analyses, we [6] have developed a methodological framework to identify roles along the interactive, cognitive, epistemic, coordination and socio-relational dimensions. We [4,6] have crossed structural analyses and message content analyses to identify profiles in the Python community, in particular the one of the boundary spanners. We shown that boundary spanners were characterized by specific interactive roles (in particular cross-participation in parallel same theme discussions in two mailing-lists), epistemic roles (transferring knowledge from application and computer sciences domains); and coordination and socio-relational roles. In online communities like usenet and wikipedia, Gleave et al. [14] have attempted to identify social role signatures on the basis of structural analyses, checking the convergence with roles identified on the basis of content analyses. Based on SNA, Sowe et al. [34] have identified knowledge brokers (or boundary spanners) as actors who participated across three mailing lists in the discussion space of the Debian OSS project.

Finally, most of these works have left aside the related question of understanding the knowledge constructed by members about others activities and roles in their community. This issue of group awareness has been addressed in a recent study by Gutwin et al. [16] in an OSS context. According to these authors, group awareness includes knowledge about who is on the project, where in the code they are working on, what they are doing, and what their plans are. In a perspective closed of Prasolova-Forland and Diviniti [27], they distinguish between general awareness of the entire team and more detailed knowledge of people that interviewed participants plan to work with. They found that social awareness is maintained primarily through text-based communication, e.g. strategies such as lurking on online discussions. Following this study, our objective is to understand social awareness in a DDP, the Python OSS community, and the distribution of such social knowledge within participants. As in Gutwin et al. [16], our methodology will be partly based on semi-structured interviews. In addition, we will also conduct contextualized interviews in order to address more properly situated knowledge of participants.

Research Questions

Techniques for analyzing interactions in OSS communities have been previously developed (e.g. [5,29]. These techniques can provide a referential view of argumentation exchange and process coordination within distributed design online communities. This view is constructed externally from the community, organizing and making visible a range of persisting traces of the whole process. Even, if such views provide a good help to understand what was going on in a particular space and at a moment of design (at least as far as traces and their treatment provide an accurate view of it), they don't convey much information about how social awareness is distributed and used to coordinate design among participants.

We would like to capture several dimensions of this specific area of design knowledge distributed within the community. This can be addressed in two directions. Firstly, social awareness can be thought as a generic –more or less shared and consistent across participants – mental model describing the participants and their participation within the design community. Secondly, each specific design process can be thought as a unique instance of such a model, that is both an entry and an output to the previous generic mental model. Looking comparatively at these two levels might provide an opportunity for identifying components, relationships and distribution of social awareness in distributed design communities.

We will adopt the notion of role to elicit this part of distributed social knowledge that refers to contributions associated to participants in the design process. Roles will be understood as knowledge about the emerging profiles of participants' contributions in the course of design.

Our research questions concern how social awareness is characterized, distributed and supported across members in distributed design. For that purpose, we propose to explore inter-subjective dimensions of roles, that is the way participants within the community identify and categorize themselves and other participants' roles and contributions to the design process. As Prasolova-Forland and Diviniti [27] and Gutwin et al. [16], we investigate social awareness by distinguishing between general vs. situated and specific levels. More detailed exploratory issues concern:

- *Content*: To what extent do participants converge upon a typology of roles or profiles in the community and how do they characterize them? What cues are preferentially exploited by participants to characterize roles?
- *Distribution*: What is the scope of distinctive roles memorized by participants and do some roles remain invisible? Are there functional/operative views of roles depending on participant's own position in the design process?
- *Articulation Between Levels*: Can we distinguish between generic roles (instantiated only in particular design process) and personalized roles (permanent at the community level)?
- *Function*: How far is knowledge about others' roles useful and mobilized by strategies for maintaining situation awareness?

A Focus on the Python Community

Our research focuses on the Python project (www.python.org) which is a dynamic and stable project. Created in 1994, this project has a group of about 100 designers and a lot of potential users of Python in various application domains (web design, scientific computing, gaming, finance...).

An interesting characteristic of this project is that its participants can engage in a specific design process: the *Python Enhancement Proposal* process (PEP). This process is used by the Python community to frame proposals of new functionalities and evolutions of the Python language.[1] Everyone can propose a PEP, whatever his/her status; the proponent is called the champion. PEPs are then discussed in two main mailing-lists of the project (use and design oriented mailing-lists). Focusing on PEPs processes enables us to select contextualised online data, in particular data concerning specific design activities.

As in other OSS projects, the design process is distributed among the three online interaction spaces [29]: the discussion, documentation and implementation spaces.

The discussion space of the Python project is composed by two main mailing lists:

- A use-oriented mailing list, *python-list*, is about general discussions and questions about Python.
- A design-oriented mailing list, *python-dev*, is for work on developing Python (fixing bugs and adding new features to the Python language).

---

[1]The PEP process is similar to other design processes in distant design communities, like the Request for Comment used by the Internet Engineering Task Force, the XEP process used by the jabber community (www.jabber.org). This formal process is also closed to the consensus-based decision making of Apache.

The documentation space is composed by all documents, website, blogs, wikis relative to the project. It contains all PEP's documents and their versions.

The implementation space contains the proper code of Python: the standard library and its modules, their versions. All the code versions related to a new functionality proposed by a PEP are archived there.

Methodology

Our methodology combines two types of interviews, each one targeting one of our principal research questions.

Our research questions concerning general social awareness are addressed by conducting semi-structured interviews with participants in the Python community.

Our research questions concerning situated social awareness are addressed by conducting semi-structured contextualized interviews with participants in a particular design process episode. The chosen design process concerns PEP XYZ.[2] Previous studies based on analyses of traces [4,6] allowed us to identify the scope and forms of participation in this PEP design process.

This PEP process occurred between October 2003 and May 2006. As our interviews were performed *a posteriori* (during 2007), this might be seen as a limitation for accessing for participants' representation in context. However, a previous work on memory of interactions in cooperation [8] has outlined that, with a long delay between the recalled interaction and the interviews, verbal content is massively forgotten but interactional and relational positions are still well remembered by interviewees.

Semi-Structured Interviews

Participants Recruitment

To recruit participants, we contacted chairs of the Python French Association (www.afpy.org) and we recruited interviewees during two Python's conferences (World Meeting on OSS – *Rencontres Mondiales du Logiciel Libre* – and Europython'06). Each interviewee was asked to recommend any other relevant participants to the researcher. We also contacted participants on the basis of observations of the mailing-lists of the Python project.

We recruited 14 interviewees. They were members of the Python community in France, United-States, Argentina and Australia. Statuses of participants in the Python community and the modalities used to conduct interviews are synthesized in Table 1. Interviewees are all users of Python, some are developers of the proper

---

[2]This PEP concerns the introduction of a module for decimal calculation, pushed by users in the financial domain.

Table 1 Interviewees statuses and modality used to conduct interviews

Statuses	Number	Modalities
Developers in application domains	5	Face to face
Developers in application domains	5	Phone
Project leader	1	Face to face
Developers of Python language	3	E-mails

Python language and some are developers of software based on Python in various application domains (web, scientific computing, financial).

Collected Data and Analysis

Face to face interviews consisted in 1–2 h of exchanges. E-mails interviews are composed of three to four messages. The interviews have been transcribed and form a corpus composed of 5,500 lines of text.

We performed a thematic qualitative analysis. Themes were categorized according to:

- Characterization of interviewee's role and participation in the project (participation in one or another mailing-lists, code contribution …)
- Types of roles and criteria reported by participants (project leader, area of expertise…)
- Strategies for constructing and maintaining knowledge about roles and design processes (reading mailing-lists, blogs or wikis, subscribing to news or RSS feeds…)

Contextualized Interviews Concerning a Design Episode

Interviewees' Recruitment and Resulting Sample

One hundred and twenty participants were involved in the use-oriented and design-oriented mailing-lists concerning the PEP XYZ process. Among them, we identified 14 common participants on both lists, from which five could be characterized as boundary spanners (for more details, see [4,6]). Seven participants contributed in the documentation and the implementation by modifying the source code and/or the PEP specification document. Actually, two participants acted in the documentation space, six in the implementation space, and one in both spaces. Thus, the technical profile related to implementation of code is concentrated in a smaller group (7) than the discussant profile (120 of which 24 are high discussants).

Among these participants, we requested 16 of the high discussants to perform an interview by email. Only four participants accepted to answer and three of them followed all the interview process. Nevertheless, the three interviewed participants are characterized by specific and complementary profiles of participation recon-structed on the basis of our previous studies [4,6] and the semi-structured interviews presented above.

Two interviewees acted in both discussion and implementation spaces:

- *Fabio*[3] is the champion of the PEP that appears to have a profile of leader during the design process characterized by a central position in communication and a tendency to perform coordination activities. He is also one of the five boundary spanners identified.
- *Nelson* was one of the most frequent participants to discussions during the design process. He is also one of the six participants who modified the source code corresponding to the PEP.

The third interviewee, *Anthony*, acted only in the discussion space. He is a well-known expert of the project (one of those identified thanks to the semi-structured interviews). He is working in the same organization than the project leader. He appears to be also one of the five boundary spanners of the design process.

Collected Data and Analysis

The questions addressed by the interviewees concerned:

- The history of the PEP XYZ process
- The participation of the interviewee in this process, his/her potential influence and his/her motivation
- The participation of others, their roles in the process, their potential influence and their motivation.

In a first phase, interviewees were asked to answer questions without looking at the PEP discussions archived online. In a second phase, in which only two interviewees (Fabio and Anthony) accepted to participate, they were allowed to consult archives.

The collected email interviews represent 1,000 lines of text.

We performed a qualitative content analysis of interviews by extracting and categorizing the descriptors of roles, and the name of participants remembered by interviewees. We analyzed both the knowledge of participants about their own participation, and the participation of other recalled people. In the following, only the results relevant for our research questions will be presented.

Results

This section is organized according to results obtained from the two types of interviews, each one targeting one of our principal research questions.

Concerning our research questions on general social awareness, semi-structured interviews leads us to identify a typology of roles within the Python Project, and strategies developed by participants for constructing and maintaining awareness.

---

[3]Faked names.

Concerning research questions on situated social awareness, semi-structured contextualized interviews with participants in PEP XYZ process allow us to specify the representations developed by participants about the roles of key actors in this process.

Typology of Roles and Strategies for Maintaining Awareness

The typology of roles presented in this section is based on an agreement between participants about dimensions they employ to identify roles at the community level and refer to general social awareness. We stress one main disagreement on the definition of a shared understanding of the roles of users and developers. We conclude this section by presenting strategies employed by participants to elaborate and use this knowledge for maintaining situation awareness.

Underlying Dimensions of Roles and Profiles

At a general level, participants elicited a partially shared view on participants' roles within the OSS community. Their knowledge about roles in their community is built on the basis of several principles. Globally, participants agreed upon three types of principles for identifying roles.

The first principle used for distinguishing roles is based on participants activities in the interaction spaces. Indeed, all participants described spontaneously different types of participants according to their activity in one or another spaces:

- *Discussants* profiles (related to evidences of activity in the discussion space of the community), are defined by participation to mailing-lists of Python (use-oriented, design-oriented or application domain) and sometimes by explicit reference to the quality of participation, as pointed by a participant: *"They are some people that construct so well-constructed their answers (in online discussions" that they are call "'bot' a robot: who write, scan all that is written online and automatically send good answers".*
- *Technical* profiles (related to evidences in the documentation and implementation spaces), are defined by software design actions (bug report, selection of bug, providing correction of bug, verifying quality of code, documentation, managing code versions...).
- *Outside of interactions spaces* persons related to activities oriented to evangelization and promotion of Python through book writing, organization of conference etc...

Furthermore, interviewees converged in eliciting one particular *discussant profile*, linked to *boundary spanning* activities [29]. Mediation and interpersonal issues are evoked and related to information transmission, support of other participants in proposing a new functionality.

The second principle is linked to reputation and expertise, as stressed by a participant:

> I think that there is no formal role with a tag. I think that they are simply people that are very visible because they contributed a lot and who have particular expertise.

These roles are most often personalized. Participants referred directly to the person name, his/her expertise domains and sometimes the context in which the person developed his/her expertise.

> For instance, when one talks about, for instance, numeric…it is always Tom…because Tom (…) is a deep expert in scientific computing. Tom worked for a while in a big scientific computing institution. Thus, if one has a problem with that if Tom says « that » that's it. It is not a formal role, it is just that he has some skills.

These roles are similar to the notion of *super-experts* or gurus as defined in the literature about software design [32]. From the interviews, we obtained a group of nine participants (identified by their names) seen as super-experts. Interestingly, the fact that five of them were administrators and four were developers of Python suggests that such role is not systematically associated to the participants' status.

The third principles is linked to the participant's status. This principle is applied only for the project leader (and not for administrators/developers/users as we will discuss in next section). The most personalised role on which every participants agree upon was the *project leader*. This is interestingly the only profile which is confounded with both a particular person and a recognized status within the community. Indeed, the project leader of Python is referred to by his status of project leader *the "Benevolent Dictator For Life" (BDFL) with veto rights over anything* but also according to his skills and his decision making activities referring to an effective profile of leader. Thus, the status of project leader of Python corresponds to his activities: his skills are recognized and power is accorded to him.

The Distinction Between Developers and Users Do Not Correspond to a Shared Understanding of Roles

Distinction between users and developers is made in the epistemology of design and in design process models. In the OSS context, these two terms keep on being used in two different ways:

- To distinguish formally users and developers' statuses in reference to ownership, and particular rights to modify the source code
- To distinguish activities in reference of a particular designed artefact (e.g. use or design of the python language)

On the basis of our interviews, it seems that there is no agreement between participants on the meaning of the developers term: some interviewees refer to discussant activities in the design-oriented mailing-lists, other to technical contributions, other to rights to modify the code, and the project leader defined developers are those who contribute significantly to the implementation of Python. Thus, as one of the interviewee put it:

[Developer's] a vague term which may in different contexts be used more or less restrictively.

Things are also made unclear by the fact that users and developers definitions are relative to the context: for instance one can be a user of the Python language and a developer in an application domain.

Python's users are developers that use Python to create products that will have their own users. They are not language developers they are developers that are using the language. Then, I feel I belong the users' community of Python, but not to the community of people that make the language evolved.

Finally these results question the classical distinction between users and developers (or designers) made in the epistemology of design.

Strategies for Constructing Knowledge About the Python Community

Two kinds of strategies are revealed by interviewees to construct social awareness, but also situation awareness (for instance what is the state of development of the project?): one is based on direct experience of participants in the three interactions spaces, another is based on mediation by online resources such as blogs or wikis. These two kinds of strategy are strongly linked to online interaction spaces of the project, in particular the discussion space.

Strategies based on experiences of participants are related to:

- Their participation in online discussions as discussants; for instance, some interviewees could not always answer to questions about roles because they did not have a look on mailing-lists for a while
- Their participation in the implementation space
- Their use of the code, as the name of the contributors is specified in the code for instance

Strategies based on mediation are related to:

- Automatically generated online resources, such as news on the website of the project or digests of online discussions

So, when that [new functionality] makes a lot of noise, that come out on Python dayly news…

On the website I go on ' what's new ?' that way I can follow evolutions

I've got also a google alert, using keywords

- Resources constructed and made publicly visible by others participants: such as blogs of project leader and super-experts, or wikis. This strategy is thus strongly related to the knowledge about roles in the community which has been constructed by the participants. As in the transactive memory approach, participants use their knowledge on "who knows what", as a pointer to relevant resources:

what makes the difference between a buddy who knows and one who doesn't know, is the buddy who spent two years polishing his sources…And then, once you know important people in the community, you point his blog and that's it.

Representations of Key Actors' Roles in a Specific Design Process

Results presented in this section are based on the contextualized semi-structured interviews about PEP XYZ process. Firstly, they concern the definition of a typology of descriptors used by interviewees to evoke roles. Secondly, they show the scope of participants recalled by interviewees. Finally, we outline that interviewees have different perspectives about roles they evoked, and that some roles can remain more or less visible for participants.

Underlying Dimensions of Contextualised Roles and Profiles

The following table (Table 2) presents a categorization of descriptors used by interviewees to evoke roles. This categorization is based on the distinction between discussant and technical profiles, and refined by more specific roles for the discussant profile [4,6].

Table 2 Interviewees' descriptors of roles

Profiles	Roles	Descriptors	Excerpt from interviews
Discussant profile	Interactive	Regularity of answers to posted messages	There were a lot of mails to the lists […]. I read them [all] at home […] preparing answers
	Epistemic	Usefulness of provided knowledge	[They helped me] with knowledge
	Cognitive	Relevance of answers	X offered useful comments
		Initiation of design idea and proposals of solution	Y was the source of the idea
	Coordination	Compilation of group input	X did all the work […] gathering feedback, incorporating it
		Consensus building	Make all this people to accord in a unique result
	Socio-relational	Mentoring help	X basically mentored Y through the process of writing the PEP
			X came and said: "you should first build the decimal data type, take a look at here and here"
			X, Y helped a lot with all this
Technical profile	Code production	Participation to pre-code or code implementation	Just the start of it [code], with a little of tests
		Coding of test	A lot of work cleaning the code and in documentation
		Participation to documentation issues	X who had a semi-worked out module […] Y who had done further work on X's module
		Code optimization	
		Reference to code ownership	

For the interactive role, participants refer to the regularity of presence in discussions, and the recurrence of answers.

For the cognitive and epistemic roles, participants refer to other participants' input in terms of usefulness of knowledge with respect to the design or relevance of the input in the discussions. They do not refer to content and type of knowledge (e.g. (application domain versus computer science or language domains) brought out by participants in the discussions. Their characterisation of roles is rather functional and normative. These characterizations are sometime embedded in a temporal description of the design process, whereas the content of the contributions remain fuzzy. Anthony, for instance, said:

> When the PEP was opened (Jan 2004) Georges gave some encouragement [...] then Michel offered useful comments; in the following month (Feb 2004) useful input was again offered by Aziz and Tom.

The coordination role, considered as most important in research on group work (e.g. [23]), is referred to only by the champion and his description remains very general.

> The rules to get a PEP accepted are simply: You have to [...] dive into thousand of mails of hundreds of people proposing absolutely useful ideas [...], read them, answer them, make all this people to accord in a unique result.

For characterising the code production roles, interviewees' descriptors may be quite precise and detailed. The participants distinguished between contributions concerning the pre-code, the code, tests, code optimization and the PEP document. Furthermore they also considered code ownership (X's module). This notion of ownership is also evoked in the cognitive role viewed by interviewees when they mention that "Y was the source of the idea".

Scope of Participants Evoked by Interviewees

The scope of identified roles, after the first phase of interviews, varies from three, for the champion (Fabio), to only one or two, for the other interviewees. The third interviewee (Anthony), who performed the second phase of interview, in which he was allowed to explore the archives of the PEP, extended a lot his scope of discussants from two to ten. Figure 1 illustrates the scope of participants evoked by the three interviewees.

Combining Fabio, Nelson and Anthony's extended views leads us to obtain a group of:

- Two participants recalled by all interviewee (Fabio and Robert)
- Three additional participants recalled by Fabio and Anthony (Tom, Aziz and Ernesto[4])

---

[4]Ernesto was not anymore part of the project at the time of the PEP, but was the owner of the first code, with Aziz, to implement decimal in Python. In this sense, it is referred by participants to be a contributor in respect of a code ownership value in OSS communities. For this reason, we do not discuss any further his profile.

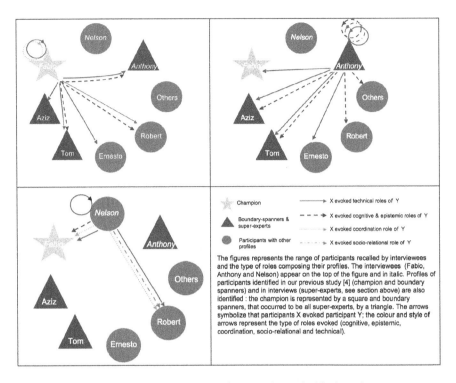

Fig. 1 Scope of participants' roles and perspectives on roles evoked by interviewees

- Four other participants recalled only by Anthony

It is interesting to note that after the first phase of interviews (without any traces support), Fabio (the champion) is the one that has the more extended view.

In the following we focus on participants recalled by at least two interviewees as presented in the figure above (Anthony, Fabio, Robert, Tim, Aziz and Ernesto), in order to compare their perspectives on roles of participants.

Interviewees' Different Perspectives on Roles

The perspectives of participants on one or another roles seem to depend on their own participation in the interaction spaces of the project.

The case of Robert is interesting as he is the only participant recalled by all three interviewees. Fabio, Anthony and Nelson agreed on his important role, but they did not characterize in the same way both his discussant and technical profiles (Fig. 1):

- Concerning Robert's technical profile, both Fabio and Nelson described it as essential. For Fabio, Robert did "*a lot of work in cleaning the code and documentation*" and for Nelson, Robert "*was the one who made all the [code modification] in the repository*". Indeed, Robert was the main code contributor (nearly 80% of actions in this code) [6]. He is an administrator of the project but is not recognized as a super-expert in our interviews. However, Anthony did not refer to the contributions of Robert in coding and documentation

- Concerning Robert's discussant profile, the three interviewees had different perspectives. Fabio acknowledged the importance of the knowledge brought by Robert. Anthony referred to it only as useful inputs. But the most interesting difference remains in Nelson's view that makes apparent a strong implication of Robert in coordinating the design process and mentoring the champion:

> Robert provided strong support to the idea as an established participant in the Python project, and basically mentored Fabio through the process of writing the PEP, submitting it and getting it accepted.

Thus, only Fabio and Nelson who were present in both the discussion and technical spaces have a broader perspective of his profile. These results seem to indicate that participants' perspectives on others' role is linked to their own implication in the spaces. Anthony who was only a discussant in the process may not be aware of the huge impact of Robert in the code implementation as himself did not participate in the technical side. By contrast, Fabio and Nelson who were involved in both spaces refer to the importance of Robert's technical profile, and their views are complementary.

A Relative Invisibility of Boundary Spanners and a Strong Visibility of Technical Profiles

Our interviewees recalled four out of the five boundary spanners that we identified in our previous research [4]: Fabio, Anthony, Tom and Aziz (Fig. 1). This result may indicate that their key participation during the design process [6] has been stressed by interviewees. Participants appearing to be boundary spanners correspond to more than half of participants evoked by Fabio and Anthony. However, if interviewees agreed upon the technical profiles of these participants, they diverged on their discussant profiles, minimizing their socio-relational and epistemic contributions.

Concerning Tom and Aziz, both interviewees recognized that they contributed to pre-code (initial versions of code) revealing their technical profile. Tom was the technical expert of the solution used to do financial calculation with Python before the PEP started. Aziz was the owner of one first attempt to implement the function proposed by the PEP. Concerning their discussant profiles, Fabio refers to the knowledge they brought ("*A lot of knowledge*") whereas Anthony spoke only of their "*useful inputs*" at the same level as for other participants.

The same type of results can be found concerning Fabio (the champion), Anthony and Nelson agreed upon Fabio's technical profiles but not on his discussant profile. Anthony emphasized the contribution of Fabio on the technical side, and did not refer to his boundary spanner and leader profiles, whereas it was essential for Fabio and Nelson. As put by Fabio himself:

> You have to dive into thousands of mails of hundreds of people proposing useful ideas and also absolutely shitty ones, read them, answer them, make all this people to accord in a unique result

On the same way, Fabio did not refer to the strong support provided by Anthony, as he noted himself and as we observed in our previous studies [4,6]. Fabio emphasized the cognitive and epistemic roles of Anthony and did not stress his socio-relational role.

These results may reflect the tendency to emphasize technical contributions in OSS communities, and to "forget" socio-relational aspects as essential for the performance of the design process. Even though participants acting as boundary spanners are recognized as key participants on the technical and sometimes on the cognitive and epistemic sides, their broader profile of boundary spanners is not acknowledged by interviewees. As a matter of fact, it is interesting to note that we showed in our previous trace-based analyses [6] that the presence of boundary spanners and socio-relational activities, performed by Fabio, Anthony and Robert, may be one of the key element explaining the success of the PEP proposal.

Discussion and Perspectives

These results help in understanding the content, development and distribution of social awareness within a large and somehow fuzzy bounded online OSS community. They reveal several dimensions of social awareness articulated across generic or personalised roles and un-contextualized or contextualized roles. Furthermore, these roles are differentially recognized by participants depending on the participant's own perspective and activities, as well as their capability in collecting relevant information.

Concerning the content, we showed that participants seem to agree upon a typology of generic roles based on evident activities performed by participants in the interaction spaces of the project and on personalized roles based on reputation and expertise of participants. They agree that the status is not relevant as a principle to distinguish between roles. Indeed, the distinction between users and developers does not capture the multiple dimensions of participation performed in design activities.

This content about general and personalized roles can be assimilated to a general mental model of participation in OSS communities. This global level of social awareness is developed and maintained by direct experience of participants within the interactions spaces of the community, as well as by gathering information through Internet resources such as blogs of participants recognized as resources for others. The knowledge about these key actors of the project would be an element supporting the transactive memory of participants [24].

Concerning the content of social awareness related to specific episodes of design within the community, our results make clear the distribution of social awareness between participants. We showed that none of the participants has an exhaustive perspective of roles. This distribution is outlined by the difference in scope of roles evoked by interviewees, as well as by the difference in their perspectives on these roles. This difference appears to be linked to their own position and activity of the interviewed participants in the design process. These various perspectives may be considered as entries for an extended social awareness as they embrace parts of a network of participants being resource for transactive memory construction.

It is interesting to discuss also the articulation between global and situated social awareness and the way it is shared or distributed across participants. Participants evoked personalized super-experts profiles, generic profiles of boundary spanner, discussant and technical profiles at a generic level of description of their community. Some of these roles or profiles are more precisely instantiated in the context of a specific design process episode in relation to evident activities of participants. We show that this instantiation is partial. Firstly, there is an emphasis on technical contribution of participants, reflecting a shared value in OSS communities regarding code production. Secondly, socio-relational and support activities – two grounds of the boundary spanning profile – are not well acknowledged by participants in design episode, whereas mediation and boundary spanning generic roles are recognized by participants at the global level. We showed in a previous study that the presence of boundary spanners was a key element of the success of the design process we studied [6]. In the same direction, literature on collaborative activities emphasizes the importance of boundary spanning and coordination in the performance of group work, suggesting also that boundary spanners are not necessarily recognized by the group [19,23]).

These results suggest that both community and team levels (seen as an *ad hoc* community subset collaborating in a specific design episode) are components of distributed social awareness in OSS design. Participants share (1) generic roles that could or should be taken in the design processes; (2) specific person-roles coupling which point on leaders or super-experts in the community; (3) detailed (although filtered) evidence-based perspectives of clearly identified participants' roles based on direct interactions during episodes of design.

This research extends previous works on group awareness and roles in online communities [17], pointing out the importance of social awareness in the elaboration of resources for participants. We propose an analysis of content, clues and dimensions of social awareness as constructed by participants in distributed design in an OSS community. Our results provide also insights on the strategies underlying the construction of awareness, such as the importance of knowledge of roles in order to select resources for maintaining situation awareness. Finally, our findings reveal that memorization of social awareness is a robust mechanism as its constituting elements (roles) can be evoked several years after a design episode. More detailed study of these strategies and how they affect the construction and maintenance of social awareness should be carried out.

Our perspectives of research concern social awareness and reflective tools or methods to support group activities [7]. In this direction, an issue is to investigate to what extent strategies developed by participants to construct situation and social awareness are efficient and how reflective tools can be incorporated in activities. Our position is that a role-based view of the communities could be interesting at least for new comers and also as a support for reflective activities on the collective dynamics. An open issue concerns the effect of revealing invisible roles or profiles on group regulation. A second phase of interviews is under progress, in which we provide the champion with our graphical representations of traces-based profiles in the PEP process.

Acknowledgements We thank our interviewees for the time they have spent to answer our questions.

References

1. d'Astous, P., Détienne, F., Visser, W., and Robillard, P. N. (2004). Changing our view on design evaluation meetings methodology: a study of software technical evaluation meetings. *Design Studies, 25,* 625–655.
2. Baker, M., Détienne, F., Lund, K., & Séjourné, A. (2009) Etude des profils interactifs dans la conception collective en architecture. In F. Détienne, V. Traverso (Eds) *Méthodologies d'analyse de situations coopératives de conception: le corpus MOSAIC,* Nancy : PUNBales, R.F. (1950). *Interaction process analysis : a method for the study of small groups.* Cambridge : Addison-Wesley.
3. Bales, R.F. (1950). *Interaction process analysis: a method for the study of small groups.* Cambridge : Addison-Wesley.
4. Barcellini, F., Détienne, F., and Burkhardt, J.M. (2008a). Users and developers mediation in an Open Source Software Community: boundary spanning through cross participation in online discussions. *International Journal of Human Computer Studies, 66(7),* 558–570.
5. Barcellini, F., Détienne, F., Burkhardt, J.M., and Sack W. (2008b). A socio-cognitive analysis of online design discussions in an Open Source Software community. *Interacting with computers, 20,* 141–165.
6. Barcellini, F., Détienne, F., and Burkhardt, J.M. (2009). Participation in online interactions spaces: design-use mediation in an Open Source Software community. *International Journal of Industrial Ergonomics, 39,* 533–540.
7. Bodker, S. and Christiansen, E. (2006) Computer Support for Social Awareness in Flexible Work. Journal of Computer Supported Cooperative Work, *15* (1), 1–28.
8. Cahour B. (2002). How the subjective memory of interactions at work makes cooperation complex. *Revue des Sciences et Technologies de l'Information, série RIA, 16* (4–5), Numéro spécial "*Cooperation and complexity in sociotechnical systems*".
9. Carroll, J.M., Rosson, M.B., Convertino, G., and Ganoe, C.H. (2006). Awareness and teamwork in computer-supported collaborations. *Interacting with Computers 18,* 21–46.
10. Cohendet, P., Creplet, F. and Dupouët, O (2000). Organizational innovation, communities of practice and epistemic communities: the case of Linux. In A Kirman & JB Zimmermann (Eds) *Economics with Heterogeneous Interacting agents.* The Netherlands: Springer.
11. Détienne, F., Boujut, J-F., and Hohmann, B. (2004) Characterization of Collaborative Design and Interaction Management Activities in a Distant Engineering Design Situation. In F. Darses, R.. Dieng, C. Simone, M. Zaklad (Eds) *Cooperative Systems design.* IOS Press, 83–98.
12. Ducheneaut, N. (2005). Socialization in an Open Source Software Community: A Socio-Technical Analysis. *Journal of Computer Supported Collaborative Work, 14,* 323–368.
13. Gacek, C., and Arief, B. (2004). The Many Meanings of Open Source. *IEEE Software, 21,* 34–40.
14. Gleave, E., Welser, H.T., Lento, T.M., and Smith, M.A. (2008). A Conceptual and Operational Definition of 'Social Role' in Online Community. *42nd Hawaii International Conference on System Sciences,* 2009, pp. 1–11.

15. Grinter, R. (1999). Systems architecture: product designing and social engineering. In Proceedings of the *international joint conference on Work activities coordination and collaboration*, pp. 11–18. ACM Press.

16. Gutwin, C., Greenberg, S., and Roseman, M. (1996). WorkspaceAwareness in Real-Time Distributed Groupware: Framework, Widgets and Evaluation. *In proceedings of HCI 1996*.

17. Gutwin, C., Penner, R., and Schneider, K. (2004) Group Awareness in Distributed Software Development. In *Proceedings of CSCW 2004* (pp. 72–81). New York, USA: ACM press.

18. Hendry, D.G. (2008) Public participation in proprietary software development through user roles and discourse. *International Journal of Human-Computer Studies, 66*, 545–557.

19. Krasner, H., Curtis, B., and Iscoe, N. (1987). Communication breakdowns and boundary spanning activities on large programming projects. In G. Olson, S. Sheppard, and E. Soloway, E. (Eds.) *Empirical Studies of programmers: Second Workshop*, pp. 47–64.

20. Lopez-Fernandez, L., Robles, G., Gonzalez-Barahona, J.M. (2004). Applying social network analysis to the information in CVS repository. In *International Workshop on Mining Software Repositories*, Edinburgh, Scotland, 25th May.

21. Mahendran, D. (2002). *Serpents and Primitives: An ethnographic excursion into an Open Source community*. Master's Thesis, University of California at Berkeley.

22. Maloney-Krichnar, D., and Preece, J. (2002). The Meaning of an online health community in the lives of its members: Roles, relationship and group dynamics. In *Proceedings of the 2002 International Symposium on Technology and Society ISTAS'02*, Social Implication of Information and Communication technology, 20–27.

23. Mathieu, JE., Heffner, TS., Goodwin, GF., Salas, E., Cannon-Bowers (2000). The influence of shared mental models on team process and performance. *Journal of Applied Psychology, 85*, 273–283.

24. Mohammed, S. and Dumville, B.C. (2001). Team mental models in a team knowledge framework: expanding theory and measurement across disciplinary boundaries. *Journal of Organizational Behavior, 22*, 89–106.

25. Olson, G.M., Olson, J.S., Carter, M.R., and Storrosten, M. (1992). Small Group Design Meetings: An Analysis of Collaboration. *Human-Computer Interaction, 7*, 347–374.

26. Olson, G. M., and Olson, J. S. (2000). Distance Matters. *Human-Computer Interaction, 15*, 139–178.

27. Prasolova-Forland, E., and Divitini, M. (2003). Supporting Social Awareness: Requirements for Educational CVE. *Third IEEE International Conference on Advanced Learning Technologies (ICALT'03)* (pp. 366).

28. Ripoche, G. and Sansonnet, J.-P. (2006). Experiences in Automating the Analysis of Linguistic Interactions for the Study of Distributed Collectives. *JCSCW, 15(2–3)*, 149–183.

29. Sack, W., Détienne, F., Ducheneaut, N., Burkhardt, J-M., Mahendran, D., and Barcellini, F., (2006) A methodological framework for socio-cognitive analyses of collaborative design of Open Source Software. Journal of *Computer Supported Cooperative Work, 15(2–3)*, 229–250.

30. Sarant, S.A. (2004). *The role of organizational boundary spanners in industry/university collaborative relationship*. Doctor of Philosophy in Psychology Dissertation Thesis. North Carolina State University, 2004.

31. Schmidt, K. (2002). The problem with 'awareness': introductory remarks on 'awareness in CSCW'. *Journal of Computer Supported Cooperative Work, 11*(3–4), 285–298.

32. Sonnentag, S. (1998) Expertise in professional software design: A process study. *Journal of applied psychology, 83(5)*, 703–715.

33. Sonnenwald, D.H. (1996). Communication role that support collaboration during the design process. *Design Studies, 17*, 277–301.

34. Sowe, S. Stamelos, I. Angelis, L. (2006). Identifying knowledge brokers that yield software engineering knowledge in OSS projects. *Information and Software Technology, 48*, 1025–1033.

35. Tollmar, K., Sandor, O., Schomer, A. (1996). Supporting SocialAwareness. @Work Design and Experience. In *proceedings of CSCW' 1996* (pp. 298–307).

Faithful to the Earth[*]: Reporting Experiences of Artifact-Centered Design in Healthcare

Federico Cabitza

Abstract In this paper we report about two design experiences in the domain of healthcare information technology that shed light on the advantages of getting rid of complex and abstract representations of hospital work and of concentrating on the artifacts that practitioners habitually use in their daily practice. We ground our approach in the recent literature on the often unintended shortcomings exhibited by healthcare information systems and propose a lightweight method to support the phases of requirement elicitation and functional design. We then discuss the main requirements expressed in our recent research activity and provide examples of how to address them in terms of modular and artifact-centered design solutions.

Background and Motivations

In this paper we report on two design experiences that we had in two different hospital settings: a Medical Oncology and Haematology Unit (MOHU) and a Medically Assisted Procreation Unit (MAPU) in a large hospital in Northern Italy. The task we were assigned to as requirement analysts was slightly different for either settings: the MOHU was involved in a process of digitization of its paper-based drug ordering system; this was based on a very well structured paper-based patient record that supported the management of approximately 15,000 hospitalizations yearly and that had been progressively and collaboratively optimized by both doctors of the MOHU and druggists from the hospital pharmacy. The MAPU, one of the most efficient units of the country with approximately 3,500 admissions yearly, was in the process of adopting a new Electronic Patient Record; this was supposed to substitute a simple, but very effective, homemade database that had been designed by the head doctor himself and had been used for 12 years in the unit

---

[*]Friedrich W. Nietzsche, Thus Spoke Zarathustra, Prologue, 3 (*bleibt der Erde treu*).

F. Cabitza (✉)
Università degli Studi di Milano Bicocca, via Bicocca degli Arcimboldi 8, 20126 Milano, Italy
e-mail: cabitza@disco.unimib.it

M. Lewkowicz et al. (eds.), *Proceedings of COOP 2010*,
DOI 10.1007/978-1-84996-211-7_3, © Springer-Verlag London Limited 2010

with general success. Both experiences motivated us in focusing on the delicate task that business and system analysts face when they are involved in the development of a software application that is intended to support healthcare practitioners in hospitals, e.g., an Electronic Patient Record (EPR) or any other collaborative healthcare information technology.

Healthcare Information Technology (HIT [1]) is an umbrella expression that includes widely different solutions, ranging from bar coding, picture archiving systems, order-communication systems, medication systems and EPRs, which often integrate several of these technologies. With respect to other organizational domains, system analysis towards the deployment of new HIT is a very delicate task, also because this usually implies the full replacement of a multi-purpose, multi-user, composite "folder" of paper-based documents, reports, charts and forms that, as a whole, has evolved over the last century to a degree of success in supporting clinical work that no HIT to date has been able to match [2]. In fact, it is now well recognized that HIT can make hospital work easier as well as harder [3], smarter as well as unsafer [4], cheaper as well as costlier [5], slower as well as faster [6], in short: better as well as worse [7]. In any case, HIT has the power to change care provision and hospital work in ways that are not always free from critical and unintended consequences [8]. In fact, despite the hype that usually surrounds the initiatives of HIT deployment, its promises for a safer, more efficient and effective healthcare have so far fallen short of expectations [9]. In the spirit of Illich [10] a new term has been recently introduced, namely technological iatrogenesis (or e-iatrogenesis), to describe the technology-induced harm to patients caused by the introduction of superimposing HIT systems that disrupt practices and trouble care providers in complex healthcare settings [11]. A mischievous observer could annotate that in the last 5 years researchers have been courageous to see the HIT King naked. It has been reported that roughly 75% of all large IT projects in health care fail [12]. In this paper we will not try to re-formulate the ever-valid question of Grudin [13] and examine "why HIT applications fail". Rather, we found it interesting that one of the main problems identified by Grudin with multi-user applications, i.e., what Norman would rephrase as simply "bad design" [14], has been restudied by sociological studies in the HIT domain claiming that a devious obstacle to the full success of EPRs are the *models* on which EPRs are based [15]. In fact, abstract models are an easy suspect, since to our personal experience as analysts in some of the largest IT projects in our region, roughly 100% of large IT projects are initiated on the basis of complex abstract models delivered in the phases of business modeling and requirements analysis. Yet, for the healthcare domain, suspicions could be better-grounded than for other organizational domains.

Generally, the importance of abstraction and modeling in software development is well recognized: abstract models facilitate the interaction with users in eliciting requirements and embedding them in the design [16] since they allow to conceive of programs in terms of user-centered functionalities, rather than the mere capabilities of the computing environment [17]. On the other hand, as candidly and wittily expressed in the Spolsky's Law ("All non-trivial abstractions, to some degree, are leaky" [18]), models can be ambiguous, incomplete, internally inconsistent, prone to fast obsolescence or just plain wrong. More suggestively, in the CSCW domain Robinson and Bannon wondered if complex and abstract models, by which work processes are represented, information needs and functionalities would not just end up by contributing in "automating a fiction": "The language of work is abstracted in a language of representation, useful to analysts. This is transformed again into an abstract formalism, chosen for its usefulness to the system implementers. The resulting system is then imposed on workers/users, taking a critical perspective, and changes the nature of the work that the representation was built on. This is a cycle that has clear potential for catastrophic change via a positive feedback loop" [19, p. 223]. Also in the organizational literature, the point is made that "Embedding fully-fledged and logically refined models in [...*computer-based*] tools [...] is not necessary – worse, they would more likely than not obstruct the work they are intended to 'support'".[1] In particular in the domain of HIT, sociological contributions suggest that the models underlying the EPR design contain a rationalistic projection of hospital work, which does not match how health practitioners actually work in a ward. Accordingly, to fill the gap between theory and clinical practice, researchers from the ICT communities who are more sensitive to the sociological debate (e.g., CHI and CSCW) have recently proposed methods for user needs analysis and requirement specification that call for a design process that is more collaborative [20,21] and involves users as well as human factor specialists [22]. Yet, other researchers question if the very objects of abstraction in healthcare, i.e., medical knowledge and clinical practice, can be modeled at all, irrespectively of whether HIT models are used in the closest collaboration with health practitioners [2].

But even so, if "logically refined models are not necessary", we address the following research question: *what could be an alternative and appropriate design approach to HIT?* To this aim, we share with Berg and Toussaint the point that models have to be "repositioned" in the HIT development process starting from the observation that documents and forms in regular paper-based records are only parts of a socio-technical environment where physicians, nurses, patients, organizational routines, all play their role in constituting memory of interventions and coordinating work [23]; in this view, artifacts need only to "cover their part", i.e., hold inscriptions and allow their manipulation, while their electronic counterparts do not need to embed any explicit and entity-based model to reflect and bridle the intelligent behavior that healthcare practitioners bring to the scene (or, better yet, let *emerge*) by using the record. Thus, determined to unearth the hidden "wisdom of artifacts" and persuaded that "doctors do not (want to) play the model game", we have applied a method that derives the information structures and conceptual operations of an EPR, by avoiding the construction of abstract models representing either work processes, information flows between actors, distribution of responsibilities (i.e., roles) or the mutual relationships between tasks, roles and data. Rather, we

---

[1] Technology in working order. Studies of work, interaction, and technology (Eds: Button G), Routledge, London, 1993, cited in [2].

have tried to examine "what the record does" [23], how its internal structure works in sequencing the work of health practitioners – as a workflow system avant-la-lettre [23] – how its fields and boxes act as reminders and ordering systems [24] of relevant information, how its affordances succeed in evoking pertinent knowledge in the minds of practitioners. This approach leads to adopting a real bottom-up approach that recognizes that artifacts used in healthcare are usually the result of a long-lasting, collective, experiential and almost unconscious design process, which is made up of attempts to improve how physicians document their decisions, represent illness trajectories [25], retrieve facts and interpretations, or cooperate with their colleagues [26]. In the next section, we explain what we mean about artifact-centered and bottom-up approach and provide some detail of the informal method we employed in our last field study. Then, in Section Reconciling Requirements and Artifacts, we will interpret the main requirements we collected in our research activity in the hospital domain in light of the artifact-centered approach, and we will report how this led us to conceive a framework we propose for the design of innovative EPRs and document systems in organizational settings. Section Summing Things Up discusses and summarizes the main findings of our research.

From Entities, Back to Artifacts

According to Silverston [28], there are two general approaches to the understanding of a domain and to the conception of its supportive software systems: the so called top-down and bottom-up approaches. They can be used combined or in some sort of integrated manner, but due to their profound differences, each approach polarizes system design in ways that are substantially irreducible.

In the top-down approach the design process starts by specifying an abstract model of the global system and what information flows take place within and outside the system. In the organizational domain, the model necessary has to include the users' milieu, and to this aim, it is (hopefully) built by interacting with the so called "domain experts" or "key users". On the basis of the experts' accounts and their good resolutions to improve practices, top-down designers get a picture of how practitioners should produce and consume data, and then formalize that picture into a list of necessarily pigeonholed and often very fine-grainedly defined entities, which the application (e.g., the EPR) will represent in its internal state and whose mutual interactions it will support by corresponding functionalities. To bear witness to the success of the top-down approach, it is sufficient to say that the methods proposed in the 1970s to both support data modelling [29] and structured programming [30] are by far the most widely and pervasively used in everyday requirement analysis and design. In regard to data modelling, for instance, designers follow the top-down tenet whenever they take conceptual entity-relationship models, and thorough a series of normalization techniques [31], they build the logical model of software applications and identify the main tables and constraints of the data base underlying these applications, as well as the main functionalities to access and manipulate their data. In this view, top-down approaches can also be called entity-centered approaches, since their main objective is to identify what (types of) entities are involved in a work setting (with either an active or passive role), to translate these entities into computational counterparts (i.e., classes and objects) and to design (and implement) interactions between these entities so that their "proxies" in the field of work (that is, the human users of the computational system) can manage and perform parceled tasks more efficiently.

This, in our opinion, outlines the first and foremost difference with bottom-up approaches in the analysis of collaborative domains as we intend them. In fact, we refer to bottom-up approaches (in system design[2]) to denote those methods that first of all, focus on the concrete artifacts that are used within a work arrangement to specify their requirements and capabilities; and that then, build a system of digital counterparts of the artifacts, which are augmented to some respect in the assumption that the complex behavior of the overall system will emerge out of interactions among its components and between components and the environment. Since in this approach artifacts are both the starting point and the final result of the digitization project, for us to say bottom-up is equivalent to say "artifact-centered". An artifact-centered approach is a method that is aimed at understanding, for each single artifact used in a work arrangement, its structure; its scope (i.e., what it is about) and aim (i.e., what it is used for); the duties and expectations its users have about it; how it works (i.e., its functions and operations), and how it can be (computationally) improved in supporting duties and in satisfying expectations; in short, we mean an artifact-centered method as aimed at (i) understanding the artifact's current and intended role within the *web of artifacts* [32] and resources that practitioners can use in their daily practice to get things done; and (ii) translating this understanding into precise functionalities that embedded in the artifacts and associated with precise uses or contexts of use, either enable, promote or augment human behaviors that *fit* into their work practices [53]. For all these reasons, despite the name, such an approach does not focus only on the *materiality* of artifacts, but rather on the "artifacts in use", i.e., on those objects that, intended to reify processes and their articulation, have come to congeal experiences, conventions and practices of participated and situated collaboration into "thingness" [52]. As other approaches that are more overtly user-centered (e.g., [27]), ours also observes and focuses on what users do, and how; but it also differs in that it focuses on *what* users use, and how, without relying much on users' accounts of work or on any representation (either mental or iconic) of their practices that cannot be traced back to some activity on artifacts. In other words, this approach is user-centered in that it addresses *their*

---

[2]We are then not referring to the general meaning that "bottom-up" has in strategies that are mentioned in methodologies of either relational schemas drafting, model integration or procedural programming; in these contexts strategies are called bottom-up in that they, respectively, integrate small portions of a conceptual model into a bigger/more abstract one, or support the construction of complex software applications from smaller modules (as it is common in Object-Oriented programming).

(emphasis intended) actual tools but it is also artifact-centered since it tries to minimize design misunderstandings coming from either unfocused observations of (too) complex behaviors, polarized descriptions of work (since users can be even more biased than ICT designers in narrating their own work or they can be just wrong in good faith) or too abstract and polished representations of work (since any explicit representation is only about the "thing", it is *not* the thing).

Obviously, no approach can be deemed perfect per se: both entity- and artifact-centered approaches can indeed present known shortcomings. Integrated approaches that take both into (some) account are probably the best choice in most cases, *once* designers have understood what the main pitfalls to avoid are and what they are prepared to trade off for the success of the project. For instance, artifact-centered approaches can "complicate" information retrieval that is performed outside the tasks that usually operate on artifacts; the same holds true in regard to post-hoc data organization according to grouping criteria that are orthogonal with respect to the artifact structure; also information sharing with external information systems can be complex to achieve in strict artifact-centered approaches. These limitations are mainly due to the fact that data structures and values in artifact-centered design can be hardly abstracted from their local context of use (i.e., the artifacts containing them) and that standard-compliant data models can be hardly subsumed when data definition and semantics is driven according to actual and locally agreed artifacts. In other words, strong points of this approach towards technologies that are smoothly included in a local and peculiar setting can play against the compatibility of these technologies with other standard systems, unless additional effort is paid toward the development of proper wrappers and extractors of the artifacts' content.

On the other hand, entity-based approaches lay ICT projects open to other risks. In regard to standardization, model reconciliation in healthcare and the adoption of common classifications towards better integration are still a highly debatable issue (e.g., [33,34]). Model-based approaches usually lead to embed entities' fixed characteristics and the associated business rules (i.e., what to do with data, what they are for) into the data models and the application logic, respectively; this can make even small changes in either entities, information flows or processes unfeasible, since changing the underlying model would require large changes in the underlying database and in the application logic of information systems. Moreover, top-down approaches are usually accomplished on a dialectical and speculative level: that is, designers reconstruct the relevant entities involved in work practices on the basis of narrations told by relatively few key-users, which often unawares tend to depict practices as they *should* be performed rather than how they *actually* are. For this reason, the reliability of entity-based data models can be jeopardized whenever important entity types are not identified, are incorrectly characterized (e.g., in terms of attributes and their formats), or just change some of their aspects over time [35].

It's All a Matter of "Observance"

In order to enable the development of an EPR at the MOHU and MAPU, we organized our analysis in three steps: for convenience we can call them

- Artifact reconstruction
- Mapping between artifacts and functionalities
- Mapping between content and behaviors

The intended goal of the first step was to get the structure of the artifacts and the type, attributes and main characteristics of the information they contain. To this aim, we proceeded using a list of open questions that supported both the interviews with key representatives and the observations we undertook in the hospital units (see Fig. 1). At the end of this first step, we identified all the relevant artifacts used in the ward; in particular, through questions no. 1 and 2 we agreed with the practitioners on meaningful ways to partition the artifacts into "building blocks", i.e., portions that group together inscriptions and fields that pertain to specific aspects of patient health and care. For each of these portions we also specified its "local" schema, i.e., data types, conventional value ranges, intrinsic constraints and access rights (cf. question no.3).

In order to balance an objective but still external approach with a subjective and informal view "from within", we administered an anonymous and brief questionnaire in which all doctors and nurses were asked to informally assess on a five-point scale the frequency of use and the perceived "importance" of each artifact identified. This provided a coarse feedback on what artifacts could be simply abandoned or integrated in others in the digitization process and also on what would be a

---

1) What sections can be detected in the artifact? What fields and inscriptions can be grouped together as pertaining to the same aspect of the patient's health and care process?

2) What are the constraints (if any) regarding the artifact sections/fields in terms of either type, value range or mutual consistency (with other sections/fields of possibly other artifacts)?

3) Who can write what in the above detected sections? More generally, what role(s) can use the artifact (either by reading or writing)?

[...]

12) Does the artifact contain data that must be replicated into some other artifact, or data that can be used for some aggregate or summary report (e.g., a weekly or monthly report)? Conversely, is some field of the artifact supposed to contain entries that are either duplicated or directly derived [34] from other artifacts?

13) What are the relevant conditions (on data or their absence) that practitioners must be aware of, or alerted/reminded/warned about, also according to the context (e.g., according to what time it is, or if an exam report has become available)? What practitioners should do in virtue of awareness of these condition?

14) Can the artifact be annotated by practitioners or contain explicit references to other artifacts/documents/media (e.g., exam reports, digital images).

Fig. 1 Excerpts from the check-list used for the artifact reconstruction. The full list is available at http://www.gl-iss.org/woad/checklist.htm

priority (and, at the same time, delicate) objective for digital replacement; for instance, from the survey, we found evidence that one shared artifact between nurses and physicians was particularly important for their mutual collaboration, i.e., the Drug Order Form; further inquiring into user habits for this artifact helped us understand that constraints regarding authorized access and writing rights should be flexible enough to allow for occasional rule infringements. Moreover, we received confirmation that the artifacts that were less structured and more independent from schedulable tasks for either professional categories (i.e., the Doctors' Diary DD and Nurses' Notes NN) were instead the most important ones which were most often used in daily practice. For its role in providing cues and starting points for further discussions, the survey also helped us in gaining trust from the "shop floor" staff in that they perceived that their opinions, even if highly qualitative, were taken into consideration by the "ICT guys".

The second step was aimed at understanding what actors do with their records, whereas just 'reading' and 'writing' is certainly restrictive. In this step, we then built a mapping between each meaningful portion of each artifact and any behavior we found applicable from a set of elementary operations that were inferred from direct observations of artifact use (see Fig. 2). We speak of behaviors since these involve users (not only the computer system) and can be seen as the goal-oriented execution of sequences of elementary operations upon artifacts within a work context. The output of the second step is then a set of associations between each artifact and all the operations that users could (potentially) need to make either *about, upon* or *by means of* that artifact. To draw an analogy with the design of regular graphical user interfaces, it is as if we had the entries of the context menu for each screen (or frame) of a prospective application.

From the list reported in Fig. 2, it is clear that some of the behaviors more easily than others can be automatized in an information technology without the direct intervention or supervision of users (e.g., operations no. i, ii, vi, vii, viii, ix, x). Moreover, from the perspective of system design, operations can be combined in more complex procedures, which are possibly transparent to users; for instance, the affordance of a button by which users can open an artifact directly from another can be associated with the execution of the sequence `consolidate`, `retrieve` and `open`; a button at the bottom of a page by which the user can "save the page" with the sequence `write` and `consolidate`. Usual operations on the artifact's content

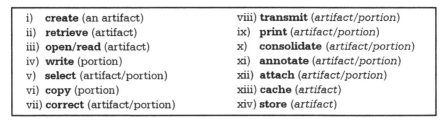

i) **create** (an artifact)	viii) **transmit** (*artifact/portion*)
ii) **retrieve** (artifact)	ix) **print** (*artifact/portion*)
iii) **open/read** (artifact)	x) **consolidate** (*artifact/portion*)
iv) **write** (portion)	xi) **annotate** (*artifact/portion*)
v) **select** (artifact/portion)	xii) **attach** (*artifact/portion*)
vi) **copy** (portion)	xiii) **cache** (*artifact*)
vii) **correct** (artifact/portion)	xiv) **store** (*artifact*)

Fig. 2 Elementary operations in artifact use. Detailed descriptions for each operation are available at http://www.gl-iss.org/woad/operations.htm

like "cut" and "paste" are combinations of `select`, `copy`, `write` (a blank) and `select`, `write` respectively. All things considered then, we see the identification of the associations between the artifacts (or, better yet, their parts) and what users may want to do with them (or may want the artifacts to do for them automatically), as a list of functionalities that are neutral with respect to how the electronic counterparts of the artifacts will exhibit them.

The third step of the method takes this list of functionalities as input and aims to identify an association between patterns of prospective content and the timely triggering of proper sequences of operations: these "associations" can be seen as a sort of *relations* between particular conditions upon both content and context (e.g., what time it is), and behaviors to exhibit in that particular case. Consequently, as output this step produces a list of modular and self-bounded if-then "bunches" of application logic that either triggers timely reminders and alerts, enables commands and operations at the GUI level or executes specific automatic tasks. For instance, a simple "workflow rule" after completing a form would be expressed (in any convenient language) in these terms: *if* 'each portion of the form is filled in' and 'the user `consolidates` the form', *then* 'the system `transmits` the form to the Lab and (`creates`/`retrieves` and) `opens` an other specific artifact'. We will see more examples of conditional rules like this in Section Design to the Test of Ward Life.

Reconciling Requirements and Artifacts

In our field analysis, we employed the method described in Section It's All a Matter of "Observance" the same way as we presented it, i.e., as a simple checklist not to neglect any relevant aspect of artifact use that could have an impact on the design of the EPR. Since the method has been developed almost 'on the fly' while it was experienced, it is not to be taken too strictly. Moreover, this method would have been of little value for us if we had not been able to interpret its outputs, i.e. the schema specification, artifact association with elementary functionalities/behaviors, and the rules for their automatical activation and promotion (respectively), in the light of the general requirements that we had come to identify in our research in the hospital domain (see, e.g., [36–38]).

During our observational studies, we saw doctors and nurses express the same request in many different but converging ways: i.e., the request for a tool capable of evolving with their practice, a tool to work *with* and *through* to pursue their professional goals, e.g. timely and accurate diagnosis, appropriate treatment, effective care. Conversely, in our informal conversations with doctors they all dreaded a tool that was customized once and for all, according to an abstract idea of their work, to work *on* and *for*. But how can this very general request be reflected in precise system requirements for successful HIT?

The analysis task undertaken at the MOHU allowed us to formalize 149 functional requirements and 250 information requirements; the analysis at MAPU detected 168 functional requirements and 1,694 information requirements of 29 different charts. Despite the relatively big numbers here involved, most of these requirements can be traced back to three main dimensions: Support, Autonomy, Flexibility. These dimensions stand for functionalities that, respectively, (i) support the use of information for both clinical activities and "secondary" activities (e.g., management, resource planning, billing, clinical research); (ii) preserve and enhance practitioners' autonomy and creativity; (iii) uphold the informality and flexibility typical of paper-based record keeping. In what follows, we discuss these three dimensions in some details.

Support (or, "fly me to the moon")   This is a common-place requirement. Since HIT is Information Technology, and medicine is an information-intensive discipline, it is no wonder that health practitioners ask HIT to support them in producing and consuming better information in better ways. Notwithstanding, a tool conceived for the administrative side of hospital work (e.g., management) can turn out to be a double-edged tool for other ambits (e.g., care). Doctors and nurses are very aware that their primary job is to identify and solve health problems, to assist and cure patients; they often advocate the introduction of HIT in their setting by mentioning reports (e.g., [39]) that back up their own experience, claiming that in modern hospitals every hour of patient care requires up to 1 h of *paper*work. Too much. This translates into the often-heard requirement of health practitioners to relieve them of the burden of secretarial and administrative tasks and to give them back time to concentrate on the many clinical works that are invisible to formal registration (e.g., sentimental, negotiative, interactional, safety work [40]). In our field studies, we collected a series of requests that regarded operations performed on the artifacts that doctors envisioned could be accomplished by the EPR alone: e.g., to control whether charts were completely filled in and "go after" the defaulters; to create re-supply orders according to cancellations in the stock book; to arrange the scheduling of tasks and orders according to the availability reported in the daily schedule; to plan shifts and leaves according to workloads reported in the monthly schedule; to wrap up reports and accounts for local departments and regional agencies. Paradoxically (but only apparently), doctors would be the first ones to be surprised if designers proposed to talk about how EPRs could support them in the *care* of their patients. This ends up as a subtle lesson: doctors are not "asking for the moon" but, rather to "thrust (or better yet, unballast) their rockets" to reach it. Adopting an artifact-centered approach allows then to focus on the practitioners's real needs exactly where they originate (cf. step one of the method) and to address them with a composite palette of artifact-centered operations (cf. step two), which the system must be able to timely call and assemble together (cf. step three), quite like a scrupulous head nurse would do, but faster and completely error-free.

Autonomy (or, "oh, don't bother opening a ticket for that")   Since no technology is (or remains for long) perfect, especially in a demanding and dynamic domain like hospital work is [41], several times practitioners expressed to us the need to be able to fine-tune and tailor HIT to their demands autonomously, i.e., without the direct involvement of either the HIT supplier or ICT professionals after the official release of the application, unless for failures or problems. This was mainly due to two overt reasons plus one which is more tacit. First, to obtain any kind of improvement or minor adjustment for a complex application (as EPRs are) usually takes a lot of time and bureaucracy. Second, it can be costly, since after-sales support usually only covers standard corrective maintenance, and any request for improvement is seen by HIT suppliers as a new business opportunity when not a pain. Third, doctors and nurses, since they are the closest users of the EPR, know all too well that their needs change over time, that they can fail to externalize them and that ICT professionals usually just do not get the point or insist on claiming that the small changes doctors solicit actually imply major interventions to the application. A do-it-yourself approach would be welcome by both professional categories as a panacea. But there is a subtle divide between fine-tuning, which usually designers interpret as the ability to configure predefined parameters, and tailoring an application to changing and extemporaneous demands, as requested by practitioners. More precisely, practitioners advocated the capability:

1. To modify the artifacts' *affordance*, in the widest meaning of the word, i.e., in terms of either how the interface looks like or what it allows users to do, on the basis of the continuous feedback from the field of work. This point regards the fact that when the patient record is made of paper-based forms and documents, doctors can tweak templates by themselves with programs that are widely known and require no particular ICT skill, such as regular word processors to, e.g., add a row to a table, move a field, insert a key or note, change an inscription. Obviously, for these modifications to become official and adopted in all the wards that have requested them, they must also be validated by the hospital management, and this can be more difficult than just changing the doc template. Yet we stress the importance of providing the practitioners with some capacity to "tweak" the interface: many of the practitioners we interacted with in our researches were in some way involved in the design of their paper-based patient record, or in its progressive tuning over the years; for some of them it was something as easy as printing drafts of templates and handing them out in the ward for validation. Others were also involved in official task forces organized by the top management to optimize how records had to look like also at the regional level. We believe that this involvement in co-building their own tools helped these practitioners in becoming more conscious users and more prepared interlocutors for both discussing and exploiting innovations in their work. The artifact-centered approach we described in Section It's All a Matter of "Observance" facilitates the parcellization of the interface into reusable "building blocks" (cf. questions no. 1–3 in Fig. 1), and thus it conceptually opens the doors to a solution where users can arrange their blocks into full-fledged forms, similar to users of a friendly DBMS who can build their own masks to the DB in a direct and visual way.

2. To formulate queries over the data stored in the patient record, both for managerial purposes and especially for research-oriented needs. This point regards how doctors formulate scientific hypotheses repeatedly as they see new cases (e.g., the idea to investigate the correlation between the odds of a negative outcome and the presence of a potential risk factor can flash more likely while discussing

a case presenting that risk factor). In these situations, practitioners found it natural to get a list of all the patients that in their records had a particular value in a specific field, i.e., to conceive conditions on clinical data where they were used to fill in these data. In other words, we observed how they preferred to reason more in terms of "fields" from forms and charts than in terms of entity attributes. Moreover, they formulated this extemporaneous kind of research questions with a frequency that would be unmanageable even if they just had to refer to the employees of the IT department to launch a standard query over the corporate database. Consequently, being autonomous in formulating queries calls for a technology that enables practitioners to build their data-centered queries in a visual manner, e.g., by picking fields from the artifacts they use more often and defining local inclusion and exclusion criteria on the values they can contain.

3. To create simple alerts and reminders that could be defined upon either data or particular recurring events, as well as to modify and disable those that for any reasons are not perceived as useful any longer. As in the case of record retrieval by field-based queries, we noticed that practitioners tended to associate these kinds of alerts and reminders with single fields and with contextual information that could be easily retrieved from the application (e.g., time, arrivals of messages and documents). This kind of local and conventional knowledge on how artifacts make sense in recurring situations is specifically addressed by the third step of our method where relationships between context and functionalities promoting awareness are made explicit. Once this knowledge has been externalized (also on the basis of question no. 13 in Fig. 1), the autonomy requirement for this calls for a solution whose complexity lays between that of reactive and computable components that are developed directly by end-users [43] and that of articulated parametric structures that, conceived at design time with the highest degree of flexibility, are then configured by the practitioners to build triggers on the basis of local conventions and extemporaneous needs [49].

Flexibility (or, "if it ain't written, there is a reason!") It is now common for researchers in healthcare to acknowledge that health practitioners can be "bad users" of HIT for very good reasons [44]. As also reported in [45], many practitioners confirmed to us that they feel uneasy in using a computer during health encounters, that it has the power to distract them from the point, that computers at the bedside can alienate the patient or worse yet, spoil the personal relationship between her and the care providers. Regarding urgent care, moreover, we also observed what has been reported in [46], i.e., that nurses tend to refuse to follow data-entry rules requiring physician pre-authorization, and that physicians often indulge in working around cumbersome procedures that they feel could hamper their actions. We also observed nurses in frantic day-hospital settings bypassing the precept to use personal credentials to log in to the system, doctors in intensive care unit refuse to open the application in the "right" sequence to get a specific page and to fill in orders with the intended level of granularity and precision: "nurses would understand all the same" was their usual justification. But flexibility does not necessarily means disorder, or anarchy. It is the *opportunity* to enjoy structured order entry and well-timed confirmations when work proceeds as smoothly as routine; as well as to improvise and cope with unexpected problems. It is the likelihood of finding a useful piece of information in multiple places instead of having to remember where it could be stored. Paradoxically, this latter requirement is clear when HIT admirers exalt the information mobility allowed by portable devices and the concurrent access to the same datum by multiple users where they are. Yet we were invited by practitioners to think of this requirement also in terms of the inner structure of the record itself. As reported in regard to the phenomenon of positive redundancy, practitioners appreciate being able to insert and view the same datum in multiple places: in fact, they explained to us that they could have to record the same datum during different activities (and hence while having different charts to handle) as well as to consult a datum while engaged in tasks that, in name, would not refer to it. This valuable insight from the field motivated us to pay particular attention to what answers practitioners may give to question no. 12 reported in Fig. 1.

Also informality is another way of seeing flexibility in action. Paper-based forms and charts often host extemporaneous inscriptions and informal annotations (e.g., underlinings, marks and marginalia). Practitioners add them to formal arti-facts for several reasons [47] but especially to enrich their records so that relevant information, they said, could "leap out" at their colleagues as well at themselves in the next shifts. This operation of enriching artifacts with something that can not be reduced to any official "datum" or to any pre-established information need is then accomplished in an informal and asynchronous way that is substantially unpredictable at design time; for this reason, the logic underlying the provision of this kind of meta-information can be also correlated with the third point discussed about practitioners' autonomy. By recognizing the important role of this informal stratification of inscriptions that artifacts naturally support and on the basis of what we could collect from question no. 14 (Fig. 1) about the annotate operation (xi in Fig. 2), we were brought by practitioners to concentrate on this functional-ity: that the system's GUI could host, as well as proactively convey, what we previ-ously called awareness promoting information [37] to indicate its subsidiary nature with respect to both the functional level (it is just some graphical or textual cue intended to promote a human capability) and the cognitive level (it regards "awareness", that is a human and intimate state of mind).

In summary, our experiences in HIT design and adoption have provided us with sufficient evidence that the dimensions of support, autonomy and flexibility must be taken seriously into account in order to minimize the odds of falling short of meeting the needs and (even tacit) expectations of care providers. In terms of the method we employed, we can recognize that the step of schema reconstruction is especially devoted to collecting knowledge to address claims of increased autonomy and flexibility, while the design of relationships (between artifacts' content and behaviors) addresses all three dimensions of general requirements and the step of associating artifacts with functionalities is aimed at identifying system capabilities in support of the daily practice as we will see in the next section.

Design to the Test of Ward Life

The first two steps of the analysis method could be associated to the development of almost any (traditional) software application, since they simply regard the (bottom-up) analysis of the application domain. Conversely, the third step can not fit (or support) the development of just any application. As said in Section It's All a Matter of "Observance", it regards the specification of small and self-contained modules of application logic; we propose this approach as a way to rethink how the requirement of autonomy could be actually delivered to users, and hence it deserves some further discussion. In [49] we proposed a high-level language so that users with a short training could directly express conditional relations in terms of computable specification, i.e., if-then statements that a (still prototypical) interpreter could execute without further intervention of professional programmers. At MOHU and MAPU, we did not propose this language. However, in order to involve practitioners with no special inclination towards formal specifications in the design of what "their record does" (see Section Background and Motivations), we invited them to express any conditional rule between situations and the system's behaviors candidly, in their own language. Real cases from the settings can help illustrate the importance of this modular approach to involve users in the direct specification of the EPR's application logic.

In Italy some very expensive chemotherapy drugs (e.g., Rituximab) are reimbursed by the National Health Service only through a specific process that allows for stricter verification. To trigger this process and give the hospital the right to reimbursement, the doctor who prescribes one of these drugs by means of the Drug Order Form (DOF) is supposed to also compile a special form (Reimbursement Form, RF), which is collected by the Hospital Pharmacy and then transmitted to the Regional Health Agency. An EPR could support this practice in two ways: either by forcing the doctor to consolidate and transmit the RF to the Pharmacy, otherwise she can not consolidate or even write the DOF at all (a solution strongly advocated by the Pharmacy); or by automatically annotating the single inscription of the prescription (e.g., by underlining it in red) in case one of these drugs was inserted in the DOF, in order to remind doctors to also fill in the RF (a solution of awareness promotion that was proposed by the head physician). The first solution could be expressed as follows: *if* 'the doctor has written *Rituximab* in a portion of the *DOF* named *drug-prescribed*' *then* "create a RF, write it by copying the prescription details from the field *drug-prescribed* and disable consolidate of the DOF until also the RF is consolidated". The second and blander behavior would be like the former one, but with a slightly different then-part: '[...] annotate the *drug-prescribed* field in red'. This business rule (which is local to *that* hospital in *that* region) could have been embedded in any traditional (but highly customized) EPR. Yet from one day to the next, the Regional Agency changed the rules and demanded that an RF would be compiled for every *other* drug prescribed in the same chemotherapy cycle of, for example, Rituximab, irrespective of its typology. While hospitals would have paid a fortune to have this functionality "quick and clean", to enact such new business rules on a standard EPR could be a pain. Instead, in terms of conditional rules, enacting this new behavior would just imply changing the if-part of the above mentioned rule as follows: "if the doctor has `written` *Rituximab* [...] and there is another *drug-prescribed* field compiled for the same cycle, then...".[3] In hospital work, cases in which business rules change unpredictably that have the potential ground-breaking impact on the hospital balance (or doctors' routine) are not that rare as in other business settings; this is mainly because many of these cases depend on external variables (e.g., national laws, ethical committees, risk management commissions) that the management cannot control.

A similar situation also occurred at the MAPU regarding the 'informed consent' procedure. The form used to document the procedure of gamete pick-up was designed when cryopreservation was a pioneer method and practitioners used to transfer male gametes into the partner's womb during the same day. Over time, cryopreservation became more popular and the government issued a specific law to regulate the times and ways of the procedure. Accordingly, all the pickup forms at the MAPU had to be changed to also contain a series of checkboxes in the header by which nurses could indicate if patients and partners had given their consent to cryopreserve their gametes for later use before undertaking the procedure. The almost sudden and unexpected need to adopt a new form again refers to the requirement of autonomy; yet having an EPR store a new variable (consent yes/no) and manage the workflow according to that (e.g., to avoid editing if the consent checkbox had not been checked) calls for an EPR whose application logic is modular as checkbox elements in the GUI are. In such an EPR, the logic would be almost effortlessly updated to comply with the new legislation by adding a simple rule that checks whether "the *informed-consent* checkbox of the *gamete pickup* form has been ticked off" and accordingly "enables the `writing` of all other fields, otherwise it disables that". Conversely, a nurse coming from another hospital told us how she felt frustrated then when she realized that just to add the checkbox in the pickup mask of the hospital's brand new EPR, she would have had to organize a meeting with a commercial agent of the ICT firm that supplied the EPR.

Another example will illustrate how it is important to flexibly support local conventions. At the MOHU, DOFs are daily sheets. Yet some drugs are to be administered several times a day at regular intervals. Occasionally, the last administration of a drug can be scheduled after midnight. In that case, the nurse who is going off duty usually puts the time of administration for the drug at exactly midnight (the last time-slot available on the DOF) and annotates a sign beside it. Then, the nurse on the next shift has to remember to copy the last scheduled administration at the right hour into the DOF of the next day. The local and conventional nature of this habit is evident [37]. The rule coping with this simple need for data redundancy [36] is almost trivial: it just `copies` values from a field to another in presence of a specific annotation. Yet, this situation is so delicate in current EPRs to have generated a recurring deadlock, known as 'midnight problem' in the literature [46].

---

[3]Discussing this conditional pattern would make it necessary to dwell on the details of rule-based programming (or on the specific artifact logic of partitioning) and would be out of the scope of this paper.

In regard to workflow: Usually this term, understood as a way to foster (or impose) pipelined clinical processes and rigid transaction patterns between facilities, makes doctors suspicious, especially if they think of how they actually use their patient records. In Section It's All a Matter of "Observance", we have seen how "workflow rules" can be conceived in terms of autonomous and local (to artifacts) constraints to user's interaction. Parcelling a workflow into a set of atomic and independent conditional mechanisms can be fruitful, since it allows to relax punctual bonds while preserving others in a selective way. For instance, some constraints could be temporarily relaxed if and only if some conditions occur, e.g., if a patient is in danger of death. Other constraints could be notified to doctors, to be sure they are aware of them although they could willingly and consciously break them and proceed. In still other cases, specific limits could be raised to force doctors to comply with the rules and prevent any workaround if some other condition holds true (e.g., a particular health condition that calls for extraordinary safety measures).

This flexibility in articulating a workflow through autonomous modules could also help smooth some "design severities". For instance, the head doctor at MAPU, tired of reviewing incomplete charts in the consolidated records of his unit, insisted on putting a "block" (as he called it) into the EPR that would prevent physicians from prescribing any drug (i.e., `write` the DOF) unless they had gone through two formalities: that first they had formulated at least two probable diagnoses on the Clinical Examination Chart, in order to comply to a regional recommendation and enable better correlational studies; and that they had asked the patient for any known allergy affecting her, thus checking at least the box 'none known' on the Anamnesis Chart, under their own responsibility. The head doctor deemed this capability of the electronic record (i.e., hindering recording!) as one of the most important ones for the improvement of the clinical profession; he is not the only one who thinks this way. Whether the doctors from his unit will always put the second most probable diagnostic hypothesis in writing or not depends on several factors, but few can be traced back to how the patient record is designed. Yet, how many doctors would appreciate that such a single block to their core activity could be relaxed according to some condition (e.g., doctor's seniority) or be just removed when the regional recommendation will be withdrawn?

Summing Things Up

In this paper we have reported the main findings of an analysis & design experience, where we took seriously the provocation, murmured by different observers of ICT projects in healthcare that abstract and entity-based modeling, as it is applied in the top-down approach to the design of HIT, could contribute to its inevitable failure. In two field studies organized within two major digitization projects at the same hospital, we adopted a bottom-up approach to domain analysis and pursued a step-wise method to focus on collaborative artifacts. These were paper-based artifacts at the MOHU and already electronic at the MAPU, but in both cases they were artifacts that had been used proficiently by doctors, pharmacists, nurses and biologists for several years and that in this time span had embodied a whole stratification of changes and adjustments that made them stick to the field of work with an exemplary accuracy.

The method we reported in Section It's All a Matter of "Observance" can be seen as part of a wider design-oriented framework, which we called WOAD [50]; within this framework, we are refining an architecture that can *natively* leverage the indications collected during an artifact-centered analysis, "close the loop" of software development and therefore provide practitioners with a platform that supports them in both tuning their tools by themselves and in progressively programming the modular logic of their EPR. To the former aim, we designed a *template editor* that allows users draw their charts by positioning reusable 'field groups' (which we called didgets [38]) in blank documents like they would do in regular WYSIWYG word processors. To the latter aim, we designed a *mechanism editor*, with which users could associate business and conventional rules with the proper situations in which these rules could turn out to be useful. Unfortunately, we are not in control of the implementation choices that project managers will choose for the development of the two EPRs that will be deployed at the MOHU and MAPU: the overall development process will end only in mid-2010, if no delay occurs. Therefore, we cannot say if the application that has been designed by taking a full artifact-centered approach will raise less unintended consequences than regular ones or if the method we followed is a recipe that, when applied elsewhere, will certainly avoid disaster. In previous researches [38], we observed that the doctors were able to address the construction of chart templates in relatively short time and were willing to modularize the application logic of a prospective EPR in terms of reactive and self-contained mechanisms. Yet, we cannot generalize these previous findings to the MOHU and MAPU cases.

All things considered, then, we are aware of the qualitative nature of the experiences we gained from our field studies; yet these experiences represent a concrete contribution to the debate on whether the bottom-up and artifact-centered approach to requirement definition and system design can be a feasible alternative to top-down and entity-based strategies in the deployment of HIT in hospitals. As far as we put this approach to the test, we witnessed how practitioners felt more at ease in discussing fields and tables from real records rather than of abstract (yet somehow familiar) concepts like health episodes, exam requests and drug prescriptions; we also observed how practitioners who were marginally involved in the requirement analysis could join participative discussion sessions more easily when they were organized with little or no advance planning; and how key users could focus more quickly on the hot points left suspended from previous meetings when regular talks were organized on a loose schedule. From our experience, then, we can claim that enabling a deeper involvement of health practitioners in the autonomous development of their HIT, in virtue of an artifact-centered analysis and design that provides them with self-contained building boxes, can embrace all the three general requirements that we drew in the light of our research in the field (see Section Reconciling Requirements and Artifacts): in fact, it addresses the banal fact that to *build* an EPR that is complete and able to fulfill all the stakeholders that are involved in its use is irremediably utopistic, even if for its deployment developers adopt a truly iterative, incremental and participatory development process. In fact, the same models that underpin how actors and activities are supported by the application risk to become rapidly outdated [35] and hence hinder real close-loop feedback from the field of work. Thus, the need for users to be as autonomous as possible from suppliers (and even, from IT staff) and the need to prearrange localized and tailored sets of functionalities that promote collaboration awareness call for an approach where designers abandon the concept of *building* and instead adopt the concept of *growing* an information system and, in particular, a HIT. As proposed in [51], the metaphor of growing (or, we would say, cultivating) an EPR suggests that the evolutionary process of developing it and continuously tuning and adjusting it are more organic than predictable and more systemic than mechanistic, as we verified in our field studies.

References

1. Bower, A.G.: The diffusion and value of healthcare information technology. The CERNER Quarterly **Q3** (2005) 16–26
2. Goorman, E., Berg, M.: Modelling nursing activities: electronic patient records and their discontents. Nursing Inquiry **7**(1) (2001) 3–9
3. Hartswood, M., Procter, R., et al.: Making a case in medical work: Implications for the electronic medical record. CSCW **12** (2003) 241–266
4. Koppel, R., Metlay, J.P., et al.: Role of computerized physician order entry systems in facilitating medication errors. JAMA **293** (2005) 1197–1203
5. Sidorov, J.: It ain't necessarily so: The electronic health record and the unlikely prospect of reducing health care costs. Health Affairs **25**(4) (2006) 1079–1085
6. Poissant, L., Pereira, J., et al.: The impact of electronic health records on time efficiency of physicians and nurses: A systematic review. JAMIA **12**(5) (2005) 505–516
7. Chaudhry, B., Wang, J., Wu, S., et al.: Systematic review: Impact of health information technology on quality, efficiency, and costs of medical care. Annals of Internal Medicine **144** (2006) 12–22
8. Ash, J.S., Sittig, D.F., et al.: The extent and importance of unintended consequences related to computerized provider order entry. JAMIA **14**(4) (2007) 415–423
9. Harrison, M.I., Koppel, R., Bar-Lev, S.: Unintended consequences of information technologies in health care – an interactive sociotechnical analysis. JAMIA **14** (2007) 542–549
10. Illich, I.: Medical nemesis, the expropriation of health. Marion Boyars Publishers Ltd, London (2000/1975)
11. Palmieri, P.A., Peterson, L.T.: Technological iatrogenesis: An expansion of the medical nemesis framework to improve modern healthcare organization performance. Proceedings of the Western Academy of Management 2008, Oakland, California, USA (2008)
12. Wears, R.L., Berg, M.: Computer technology and clinical work still waiting for godot. JAMA **293**(10) (2005) 1261–1263
13. Grudin, J.: Why CSCW applications fail: Problems in the design and evalutation of organizational interfaces. In CSCW '88, Portland, Oregon, USA, ACM Press (1988) 85–93
14. Norman, D.A.: The design of everyday things. Doubleday, New York (1990)
15. Berg, M.: Medical work and the computer-based patient record: A sociological perspective. Meth Inform Med **37** (1998) 294–301

16. Wieringa, R.J.: Requirements engineering: frameworks for understanding. Addison-Wesley, Reading, MA (1996)
17. Schmidt, D.: Model-driven engineering. IEEE Computer **39**(2) (February 2006) 25–31
18. Spolsky, J.: Joel on software: And on diverse and occasionally related matters that will prove of interest to software developers, designers, and managers. Apress (2004)
19. Robinson, M., Bannon, L.: Questioning representations. In ECSCW'91, Amsterdam, The Netherlands (1991)
20. Kensing, F., Sigurdardottir, H., Stoop, A.: MUST – a participatory method for designing sustainable health IT. Studies in Health Technology & Informatics **129**(2) (2007) 1204–1208
21. Scandurra, I., Haegglund, M., Koch, S.: From user needs to system specifications: Multi-disciplinary thematic seminars as a collaborative design method for development of health information systems. Journal of Biomedical Informatics **41**(4) (2008)
22. Nièsa, J., Pelayo, S.: From users involvement to users' needs understanding: A case study. In press International Journal of Medical Informatics (2009)
23. Berg, M., Toussaint, P.: The mantra of modeling and the forgotten powers of paper: A socio-technical view on the development of process-oriented ICT in health care. International Journal of Medical Informatics (2002) **69**(2–3):223–234
24. Schmidt, K., Wagner, I.: Ordering systems: Coordinative practices and artifacts in architectural design and planning. CSCW **13**(5–6) (2004) 349–408
25. Strauss, A.: Work and the division of labor. TSQ **26**(1) (1985) 1–19
26. Berg, M.: Of forms, containers, and the electronic medical record: Some tools for a sociology of the formal. Science, Technology and Human Values **22**(4) (1997) 403–433
27. Hartswood, M., Procter, R. et al.: Co-realisation: towards a principled synthesis of ethnomethodology and participatory design. Scandinavian Journal of Information Systems 14(2) (2002), 9–30
28. Silverston, L.: The Data Model Resource Book. Wiley, New York (2007)
29. Chen, P.: The entity-relationship model: Toward a unified view of data. ACM Transactions on Database Systems **1**(1) (1976) 9–36
30. Wirth, N.: Program development by stepwise refinement. Communications of the ACM **14**(4) (1971) 221–227
31. Batini, C., Ceri, S., Navathe, S.B.: Conceptual database design: an entity-relationship approach. Benjamin-Cummings Publishing Co., Inc., Redwood City, CA, USA (1992)
32. Bardram, J.E., Bossen, C.: A web of coordinative artifacts: collaborative work at a hospital ward. In GROUP'05, New York, USA, ACM Press (2005) 168–176
33. Winthereik, B.R., Vikkelso, S.: Ict and integrated care: Some dilemmas of standardising inter-organisational communication. CSCW **14**(1) (2005) 43–67
34. Ellingsen, G., Monteiro, E.: Seamless integration: Standardisation across multiple local settings. CSCW **15**(5–6) (2006) 443–466
35. Suchman, L.A.: Plans and situated actions: The problem of human-machine communication. Cambridge University Press, Cambridge (1987)
36. Cabitza, F., Sarini, M., et al.: "When Once Is Not Enough": The role of redundancy in a hospital ward setting. In GROUP'05, Sanibel Island, Florida, USA, ACM Press (2005) 158–167
37. Cabitza, F., Simone, C., Sarini, M.: Leveraging coordinative conventions to promote collaboration awareness. CSCW **18** (2009) 301–330
38. Cabitza, F., Simone, C., Zorzato, G.: ProDoc: an electronic patient record to foster process-oriented practices. In ECSW'09, Vienna, Austria, Springer, September 9–11 (2009)
39. PricewaterhouseCoopers: Patients or paperwork? The regulatory burden facing america's hospitals. Technical report, American Hospital Association (2001)
40. Strauss, A., Fagerhaugh, S., Suczek, B., Wiener, C.: The social organization of medical work. University of Chicago Press, Chicago, IL (1985)
41. Dyro, J.F.: Clinical engineering handbook. Academic Press series in biomedical engineering Biomedical Engineering Series. Academic (2004)
42. Illich, I.: Tools for conviviality. Harper & Row, New York, NY, USA (1973)
43. Henry Lieberman, F.P., Wulf, V. (Eds.) End-user development. Springer, Berlin (2006)

44. Garfinkel, H.: "Good" organizational reasons for "bad" clinic records. In Studies in Ethnomethodology, Prentice-Hall, NJ, USA (1967) 186–2006

45. Gadd, C.S., Penrod, L.E.: Dichotomy between physicians' and patients' attitudes regarding emr use during outpatient encounters. AMIA Symposium (2000) 275–279

46. Ash, J.S., Berg, M., Coiera, E.: Some unintended consequences of information technology in health care: The nature of patient care information system-related errors. JAMIA **11** (2004) 104–112

47. Bringay, S., Barry, C., Charlet, J.: Annotations: A functionality to support cooperation, coordination and awareness in the electronic medical record. In COOP'06, France, Provence (2006)

48. Campbell, E.M., Sittig, D.F., et al.: Types of unintended consequences related to computerized provider order entry. JAMIA **13**(5) (2006) 547–556

49. Cabitza, F., Simone, C.: LWOAD: A specification language to enable the end-user development of coordinative functionalities. LNCS 5435, Springer (2009) 146–165

50. Cabitza, F., Simone, C.: WOAD: A framework to enable the end-user development of coordination oriented functionalities. Journal of Organizational and End User Computing **22**(1) (2009)

51. Atkinson, C.J., Peel, V.J.: Transforming a hospital through growing, not building, an electronic patient record system. Methods of Information in Medicine **37**(3) (1998) 285–293

52. Wenger, E.: Communities of practice. Learning, Meaning and Identity. Cambridge University Press, Cambridge (1998)

53. Aarts, J., et al.: Understanding implementation: The case of a computerized physician order entry system in a large Dutch University medical center. JAMIA **11**(3) (2004) 207–216

A Reformulation of the Semantic Gap Problem in Content-Based Image Retrieval Scenarios

Tommaso Colombino, Dave Martin, Antonietta Grasso, and Luca Marchesotti

Abstract This paper considers the notion of the "semantic gap" problem – i.e. how to enable a machine to recognize the semantic properties of an image – as it is commonly formulated in the domain of content-based image retrieval. Drawing on ethnographic studies of design professionals who routinely engage in image search tasks we seek to demonstrate the means by which aesthetic and affective concepts become associated with images and elements of images within a cooperative design process of selection, discussion and refinement and how these often do not correspond to the unused semantic tags provided in image libraries. We discuss how we believe the problem of the semantic gap is misconstrued and discuss some of the technology implications of this.

Introduction

This paper is the outcome of our ongoing research on content-based image processing technologies and of a series of ethnographic studies of professionals – namely graphic designers and editorial photo researchers – whose work involves, among other things, performing image search tasks. The goal of the paper is to challenge some common assumptions about the way user behaviour and requirements are modeled in content-based image retrieval (CBIR) research, and provide some insight into how the "semantic gap" problem is really experienced by professionals who, as a routine part of their work, engage in extensive image search and retrieval activities.

In general terms, the semantic gap is characterized as the difference between a computational representation of an image's content, which is restricted to low-level

T. Colombino (✉), D. Martin, A. Grasso, and L. Marchesotti
Xerox Research Centre Europe, 6, chemin de Maupertuis, 38240 Meylan, France
e-mail: Tommaso.Colombino@xerox.com; David.Martin@xerox.com;
Antonietta.Grasso@xerox.com; Luca.Marchesotti@xerox.com

M. Lewkowicz et al. (eds.), *Proceedings of COOP 2010*,
DOI 10.1007/978-1-84996-211-7_4, © Springer-Verlag London Limited 2010

pixel data, and the high level semantic descriptions that users might employ in any given context [4,6]. From a user's perspective the problem can be compounded by the limits of current image retrieval tools and technologies, and a more generalized difficulty in characterizing just exactly what it is that one is looking for:

> There are times and situations when we imagine what we desire, but are unable to express this desire in precise wording. Take, for instance, a desire to find the perfect portrait from a collection. Any attempt to express what makes a portrait "perfect" may end up undervaluing the beauty of imagination. In some sense, it may be easier to find such a picture by looking through the collection and making unconscious "matches" with the one drawn by imagination, than to use textual descriptions that fail to capture the very essence of perfection. One way to appreciate the importance of visual interpretation of picture content for indexing and retrieval is this [3, 5:1–5:2].

There is truth in the assertion that just what one is looking for can be difficult to articulate, in high-level language or in terms of low-level features of an image. There is also a subtle, but consequential, assumption in this type of assertion that warrants further thought – the assumption that when people search for an image, it is an act of looking for a match between an 'idea image' in their 'mind's eye' and a digital image in a collection. It is an assumption that has been borrowed somewhat non-problematically from cognitive-psychological theories, which treat visual perception and recollection as neuro-cognitive computational processes which somehow involve, literally, the presence of an image in the brain (or the mind) – presumably as a neuro-chemical state – which can be compared and matched (consciously or otherwise) to visual perceptual stimuli [8].

We are not seeking here to do a full blown conceptual critique of cognitive psychological theories of visual perception. This has been done elsewhere [1,2]. However we would urge researchers involved in content-based image retrieval technologies and in the design of novel visual asset search and management tools to remember that the metaphor of the brain as a computer and cognition as a computational process is just that – a metaphor, and the fact that it appears to fit rather nicely the formulation of the semantic gap as a computational problem that can be solved by purely computational means does not in itself, support its literal interpretation.

We want to demonstrate and argue two things. Firstly, that the notion of image matching is not borne out in real-life examples where suitable images are actually *discovered* through a search process – i.e. even when they seem to have a clear idea of what they want in advance of a search, professionals very much work out just-what-it-is that they want and how it might be appropriate through looking and associated activities. Furthermore, browsing widely is often a means of finding inspiration. Secondly, the problem of semantic labeling is not in many cases a problem about the user being unable to express what they want in aesthetic or affective terms, it is the fact that their choice of terms, as matched by a system often will not lead them to appropriate images. We want to argue that this is not due to simply needing better refinement of the mapping of semantic terms to features but is a consequence of the way semantic terms work and are applied in relation to images.

We do this because we think that it is important to clarify the conceptual relationship (and distinction) between technological–computational challenges in the field of image processing (of which content-based image retrieval is a prominent one), and the real life activities the technologies might be used to support.

We want to draw attention to the way the semantic properties of an image emerge in the course of a series of embodied and interconnected activities (an image search query, followed by browsing of the results, and the selection of a subset of relevant or candidate images, for example) which usually are in turn part of a larger, often *collaborative* applicative context (product design, or an editorial project). We will argue that in such a real-life applicative context, an image search is part of a creative process where the given requirements may be difficult to successfully map onto semantic categorisations used in image libraries.

But what is the practical consequence of this assumption? Why does it matter? There is a subtle difference between treating the semantic properties of an image as emergent (the product of embodied activities and situated collaboration) and treating images as being *statically polysemic*, i.e. being subject to several persistent semantic connotations. The notion that images are statically polysemic enforces the idea that the semantic connotations are properties of the image itself, which can be recognized (by a human or a machine) where a proper disambiguation of the right connotation can be achieved, for example, by applying the proper domain knowledge. We contend that images *are* polysemic but 'indexically' (not statically) so – i.e. the semantic meaning(s) of images are fixed repeatedly, differently, within particular sets of activities such as graphic design. The lifetime of any given meaning can be a singular situation. During a design project semantic meanings are worked up – produced, evaluated, changed, discarded, crystallized. The semantic meaning of an image is dynamic, even in the hands of a single group of users, never mind many different groups in many different places.

Furthermore, as [1] point out, "it is true that machine recognition – that is, the ability of a machine to register an object it has been programmed to pick out ('recognize') – involves matching input with electronically stored image". We suggest that when it comes to a human user, the semantic properties of an image – the ones that we're interested in – are better understood as emergent characterizations. They are not image properties which are recognized thus producing a semantic perception. However, a semantic perception or aesthetic appraisal may be mapped to image properties *after the fact*. However, this is not a necessary condition of providing a semantic description of an image.

By providing concrete examples, drawn from our ethnographic field studies, of image searches conducted by professionals (graphic designers and editorial photo researchers) we propose to show the practical ways in which these professionals make decisions about which images to select, and we hope to show how those "properties" are ascribed, made relevant, and therefore visible, accountable and agreed upon in the course of situated, and often collaborative, activities [6].

The Emergence of Semantic Properties Is Through Real-Life Image Searches

This section examines some real examples of image searches, and focuses in particular on the ways in which high level semantic properties 'become' visible in certain images. While not the only possible image retrieval scenario, here we will focus on the use of commercial image bases (such as Getty Images [8], or Shutterstock [9]) which are, generally speaking, accessed and searched directly on-line by users through a web interface which includes the search tools (which vary somewhat from case to case, but the primary tool inevitably is a textual, keyword-based, query) and a thumbnail viewing pane. Searches are initially conducted through a keyword query, the result of which can be initially constrained and subsequently refined through various parameters and browsing tools which vary from case to case.

This is the primary type of search that the professionals we observed conduct and that in CBIR scenarios is commonly describe as a "category" search. Smeulders et al. [8, p. 3] draw a distinction between a "category" search and a "targeted" search, where the main difference appears to be that in the case of a targeted search the user is either looking for a specific, known image, or has a specific image of an object in mind he or she wants to match.

The number of images returned by a search clearly depends on the specificity of the terms used in the formulation of the query and on the preponderance of images containing those elements. A search for images tagged with the keyword "beach" run on Getty Images [5] will return roughly 130,000 images, whereas a search using the keyword "duck-billed platypus" returns about 20 images (the exact number changes constantly over time as the image collections are updated). Browsing through 20 images to find the appropriate one clearly is not very time consuming, but browsing through 130,000 images (moreover where each page of thumbnails has to be loaded individually) obviously is not a very practical proposition.

In order to aid the browsing process the Getty Images interface offers a "refinement" toolbar (which can be seen on the left side in Fig. 1).

This toolbar basically consists of a refinement tree built with all the tags contained in the images in the current search space, organized by type of tag ("categories", editorial or creative; "people", which contains demographic tags; "location", which allows to select specific, named geographical locations; "keywords", which contains all types semantic tags ranging from content to aesthetic properties; "style", which contains tags pertaining to the technical properties of the image such as orientation, subject position, etc.). The numbers in parentheses next to each tag indicate how many images in the search space are associated to that tag. Clicking on a keyword in the toolbar will automatically refine the search space to all images associated with that tag. Because the refinements are concatenated, selecting three or four keywords will quickly reduce the search space. For example, in the case of the "beach" search, clicking in succession on the keywords "no people", "idyllic", and "panoramic" will reduce the search space to less than 200 images.

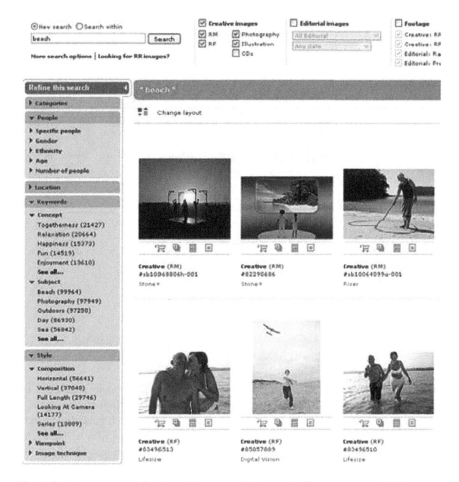

Fig. 1 Getty images search for "beach" images with keyword refinement tree on the left

It is important to note that the list of all the keywords contained in a search space of over 130,000 images is far too large to be arranged and displayed in the toolbar. There is therefore the option for the user to "see all" the tags of a particular type (Fig. 2). The tags which are actually displayed within the toolbar are simply the ones that contain the largest number of associated images (arranged in descending order).

Getty Images has, by comparison to most other commercial image bases, an advanced browsing interface which leverages the very extensive, high-level semantic tagging of all its images. The conceptual tags (such as "happiness" or "relaxation"), whether they are the product of manual or automatic indexing, are meant to capture those less tangible properties that might, for example, differentiate one picture of a beach from another which is otherwise very similar in terms of content.

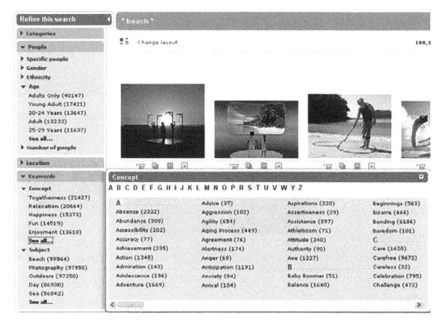

Fig. 2 Complete list of "concept" related keywords in beach search on Getty Images

The question that is relevant to our purposes here is to what extent such refinement mechanisms are useful (i.e. do they actually allow the user to efficiently navigate a search space of thousands of images to locate those images which have the desired properties).

In principle the extensive high-level semantic tagging of images provided by Getty Images is meant to address the "semantic gap".[1] The qualities they attempt to capture are precisely of those that cannot be expressed in a content-based keyword search; they apply to e.g. a mood, feeling or aesthetic in an image. However, they are not used by professionals observed by us and we would argue that this is because they immediately run up against the problem of polysemic indexicality. When we apply semantic descriptions to images there are two problems related to constancy of meaning. Firstly, there is the problem of *agreement*. Depending on the people and the context of viewing it is clear that there is variation in the semantic descriptors people deem appropriate. Yes – some archetypal image features (e.g. a smile-happiness) bring greater agreement but other many features can be shown to be far more ambiguous. Secondly, although in some cases we may find it relatively

---

[1] We would like to point out that we refer to Getty Images as a good example of a site that employs the principle of semantic tagging and browsing and that our argument is around how these types of technologies work. Our criticism is not of Getty Images per se – it is a popular site which enjoys good reputation among professionals for its high quality images.

easy to map semantic assessments onto concrete features of an image (as in the smile example) in other cases this is more intangible (something about the light and shadows) or very difficult to map (I don't know why but it makes me feel sad). It can be easier to articulate a semantic meaning than to specify why. Of course, it is possible to analyse images for features that recur when people have a tendency to give a certain response but cannot articulate what features it relates to *but this will only be possible in cases of high agreement amongst a user population*. This means that tags which are applied according to generic criteria by somebody other than the person doing the search may not, in fact, capture those properties that are being sought in a specific search.

As a case in point can be found in the work of a professional photo researcher who was asked to find some pictures for a feature on an increasingly popular drug called "spice", which up until a very recent ban was being legally sold in Germany as an herbal mixture (Fig. 3).

Among the pictures the journalist was looking for one had to include a person, perhaps in the process of smoking the drug. The problem the photo researcher was having was that a search for the drug itself only produced pictures of the package and the product, but not of anyone smoking it. To find pictures of people "smoking" she used the keyword "kiffer" (which loosely translates as "pot-smoker"), but felt that the resulting images were not unflattering enough in their depiction of "kiffers" for a newspaper that has a somewhat Christian conservative editorial line.

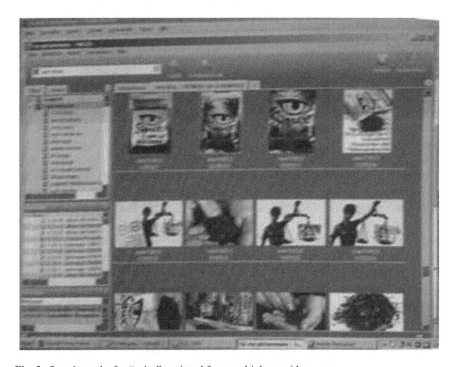

Fig. 3 Search results for "spice" retrieved from multiple providers

Fig. 4 Special feature on "spice"

A look at the picture that was ultimately printed (Fig. 4) on the paper probably shows that these judgments, while they may take up a certain amount of time and effort in the course of an image search, are difficult to characterize in terms of any properties or features the image might have that could objectively characterize it as portraying drug use in an unflattering way. In the chosen image, the fact that the whole face of the person smoking the joint was not visible seemed to reassure the photo researcher that if not unquestionably *unflattering*, the picture was at least *impersonal* enough not to contradict the overall tone of the feature itself.

The issue we want to raise with this example is whether there is in this type of search in fact a semantic gap, that could be though of as a retrieval problem, between low-level image content and the concepts such as "unflattering" or "impersonal". Ultimately, the photo-researcher was able to articulate the appropriate higher level semantic quality of the image in terms of a visual property. But this connection could not easily be articulated, or found inside the photo-researcher's head, at the moment the search itself was undertaken – it was arrived at by taking into consideration things like the content of the feature, feedback from the journalist and the art director, and the photo-researcher's knowledge through experience of selecting images that suit the paper's editorial line.

An aesthetic judgement is partly about the perception of properties (which from a practical point of view, are "looked for" when doing a search and/or choosing an image within a set) and partly about an articulation, or characterization, of those same properties which would otherwise not be "visible" and "accountable" as such in a different context. Even though it is possible to establish a link between a high-level semantic property (unflattering or impersonal) and a visual feature of the image (the partly visible face), the link would be difficult to generalize beyond the context within which it was established in the first place. And the context is not in turn reducible to a domain (such as "drug use") and they way you might model concepts such as flattering-unflattering and personal-impersonal within it.

Sketches of other observations from our studies can add to this understanding. Firstly, the notion of mind's eye matching is massively undermined by the fact that searches can often start out with apparently one target object and end up with another completely different discovered solution. For example, one of the graphic designers we observed spent some time looking for a picture of a washing machine to illustrate an article on laundry and the environment but ended up choosing a picture of clothes on a washing line because *"washing machines don't look good and clothes lines do"*!

This example can be elaborated (in terms of whether matching occurs) and enriched (in understanding emergence of semantic labels) from a look at the search and selection of fonts – a parallel but perhaps more restricted domain than photographs – for a biscuit bar wrapper design (see Fig. 5). In the picture we can see that six (three are the same) different fonts have been selected and placed on outline packets. It is a very clear example of how designers often select multiple possibilities and try them out. They don't know how an image, font, colour or whatever will work until they develop the other elements of the design, place it in context

Fig. 5 Trying out fonts for 'Bites' bars

(of images, graphics text and so forth), and they specifically assess the *candidates* with other people (colleagues, customers etc.). This process allows them to work-up and find the correct font, image, design and so forth.

Another clear feature of this comparative assessment work is that it involves making semantic articulations of what is seen and how to interpret it. Just as the photo editor could articulate why the photo 'fitted the bill' for the spice story. In the bites case the designers used the terms 'chocolatey', 'shouty', 'crunchy', 'home-made', 'it's really perfect', 'of the market' and 'for little boys' amongst others about the fonts under discussion. Are they inherent features of the fonts? Would they be seen by others? They are mapped to the fonts as part of the design articulation and assessment process. They are gestures of appreciation (perfect), sensual cross-relations (chocolatey, crunchy, shouty) and are related to the product and other expressions of what they evoke in terms of the product, consumer etc. (home-made, of the market, for little boys). Some of these can be related to concrete features of the font-images (e.g. chocolatey as a smooth edged, regular font) others not. The designers work-up an agreement on the relevant semantic labels through this process but the challenge in terms of categorisation is what number of these might travel to and be relevant in another situation of use, and also how they might relate to concrete features and as such be perceived in other font-images. We should emphasise as Wittegenstein (1966; 11) makes clear: aesthetic words can be best thought of as gestures within complex activities, such as these cooperative and organisationally circumscribed processes. Sometimes they point to concrete image features, sometimes to an overall look and feel, sometimes to an impression. And they create analogues (e.g. in different senses) and relate to all sorts of relevant features of context.

Conclusion and Technology Directions

What does this study tell us in reference to the design of search tools? It is worthwhile to reiterate our findings and suggest how they may be relevant for issues to do with design:

1. Image search is not a single order activity. Searches vary quite dramatically in terms of the concreteness or explicitness of what the person is searching for. Even with an explicit idea of required 'features', finding the right image can be time consuming. Often images can only be assessed once they are placed in various other contexts (physical layouts with other objects or cooperative and organizational situations). The 'correct' image is not a match for something held in the 'minds eye'.
2. Semantic tagging is bedeviled by the indexially polysemic nature of images; the relevance of any semantic label is always related to context (people, situation, purpose). This necessarily compromises the ability of semantic tags to be relevant cross-situationally.

3. The reliability of semantic tags – cross-situationally – will be related to at least the two following notions; *agreement across viewers* and whether they can be related to *concrete features of images* irrespective of whether these can explicitly articulated by viewers (i.e. these features could be found by machine categorisation in images people label semantically in the same way). In situations where labeling is done by a person without reference to agreement and concrete features it is likely to be problematic. We should also throw in that *fashion* dictates that once relevant categorizations may become inappropriate over time.

4. We have noted that choice of aesthetic language is not random – it is appreciative (negative-positive and otherwise), it is cross-sensual, and it makes contextual connections. These references are produced, worked-up, argued over and refined, most clearly post-selection (at least of initial candidates). The question remains as to how they can be made relevant to assist search tasks. By further investigation can we understand better whether there are patterns related to domains and how broad or narrow these domains could be. By starting small, can we create a reasonable set of semantic labels for the fonts related to biscuit bars, or images related to smokers? Should we instead concentrate on supporting archiving and the configuration of search mechanisms for small groups of designers who work together and share common perspectives and understandings, as we have seen in our studies?

5. Finally, agencies and commercial image bases may have hundreds of thousands (if not millions) of images, and any image search requires a compromise between defining and delimiting the search space through the use of explicit criteria, and browsing a sufficiently large sample of the available images to ensure that the most suitable or aesthetically appealing ones are not missed. As stated, many commercial image bases try to address this through the use of conceptual tags (such as "happiness" or "relaxation") that are meant to capture those less tangible properties that might, for example, differentiate one picture from another otherwise very similar one in terms of content. In the practices we have observed such tags were not relied upon – either in the formulation of a query or as part of a refinement/browsing process. The interesting finding – although not particularly unexpected – is that professionals inevitably conduct their searches in ways where they can have a reasonable grasp on what that search will return, hence the persistent relevance of object/feature tagging. It may not be the beach shot I want but at least it will be a beach. The key point here is that if users cannot understand the reasons for the selection of 'dreary' or 'uplifting' or 'unflattering' photos they will not use this mechanism again, it will be seen as unreliable. Users, often try to work out how something works – the decision making behind the tagging. A clear point to make, once again, is that if the means by which tags are assigned, *systematically*, can be made *visible*, in some kind of way this will clearly be more useful for users. If the tags are not added in any principled systematic manner they are unlikely to be useful.

In this paper we have sought to use ethnographic fieldwork to seek to better understand issues pertaining to the conceptualization of the nature of problems relating to the work of image categorization and the design of image search mechanisms. Given the limits of the image search tools currently available to professionals such as graphic designers and editorial photo-researchers, there are clearly opportunities for more sophisticated retrieval technologies. However, there is also a need, as part of the research program in content-based image retrieval technologies, to bring the semantic gap problem in better focus by understanding when, how and to what end a link between visual properties and aesthetic qualities in an image is established. This should in turn help to clarify what type of image properties can usefully be leveraged by users when performing real-life image search tasks.

This is also clearly relevant for the Coop/CSCW community, not just in reiterating that it is important to understand that search and related activities have cooperative and organizational features – both within the immediate situation of search but also with a wider orientation to organizational and customer requirements. Secondly, exactly the same point can be applied to semantic labeling. Through this we hope we have contributed to better understanding for these two communities and plan to continue this research to further understand this issue and contribute more directly to technology design.

References

1. Bennet, M.R., Hacker, P.M.S.: Philosophical Foundations of Neuroscience. Blackwell, Oxford (2003)
2. Coulter, J., Parsons, E.D.: The Praxiology of Perception: Visual Orientations and Practical Actions. Inquiry, Vol. 33, pp. 251–272 (1990)
3. Datta, R., Joshi, D., Li, J., Wang, J.Z.: Image Retrieval: Ideas, Influences, and Trends of the New Age. ACM Computing Surveys. Vol. 4, No. 2, Article 5 (2008)
4. Dorai, C., Venkatesh, S.: Bridging the Semantic Gap in Content Management Systems: Computational Media Aesthetics. COSIGN 2001, pp. 94–99 (2001)
5. Getty Images, http://www.gettyimages.com, accessed 21/09/2009
6. Martin, D., O'Neill, J., Randall, D. 'Talking about (my) Generation': Creativity, Practice, Technology, and Talk. ECSCW 2009, pp. 171–190 (2009)
7. Shutterstock, www.shutterstock.com, accessed 21/09/2009
8. Smeulders, A.W.M, Worring, M., Santini, S., Gupta, A., Jain, R.: Content-Based Image Retrieval at the End of the Early Years. IEEE Transactions on Pattern Analysis and Machine Intelligence, Vol. 22, No. 12, pp. 1–32 (2000)
9. Wittgenstein, L. (1966), Lectures and Conversations on Aesthetics, Psychology, and Religious Belief, ed. Cyril Barrett. Oxford: Basil Blackwell

Design of a Collaborative Disaster Response Process Management System

Jörn Franke and François Charoy

Abstract We describe in this article a framework for disaster response process management. This framework can be used to develop information systems supporting those processes. It is grounded in several research approaches: literature research, case studies, end user interviews and workshops. We compare disaster response process management with business process management and argue why it is substantial different to it. Another main result of this comparison is that business process management technology, such as flexible workflow systems, are not suitable for disaster response processes. We propose an information system supporting disaster response processes based on our developed framework. Finally we present validation of the information system design and give outlook on our future research.

Introduction

Information Communication Technology (ICT) support for disaster management has recently drawn much attention in research due to the growing awareness of disasters all over the world. The European Union (e.g. within the FP7 research framework) and research agencies of different countries (e.g. Germany or France) have granted several research projects in this area. However, none of them explicitly deals with the management of the activities of different organizations in the disaster response with ICT support. Our research has confirmed that it is an important issue.

J. Franke (✉)
Public Security, SAP Research Center (SRC) Sophia Antipolis, 805, Avenue du Docteur Maurice Donat, BP1216-06254 Mougins, France
e-mail: joern.franke@sap.com

F. Charoy
LORIA-INRIA, Nancy-Université, BP 239-54506 Vandoeuvre-lès-Nancy Cedex, France
e-mail: charoy@loria.fr

M. Lewkowicz et al. (eds.), *Proceedings of COOP 2010*,
DOI 10.1007/978-1-84996-211-7_5, © Springer-Verlag London Limited 2010

Our interviews with fire fighters and police have also shown that current practices for managing activities without or only with unsophisticated ICT support, such as e-mail, have several flaws and current practices are criticized by all stake holders.

The goal of this paper is to propose an approach for a collaborative disaster response process management system. We will follow a design science research approach [1] to achieve this goal. Following this approach, in the next chapter, we propose a framework for disaster response process management. It must support the management of activities within the disaster response on an intra-and inter-organizational level. In the third chapter, we propose an information system supporting disaster response process management based on the framework developed in the previous chapter. In the fourth chapter, we describe evaluation methods for this information system and provide initial evaluation results. Finally, we conclude and give an outlook on our future research.

Framework for Process Management for Disaster Response Processes

Definition

The term disaster is not uniquely defined in the area of disaster management. It is also used synonymously with terms like emergency or catastrophe. We distinguish between these terms and follow their definition by [2]. An emergency is a routine and is part of the day-to-day live of a public safety organization (e.g. fire fighter fight a manageable fire in one house). Each organization involved in solving the emergency is clear about its tasks and how it works together with other organizations. Major concerns in an emergency are the people affected by the event.

A disaster is significantly different to an emergency. The organizations face new and unforeseen challenges. There are far more organizations involved than in an emergency and it is not always clear what are the dependencies between them. Activities of day-to-day emergency routines may become less important than activities to fight the disaster. Goals of the organizations change depending on the evolution of the disaster response. Planning is important, but plans may change arbitrarily and new plans have to be made and integrated with other plans and activities of the own and other organizations. Execution and monitoring of new and old plans as well as activities is challenging. We use the term crisis synonymously with disaster.

A catastrophe is characterized by a very heavy impact on the community and its infrastructure, in particular the communication infrastructure. The organizations and people are overwhelmed by the impact, communication and coordination is almost impossible. One example for a catastrophe is the nuclear bomb in Hiroshima. Our proposed disaster process management approach aims at disasters and is also touches the area of emergencies, because it can be used to mitigate the risk or to manage the case when an emergency evolves into a disaster.

Disaster process management has only recently drawn some attention, but this was usually driven from the technical side without few if not any foundation in the social sciences. Disaster process management can be described by the following lifecycle phases: mitigation, preparedness, response and recovery [3]. The mitigation phase deals with risk reduction, i.e. prevention or attenuating that a disaster can actually happen. Preparedness deals with planning and training for disaster response and recovery within one organization and or between more organizations. In the response phase different organizations with low and high dependency on each other fight the disaster and its consequences. The recovery phase is about debriefing from the response (learning and discussing about the response) and reconstruction of the social processes (e.g. build houses, relocation, funds etc.) of the affected communities. We focus here mainly on the processes in the response phase. In the next section we describe our research methodology for developing the framework.

Research Methodology

In the following subsections, we introduce our different research methodologies. We begin in the next subsection with the literature review, followed by interviews in the third subsection. In the fourth subsection we describe a workshop about cross-organizational aspects of disaster response process management. In the fifths subsection we describe our analysis of disaster response plans.

Literature Review

We searched the literature in the social sciences and business process management on the topic. The goals of the literature review were (1) to understand the domain (2) to confirm the problematic (3) to provide an interdisciplinary view on the problem. Core theoretical foundation is Weick's work on sense making [4]. Weick identified the same problem as we did in our talks with public safety organizations: The main problem is to know who does what and how the corresponding activities are related. We analyzed empirical results (e.g. [5]) and we also investigated selected case studies (e.g. [6–10]). We are not aware of any work that deals with disaster response process management from an information systems perspective. Business process management (cf. [11,12]) was chosen as a reference, because it addresses, among other things, the same problematic, but in another domain. This field also provides mature technology and tools to address this issue. Business process management is used for intra- and inter-organizational coordination of activities. The management discipline encompasses methodological and technological approaches [13]. Business process management follows the lifecycle of planning/change management, implementation and monitoring of business processes [14]. The focus is mostly on operational business processes [15] that are repeated a great number of times. Strategic or tactical processes require different approaches. Most prominent technical approaches are process-aware information systems or workflow systems [16], where the operational business process is modeled, executed and monitored. Technological solutions based on these approaches have been proposed (e.g. [17–19]), but without any agreement or clear definition what disaster process management could means.

Interviews

We used the results of the interviews within the SoKNOS project for investigating them from the point of view of the problem mentioned before. The interviews were open and the goal was to find out what are the problems and challenges in the disaster and how it can be supported by ICT in general. A scenario of a flood has been developed based on previous disasters together with end users. A set of unified modeling language (UML) use cases have been developed that can be supported by various systems. Response activities have been modeled for getting an overview about the processes and activities during a disaster response. Interviews last usually 1–2 h. Interview partner have been fire fighter commanders and police commanders with several years of experience, because the focus of the project was the command center level.

Workshop

The workshop aimed at cross-organizational collaboration between command centers of different organizations. The workshop lasted 1 day. The workshop itself was open and the goal was to get the big picture of cross-organizational collaboration between public safety organizations in a disaster. It was attended by domain experts, e.g. fire fighter commanders from two different states in Germany and a police chief of one state in Germany. It was also attended by computer scientists and scientists from the information systems area. Topics covered in this workshop were: legal framework for collaboration between public safety organizations and its implementation in real disasters. We covered several real flood disasters where different public safety organizations worked together. The output was a global picture how public safety organizations, in particular police and fire fighter work together within one state and different states in Germany. The results are presented in the next section.

Plans of Organizations

During our research we had the opportunity to look at plans of fire fighters of two different states in Germany for responding to a disaster. Although both organizations have the same purpose (fire fighting), they are highly independent and follow different methods, regulations and procedures, because states in Germany are highly independent. These plans cover generic disaster activities (e.g. evacuation or treatment of injured people), but also disaster specific activities (e.g. for a pandemic).

Disaster Response Process Management

Overview

In this section we present our research results about disaster process management in the response phase. We describe challenges in modeling, executing, monitoring and cross-organizational aspects of response processes. We compare them in each corresponding subsection with business process management and summarize the results in the fifth subsection. Finally, we describe in the last subsection requirements for a disaster response process management system. These requirements can be used as a basis to develop such a system.

Modeling Processes

A first step has been to challenge business process modeling languages, using them to model disaster response processes. The main rationale behind this was that systems supporting management of processes require description of the processes as business process models. We tried to model together with end users, based on plans and their experience, the response processes for a flood and a train accident with hazardous material. We used the event-driven process chain (EPC) modeling language. We did not investigate other business process modeling languages, because research has shown that business process modeling languages are understood as similar by the different users [20]. The main problem was that most activities in the resulting plans are executed in parallel and different temporal relationships exist between activities which cannot be modeled adequately by business process modeling languages. For example, a business process modeling language cannot articulate that two activities have to be executed at the same time or that they should overlap. Business process modeling languages only support data dependencies between activities, but to very limited extent temporal dependencies (e.g. it is only possible to describe sequences of activities). In fact, the modeled processes were useless, because they just illustrated that many activities had to run in parallel.

We also tried to consider governance/management aspects of activities, but the modeling of these aspects was limited using a business process modeling language. For example, in a business process modeling language, it is only possible to model who is responsible for executing an activity, but we also needed to model other mechanisms (governance), such as only an accountable person is allowed to change an activity from a planning phase to and execution phase (i.e. giving an order for execution). When including this, resulting process models where very large (i.e. many activities and connection between activities) and could not be understood without extra explanation by the modeler. The police chief commented the models as follows:

> This is just for you (the interviewers) to get an overview what happens. It does not make much sense to represent it like this. We better do not start modeling the exceptions in this…

We also did not find use of business process modeling or similar languages (e.g. flow charts) in planning documents. Our experience has also been confirmed by others (e.g. [18,19,21]). Modeling or planning is also done in real disasters. Usually, the organizations use whiteboards or geographical maps to model/plan their actions to respond to a disaster. They rely at least initially on existing plans for responding disasters. These plans are written documents, where activities are listed. Sometimes also background information is given (e.g. scientific reasons).

Execution

Once the disaster has happened, a lot of response processes are executed by different organizations. Each organization establishes a command center managing its response. Depending on the dimension of a disaster, more than one command center might be established by one organization (e.g. one for each disaster site). A command center controls one or more field teams, which are themselves coordinated by a team leader. Usually the field teams have the right to act autonomously in case of imminent danger or threat of life (i.e. it is not comparable with a military command and control model). The different planned activities are delegated to the responsible people for execution. Accountability and responsibility (governance) for an activity are usually clear in emergencies, because each organization has clearly defined task. However, in a disaster this is not always the case. Accountability or responsibility may become unclear for several reasons, e.g. organizations have to do new tasks, because disasters have by definition new and unforeseen challenges. Another consequence of this is that availability is unclear, because organizations may be busy with new and unforeseen tasks, e.g. if some of the field team members are injured then rescuing them has priority over responding to a disaster (e.g. continue fighting a fire).

Workflow technology (cf. [15]) enables the controlled execution of operational business processes by means of an information system. It cannot be used to execute disaster response processes. Firstly, it relies on business process models, which cannot be used to model adequately response processes as mentioned before. Secondly, it enforces the execution of the processes, because business processes need to process information (e.g. invoices) in a standardized way. This does not hold for a disaster response processes: The focus is here on detecting violation of dependencies to other activities in order to deal with them adequately. Thirdly, business process models do not provide enough flexibility for change, although several change approaches have been proposed in the literature [22–26]. These approaches only apply where change is the exception and not the rule. During a disaster, change and adaption is the rule. Fourthly, the execution semantics of a workflow do not apply to a disaster response process. Each process execution (workflow) in the workflow system manages information and sequential dependencies between activities (e.g. an invoice need to be received before it can be processed). Disaster response processes do not have information dependencies between the activities, but temporal dependencies, which need a different kind of treatment. The reason for this is the inadequate description of response processes by a business process modeling language. Hence, it is very difficult to execute disaster response processes in a workflow system. The disaster response process execution in such a system would be meaningless.

Monitoring

The command center of an organization receives feedback, i.e. the state of an activity, from the field. Different organizations have different means to visualize this feedback. Some organizations, such as fire fighters, use geographical maps to present this information. Others, such as the police, use a matrix to present this information. This means they use the same tools for monitoring and modeling/planning. At the moment, they don't always have information technology support, although this is a desired feature, because using printed maps or whiteboards is quite cumbersome and information can get lost or there may be information overload.

We have argued before that execution of disaster response processes in a workflow system is meaningless and thus, monitoring of them in the same system is also meaningless. Monitoring in a workflow system is used to ensure that the processed business objects by a workflow meet business goals and key performance indicators. Disaster response processes do not have business objects and business goals are different from goals of a disaster response.

Cross-organizational Aspects

During our workshop, we discovered the importance and the multi-dimensional aspects of cross-organizational management.

There are three different kinds of collaborations between organizations:

1. Activities of one organization depend on many other activities of other organizations, i.e. temporal dependencies as mentioned already in the modeling section. This came up not only in the workshop, but also in other case studies (e.g. [10]) and interviews. It should be noted that, although activities are dependent on each other, there is no globally defined process by the different organizations. The organizations are highly independent and they deal with activities and dependencies to activities of other organization in a decentralized manner, i.e. they deal with them themselves.
2. One organization may work as a contractor for another organization.
3. One organization becomes part of the other organization, i.e. part of the organizational structure.

The problem of accountability and responsibility becomes also a new dimension on the cross-organizational level, for example, when fire fighters of different states or even countries fight together a fire. There can be a mixture of all three kinds of collaborations, which leads to unforeseen problems if accountability and responsibility is not describe properly. Security and trust was an important matter when working on the cross-organizational level. Security refers to ensuring confidentiality and integrity of information when transmitting, storing and processing them. Trust is about how much people in one organization trust people of other organizations. This affects information sharing between them. In our workshop it was noted that trust may even change during a disaster. For example, people, who have been trusted before are not trusted anymore, because of an event destroying their reputation.

Inter-organizational operational business processes can be modeled using workflow technology (e.g. [27,28]). They are suited for operational business processes and similar arguments to the ones given above apply also to them. Cross-organizational business processes have usually few well-defined complex organizational and technical interfaces between them. Those interfaces are well-designed for the given purpose. One global processes in which all organizations are part of is designed and all organizations agree to this process (cf. supply chain management). The opposite holds for cross-organizational disaster response processes: There are many simple interfaces, which are created ad-hoc. They are not well-designed for the given purpose, but functional (e.g. using phone, e-mail or fax instead of complex communication system).

Comparison

Disaster response process management is different than business process management. In the Table 1 we summarize important differences. We chose the following criteria for comparing them: Management Lifecycle, Modeling, Execution, Monitoring and cross-organizational aspects. Our experiences with end users confirm that these differences require a new approach to process management and its technology support. It should be noted that we do not only aim at an adequate description of processes, but also at their management (i.e. execution and monitoring).

Requirements

In this section we describe the main requirements for a collaborative disaster process management system based on our research described in the previous sections. These requirements are the following:

- It shall allow simple modeling (i.e. without complex constructs) of the response activities on a shared activity workspace. Humans have problems to understand complex models [29] in real time and a quick understanding of activities and dependencies is required in a disaster response.
- It shall allow the modeling of activities: Activities can be created ad-hoc because new activities, which have not been done before, will occur. Different types of activities (e.g. decision-making activity, evacuation or search and rescue) need

Table 1 Comparison between Business Process Management and Disaster Process Management

Criteria	Business Process Management	Disaster Process Management
Process Management Lifecycle	Planning, Implementation and Monitoring of processes are sequential steps, each taking a lot of time	Planning, Implementation and Monitoring of processes in parallel, no start and end of these steps, highly iterative steps
Modeling	Control-flow oriented: complex routing of information between activities. Processes can be managed in isolation to each other	Temporal dependencies between activities. Processes cannot be managed in isolation to each other
Execution	Frequently, few exceptions, change is seldom	Executed seldom/once, many exceptions, change is the rule
Monitoring	Key performance indicators and business goal violation	Activity status and violation of temporal dependencies
Cross-organizational Aspects	Global definition of inter-organizational processes, few interfaces/interactions between organizations (organization to organization)	No global definition of inter-organizational processes, many interfaces/interactions between organizations (people to people), ad hoc definition of new interfaces/interactions based on personal contacts

to be modeled differently, because there are different management processes for them. For example, activities in the field have a different management process compared to strategic activities.

- It shall allow the modeling of different kinds of dependencies: different kind of temporal dependencies can be established between activities (e.g. activities should be in the same state at the same time). This is the result of our research and currently these kinds of dependencies are not supported by process management systems.
- It shall allow the modeling of governance roles: organizations tend to be involved in networked organizational structures. This requires a clear description and enforcement of governance roles for an activity. This is essential and is still a big issue in current disaster response processes.
- It shall support the execution of activities: Execution is described as state change of activities. State changes of all activities can take place concurrently. In real case, all the activities may run in parallel. Each state change may violate dependencies and this needs to be managed by the system (e.g. by visualizing them). This supports the understanding of the disaster response processes.
- Monitoring of shared activity workspace: Each user can visualize the activities and their dependencies differently, e.g. by providing a map of activities or an activity matrix. This requirement results from the fact that each organization has already means for monitoring of the response processes. If they are not provided by the system, the end users will not accept it.

- Exchange of activities and dependencies: Activities and dependencies can be exchanged between different shared activity workspaces within and outside the organization. Exchange always takes place between people based on prior private or work-related contacts and not between organizations. Subsequent state changes of the exchanged activities needs to be propagated to all shared workspaces the activity has been exchanged with. Our research has shown that organizations are highly independent, but still they have to exchange these kinds of information. They do not plan processes in a collaborative manner, but keep other people informed about their own activities and integrate the status of activities of other organizations in their own processes.

Based on these extensive studies and requirements elicitation, we have started to work on a model that should answer these requirements. This model is centered around the concept of activities and on their dependencies.

Concept for a Disaster Response Process Management System

Overview

In this chapter we are going to describe the fundamental concepts of the disaster response process management system. We start in the next subsection with a modeling language for describing disaster response activities. A meta-model for the language is described and afterwards an example is given, which explains the elements of the meta-model. In the second subsection, we describe how the model is enacted by the system. In the third subsection, we describe how we can facilitate monitoring of the activities beyond the execution mechanism. In the last subsection we describe how activities can be exchanged between shared activity subspaces to enable cross-organizational process management.

In contrast to business process management systems, our system supports modeling, execution and monitoring at the same time in an integrated manner as it is part of the requirements we have identified.

Modeling

Overview

Our research has shown that business process modeling languages are not able to model disaster response processes adequately. The modeling approach we propose is based on the meta-model described in the next section. It is followed by an example of this modeling approach.

Meta-Model

The meta-model includes the following model elements: activity type, activity and dependency. Activities have an activity type. Activity types are used to model the different kind of activities, their life cycle and their governance rules. All activities may run in parallel as soon as they are created and dependencies can be established between them during their execution.

An **activity type** $at_i = (SA, f, G)$ is described as follows:

- S is a finite set of activity states.
- $SA \subseteq S$ is a subset of activity states for the activity.
- $f : SA \rightarrow SA$ is a transition function defining the possible transitions from one state to another for one activity type.
- $G = \{g_a, g_r, g_c, g_i\}$ describes four governance roles (accountable, responsible, consulted and informed) and their transition functions for changing an activity state. These governance roles can be found in various contexts, such as military or project management [30].
- The idea is that depending on the role only a certain subset of transitions can be made.

  - $g_a \subseteq f$ is the transition function of the accountable role for the activity. Accountability describes who decides ultimately on the activity and also the governance arrangements.
  - $g_r \subseteq f$ is the transition function of the responsible role for the activity. Responsibility describes who executes the activity.
  - $g_c \subseteq f$ is the transition function of the consulted role for the activity. Consulted describes who should be consulted prior a state change.
  - $g_i \subseteq f$ is the transition function of the informed role for the activity. Informed describes who is informed after a state change.

An **activity** $a_i = (uid, name, cs, ad, GA)$ is defined as

- uid is a unique identifier of the activity
- $name$ describes the activity
- $cs \in SA$ is the current state of the activity
- $ad \in A_t = \{at_1, ..., at_n\}$ one activity type in the set of activity types
- $GA = P \times G$
- P is the set of assigned participants/users

The activity description can be extended by further data (e.g. resources, geographical positions etc.), but we do not define how the data should be structured or interpreted.

Dependencies can be defined between states of two activities. Here, we limit ourselves to temporal dependencies.

They have been identified as very important in the requirements phase. These dependencies are not based on absolute or concrete date/times, but on relative ones (i.e. relative to states of other activities). The main reason is that absolute date/

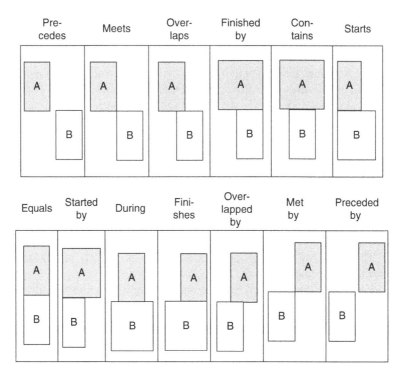

Fig. 1 Allen's proposed time interval relationships

time dependencies are difficult to plan or predict in a disaster response. However, this does not mean we cannot integrate deadlines in our model. We chose Allen's time interval relationship theory [31] as a foundation of our dependency model. Allen described 13 time interval relationships (see Fig. 1), we also use for describing dependencies between states. These dependencies are distinct, exhaustive and qualitative. This is different from business process models and provides much more flexibility. Several dependencies may exist between different states of two activities.

All these elements can be loaded from and stored into a file (similar to a response plan).

Example

Activities and dependencies can be created by users on a shared activity work space at any point in time. The model doesn't distinguish between design, execution or monitoring phase. Activities are based on activity types. Examples for activity types are decision-making activities or operation in the field. Each activity type has its own management lifecyle (see Fig. 2 for an example).

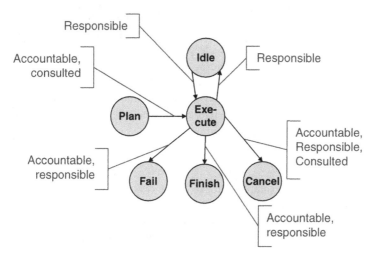

Fig. 2 Example: Activity type

As we have said before, the model is created and modified as it executes. Execution here means changing state of activities and taking care of dependencies. Therefore, we provide an example for modeling and executing activities in the next section.

Execution

Algorithm

Execution is about changing the state of activities. State change of activities has an impact on the dependencies between them. The execution algorithm can be described as follows:

1. State change of activity is requested
2. Verify if state change is allowed by governance role
3. Create a list of violated dependencies by the state change

All violated dependencies are returned by the execution algorithm. We do not describe the technical implementation here, but it has been already implemented. The system has three choices to treat the violation of dependencies: not allowing the state change (enforcing the dependency), visualization of the violation of dependencies (support) or trigger the required state changes of other activities to fulfill the dependency (automation). The treatment of dependency can be modeled together with the dependency in our system, e.g. the user defines if the dependency should be enforced, supported or automated. Selecting one or the other dependency violation management strategy is very dependent on the kind of activity and on the situation. More experimentation will be needed to understand what the best practices are. However, the need to provide very flexible management mechanisms is mandatory. Especially, always enforcing the kind of constraints that we allow to implement would certainly conduct to unproductive situation.

Each change is also recorded in the execution trace. The execution trace also records the governance role and the participant who performed the state change.

Example

Figure 3 illustrates an example for executing two activities with a dependency between the state "execution" of each activity. The dependency says that both activities have to be in the execution state at the same time. It means that the beginning and the end of their execution should be synchronized.

In the first phase, both activities are in the state "Plan". The dependency is not violated, because no activity is in a state described in the dependency. The responsible role for the activity "Build dam" switches to the state "Execute" in phase two. The systems warns the participants in the shared activity workspace that there is a dependency conflict: if the activities "Build Dam" switches into the state "Execute", the activity "Transport Sandbags" has also to switch into the state "Execute" and vice versa. In the third phase, the responsible role for the activity "Transport Sandbags" switches into the state "Execution" and the conflict is resolved.

Monitoring

Core concept of monitoring is that the participants are informed about the current state of an activity and of violated dependencies. This mechanism can be extended by visualizing the activities in different contexts based on the attached data. For example, one popular visualization method for organizations in the disaster response is to visualize the activities on the map. This is illustrated in Fig. 4. In this example, a flood of the river Seine is threatening several suburbs in Paris. Different organizations try to build a sandbag wall to protect the suburbs against the flood. The activity "Transport Sandbags" failed, because a truck broke down.

Decentralized Exchange

Overview

In this section we describe how our approach works on the cross-organizational level. The basic idea is that there is no globally defined process. People within one shared activity workspace exchange selected activities and dependencies with

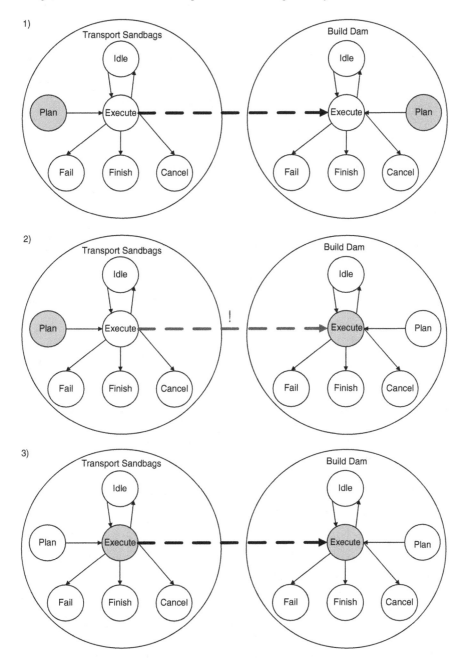

Fig. 3 Example: Execution of activities

people of other shared activity workspace. For instance, the police chief, responsible for the shared activity workspace of the police exchanges this information with the fire fighter chief responsible for shared activity workspace of the fire fighters.

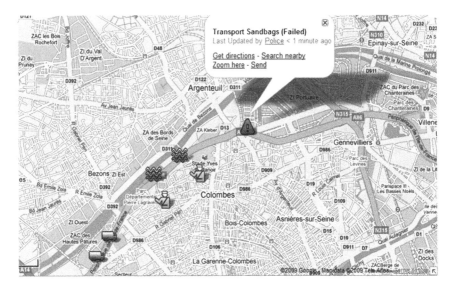

Fig. 4 Example: Monitoring

Each of them can define new dependencies of their own activities with the shared activity ones. Shared activity workspaces are not managed by a centralized server. Thus, appears the problem of the synchronization of activity states when they are shared between different activity workspaces.

In the following sections we describe a protocol for exchanging activities and dependencies. Afterwards, we describe how modeling and execution are affected by exchanging of activities and dependencies. Finally, we describe change propagation of activity state changes.

Protocol

In this section we describe how activities and dependencies can be exchanged between shared workspaces. This can be another shared workspace within one organization, but also a shared workspace of another organization. The exchange is initiated between people based on personal contacts. This is the desired method to exchange information as we have found out in our interviews and workshops. For example, the chief of the police pushes some activities and dependencies to the chief of the fire fighter. Pushing of this information can be done by various communication protocols (e.g. e-mail). This is similar to the current situation, but with the support of our more sophisticated process management approach. Each exchange follows the following process:

- Participant P of shared activity workspace X sends selected activities A_i and dependencies D_i to participant m of another shared activity workspace Y

- Participant m receives the activities A_i and the dependencies D_i and decides which activities $AS_i \subseteq A_i$ and dependencies $DS_i \subseteq D_i$ he/she wants to add to the shared activity workspace

Modeling

Exchanged activities and dependencies need to be represented in the shared workspace. Exchanged dependencies and activities are modeled the same way like not-exchanged ones. Dependencies can be defined arbitrarily between non-exchanged and exchanged activities.

Execution Support

As mentioned before, execution is defined as state change of an activity. State changes of exchanged activities are treated in the same way as state changes of non-exchanged activities. An important point is that execution may have different local effects, because in different shared workspaces different dependencies can be established to the activity. This may lead to violation of dependencies in some activity workspaces. These violations have to be resolved like any other violation (e.g. by changing the state of an activity, by removing the dependency, by communicating with people from the other shared workspace or by waiting).

Change Propagation

Exchanged activities may change their state after the exchange. This state change needs to be propagated. We distinguish between two cases for change propagation, which are based on current practices on how information is exchanged between organizations in a disaster response:

- If the state change occurred in the own shared activity workspace then it has to be propagated to all organizations the activity has been forwarded to (e.g. the fire fighter inform the police about canceling the activity "Protect residential area from flood").
- If the state change occurred in another shared activity workspaces and has been received to update an exchanged activity, it has to be propagated to all shared activity workspace the exchanged activity has been forwarded to (e.g. the police informs the red cross about the cancellation of the activity "Protect residential area from flood" by the fire fighters).

We have identified the following problem cases when propagating change in the shared activity workspace:

- Missing updates: An organization may not receive all updates, because it has been disconnected or other organizations, responsible for propagating the change, have been disconnected.

- Incomplete Propagation: State changes may never be propagated to all parties involved or different shared activity workspaces may have different states of the same activity.
- Conflicting Updates: State changes can be conflicting, for example if, an activity is changed in more than one shared activity workspace to different states. This leads to conflicting updates.
- Ensuring governance on the cross-organizational level (i.e. who is allowed to do state changes).

These problems may also occur by using the traditional methods as outlined above. We have developed several mechanisms for avoiding or mitigating these conflicts, which go beyond the scope of this paper. They are currently evaluated by researchers and end users.

Example

In this example we illustrate the exchange mechanism. Figure 5 provides an example for exchanging activities and dependencies between different shared activity workspaces. In this example the police exchanges activities and dependencies with the fire fighters in the first step. The fire fighters integrate them in their shared activity workspace and create new dependencies to their own activities in the second step.

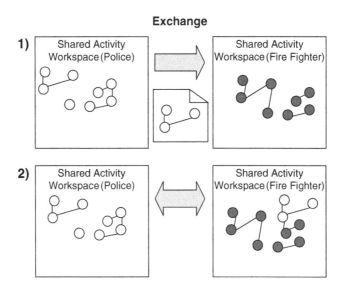

Fig. 5 Example: Exchange

Discussion

Our concept meets the requirements mentioned before. It provides support for modeling, execution, monitoring and cross-organizational aspects of disaster response processes. It should be noted that it just represent one possible solution. We discussed with three business process experts from our lab, not involved in our project, our approach based on a given flood scenario. The experts modeled some response processes based on our solution. A paper prototyping approach has been chosen for this, because at that time our prototype is not usable. We explained them our model approach and based on this approach they drew the activities and dependencies on a piece of paper. The experts agreed that this modeling approach is more suitable to model disaster response activities. They were concerned that, although the models are much more simpler compared to business process models, they may also get complex, because in a disaster there are usually many activities. This can be limited in an implementation by providing filters by criteria, so that only relevant activities are shown. Other critics are based on the limitation of the paper-based approach (drawing takes time, mistakes cannot be easily made undone etc.). We provided some examples of execution of the models based on the models the experts created. They recognized that warning of dependency violation is helpful in those scenarios. We did not evaluate cross-organizational aspects, because they do not really change modeling, execution and monitoring. We are aware that these are just a limited validation, but it shows us that we are heading in a good direction.

Conclusion

Our contribution in this paper is threefold. First, we proposed the foundation of process management model for disaster response that can be used to build information systems supporting disaster response process management. Such a foundation is strongly required, because existing means have their limitations and people from the technical community have little knowledge about disaster response processes. The opposite holds for the disaster domain perspective: They are not aware of possible technological solutions. Secondly, we have described a new approach for managing processes in the disaster response, because our research has shown that existing technology for operational business processes does not fit with this kind of scenario. Our approach encompasses modeling, execution and monitoring of disaster response processes on the intra- and inter-organizational level. Central concepts of our approach are activities on multiple shared activity workspaces and exchange of activity information between them. We strongly believe that we can contribute with this to the recently opened discussion on alternative process modeling and management approaches (e.g. [32]). Thirdly, we described initial validation of our approach by discussion with experts. We are aware that this validation is only a small first step towards a more sophisticated validation, but we think that even this little validation initially confirms that we are on the right track. We plan to have a similar test of our approach with end users in the near future based on an implemented prototype to avoid limitations of the paper-based approach. We plan to test our approach with different end users, e.g. police and fire fighters. Feedback will be used to improve the concept and the prototype. Finally, we plan to test the prototype in real disaster exercises. Our end users are very open for testing the prototype in a real exercise. We plan two different kinds of exercises. One exercise will have a predefined story, which is known by all participants. This exercise resembles more an emergency than a disaster. Goal of this exercise is to understand the prototype and to learn about different possibilities to model a situation. In the second exercise we will also use a script, but only the high level part of this script is known by the end users who use the prototype. The detailed parts are developed by other end users during the exercise to make it more realistic. With this exercise we want to evaluate how well the prototype works in not predictable scenarios, such as disasters.

Acknowledgement The research was partially funded by means of the German Federal Ministry of Education and Research under the promotional reference 01ISO7009. The authors take the responsibility for the content. Another part was funded by the research organization of the French government.

References

1. Hevner, A.R., S.T. March, and J. Park, *Design Science in Information Systems Research.* Management Information Systems Quarterly (MISQ), 2004. **28**(1): 75–105.
2. Quarantelli, E.L., *Catastrophes Are Different From Disasters: Some Implications for Crisis Planning and Managing Drawn From Katrina.* 2005, Disaster Research Center (DRC), University of Delaware, Delaware.
3. Choi, S.O., *Emergency Management: Implications from a Strategic Management Perspective.* Journal of Homeland Security and Emergency Management, 2008. **5**(1): 1.
4. Weick, K., *Making Sense of the Organization.* 2000: Blackwell, Oxford.
5. Drabek, T.E., *Strategies for Coordinating Disaster Responses.* 2003: Institute of Behavior Sciences, University of Colorado, Colorado.
6. *Beyond September 11th – An Account of Post-Disaster Research*, ed. J.L. Monday. 2003: Institute of Behavioral Science, Natural Hazards Research and Applications Information Center, University of Colorado, Colorado.
7. GovernmentSaxony, *Bericht der Sachsischen Staatsregierung zur Hochwasserkatastrophe im August 2002 (Report of the government of Saxony on the flood disaster in August 2002).* 2003, Freistaat achsen.
8. Larsson, S., E.-K. Olsson, and B. Ramberg, *Crisis Decision Making in the European Union.* 2005: Crisis Management Europe Research Program, Stockholm.
9. Townsend, F.F., *The Federal Response to Hurricane Katrina – Lessons Learned.* 2006, The White House, Washington, DC.
10. Wachtendorf, T., *Interaction Between Canadian and American Governmental and Non-Governmental Organizations During the Red River Flood of 1997.* 2000, Disaster Research Center, University of Delaware, Delaware.
11. *Process Management*, ed. J. Becker, M. Rosemann, and M. Kugeler. 2003: Springer, Berlin.

12. Hammer, M. and J. Champy, *Reengineering the Cooperation: A Manifesto for Business Revolution*. 2001. Nicholas Brealey, London.
13. van der Aalst, W.M.P., A.H.M. ter Hofstede, and M. Weske. *Business Process Management: A Survey*. In *1st International Conference on Business Process Management*. 2003. Eindhoven, The Netherlands.
14. Zur Muehlen, M., *Organizational Management in Workflow Management – Issues and Perspectives*. Information Technology and Management Journal, 2004. **2004**(3): 271–291.
15. Dumas, M., W.M.P. van der Aalst, and A.H. ter Hofstede, M., *Introduction*, in *Process-Aware Information Systems*, M. Dumas, W.M.P. van der Aalst, and A.H. ter Hofstede, M., Editors. 2005, Wiley Interscience: Hoboken, NJ.
16. Dumas, M., W.M.P. van der Aalst, and A.H.M. ter Hofstede, *Process-Aware Information Systems*, M. Dumas, W.M.P. van der Aalst, and A.H.M. ter Hofstede, Editors. 2005, Wiley, New York, pp. 3–21.
17. de Leoni, M., M. Mecella, and G. de Giacomo. *Highly Dynamic Adaptation in Process Management Systems Through Execution in Monitoring*. In *International Conference on Business Process Management Systems*. 2007. Brisbane, Australia.
18. Fahland, D. and H. Woith. *Towards Process Models for Disaster Response*. In *Process Management for Highly Dynamic and Pervasive Scenarios*. 2008. Milan, Italy.
19. Georgakopoulos, D., et al. *Managing Escalation of Collaboration Processes in Crisis Mititgation Situations*. In *16th International Conference on Data Engineering*. 2000. San Diego, CA.
20. Recker, J., *Understanding Process Modelling Grammer Continuance – A Study of the Consequences of Representational Capabilities*. 2008, School of Information Systems, Queensland University of Technology, Brisbane, Australia.
21. Denning, P.J., *Infoglut*. Communications Of The ACM, 2006. **49**(7): 15–19.
22. Dadam, P. and M. Reichert, *The ADEPT Project: A Decade of Research and Development for Robust and Flexible Process Support – Challenges and Achievements*. Computer Science – Research and Development, 2009. **23**(2): 81–97.
23. Grigori, D., F. Charoy, and C. Godart. *Anticipation to Enhance Flexibility of Workflow Execution*. In *Database and Expert Systems Applications (DEXA'2001)*. 2001. Munich, Germany.
24. van der Aalst, W.M.P., et al., *Proclets: A Framework for Lightweight Interacting Workflow Processes*. International Journal of Cooperative Information Systems, 2001. **10**(4): 443–481.
25. van der Aalst, W.M.P. and M. Pesic. *DecSerFlow: Towards a Truly Declarative Service Flow Language*. In Lecture Notes in Computer Science, *Web Services and Formal Methods*. 4184: 1–23, 2006.
26. van der Aalst, W.M.P., M. Weske, and D. Grünbauer, *Case Handling: A New Paradigm for Business Process Support*. Data & Knowledge Engineering, 2005. **53**: 129–162.
27. Montagut, F., *Pervasive Workflows – Architecture, Reliability and Security*. Computer Science and Networks, Ecole Nationale Supérieure des Télécommunications, 2007. Sophia Antipolis, France.
28. Schulz, K.A. and M.E. Orlowska, *Facilitating cross-organisational workflows with a workflow view approach*. Data & Knowledge Engineering, 2004. **51**(1): 109–147.
29. Miller, G.A., *The Magical Number Seven, Plus or Minus Two: Some Limits on our Capacity for Processing Information*. Psychological Review, 1956. **63**(2): 81–97.
30. Smith, M.L. and J. Erwin. *Role & Responsibility Charting (RACI)*. 2007 [cited 03.06.2009]; Available from: http://www.pmforum.org/library/tips/pdf_files/RACI_R_Web3_1.pdf.
31. Allen, J.F., *Maintaining Knowledge about Temporal Intervals*. Communications Of The ACM, 1983. **26**(11): 832–843.
32. Fahland, D., et al. *Declarative versus Imperative Process Modeling Languages: The Issue of Understandability*. In *1st Workshop on Empirical Research in BPM (ER-BPM'2009)*. 2009. Ulm, Germany.

Supporting Collaborative Workflows of Digital Multimedia Annotation

Cristian Hofmann and Dieter W. Fellner

Abstract Collaborative annotation techniques for digital multimedia contents have found their way into a vast amount of areas of daily use as well as professional fields. Attendant research has issued a large number of research projects that can be assigned to different specific subareas of annotation. These projects focus on one or only few aspects of digital annotation. However, the whole annotation process as a operative unit has not sufficiently been taken into consideration, especially for the case of collaborative settings. In order to attend to that lack of research, we present a framework that supports multiple collaborative workflows related to digital multimedia annotation. In that context, we introduce an process-based architecture model, a formalized specification of collaborative annotation processes, and a concept for personalized workflow visualization and user assistance.

Introduction

As means of enriching digital content by additional information, collaborative annotation techniques for digital multimedia contents have found their way into a vast amount of areas of daily use as well as professional fields. In the Web, popular platforms can be identified such as *Flickr.com*, *Youtube.com*, or *Delicious.com*, which enable shared manual classification and bookmarking of contents of various media formats in order to organize such files in a structured form and facilitate later retrieval. In addition to these simple ways of applying annotations, more complex environments are utilized for various purposes and objectives, such as information retrieval, content analysis, or group communication, and in the scope of different

C. Hofmann (✉) and D.W. Fellner
Fraunhofer Institute for Computer Graphics Research/TU Darmstadt,
Interactive Graphics Systems Group, Fraunhoferstr. 5, 64283 Darmstadt, Germany
e-mail: cristian.hofmann@igd.fraunhofer.de; d.fellner@igd.fraunhofer.de

M. Lewkowicz et al. (eds.), *Proceedings of COOP 2010*,
DOI 10.1007/978-1-84996-211-7_6, © Springer-Verlag London Limited 2010

application areas and practices, e.g., computer-supported collaborative learning, medicines, engineering, human science, sports science, e-Commerce, edutainment, or gaming [4, 30, 31, 33]. In our research work we focus on two concrete scenarios of collaborative multimedia annotation. The first case deals with annotation of multimedia content with semantic information. At this, users first annotate multimedia documents (e.g., websites, videos, images, etc.) or parts of a document (e.g., single video scenes, image sections, etc.) with simple metadata such as descriptors or textual tags. Subsequently, documents or document parts are assigned to a given ontology. The second annotation scenario is concerned with video content analysis. In that case, users collaboratively select video segments by performing shot detection, write transcriptions, categorize video segments using a predefined vocabulary, enter own ratings and interpretations of the observed content, and discuss their results. In the following, the differing variants of digital multimedia annotation are going to be illuminated.

Digital Multimedia Annotation: A General Overview

In order to comprehend the background of this work, it is important to briefly overview the wide range of the area of digital annotation concerning its various forms and usages. In a general view, annotations are means of enriching arbitrary content by additional information. Thus, from a user's point of view, annotations enable persons to associate own information with provided documents [2]. That personal information can manifest different types and purposes such as commentary, elucidation, explanation, footnote, interpretation, reflection, linking, classification, or linking [1, 26, 30]. In the scope of such usages, annotations may appear as *metadata*, *content*, or *dialog act*. Annotations as metadata serve as additional data associated to existing contents, defining their properties and structure [1, 2]. Annotations also can be applied as content, enriching existing content by a further layer of explanation or interpretation [1, 2, 26]. As part of a collaborative discourse respecting a certain subject, content-annotations can be regarded as dialog acts [1, 14]. Different media formats such as text [36], images [40, 41], audio files [5], video [12, 20, 40], or 3D-models [19, 23] are involved in digital annotation referring to the contents that are annotated on the one hand and the coding of annotations on the other hand [2, 13, 32]. In general, annotation techniques aim the exposure and elucidation of the semantics of given information [2]. In line with that superior objective, annotation environments are used in various application areas such as indexing and retrieval, information classification, content analysis, sharing and discussion, or collaborative authoring. The latter forms of usage reveal that annotations also can be means of exchanging and sharing ideas and opinions of a collaborating community with respect to mutual accessible digital contents [2, 10, 11, 14, 43]. In that context, different types of annotations are identified: annotations written by the producer of the content, and annotations created by the recipients of the provided contents [1]. Furthermore, annotations can be private, shared, or public [27]. Private annotations are visible and accessible only to their authors, whereas shared and public annotations are treated by a certain team or all participating users. In cases of collaborative working, user groups obtain multiple views of the handled information [27]. Thus, annotations support the discourse and information exchange within specific communities improving various forms of collaborative work scenarios [2, 11, 13]. In conclusion, the area of (collaborative) digital annotation includes a large set of different workflows that embrace several research topics.

Support of Collaborative Annotation Workflows: Key Challenges and Our Contribution

Beginning from the times of manual annotation of textual documents, research on annotation has long tradition and issued a large number of research projects that can be assigned to different specific subareas of annotation. These projects focus on one or only few aspects of digital annotation [20, 21]. However, the annotation process, as a whole operative unit which issues several different workflows, has not sufficiently been taken into consideration, especially in cases of collaborative work [1, 17, 20, 21]. The exploration of workflows of collaborative multimedia annotation is a relevant research topic due to user-specific requirements and challenges of application design. First, from a *user's point of view*, problems can be identified with respect to the usage of annotations systems. To take an example, within the process of collaborative video analysis, an amount of tasks or sub-processes can be registered: configuration of specific application and community settings, marking and chunking contents, classification of selected contents, generate transcriptions, writing (shared) interpretations and ratings with respect to the observed facts, searching and commenting of co-analysts results, leading discussions about disagreements, subsequently re-editing of configurations and own contributions, and publishing of results [17, 21, 29, 30, 35]. Different annotation tools, algorithms, etc. can be used to accomplish that large number of analytic (annotation) tasks. Commonly, the amount of available services leads to multi-optional and complex user interfaces. Thus, users struggle in understanding and learning how to use the system's set of tools and have problems in recognizing their current state and the next steps within the process [37]. In that context, annotators have to make an effort in recognizing contents that are to be executed by them and not by other community members. Furthermore, annotation can be an elaborate and time-consuming work, especially when it is conducted in a "manual" way [3]. Second, from an *application design point of view*, relevant key features have been declared with respect to flexibility in order to support different ways of using annotations and integration of different services [1, 11].

In order to attend to the lack of research on the annotation process as (collaborative) workflows, and based on the described challenges and problems which arise from a user's and an application design points of view, the main contribution of this paper is the illustration of a generic framework to support collaborative workflows related to digital multimedia annotation. By workflow-support, we mean the facilitation of loops and transitions between the single workflow steps and tasks in general. More precisely, appropriate services and information shall be provided at the proper time, depending on the current individual or group's state of the work. Consequently, we expect a reduction of the users' load with regard to the use of such applications and hence enhancement of efficiency. In addition to that, we enable the integration of different annotation services by applying a service-oriented infrastructure. Thus, previously declared demand on flexibility can be complied. The annotation framework has been developed in the scope of the THESEUS program. THESEUS is a research program, initiated by the Federal Ministry of Economy and Technology (BMWi), to develop a new internet-based infrastructure in order to better use and utilize the knowledge available on the internet.

In Section Related Work, the identified related work concerning research on support of annotation workflows and practices is illuminated. Section Process of Collaborative Multimedia Annotation gives a brief overview of an abstract model describing annotation processes and tasks. Following, an integrable generic framework for workflow-based collaborative annotation is presented in Section A Framework to Support Collaborative Annotation Workflows. In that context, we illustrate an architecture model that is based on a process model for digital annotation, as well as a concept for workflow visualization and user assistance by interpreting process specifications. Concluding, we summarize the presented results and assume our future work.

Related Work

Bertino, Trombetta, and Montesi present a framework and a modular architecture for interactive video consisting of various information systems. The coordination of these components is realized by identifying inter-task dependencies with interactive rules, based on a workflow management system [4]. The Digital Video Album (DVA) system is an integration of different subsystems that refer to specific aspects of video processing and retrieval. In particular, the workflow for semiautomatic indexing and annotation is focused [31]. Pea and Hoffert illustrate a basic idea of the video research workflow in the learning sciences [22]. In contrast to our research work, the projects mentioned above do not or only to some degree consider the process for collaborative use cases. The reconsideration of such communicative and collaborative aspects requires modifications and enhancements of the existing approaches and concepts.

Processes of Collaborative Multimedia Annotation

In this section, workflows of digital annotation are illustrated in a general view by means of an abstract process model. That model arises from an empirical study of multiple identified annotation workflows of real practices, primarily focusing on

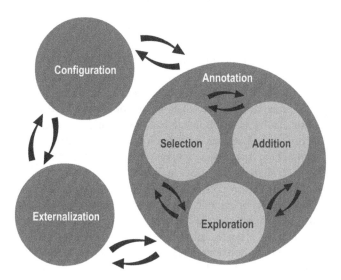

Fig. 1 Abstract process model for digital multimedia annotation

collaborative usage settings [21]. As shown in Fig. 1, the annotation process is divided into the sub-processes *configuration*, *annotation*, and *externalization*. Annotation is subdivided again into the sub-processes *selection*, *addition*, and *exploration*. These sub-processes consist of one or more different tasks that have to be accomplished by certain users or groups applying differing tools and algorithms. Although these sub-processes are subsequent in a first sight, this section shows that annotation workflows have to be regarded as networks including options, iterations, loops and re-entries to previous steps. In the following, the sub-processes of digital multimedia annotation are illustrated as tasks of the annotation process.

Configuration

Before starting an annotation project, the environment has to be configured. Specific project preferences can be adjusted and the graphical user interface may be customized [9]. Furthermore, participants are assigned to accounts and user groups that are associated with specific roles and access rights. The annotation tasks can be distributed among the individual users [9, 25, 40]. For example, tasks of a project are assigned to predefined groups, and furthermore a group administrator is able to distribute the annotation tasks among the individual users [25, 40]. Since annotation processes are iterative and contain loops and re-entries to previous process states [30, 38], predefined configurations of the used environment often need to be modified during a running annotation process.

Annotation

The following phases selection, addition, and exploration can be regarded as one operative unit. The conducted expert interviews revealed that no specific operative sequences can be identified referring to these "real" acts of annotating [30]. Note on video analysis processes that activities of de-composition (segmentation, coding, categorization, and transcription) and re-composition (rating, interpretation, reflection, comparison, and collocation) are closely interrelated. They depict video annotation as a complex process that contains circular and recursive loops, in which the analyst alternately marks, transcribes and categorizes, analyzes and reflects, and needs to conduct searches [28]. Performed a field study with respect of the annotation of digital libraries, reporting that acts of searching, reading and annotating are performed at the same time and can be done together with other activities, e.g. working with colleagues. Hence, selection, addition, and exploration, as higher-level categories, have to be considered related to each other. In the following, these three items are explicitly described.

Selection

Annotators need to mark concrete contents of interest that annotations shall refer to. The simplest variant is marking a whole document such as a website. A second variant is the selection of elements contained within a document. Let us assume that a considered website consists of a text, various graphics, and a video. An annotator is able to mark each of these elements as an independent unit, or select two or more of these elements as a composed unit, and consequently annotate a unit with different information [13, 32]. As a third variant, these single elements can be again subdivided into segments. For example, annotations may be associated to a whole text, or to one or more special parts of the text [11]. How exactly segments are defined depends on the media format of the original content and the specific media properties, as well as the purpose of annotation. Segments can also be artifacts of collaborative work. In some of the investigated use cases, the segmentation task is partitioned and assigned to individual users or groups. For example, group A chunks the video according to a certain characteristic 1, group B seeks for characteristic 2, and so on. Furthermore, in content analysis use cases, users or groups may also work with different classification systems, vocabularies, ontologies, etc.

Addition

After marking the relevant documents, document subsets, or object segments, co-annotators continue adding annotations as additional information to these elements. As already mentioned, a relevant objective of annotation is the classification of given information resources or parts of it, in order to facilitate archiving and later retrieval [3]. Collaborative practices are supported by allowing shared information organization activities and exploiting of information structures establish by collaborators. For example, widespread approaches are *Collaborative Tagging*, *Social Bookmarking*, and *Semantic Annotation* [3, 10, 26]. In a further context, users may describe observed facts, e.g. behaviors and events of a video, objects within an image, sequences of an audio file, etc. In order to explain, elucidate, interpret, or comment on the given contents, users need to give descriptions in a more free way than assigning metadata [35]. In most cases, they are allowed to enter free textual annotations that can be regarded as additional content [1, 2, 26]. Like the selection task, the addition of annotations may be distributed to different users and groups. In that case, annotated information becomes a shared contribution [2, 11, 14, 43]. Shared contributions are an important part of collaborative work. They enable the communication between co-annotators as well as the organization of common tasks and are regarded as dialog acts [1, 14]. Organization and coordination of collaborative activities are essential in the context of co-writing or co-authoring with respect to granulated information exchanges between collaborators creating a shared document [10, 43]. Furthermore, when users work separately, they need to discuss their annotations, conclusions, and the annotation process with other participants [9]. Particularly in the context of consensual approaches applied in content analysis, discussion is a means of agreement and consistency of different annotators' results. Thus, discussion often leads to a return to previous steps of the annotation process [29, 30, 35]. In the end, the final results of the annotation project arise from iterative loops through the process, in which the data is continually modified and adjusted.

Exploration

Selection and information addition always go along with searching, browsing, and reception activities [28, 30]. Especially in collaborative annotation situations, users also need to search for their own results but also for results of co-annotators, experts, or other sources [22, 30]. Exploration of co-annotator's data also can be an issue in asynchronous collaborative projects which proceed over a long time frame. After being absent, users may need to track the changes performed by other annotators involved in the project. Exploration also includes restructuring of the data representation. With regard to this, annotators are allowed to contrast relevant data with each other, or to hide less important information. According to this, exploration also supports reflection. It facilitates the consideration of multiple views of the video where users are allowed to obtain perspectives beyond their subjective point of view [27, 38, 40].

Externalization

The externalization phase refers to two different aspects at the end of the annotation process: Publication of the process' results and export of data for the purpose of processing the data with external applications. Public annotations are treated by all participating users [2, 26]. Normally, publication begins with editing and converting the data into several formats, and moves on to presenting this information by means of corresponding media [30]. Published results can be used for demonstration purposes [29]. Also databases of already annotated material can serve as digital resource for information retrieval in following annotation sessions [35]. Furthermore, a goal of annotation can be obtaining (mostly automatically) generated surveys and assemblies of similarly categorized content subsets, e.g. video summaries [3]. Furthermore, it is often necessary to export data for further processing by means of more specific applications.

A Framework to Support Collaborative Annotation Workflows

In this section, a generic and integrable framework that supports different concrete annotation workflows is presented. First, general requirements with respect to workflow-support and collaboration are derived. Subsequently, we present a developed the architecture model that is based on the sub-processes of collaborative annotation illustrated in the previous section. In particular, it is shown that the architecture aims at establishing a framework that can be integrated in superior systems. Furthermore, we propose a formal specification of processes that is used for the purpose of workflow control and visualization, as well as a process-driven user assistance. Workflow visualization and process-driven assistance are presented as concepts in the last part of this section.

Process-Based Requirements

Conceptual design decisions particularly base on our endeavor to support given operating procedures within the annotation workflow. In that context, we identified basic requirements that have to be fulfilled by the framework. In general, the following requirements result from our explicit consideration of annotation workflows on the one hand, and collaborative practices on the other hand. The requirements are based on a comparative analysis of current annotation environments.

1. *Workflow Control.* Workflows of collaborative multimedia annotation can be complex, since they are network-like and may contain several iterations. Thus, transitions between workflow phases and the control of sequences of sub operations have to be supported. Also loops and re-entries to other phases of the workflow must be considered.
2. *Sub-Process Enclosure.* In order to guarantee workflow control, sub-processes of annotation must be made "tangible" for a certain control instance. Thus, the identified phases and tasks of collaborative annotation workflows need to be pooled into functional units that are mutually delimited. In doing so, task areas can be typecasted and invoked by addressing respective modules.

3. *Process Awareness.* In order to support operating flows of annotation, users must be enabled to monitor the current process. That is, he or she needs to obtain information about the current state as well as actual and upcoming activities or tasks. Thus, users are "aware of process". For example, Process Aware Systems use work lists to offer work items that have to be performed by people [24]. In that context, especially in the case of collaborative work, that kind of visualization needs to be personalized due to the different needs of varying user groups and roles [7, 8].

4. *Service Integration and Providing.* As mentioned in that paper's introduction, a large number of potential functionalities can lead to complex and multi-optional user interfaces that obstruct especially unexperienced users. Furthermore, Agosti et al. (2007) and Constantopoulos et al. (2004) note that flexibility in order to support different ways of annotation as well as integration of different services are key aspects of the design of annotation systems [1, 11]. As a result, integration of different annotation services and providing these services to users in an appropriate way have to be supported.

5. *Extensibility.* Flexibility and service integration require a framework that provides interfaces or "docking ports" for multiple tools or external services. In addition to that, the system must enable administrators to integrate, replace and remove tools that can be assigned to task-related modules.

6. *Consistency.* As a consequence of extensibility, since multiple tools read and possibly write on the same data. Thus, the consistency of shared parts of the data set has to be ensured at every point of the annotation process. Furthermore, with respect to collaborative practices in which data is exchanged between members of a community, consistency of data must also be warranted for every peer in the shared system.

7. *Selection Support.* It is essential to select the concrete contents that are to be annotated. In doing so, there are two levels of different kinds of contents. First, a whole multimedia document, one or more media elements contained in a document, or segments of single media elements can be marked. Second, information may be coded in different media formats [2, 11, 13, 32]. In order to support the annotation workflow, selection of the desired contents must be alleviated.

8. *User Management.* User management is required due to the following reasons: Users have to be assigned to accounts, user groups, and roles with respective access rights. In collaborative settings, the annotation task may be portioned and distributed to users and user groups in several ways. As a consequence, a personalized view on the workflow for varying roles of users must be provided [7, 8].

9. *Data Exchange.* In collaborative use cases, the annotation environment has to realize the data exchange between multiple users of the application that are potentially separated over space. For this purpose, stored information must be made available to every participant of the group.

10. *Correct Data Handling.* In the scope of collaborative work, in which each group
    member has full access to shared contents, Stahl et al. regard the emerged informa-
    tion set as a *Dynamic Information Space*. That is, the information set is continually
    change and extended [38]. In addition to that, annotations can be assigned to dif-
    ferent kinds of contents. Thus, an appropriate handling of media files, its annotated
    information, as well as their organizational structure must be provided.

Process-Based Architecture Model

In this section, the general assembly of the framework's underlying architecture are
presented. In that context, components of the architecture that are related to the
sub-processes of annotation are illustrated.

The architecture model of the collaborative annotation framework was drafted relying
on the presented requirements on the one hand, and on the identified sub-processes
and tasks of collaborative annotation on the other hand. As a result, the key features of
the concept are (a) a *Client-Server-Architecture*, (b) a *Component-based Environment*,
(c) the realization of an *Model-View-Controller* (MVC) and the *Mediator* design patterns,
(d) an *Event-based Communication*, and (e) a *Service-oriented Infrastructure*. The
single features of the architecture are illustrated in the following (Fig. 2).

Client-Server Model

A fundamental condition for collaborative processes is the interconnectedness of
every peer taking part for information exchanging purposes [9, 13]. Within a range

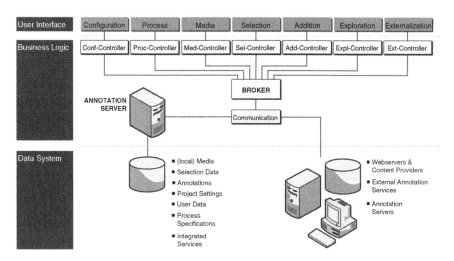

Fig. 2 Process-based architecture model

of optional models that can be considered, e.g., client-server, peer-to-peer, or web-based approaches. We suggest a client-server architecture, not only due to its wide spreading in the area of information systems [9]. In general, data consistency, shared data exchange, and user management are enabled. A centralized *Multimedia Annotation Server* realizes a centralization of the information space. In doing so, the data system is available for any client that is connected. Additionally, it provides several services such as authentication of annotators, and management of accounts and access rights. In that context, modifications of the data set by the community are managed and provided to respective group members. The server is also responsible for a consistent storage and management of local media files, global project configurations, and annotation information, but also workflow-related data like predefined process specification files or integrated services. Centralized management also provides support for distributed authoring processes, e.g. tracking of changes made by co-annotators. With respect to our specific research focus, a relevant function of the server application is to provide predefined workflow specifications. Suchlike description files can be accessed by the local Workflow Management Environment in order to perform controlling activities. For example, one prototype of our annotation framework transmits workflow descriptions coded in *XPDL* (XML Process Definition Language) via HTTP. The client application handles user entries and interaction on the graphical user interface. It provides authoring options and assigned tools for media and annotation editing purposes. Here, the views of the MVC model are pooled as graphical representation of services.

Component-Based Environment

The identified sub-processes of annotation need to be pooled into functional units that are mutually delimited in order to typecast task areas that can be invoked by a central control unit. Furthermore, the architecture must enable administrators to integrate, replace and remove tools that can be assigned to these task-related modules. Thus, the phases of the workflow are implemented as software components. A software component can be seen as an enclosed unit which provides specific services. It can be embedded into a higher-level system and combined with other components. The concrete implementation of a component is concealed from its accessing instance, the communication is provided by specific interfaces [29]. Within our architecture model, the components are abstract and serve as containers for previously assigned tools and methods. Furthermore, they may be implemented several times. To sum up, sub-process enclosure, service integration, and extensibility are guaranteed. Central components are the *Broker Component*, *Process*, *Media*, and the *Communication Component*. The Broker implements the Mediator component as global controller of the MVC model. The Process Component is responsible for process visualization and process-driven user assistance which are going to be explained in the next section. The Media Component serves as display component for selected media files. The Communication component realizes the connection between elements of the shared framework. First, the communication between the framework's central Multimedia Annotation Server is establish. Additionally, access is warranted to external information resources such as web servers, external annotation services, or external annotation servers, e.g., providing and storing semantic annotations or ontologies. Based on the identified process phases and tasks, we conceived and included the abstract components *Configuration*, *Selection*, *Addition*, *Exploration*, and *Externalization*. The Configuration Component is responsible for any administrative task performed by authorized users. It provides input interfaces for several configuration options such as users and task management, process specification, or project settings. Selection components represent any service for content selection or segmentation. For that purpose, interfaces must be provided that support interaction with media players and data visualization components. Analogously, addition components are responsible for the conjunction of any kind of annotation. Exploration components serve as means of reception, browsing, navigation, and searching. Basically, information is visualized, and services for manipulation of the data representation such as filtering or sorting are provided. In addition to that, specific search functionalities may be integrated. Examples are specific timeline views for continuous media like audio or video, or annotation structure visualization tools. Externalization tools are responsible for data processing for the use in external environments.

Model View Controller and Mediator Pattern

In order to realize an appropriate management of media files and its annotated information, we rely on existing approaches with regard to content annotation or linking. In the area of hypermedia research, several models can be identified, e.g. the *Dexter Hypertext Reference Model*. That model divides the system into three delimited layers, separating data, the given hyper structure, and its representation [18]. The *Model View Controller Model* (MVC) equally divides the application into three levels: the model layer represents the involved data, views display the information and assume user interaction, the controller layer processes user entries and is enabled to modify data in the model. Furthermore, data consistency is warranted through a specific notification policy. In the presented process-based architecture, the model layer consists of data and information from contents and assigned annotations to project configuration information, etc. In that context, the storage of predefinable process specifications and (references to) the available services are a central part of our work. The view layer represents any visual component at the graphical user interface. Besides the general elements of the user interface, the single views display the available tools or services that are previously assigned to respective tasks of the annotation workflow. The controller layer includes two different kinds of controllers: local controllers are assigned to every component of the view (as well as the server communication component) and act as interfaces between component and application. A central component serves as global controller and implements the included Mediator pattern. The Mediator pattern provides a central instance, called *Broker Component*, which defines the cooperation and interaction of multiple objects. This central unit holds an intermediary role and coordinates the overall behavior of the system [15]. Thus, workflow control can be supported with regard to transitions between workflow phases, sequences of sub operations, passing through loops, and re-entries to other phases of the workflow. The specific processes and sequences within the annotation workflow are defined by task groups and sub operations, which can be pooled into several system components. The global controller is key component with respect to the realization of *Event-based Communication* and the establishment of a *Service-oriented Infrastructure*. A event-based system is a shared environment composed of multiple active software components and an service that realizes event transmission, commonly called Event-Broker or Event-Dispatcher [34]. There, active software components may obtain the role of an event publisher or an event consumer. The Broker component appears as event transmitter and is responsible for inter-service communication and interoperability, as well as workflow control and governing. Thus, a service-oriented infrastructure can be implemented. Service-oriented infrastructures focus on the realization of components as modular services that can be invoked by certain clients. Thus, based on a service-oriented infrastructure that is enabled by the global controller, modularized sub-processes of collaborative annotation can be individually invoked and controlled.

Process Management I: Specifying Processes

The main objective of our work is to support different workflows by dealing with user-specific problems that arise from multi-optional tool sets and complex user interfaces, and design-specific requirements. More precisely, we enable the integration of different annotation services and realize service providing at the proper time, depending on the current individual or group's state of the work. For that purpose, we applied a service-oriented infrastructure. Hence, the emphasis is to handle components as modular services that are provided to clients [16]. An essential requirement for process management within service-oriented infrastructures is the coordination of shared resources [16]. In general, among these resources are the available annotation services and the single users or user groups. In order to enable management of process-related resources, an appropriate workflow management concept is necessary. Workflow Management comprises all tasks that are to be accomplished at modeling, simulation, and execution and supervision of workflows [34]. A workflow can be regarded as a business process that is executed by means of computing devices [34]. Such processes are automatized, and documents, tasks, or contents are transferred according to specified rules [42]. A process-based system must be driven by a specific process model [24]. According to that, the concrete applied processes must be modeled and fed into the framework in forms of a schema or workflow specification [16]. Workflow schemata describe a process by means of a workflow modeling language for the purpose of documentation, analysis, or execution within a workflow management system [34]. In the following, we specify a formal description of collaborative multimedia annotation processes.

That formal specification aims at supplying relevant requirements for workflow-support in collaborative annotation settings. First, the general tasks (work items), involved annotation services, multimedia contents, and users are specified. Additionally, essential attributes for user assistance within a workflow can be set, such as the state of a task, service types in order to also realize real-time service assignment, e.g. "selection of video segment", and definition of content types. Tasks may be structured in an hierarchical order, e.g., the superior task "addition" can obtain the sub-tasks "annotate metadata" or "add comment" [24, 39]. Transitions between related or subsequent tasks are defined. Thus, the operative flow is specified and workflow control procedures are driven. Furthermore, transitions are linked with contents that are transfered from one task to the following. In doing so, the data flow referring the annotation flow can be defined. Tasks are also assigned to available services, as well as to the single users or user groups that have to execute them. As a result, service providing is supported at a user interface level. In addition to that, on user interfaces, personalized views of the workflow can be provided. As stated in [7, 8] personalization is a key requirement at workflow visualization. Here, personalization is realized at two areas: first, at the area of tasks that have been assigned to users and groups with respective authorizations and, second, the concrete contents that are processed by a user or group. In particular, the latter case can be regarded as useful for selection support. In the following, a formal specification of (collaborative) multimedia annotation workflows, is presented.

Definition 1. An annotation process is defined by a tuple $p = (i_p, W, T, S, C, G, WS, ST, CT)$ where:

- ip is the unique identifier of p.
- $W = \{w_1, w_2, \ldots, w_n\}$ is a finite set of work items which assemble p.
- $T = \{t_1, t_2, \ldots, t_n\}$ is a finite set of transitions located between consecutive work items.
- $S = \{s_1, s_2, \ldots, s_n\}$ is a finite set of services which are offered to perform the single work items included in p.
- $C = \{c_1, c_2, \ldots, c_n\}$ is a finite set of contents that are transfered in between work items.
- $G = \{g_1, g_2, \ldots, g_n\}$ is a finite set of user groups which execute the single work items included in p.
- $WS : W \rightarrow WorkItemStates := \{NotEnabled, Enabled, Active, Accomplised\}$ indicates the state for each work item $w \in W$.
- $ST : S \rightarrow ServiceTypes := \{Configuration, Selection, Addition, Exploration, Externalization, Document, Element, ElementComposition, ElementSubset, Text, Graphic, Audio, Video, 3D, GenericFormat\}$ assigns a set of service types for each service $s \in S$, indicating for what kind of tasks and contents a service can be used.

- $CT : C \rightarrow ContentTypes := \{Document, Element, ElementComposition,$ $ElementSubset, Text, Graphic, Audio, Video, 3D, GenericFormat\}$ indicates the content type for each content $c \in C$ transfered in p.

Definition 2. A work item is defined by a tuple $w = \left(i_w, i_{pw}, d, S_w\right)$ where:

- i_w is the unique identifier of w.
- i_{pw} is the unique identifier of the parent work item of w (optional).
- d is the deadline of w (optional).
- $S_w \subseteq S = \{s_{w1}, s_{w2}, ..., s_{wn}\}$ is a finite set of one or more services which are offered to perform w.

Definition 3. A transition is defined by a tuple $t = (i_t, i_o, i_d, C_o, C_i)$ where:

- i_t is the unique identifier of t.
- i_o is the unique identifier of the origin work item, from which the transition t is launched.
- i_d is the unique identifier of the destination work item, at which the transition t targets.
- $C_o \subseteq C$ is a finite set of contents that are output data of the origin work item.
- $C_i \subseteq C$ is a finite set of contents that are input data for the destination work item.

Definition 4. A service is defined by a tuple $s = (i_s, l_s)$ where:

- i_s is the unique identifier of s.
- l_s indicates the location of s.

Definition 5. A user group is defined by a tuple $g = (i_g, U_g, W_g)$ where:

- i_g is the unique identifier of g.
- U_g is a finite set of users belonging to g.
- $W_g \subseteq W$ is a finite set of work items which are to be accomplished by the group g (optional).

Definition 6. A user is defined by a tuple $u = (i_u, g, W_u, R)$ where:

- i_u is the unique identifier of u.
- $g \in G$ is the group that the user belongs to.
- $W_u \subseteq W$ is a finite set of work items which are to be accomplished by the user u (optional).
- $R = \{r_1, r_2, ..., r_n\}$ is a finite set of roles that are assigned to u. Role assignment also implicates several access rights respecting the content(s) that are to be handled.

Definition 7. A content is defined by a tuple $c = (i_c, i_{pc}, l_c)$ where:

- i_c is the unique identifier of c.
- i_{pc} is the unique identifier of the parent content of c (optional).
- l_s indicates the location of c.

Process Management II – Workflow Visualization and Process-Driven Assistance

The specification of concrete workflows is fundament for workflow execution. Within the presented concept, workflow management particularly focuses on workflow visualization and process-driven assistance. The general objectives of these aspects are to provide users information about what are the current state and task(s), which contents are involved, and which services can be selected in order to accomplish a respective tasks. In that context, a visual-interactive concept for *Workflow Visualization* and *Process-driven User Assistance* is illustrated. Especially in the scope of collaborative annotation scenarios, the processes may be long-running, include a large number of activities, and involves several user groups and roles [7]. In that case, users have different tasks and knowledge about the process. Thus, a uniform workflow visualization for all participants can not cover all expectations and individual requirements [8]. The process must be presented in various ways, including a personalized visualization with an appropriate level of granularity [6–8]. In doing so, the specific needs of different user groups can be fulfilled. For that purpose (a) the process visualization must be able to be reduced by hiding not-relevant information, (b) the representation of process elements such as activities or data must be customizable [6, 7]. In particular, we refer to two dimensions of personalization: control and data flow. Control flow includes a personalized process visualization referring to the activities or tasks that a certain user has to perform. For example, a user with an administrator role may be allowed to conduct any tasks, especially system configuration. Whereas, a "normal annotator" will have only authorization for selecting and adding additional information. From a data flow perspective, personalized process representation only shows the contents that are assigned to the current user and/or his assigned group. Assuming that two groups have created video segments with respect to different topical categories. In the next step, addition of textual contributions, the process representation only highlights the video segments that were created by the group of the current user. Process-driven assistance is a part of the presented workflow visualization concept. First, it includes guidance of users when they specify the necessary parameters before effectively performing a task. Furthermore, assistance is given by indicating the available services that are to be used in the scope of the current state of process depending on the predefined process-related parameters on the one hand, and on the other hand further attributes that are gathered from a process-specification. Such as for process visualization, also user assistance has to consider different types of users, since the expertise of a single user referring to the operation of the application determines the level of assistance that is required. In the following, the concepts of workflow visualization and process-driven user assistance are illustrated. For that purpose, we refer to the prototype application *SemaWeb* that allows semantic annotation of web contents. Here, the multimedia annotation framework and a workflow visualization component are integrated.

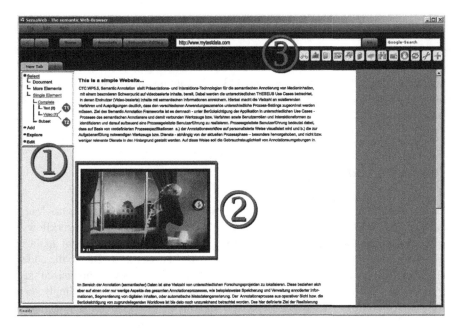

Fig. 3 Workflow visualization and process-driven assistance in *SemaWeb*

As shown in Fig. 3 (1), predefined processes are presented by means of a tree visualization. On the first level, the general superior tasks of the project are listed. Child nodes of all tiers map the next category within a thread of decisions that have to be made by the user in order to initiate the required task. That is, various properties are requested by the system that determine the parameters of task execution. The general idea of the tree view concept is that users are enabled to select a path of the tree structure which guides them through the several options, feeding the system with required information at the same time. Thus, the leafs of the tree are always available services that match to the activated path options. The items displayed by that component are personalized: only the relevant data is shown based on task distribution defined in the loaded process specification and the user management data. The simple example in Fig. 3 shows that a user wants to select a whole video on a website in order to annotate some descriptive metadata. For that purpose, the user clicked the options *select*, *single element*, *whole element* (and not a segment), and *video media*. The available videos are shown in the tree, and after selection of the video two existing video selection tools are faded in. That way of interaction supports users in small steps, and we suggest that especially users with less experience concerning the usage of annotation systems will benefit. Still, other types of more experienced users may not accept that kind of step-by-step guidance. Consequently, we distinguish between the three user types novices, advanced, and expert. According to that, as shown in Fig. 3 (2), advanced or expert users are also able to select the desired contents by means of mouse actions upon the website.

In that case, the tree view responds to that activities and adopts the representation, so that advanced users are still able to localize applicable services by means of the process visualization. Thus, they are allowed to overleap single steps within the tree path. At an expert level, users are also able to select the right tools directly without using the tree view component (see Fig. 3 (3)). To sum up, the process visualization and assistance concept covers multiple forms of habit, knowledge, experience, and specific tasks of the different users and user groups.

Conclusion and Future Work

We illustrated that even though research in the area of digital annotation has long tradition and includes an amount of respective projects the practices and workflows of annotation has not been sufficiently considered to date. Particularly, that applies to collaborative practices which gain more and more in importance. Due to the wide range with respect to types, usages, application areas, and users we emphasized the large number of different workflows of (collaborative) annotation. Accordingly, the main contribution of this paper is the illustration of a concept for a integrable framework that supports multiple collaborative workflows of digital multimedia annotation. Based on a model that describes the annotation process in an abstract way, we introduced a respective architecture model. The significant aspects of the architecture are the separation of the basic elements included, so that the framework can be integrated as a subsystem into existing environments. By means of a service-oriented infrastructure, different components that serve as specific annotation services can be integrated and coordinated. In addition, we presented a formalized specification of the collaborative annotation process including its essential aspects and elements. Based on that formalization, concrete workflow specifications can be generated in order to realize workflow management. In the scope of workflow management, a visual-interactive approach for user-centered support by means of workflow visualization and process-driven assistance was introduced. Basically, that approach deals with providing users with information about the workflow tasks and the services or user interface elements that are to be used with the respect to the current state within the annotation process. There, personalization of the view and the interactive access on the workflows are means of supporting collaboration. In doing so, various levels of knowledge and expertise, as well as use styles and preferences are considered. In summary, the presented concept aims at improving the use of annotation systems, especially in the scope of collaborative scenarios. Up next, the concepts included in the presented framework are going to be evaluated with the aid of usability tests and case studies.

Due to the wide range and complexity of the annotation field, several points of contact for future research work can be identified. Especially in the scope of our research work, two topics are of special interest concerning annotation workflow visualization and assistance through service providing. The first question refers to how process representation and recommending of services can be improved by machine-learning approaches, e.g., by realizing adaption based on automatic interaction analysis. Second, service providing and retrieval can be evolved by advanced approaches from the semantics field, such as research on specific service ontologies.

References

1. Agosti, M., Bonfiglio-Dosio, G.,Ferro, N.: A historical and contemporary study on annotations to derive key features for systems design. Int. J. Digit. Libr. 8(1), 1–19 (2007)
2. Agosti, M., Ferro, N.: A formal model of annotations of digital content. ACM Trans. Inf. Syst. 26(1), 3 (2007)
3. Bertini, M., Bimbo, A. D., Nunziati, W.: Automatic Annotation of Sport Video Content. Alberto Sanfeliu, Manuel Lazo-Cortés (ed.): CIARP, Springer, 1066–1078 (2005)
4. Bertino, E., Trombetta, A., Montesi, D.: Workflow Architecture for Interactive Video Management Systems. Distrib. Parallel Databases 11(1), 33–51 (2002)
5. Bischoff, K., Firan, C. S., Paiu, R.: Deriving music theme annotations from user tags. WWW '09: Proceedings of the 18th international conference on World wide web, ACM, New York, USA, 1193–1194 (2009)
6. Bobrik, R., Bauer, T.: Towards Configurable Process Visualizations with Proviado. WETICE, IEEE Computer Society, pp. 367–369 (2007)
7. Bobrik, R., Reichert, M., Bauer, T.: View-Based Process Visualization. Gustavo Alonso, Peter Dadam, Michael Rosemann, ed., BPM, Springer, pp. 88–95 (2007)
8. Bobrik, R., Reichert, M, Bauer, T.: Requirements for the Visualization of System-Spanning Business Processes. DEXA Workshops, IEEE Computer Society, pp. 948–954 (2005)
9. Brugman, H., Russel, A.: Annotating Multi-media/Multi-modal resources with ELAN. Proceedings of the 4th International Conference on Language Resources and Language Evaluation (LREC 2004), European Language Resources Association, Paris, pp. 2065–2068 (2004)
10. Cadiz, J. J., Gupta, A, Grudin, J.: Using Web annotations for asynchronous collaboration around documents. CSCW '00: Proceedings of the 2000 ACM conference on Computer supported cooperative work, ACM, New York, USA, pp. 309–318 (2000)
11. Constantopoulos, P., Doerr, M., Theodoridou, M., Tzobanakis, M.: On Information Organization in Annotation Systems. Intuitive Human Interfaces for Organizing and Accessing Intellectual Assets, pp. 189–200 (2004)
12. Costa, M., Correia, N., Guimaraes, N.: Annotations as multiple perspectives of video content. MULTIMEDIA '02: Proceedings of the tenth ACM international conference on Multimedia, ACM, New York, USA, pp. 283–286 (2002)
13. Finke, M.: Unterstuetzung des kooperativen Wissenserwerbs durch Hypervideo-Inhalte. Universitäts- und Landesbibliothek Darmstadt (2005)
14. Frommholz, I., Brocks, H., Thiel, U., Neuhold, E. J., Iannone, L., Semeraro, G., Berardi, M., Ceci, M.: Document-Centered Collaboration for Scholars in the Humanities – The COLLATE System. ECDL '03, Springer, pp. 434–445 (2003)
15. Gamma, E., Helm, R., Johnson, R., Vlissides, J.: Design Patterns. Elements of Reusable Object-Oriented Software, Addison-Wesley, Reading, MA (1995)
16. Gogouvitis, S. V., Kousiouris, G., Konstanteli, K., Polychniatis, T., Menychtas, A., Kyriazis, D., Varvarigou, T.: Realtime-enabled workflow management in service oriented infrastructures. AREA '08: Proceeding of the 1st ACM workshop on Analysis and retrieval of events/actions and workflows in video streams, ACM, New York, USA, pp. 119–124 (2008)
17. Hagedorn, J., Hailpern, J., Karahalios, K. G.: VCode and VData: illustrating a new framework for supporting the video annotation workflow. AVI '08: Proceedings of the working conference on Advanced visual interfaces', ACM, New York, USA, pp. 317–321 (2008)

18. Halasz, F. G., Schwartz, M.: The Dexter Hypertext Reference Model. Communications of the ACM 37(2), 30–39 (1994)
19. Havemann, S., Fellner, D. W.: Seven Research Challenges of Generalized 3D Documents. IEEE Comput. Graph. Appl. 27(3), 70–76 (2007)
20. Hofmann, C., Hollender, N., Fellner, D. W.: Workflow-Based Architecture for Collaborative Video Annotation. A. Ant Ozok, Panayiotis Zaphiris (ed.), HCI (12), Springer, The Netherlands, pp. 33–42 (2009)
21. Hofmann, C., Hollender, N., Fellner, D. W.: A WORKFLOW MODEL FOR COLLABORATIVE VIDEO ANNOTATION – Supporting the Workflow of Collaborative Video Annotation and Analysis performed in Educational Settings. Proceedings of the International Conference on Computer Supported Education (CSEDU 09), INSTICC Press, Lissabon, Portugal, pp. 199–204 (2009)
22. Hollender, N., Hofmann, C., Deneke, M.: Principles to reduce extraneous load in web-based generative learning settings. Workshop on Cognition and the Web 2008, pp. 7–14 (2008)
23. Kadobayashi, R., Lombardi, J., McCahill, M. P., Stearns, H., Tanaka, K., Kay, A.: Annotation authoring in collaborative 3D virtual environments. ICAT '05: Proceedings of the 2005 international conference on Augmented tele-existence, ACM, New York, USA, pp. 255–256 (2005)
24. Leoni, M.; Aalst, W. M. & Hofstede, A. H.: Visual Support for Work Assignment in Process-Aware Information Systems. BPM '08: Proceedings of the 6th International Conference on Business Process Management, Springer-Verlag, Berlin, Heidelberg, pp. 67–83 (2008)
25. Lin, C.Y., Tseng, B. L., Smith, J. R.: Video collaborative annotation forum: Establishing ground-truth labels on large multimedia datasets. Proceedings of the TRECVID 2003 Workshop (2003)
26. Marshall, C. C.: Toward an ecology of hypertext annotation. HYPERTEXT '98: Proceedings of the ninth ACM conference on Hypertext and hypermedia: links, objects, time and space—structure in hypermedia systems, ACM, New York, USA, pp. 40–49 (1998)
27. Marshall, C. C., Brush, A. J. B.: Exploring the relationship between personal and public annotations. JCDL '04: Proceedings of the 4th ACM/IEEE-CS joint conference on Digital libraries, ACM, New York, USA, pp. 349–357 (2004)
28. Marshall, C. C., Ruotolo, C.: Reading-in-the-small: a study of reading on small form factor devices. JCDL '02: Proceedings of the 2nd ACM/IEEE-CS joint conference on Digital libraries, ACM, New York, USA, pp. 56–64 (2002)
29. Mikova, M., Janik, T.: Analysis of elements supporting health in physical education: Methodological approach of video study. Janík T. Wagner R. Mužík, V., ed.,'Mužík, V., Janík, T., Wagner, R. (ed.) Neue Herausforderungen im Gesundheitsbereich an der Schule. Was kann der Sportunterricht dazu beitragen?, MU, Brno, pp. 248–260 (2006)
30. Pea, R.,Hoffert, E.: Video Research in the Learning Sciences. Goldman, R., Pea, R., Barron, B., Derry, S.J. (ed.) Video workflow in the learning sciences: Prospects of emerging technologies for augmenting work practices. Lawrence Erlbaum, London, pp. 427–460 (2007)
31. Pea, R., Mills, M., Rosen, J., Dauber, K., Effelsberg, W., Hoffert, E. The Diver Project: Interactive Digital Video Repurposing. IEEE MultiMedia 11(1), 54–61 (2004)
32. Reif, G.: Semantische Annotation. Semantic Web - Wege zur vernetzten Wissensgesellschaft 5(4), 405–418 (2006)
33. Richter, K., Finke, M., Hofmann, C., Balfanz, D.: Hypervideo. Pagani, M. (ed.) Encyclopedia of Multimedia Technology and Networking, 2nd ed., Idea Group Pub., USA, pp. 641–647 (2009)
34. Schaetzle, R.: Workflow-Management – ein ereignisbasierter Ansatz. PhD thesis, Universitat Karlsruhe (TH) (2000)
35. Seidel, T., Prenzel, M., Kobarg, M. (Eds.): How to run a video study. Technical report of the IPN Video Study. Waxmann, Münster (2005)
36. Sesink, W., Goeller, S., Roeßling, G., Hofmann, D.: emargo: Eine Digitale Randspalte zum Selbststudium (nicht nur) der Informatik. Proceedings der Pre-Conference Workshops der 5. e-Learning Fachtagung Informatik (DeLFI 2007), Logos Verlag, Berlin, pp. 101–108 (2007)

37. Sliski, T. J., Billmers, M. P., Clarke, L. A., Osterweil, L. J.: An architecture for flexible, evolv-able process-driven user-guidance environments, SIGSOFT Softw. Eng. Notes 26(5), 33–43 (2001)
38. Stahl, E., Finke, M., Zahn, C.: Knowledge Acquisition by Hypervideo Design: An Instructional Program for University Courses. Journal of Educational Multimedia and Hypermedia 15(3), 285–302 (2006)
39. Streit, A., Pham, B., Brown, R.: Visualization Support for Managing Large Business Process Specifications. Business Process Management, 3649, 205–219 (2005)
40. Volkmer, T., Smith, J. R., Natsev, A.: A web-based system for collaborative annotation of large image and video collections: an evaluation and user study. MULTIMEDIA '05: Proceedings of the 13th annual ACM international conference on Multimedia, ACM, New York, USA, pp. 892–901 (2005)
41. Wang, M., Zhou, X., Chua, T.-S.: Automatic image annotation via local multi-label classifica-tion. CIVR '08: Proceedings of the 2008 international conference on Content-based image and video retrieval, ACM, New York, USA, pp. 17–26 (2008)
42. Workflow Management Coalition Terminology & Glossary. Document Number WFMC-TC-1011, Issues 3.0, Technical report (1999)
43. Zheng, Q., Booth, K., McGrenere, J.: Co-authoring with structured annotations. CHI '06: Proceedings of the SIGCHI conference on Human Factors in computing systems, ACM, New York, USA, pp. 131–140 (2006)

Change Awareness for Collaborative Video Annotation

Cristian Hofmann, Uwe Boettcher, and Dieter W. Fellner

Abstract Collaborative Video Annotation is a broad field of research and is widely used in productive environments. While it is easy to follow changes in small systems with few users, keeping in touch with all changes in large environments can easily get overwhelming. The easiest way and a first approach to prevent the users from getting lost is to show them all changes in an appropriate way. This list of changes can also become very large when many contributors add new information to shared data resources. To prevent users from getting lost while having a list of changes, this paper introduces a way to subscribe to parts of the system and only to have the relevant changes shown. To achieve this goal, the framework provides an approach to check the relevance of changes, which is not trivial in three dimensional spaces, and to be accumulated for later reference by the subscribing user. The benefit for users is to need fewer time to be up-to-date and to have more time for applying own changes.

Introduction

When working alone on a single document the user always knows what and where changes occur. But as soon as more users collaborate on one or more documents, they need to realize all changes made to the documents that are modified by the

C. Hofmann (✉) and D.W. Fellner
Fraunhofer Institute for Computer Graphics Research Darmstadt, Fraunhoferstr. 5,
64283 Darmstadt, Germany
and
Technische Universtät Darmstadt, Interactive Graphics Systems Group, Fraunhoferstr. 5,
64283 Darmstadt, Germany
e-mail: cristian.hofmann@igd.fraunhofer.de; d.fellner@igd.fraunhofer.de

U. Boettcher
Technische Universtät Darmstadt, Interactive Graphics Systems Group, Fraunhoferstr. 5,
64283 Darmstadt, Germany
e-mail: boettcher@gris.informatik.tu-darmstadt.de

M. Lewkowicz et al. (eds.), *Proceedings of COOP 2010*,   101
DOI 10.1007/978-1-84996-211-7_7, © Springer-Verlag London Limited 2010

community. If the applied collaborative system only provides viewing and modifying of documents, any user has to inspect all documents carefully to notice all changes which have been made. As that may be a time consuming and defective activity, users must spend much of their productivity to avoid errors and track the new modifications in an appropriate way. Thus the system does not scale well with increasing number of users. The more users there are, the more changes must be inspected prior to applying own changes. But the main goal of collaborative systems is to scale well with increasing number of users to multiply productivity. Consequently, there must be a way to avoid spending much time on getting up-to-date. The system has to announce changes to the users, so they do not have to search for them. This protects collaborating users from missing any change that has been made. Particularly, that also reduces the time needed to inspect all changes for relevance. As a second step, in order to additionally reduce the time needed to get up-to-date, certain filters can be implemented to further reduce the time needed to get up-to-date. The user selects videos or parts thereof to follow and only changes of these specific elements are shown. In doing so, the user can spend a great share of actual productive time. When trying to apply filters to videos, there are specific constraints to be solved.

The main contribution of this paper is to present an environment for Collaborative Video Annotation that supports tracking of changes by applying suchlike filters to video-based media. In doing so, we expect to alleviate essential activities that users have to perform when annotating videos in collaborative settings. Here, we introduce a way to support filters in Collaborative Video Annotation to assist the users with *Change Awareness*. By allowing the user to select which informations to be filtered and which not (rather than filtering automatically), a maximum control for the user is assured. The presented concepts have been developed in the scope of the THESEUS program. THESEUS is a research program, initiated by the Federal Ministry of Economy and Technology (BMWi), to develop a new internet-based infrastructure in order to better use and utilize the knowledge available on the internet.

Fundamentals

First, we introduce the involved fundamentals and specific characteristics Video Annotation and Collaborative Video Annotation as a sub-category. Finally the field of Change Awareness will be illuminated. There, the main question is: Why do you need Change Awareness?

Video Annotation

In general, Video Annotation means applying additional content to videos. This content can be of different types, for example metadata or additional multimedia content. Metadata can either be descriptive [1, 5] or semantic [3]. Additional content can be of numerous formats: texts (notes, comments, discussions, etc. [5]), multimedia (sounds, videos, etc.) [1] or other formats containing certain information.

Fig. 1 Comparison of annotations in books and in videos [7]

While metadata is usually designed to be read by machines, additional content should be displayed to the users [1].

This concept is closely related to side notes applied to books by readers. These are applied to make it easy to understand difficult parts of the book either for oneself of for fellow readers. Sometimes they are applied to remember additional information found in other books or own thoughts to be followed later on. Annotation to books is obviously of the second type: additional user information, and can only be used for texts or user drawn graphics. In the scope of digital video content, this limitation is obsolete, since you can display a much broader selection of content. Figure 1 shows the concepts of Annotation to books and to videos. You can easily realize the similarities and the differences.

While annotation to books is easy and only a pen is needed, annotation to videos has to be supported by the applied video player [5]. This is an important difference between the two worlds, as book writers can be sure that readers are able annotate, while video creators do not have that guarantee. This problem has to be solved with a specific player for videos supporting annotations. Also videos have a different structure compared to books. Videos consist of events, objects, and scenes as temporal parts and they show moves as spatial parts [5, 9].

Within or upon a video, annotations consist of three parts: an anchor in the source video selecting the topic to be annotated, the annotation (of any player supported type which might also include other videos or annotated videos) and the link connecting these two items. The anchor can be any spatiotemporal object contained in the source video, for example a scene or a specific object shown. Figure 2 shows the principal structure of annotated videos. It shows the videos, annotated objects and the links connecting them.

Collaborative Video Annotation

Collaborative Video Annotation means having the principles of Video Annotation in collaborative environments, whereat many users annotate the same video or videos. It can be used in different contexts and use cases such as learning environments

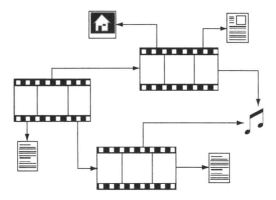

Fig. 2 Structure of annotated videos [7]

[5, 8, 18] or video analysis [6, 13]. A growing number of application scenarios for (collaborative) video analysis in education can be identified. Pea and colleagues report on a university course of a film science department, in which two different movie versions of the play "Henry V" are analysed by a group of students with respect to the text transposition by different actors and directors [13]. Other examples for the application of video analysis in education are motion analyses in sports and physical education, or the acquisition of soft skills such as presentation or argumentation techniques [10, 13, 14]. Brugmann et al. [4] describe another example where a shared group of scientists work on papers about sign language [4]. As this topic is underrepresented in science, scientists are far away from each other. These ways are commonly overcome by travel which requires much time. As the scientists are often deaf-mute themselves, telephone conferences are no solution. Video conferences could be used, but the sign language demands a great share of the scientists attention and leads to few attention for the topic discussed over. The participants must have two videos in attention, one showing the speech and the other the topic. With video annotation the speech can be textual and the scientists can rewind and see the same part again if that matters [4].

In greater projects many people are working together on one document. The number of modifications can rapidly become overwhelming especially in asynchronous systems, because the numerous modifications and points of modification exceeds the humanly possible [2, 16]. Thus the participants coherent work can no longer be ensured [13] and mistakes will happen.

Change Awareness

Mentioned problems (having overwhelmingly numerous changes and thus loosing coherence) can be mitigated by providing Change Awareness. That basically means to track down every change in any document contained by the system and to inform the user about these changes. "Information elements include: knowing who changed the artifact, what those changes involve, where changes occur, when changes were made, how things have changed and why people made the changes" [17]. Thus the information is supporting the user in his work and may yield to more productivity. Papadopoulou [12] defines Change Awareness as "the ability of a person to track the changes that other collaborators make to a group project at any time while interacting with it" [12].

Change Awareness can have two different underlying principles. The first system is that one user does changes in the system and the other users follow these changes live while having some sort of communication (e.g. telephone conference). This way does automatically fulfill all the aspects called for by Tam and Greenberg (who, what, where, when, how, why) [17]. But this way does only work in synchronous systems as all users have to follow the changes live, while the framework presented in this paper should be indifferent about synchronous and asynchronous. The second way is to accumulate the changes and save them into the database. Then the server informs the user about the changes made (either with login or with some other message the user sends to the server). This results in the user being always well-informed about all changes made, knowing what happens where, and able to make own changes without interfering with others [12].

This basic principle must be further enhanced when larger projects should be handled by the server. If projects grow larger, the number of changes increases proportionally. That results in the changes itself becoming overwhelmingly numerous. So a strategy must be found to show only relevant changes. That means a type of filter must be implemented. The basic variant of filtering in this case is to have the user decide which parts of the project are relevant to him.

This yields to a new problem in regard to Video Annotation: the annotations are connected with anchors, which may be three dimensional spatiotemporal objects contained in a video, as there are two dimensions in space (x-axis and y-axis) and the time as third dimension. These anchors can and will overlap with other anchors and if the user for example is interested in the car shown in a video, he may also want to know about changes concerning the tire. That means the tracking system should include some sort of test for overlapping anchors.

To gain Change Awareness, the system has to track every change the users commit to the documents. The tracking objects are known as Awareness Information: "... the value of information elements that need to be collected and presented to users, to preserve their awareness" [12]. Tracking changes may result in a higher productivity because the users need fewer time to get up-to-date while staying sure not to miss any relevant change [11].

However it should be remembered that some contributors will want to have all changes in any document displayed. Papadopoulou describes this as role dependent: "The awareness information people require when collaboratively authoring a document is highly related to their roles as well. Some users may need to be informed about every last detail of changes made to a document while others may be satisfied with information showing only major revisions" [12]. She explains further that lawyers for example have to know every change of a contract while professors only need to have an overall view to the documents and need only be informed about major changes [12].

Related Work

Tam and Greenberg [17] introduce asynchronous Change Awareness to Collaborative Systems. They take a broad view on Collaborative Systems in general and show in detail what is needed to make the user able to be change aware. The theoretical basics for tracking changes are discussed and a framework is introduced. But the main goal for Tam and Greenberg is to provide theoretical background for others to research further on. They neither built a prototype nor applied their findings to any real case. In their conclusion they say that "we have to analyse the need for change awareness in particular application domains. By understanding these differences, custom versions of the framework tailored to that domain may be produced" [17].

Papadopoulou [12] introduces a framework for change awareness in collaborative systems. In her dissertation she describes how this framework can be used to enhance a text editor with contributor's awareness for changes. She also discusses the problems related with concurrent work of multiple users on the same document, which may lead to users change documents which already changed after they downloaded the contents. Additionally she discusses the privacy issues of collaborative systems in detail and concludes with further uses of her framework for other fields of work. She states that if "more than one user has worked on the same document part, possible conflicts to be resolved may arise. In the worst case, the changes of one user might have to be discarded, which could be disappointing and time-consuming for the users" [12]. While this is very similar to this paper, she focuses on texts and graphics and did neither discuss nor examine the specific hindrances to be solved when implementing Change Awareness into Collaborative Video Annotation Systems.

The Vannotea project [15, 19] implements some rudimentary forms of change tracking. But it reveals that the method collaborators are made aware of changes is not tailored to the special needs of video annotation. The changes are announced via RSS feeds delivered by the annotation servers. These feeds include all changes made. The filtering should be further improved to be configurable to the special needs of any contributor. As Papadopoulou [12] figured out there are different roles which contributors may take on. Depending on these roles, different filtering methods should be applied [12].

Framework Requirements Analysis

Based on the aspects pointed out in the fundamentals section with respect to Change Awareness, we examined existing systems for Video Annotation. We checked if and how these systems provide Change Awareness to their users and if any filtering is provided.

Many state of the art-systems do not provide any Change Awareness explicitly. Those which do, only provide some basic level of Change Awareness. They do not track all changes, or they track all changes but do not provide filtering in a satisfying way. None of the systems which are state-of-the-art does provide filtering of the Awareness Information for specific spatiotemporal parts of the video(s) (which is essential as figured out above).

By means of that state-of-the-art analysis, we were able to model the following requirements for our framework: *Subscriptions*, *Overlap Detection*, *Event Triggering*, *Change Tracking*, *Awareness Information Providing*, *Server Messages Enrichment*, and *Client Enrichment*. In the following, these requirements are described.

Subscriptions

The system has to provide a way to subscribe to certain parts of the database. As we discussed earlier this should not only target videos but also parts of a video. To achieve this goal, the underlying Object Model must be enriched to allow to attach subscriptions to any object representing content. This includes (not intended to be exhaustive): Accumulations of videos, videos itself, scenes or objects contained in videos, or comments attached to videos.

Additionally any change to an object should be detected and provided to the corresponding subscriptions. This should be least intrusive to the Object Model to allow for easy integration into existing systems or reuse.

Overlap Detection

The objects or scenes shown in videos do naturally overlap. Cars shown have tires, a dialog has different speakers involved, and chapters are divided into several locations shown. When a change occurs on any object contained in or overlapped by another one, the Subscriptions to this other object should also be informed.

While this goal seems trivial at first and is easy to implement for video aggregations (e.g. documents) or scenes of videos, there are much more hindrances when it comes to parts of videos (e.g. objects contained in the video). Parts of videos are three dimensional spatiotemporal objects, so detecting if two parts overlap means solving a three dimensional overlapping problem.

To minimize time needed to announce changes, which is crucial to synchronous systems, overlaps should be precalculated. This can easily be implemented using adapters for the objects to which Subscriptions are applied. These adapters track which other objects (adapters) are overlapping to themselves. If a change occurs the object informs the corresponding adapter, which acts like a single subscription to the object. These adapters inform not only their subscribers but also the overlapping object's adapters.

Event Triggering

The server's implementation has to be enhanced with an event triggering system for change events. Any change made should trigger an event which is passed to the subscription system. This system handles the event appropriately. All (straight or oblique) subscribers should be informed about the change event and the triggering action.

Change Tracking

Any change made to an object should be announced to all of the object's subscribers. The awareness information should include [17]:

- Who changed the artifact?
- What are those changes involving?
- Where occurred these changes?
- When were the changes made?
- How have things changed?
- Why made people these changes?

As this should also work asynchronously, the tracked changes have to be persisted. The awareness information is saved for future use by the subscriber, and should be persisted and later presented to the user.

While the first five items are automatically known when a change occurs, the last item is different and needs specific handling by the client. As it is not clear how the user reacts on having to provide a reason for every changes he does, this part of the Awareness Information is optional on the server side of our implementation and not supported by the client.

Awareness Information Providing

Finally the server should be enhanced to be able to provide the awareness information to clients. That means a message should be implemented which retrieves the awareness information. This message should be parameterized:

- Show changes since last message by client
- Show messages marked to be read later
- Show all changes saved in database for the user

The default setting should be to provide all changes since last message exchange between server and client, and the messages marked for later reading. With parameters the client can additionally choose any of the three items above.

Also the client should be able to delete any awareness information in the database. To provide this option, the server should remember the awareness information individually for each user.

Server Messages Enrichment

While most changes to the system will occur while the user is not logged in, some will happen while the user is present. So the user should not only be informed about changes with login but instead be informed with any message submitted.

To slim the message exchange, only key information should be added to messages. Each message should be enriched with a short note providing information if any new change happened. Additionally the client should receive a note about messages marked to be read later when the user logs in. It is the clients responsibility to act properly on the information provided (e.g. to inform the user and to allow the user to retrieve the awareness information).

Client Enrichment

The only step taken regarding the client is to implement a notice to the user, which is shown whenever the server notifies the client about any change made. The user then decides how to react on the changes. He may disregard the notice, take a short look and continue his work, or interrupt to respond on the changes.

This message the server shows to the user should be non-disturbing with regard to the work flow of the user, but prominent enough to be recognized in any circumstances.

Results of the Requirements Analysis

As a result to this analysis, the server should be divided into five parts: the Message Interface, the Command Execution Logic, the Object Model, the Subscription Management, and the Persistence Interface. These are shown in Fig. 3 and be described as follows:

– *Message Interface.* This part of the server receives the messages of the client, parses the relevant data and hands it to the appropriate part of the Command Execution.
– *Command Execution Logic.* In this part the program logic resides. The relevant objects are retrieved from the Persistence Interface, the modifications are applied, and the objects are persisted again.

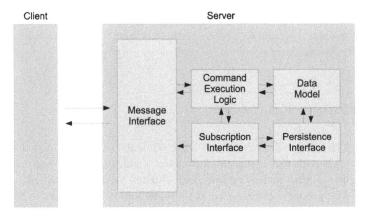

Fig. 3 Global model of the server

- *Object Model.* The Object Model will be described in detail in Chapter 5.
- *Subscription Management.* All changes in any object are handed over to the Subscription Management to be persisted for later use by any user of the system.
- *Persistence Interface.* The Persistence Interface provides simple methods to store and retrieve objects. All objects stored are persisted.

A Framework for Change Awareness in Collaborative Video Annotation Systems

We implemented a video annotation system providing Change Awareness as described in this paper. The application consists of a server and a client application. Our implementation can be used as a framework to enrich other servers with Change Awareness or to implement own servers for other topics. Following, we will describe what we did in general.

Object Model

The object model of the server is based on Finke's model for hyperlinked video [5]. In order to support Change awareness, we enlarged that model with specific classes which are going to be explained below. In Finke's hypervideo model, the base classes are modeled to represent the general objects needed to provide different projects containing annotated videos or other information to the users. These classes shown in Fig. 4 are:

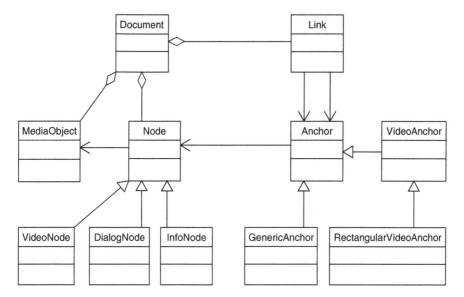

Fig. 4 The object model, which this framework is based on [5]

- *Document.* This class is the container class representing a project. All informations contained in a Document belong to a single context. This context usually is a base video to be discussed by the community. To this base video all comments (which may be of any media type as already figured out) are added either directly or indirectly.
- *Node.* Any information fragment of a specific type is contained in a Node object. A Document may and will contain different Nodes referencing to each other as annotations. In general the server is able to annotate an annotated video to another video, thus chaining nodes together.
- *VideoNode.* The base Node of a Document in our field of work will be a VideoNode, which contains a video able to be annotated. In the Object Model, any media will be able to be annotated.
- *DialogNode.* Not all annotations to the base video will be other videos. In fact, most will be texts, which are stored in DialogNodes. These are also able to be annotated, but in our implementation only the whole DialogNode may be annotated. This could be different for other fields of work. DialogNodes may additionally have sub nodes, which have to be DialogNodes, too. This enables a forum-like discussion contained in a tree of DialogNodes.
- *InfoNode.* All other informations are stored in InfoNodes. These can form a tree, too.
- *MediaObject.* Any Node contains a MediaObject, in which the data is encapsulated. A video for example could have different formats like MPEG or Flash. This information is encapsulated in the MediaObject class to free the VideoNode of this differentiation. Thus the VideoNode can reference to any video with the same methods, regardless of format.

- *Anchor*. This class implements a way to select parts of any media contained in a Node. These are used to select the topic of annotations. Anchors may have different types, depending on the data.
- *VideoAnchor*. These select any spatiotemporal part of a video to make this part able to be referenced and annotated. VideoAnchors may have different shape depending on the object to be annotated. These shapes have to be implemented. In our implementation only a rectangular shape is available, but this can easily be enhanced with additional types of shape.
- *GenericAnchor*. When no other type of Anchor fits, this type can be utilized to refer to the whole Node.
- *Link*. Links connect anchors to enable annotations as described in Fundamentals. Links connect a source Anchor representing the object which should get an annotation with a destination Anchor representing the annotated object. In general, this could also be only part of a video, but in our implementation only GenericAnchors are used for destinations.

To provide Change Awareness, there has to be a way for users to select which parts of a project should be tracked. Thus, some objects must be added to this Object Model to support Change Awareness. These additions are shown in Fig. 5 in gray and described here:

- *Subscriber*. This interface represents any Subscriber. This interface just provides a way to announce a change. All objects containing data that may be changed

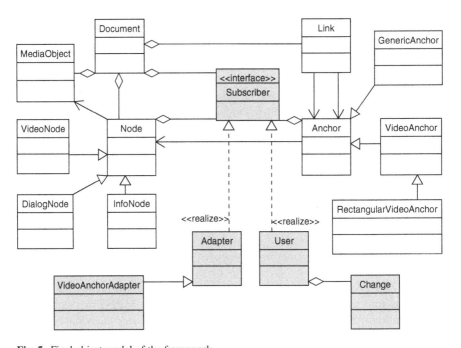

Fig. 5 Final object model of the framework

and tracked provide a way to register Subscribers with them. These Subscribers can be of different type to allow for Overlap Detection.

- *User.* User are the standard Subscriber. User represents any user registered with the system. All User objects keep track of Changes to be prepared to present them to the corresponding human. User may additionally hold any login credentials or user defined settings (e.g. default project to open).
- *Adapter.* The other type of Subscriber is an Adapter to other Subscribers. Whenever an object could overlap with other objects of the same type, an Adapter is created to keep track of all overlaps. This means, whenever an object is created for which an Adapter exists, a corresponding adapter is also created. This adapter is attached to the object and functions as a hook for other subscriptions to that object as an Adapter can also be subscribed to. Secondly any created adapter checks, if any already existing adapter represents an object which overlaps with its own object. If there is any, it saves this overlap for future use and announces that overlap to the other anchor as well.
- *VideoAnchorAdapter.* In our field of work, only VideoAnchors can have relevant overlaps. Thus we only implemented this specific Adapter. Other adapters could be implemented as well taking this one as an example.
- *Change.* This object represents any change made to any object. It stores the Awareness Information that should later be presented to the user.

All objects supporting subscriptions announce their changes to all subscribers, either an adapter or a Subscription object.

Overlap Detection and Change Tracking

The adapters provide methods for detecting overlaps. As there are anchors tailored to special needs, the adapters must also be tailored to a specific Anchor class. Each tailored anchor may or may not have an adapter class, as there could be anchors which can never overlap. With regard to video objects the adapter class has to solve a three dimensional overlapping problem. The adapter first determines if one of the two Anchors is wholly included in the other. Thereafter it checks if any edge of one anchor penetrates the surface of the other anchor. If either of these conditions applies, an overlap is found. Each anchor represents a three dimensional object. Mathematically these objects have 12 edges and six surfaces. These edges can be defined as follows (with g and h being points on the edge):

$$e = \left\{ x \in R \mid x = g + k \cdot (h - g) \right\} \tag{1}$$

The surfaces are inside planes. These planes are in vectorial form and in Hesse-Normalform (with p, q and r being corners of the surfaces, n the normal vector of the plane, and a the distance between the plane and the origin):

$$P = \left\{ x \in R \mid x = p + m \cdot (q - p) + n \cdot (r - p) \right\} = \left\{ x \in R \mid x \cdot n = a \right\} \tag{2}$$

The Anchor can mathematically be defined as intersection of six half-planes defined by the six surfaces. These half-planes are:

$$H_k = \left\{ x \in R \,|\, x \cdot n_k \geq a_k \right\}$$ (3)

The anchor can thus be written as:

$$A = \bigcap_{k=1}^{6} \left\{ x \in R \,|\, x \cdot n_k \geq a_k \right\}$$ (4)

To check for an overlap, you simply calculate the intersections of the 12 edges of one Anchor with the six surfaces of the other Anchor. This results in 72 points. These 72 points are then checked, if one of them is inside both Anchors. (There fortunately must only be checked once, as you used the edges of one Anchor, thus the points are by design inside this Anchor.) If one of the points is inside both anchors, an Overlap is found.

If an overlap is found, the overlapping anchor's adapters save this information for later use. Whenever any change occurs in one of these two connected anchors, the subscribers of both anchors receive the corresponding Change object.

Visualization

This section describes how users are informed of changes occurred on runtime or during absence. As already mentioned, the user notice should be displayed in a non-disturbing way. However, notices should be distinctive enough, so that the user is able to recognize them whatever he is doing in that moment. Figure 6 shows a screenshot of the client noticing the user that parts of the annotated video have been modified. The client uses no popup window to notify the user, since this would disturb users in the context of their actual activities. Instead, the client provides a panel in the upper right corner of the graphical user interface. In that panel, a red dot indicates new changes drawing only necessary attention to be noticed in any circumstance. The user realizes that something requires his attention, but can work on until a state is reached in which the current work can be interrupted in order to focus on the adviced changes. Additionally, the user is instantly informed if a change is connected to a part of his actual work. To accomplish this, the client shows a red sign on the upper corner of each anchor which is connected to a change event (see Fig. 6).

After selecting the "Changes occurred" button, a list of actual modifications are displayed on the changes panel. Figure 7 gives an example, how the changes list is presented to the user. The changes list is linked to the related object. A click on any element opens the related object in the browser window. Thus, users are enabled to follow respective changes in a direct way (see red line in Fig. 7). Furthermore, three

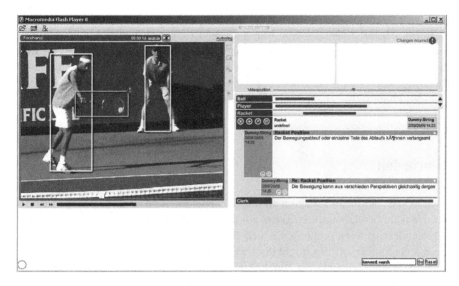

Fig. 6 Client notifying new changes to the user

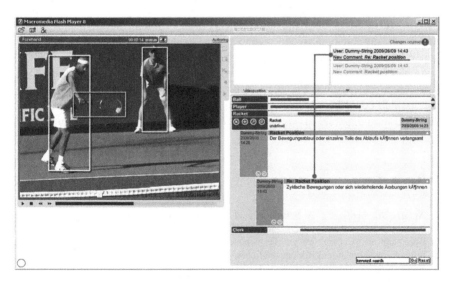

Fig. 7 Client presenting the changes list to the user

of the relevant questions are answered on the spot: You see who made the change, when the change was made, and how things changed. With a simple click the user can open this related object and inspect the changes (which are still marked as new). This link answers the other two questions (what and where), which cannot be answered in textual form in the changes list.

To sum up, users are notified about changes made in the current video project by means of a specific visualization. The integrated changes list provides information about who, when, and how changes where made. Furthermore, elements of the change list are connected to the respective area on the video. Thus, users can follow the changes by viewing the respective contents on the one hand, and information is provided about where changes occurred and what has been modified.

Conclusion

Keeping the user informed about all that is happening is an important field of work when working collaboratively. Users not knowing what others do cannot contribute to the collective work properly, because they might miss others work and can thus leave no comment, or they might do work which is already done.

While some Collaborative Video Annotation systems already support keeping track of changes, they still do not allow users to select specific parts of interest instead of a whole entity. But, as we have seen, it is necessary to provide that information properly.

We pointed out how the system should be designed, and what circumstances must be fulfilled to help the user solving this problem. With the presented framework, any collaborative video annotation systems can be enhanced by providing proper Awareness Information to keep the user up-to-date.

As part of future research activities, we did not implement or suggest any kind of recommender system. These could be used to assist the user in finding more filters which could be relevant to the annotators' interests. We did not bring any illumination to this field of work, which could enhance the productivity further.

References

1. Agosti, M., Ferro, N.: A Formal Model of Annotations of Digital Content. In: ACM Transactions on Information Systems (TOIS), 26,1(3). 2007
2. Bergmann, R., Niederholtmeyer, C.: Arbeiten im Internet. Virtuelle Arbeitsgruppen in Non-Profit-Unternehmen und Bildungseinrichtungen. hiba Forum Band 24. hiba Verlag. 2003
3. Berners-Lee, T., Hendler, J., Lassila, O.: The Semantic Web. In: Scientific American, 284(5): 34–43. 2001
4. Brugman, H., Crasborn, O., Russel, A.: Collaborative annotation of sign language data with peer-to-peer technology. In: Proceedings of the 4th International Conference on Language Resources and Evaluation, pp 213–216. European Language Resources Association, Paris. 2004
5. Finke, M.: Unterstuetzung des kooperativen Wissenserwerbs durch Hypervideo-Inhalte. Universitäts- und Landesbibliothek Darmstadt (2005)
6. Hagedorn, J., Hailpern, J., Karahalios, K.G.: VCode and VData: illustrating a new framework for supporting the video annotation workflow. In: Proceedings of the working conference on Advanced visual interfaces, Napoli, Italy. pp 317–321. 2008

7. Hofmann, C.: Entwurf und Neuimplementierung einer Hypervideoanwendung für kooperativen Wissenserwerb. Diploma Thesis, Universität Siegen. 2006
8. Hofmann, C., Hollender, N.: Kooperativer Informationsaustausch mit Hypervideo: Potentiale für das Web 2.0. In: Proceedings of the Pre-Conference Workshops of the DeLFI 2007, Logos Verlag, Berlin. 2007
9. Hofmann, C., Hollender, N.: Kooperativer Informationserwerb und -Austausch durch Hypervideo. In: M & C '07: Proceedings of the Mensch & Computer 2007: Konferenz für interaktive und kooperative Medien, Oldenbourg, pp 269–272. 2007
10. Hollender, N., Hofmann, C., Deneke, M.: Principles to reduce extraneous load in web-based generative learning settings. In: Workshop on Cognition and the Web 2008, Granada, Spain, pp 7–14. 2008
11. Kim, H., Erklundh, K.S.: Collaboration between Writer and Reviewer through Change Representation Tools. In: Proceedings of the 35th Annual Hawaii International Conference on System Sciences, IEEE Computer Society, Washington, DC, USA. 2002
12. Papadopoulou, S.: Multi–Level Change Awareness for Collaborative Authoring Applications. Dissertation at the ETH Zürich, Zürich, Switzerland. 2009
13. Pea, R., Lindgren, R., Rosen, J.: Computer-supported collaborative video analysis. In: 7th International Conference on Learning Sciences, pp 516–521. International Society of the Learning Sciences, Bloomington, IN. 2006
14. Richter, K., Finke, M., Hofmann, C., Balfanz, D.: Hypervideo. In: Pagani, M. (ed.) Encyclopedia of Multimedia Technology and Networking, 2nd edition, pp 641–647. Idea Group Pub, Hershey, PA. 2007
15. Schroeter, R., Hunter, J., Guerin, J., Khan, I., Henderson, M.: A Synchronous Multimedia Annotation System for Secure Collaboratories. In: Proceedings of the 2nd IEEE International Conference on E-Science and Grid Computing, Amsterdam, The Netherlands (eScience 2006), p 41. 2006
16. Schulmeister, R.: Grundlagen hypermedialer Lernsysteme: Theorie – Didaktik – Design. Addison-Wesley, Bonn. 2002
17. Tam, J., Greenberg, S.: A framework for asynchronous change awareness in collaborative documents and workspaces. In: Int. J. Hum.-Comput. Stud. 64, 7 (Jul. 2006), 583–598. 2006
18. Zahn, C., Finke, M.: Collaborative knowledge building based on hyperlinked video. In: Wasson, B., Baggetun, R., Hoppe, U., Ludvigsen, S. (ed.): Proceedings of the International Conference on Computer Support for Collaborative Learning, Dordrecht, The Netherlands, pp 173–175. 2003
19. http://www.itee.uq.edu.au/ eresearch/projects/vannotea/

Rethinking Laboratory Notebooks

Clemens Nylandsted Klokmose and Pär-Ola Zander

Abstract We take digitalization of laboratory work practice as a challenging design domain to explore. There are obvious drawbacks with the use of paper instead of ICT in the collaborative writing that takes place in laboratory notebooks; yet paper persist in being the most common solution. The ultimate aim with our study is to produce design relevant knowledge that can envisage an ICT solution that keeps as many advantages of paper as possible, but with the strength of electronic laboratory notebooks as well. Rather than assuming that users are technophobic and unable to appropriate state of the art software, we explore whether there are something inherent in current ICT infrastructure that invites resistance from the users. The method used is interviews, combined with a modified version of future workshops and the data are analyzed with activity theory. Our results concern issues of configurability, mobility, and the barrier between documentation and control, amongst other things.

Introduction

IT tools give an obvious advantage over the analogue counterpart for our inscription-based activities in many aspects of our everyday life. We write our papers, manipulate images, create music and build detailed three-dimensional models with the hassles of doing it by hand long forgotten. Computer supported collaboration with inscriptions have many success stories; Wikipedia is but one of them.

C.N. Klokmose (✉) and P.-O. Zander
Department of Computer Science, Aarhus University, Aabogade 34, 8200 Aarhus N, Denmark
e-mail: clemens@cs.au.dk; poz@cs.au.dk

C.N. Klokmose
Laboratorie de Recherche en Informatique, Université Paris-Sud, Bâtiment 490,
F-91405 Orsay, France
e-mail: clemens@lri.fr

M. Lewkowicz et al. (eds.), *Proceedings of COOP 2010*,
DOI 10.1007/978-1-84996-211-7_8, © Springer-Verlag London Limited 2010

However, there are some domains where the flexibility of paper seemingly overweighs the benefits of digital solutions. An example is laboratory notebooks, which are interesting, because many laboratory workers are highly computer literate, autonomous, thus some form of computer illiteracy or unwillingness to experiment cannot explain their resistance to collaboration technology. This was a main reason to conduct a case study on the work practice of laboratory notebooks and work in a Physics and Astronomy department.

Systems for electronic laboratory notebooks (ELN) are beginning to emerge especially in the biochemistry and pharmaceutical industry. But in the academic research laboratories around the globe the paper-based laboratory notebook is still the referential source of documentation [1, 2]. However, given the increasing complexity of modern research, and the computerisation of the majority of the experimental equipment the traditional paper-based laboratory notebook is beginning to age. Paper has a number of advantages in the context of laboratory note-books: It is lightweight, ubiquitous, cheap, and easy to use [3, 4]. Sometimes legislation has a favourable view on paper [5]. And the possibility to flexibly file and spatially organize paper in a physical space at a low time cost and without needing to organize it in a hierarchical (or tag cloud) structure is relatively efficient [6]. It is easy to place a paper document into their task-related context, and since many types of research involves moving around in the laboratory, that context is potentially the whole room.

Tabard et al. [7] augment paper-based laboratory notebooks through the use of Anoto technology (http://www.anoto.com/), hence, bridging the gap between the analogue and digital. This appears to be a promising approach, however we want to explore whether some of the inherent problems in creating a purely digital labora-tory notebook system can be addressed by diverting from traditions and funda-mental assumptions in how we design information systems. In particular if we divert from the assumptions of the desktop metaphor or the assumptions of that all human-computer interaction must based on applications. With 'application' we mean a set of tools bound together with a specific work domain in mind. This is for instance to produce printable documents, creating PowerPoint presentations or constructing CAD models of buildings. An example of an application such as Microsoft Word embodies a specific understanding of how we produce written documents. If we want to do something out of the ordinary, e.g. make free-hand annotations with a tablet pen, we need to look within Word for a tool to do so. If it is not possible we can hope it will be in the next release. In this paper we argue that seen through our theoretical lens, this static nature of applications stands in a problematic contrast to the nature of the use of laboratory notebooks by the participants of our study.

The definite majority of related work on ELNs as well as products on the market [e.g. 2, 8, 9] subscribe to the assumptions of applications. We want to complement their views with a non-application-centric view on cooperation with laboratory notebooks. Therefore, we have conducted interviews and workshops that try to enable thinking among users outside these beaten paths. We describe this in the next section.

Method

During the fall of 2008, a group of researchers from the Department of Physics and Astronomy at Aarhus University were invited to participate in a series of workshops and interviews discussing the future of laboratory notebooks. Our aim was to contribute to a technological solution to lab workers' actual problems. We structured our research around the question: What are the central characteristics of a set of lab book artefacts that retain the advantages of a paper-based lab book, but do not reinstate its disadvantages? In order not to merely repeat previous laboratory notebook work, we used an approach where we did not assume, or make the participants take for granted, desktop metaphors and applications; this becomes especially evident in the workshop setups.

Our study did not include any construction or evaluation of an actual prototype, but concentrated on the current state of work practice and visions for a future practice. However, the study can be seen as a first step towards a future system development project – this potential was also discussed with the physicists.

The group consisted of five PhD students with a focus on experimental physics but with different fields of study: Photoemission, semiconducting, high-energy physics, laser physics and mass spectrometry. Four of the five participants had extensive experience in using paper-based collaboratory laboratory notebooks. The fifth had discarded the use of paper-based notebooks for a partly digital solution – a choice, however, leaving him with some amount of bad conscience. One of the participants had been involved in larger experiments at CERN where both paper-based and makeshift web-based laboratory notebooks were used.

The study consisted of individual interviews, two workshops and an introductory meeting. The introductory meeting was setup for the participating physicists to meet the researchers, and to present them with the point and plan of the study.

Interviews

Each participant was interviewed about his or her use and understanding of laboratory notebooks and asked to give a tour of his or her laboratory where more informal conversation took place. Four of the participants were able to show us around their laboratories.

The interviews were aimed at uncovering the role played by the laboratory notebook to the physicists and their work. We wanted to know how they characterized a laboratory notebook, whether it was used for documentation only, if it was used in communication, and if it was used collaboratively. All interviews were recorded and transcribed.

We used an interview guide, constructed in order to generate data relevant to our theoretical framework. The interviews were semi-structured [10].

The interpretation of our data has been informed by realist evaluation. This paradigm posits that outcomes of activity (i.e. outcome patterns or regularities) follow from mechanisms in contingently configured contexts [11]. Hence, the use of laboratory notebooks must be understood in its socially situated location. The investigation of laboratory work is concerned with the real, but it is a reality that is stratified and acknowledges the interplay between these different strata of reality [12]. The goal is to reveal the complex and contingent causal mechanisms of laboratory work that are not necessarily directly accessible for us via our senses, i.e. contradictions that do not produce immediate breakdown. Realist evaluation is also applied and concerned with praxis, and should have as its goal to transform this (real) praxis, in this case use of laboratory notebooks. Another tenet of realist evaluation is that it should not be purely measurement-driven but instead be founded on theory in the evaluation process [13]. Accordingly, our conceptual framework shaped our interview guides and data analysis.

Future Workshops

We conducted two workshops with the physicists aimed at on the one hand addressing the weaknesses of the current paper-based notebook and on the other hand bringing forth their visions of a future electronic laboratory notebook system. The two workshops were approximately 3 h of length each. The workshops were structured as future workshops [14], though with an important alternation described below. Future workshops were originally used as methods for democratic brainstorming on social and community issues [14]. However the method has shown itself useful from a design and HCI perspective [15]. Future workshops consist of three phases:

- A *critique phase* aiming at elucidating all problems and issues regarding, in this case, the physicists' use of paper-based laboratory notebooks.
- The *fantasy phase*, where ideas, no matter how far-fetched, for solutions to the problems in the previous phase are stimulated and brought to the table.
- And finally the *realisation phase* where the potentials in realising the ideas of the last phase are discussed.

The first workshop was held as a regular future workshop beginning with a critique phase where the physicists were encouraged to list the problems and issues they had with their current paper-based laboratory notebooks. This was followed by a fantasy phase where the goal was to get as many visions for a future laboratory notebook in the open, no matter how far fetched they may have seemed. Finally in the realization phase we encouraged the physicists to reflect on how their visions could be implemented through contemporary technology. Each phase was finished with a vote on what the physicists believed to be the most important critiques or visions. Each physicist was given six votes to cast in each voting session.

As introduction to the second workshop we gave the physicists a 1-h presentation of the visions of ubiquitous instrumental interaction (presented in "Springboard: Ubiquitous Instrumental Interaction"). The physicists were presented example scenarios and demonstrations illustrating the technological potentials of the vision.

It should be noted that this presentation was purposely devoid of examples taken from the context of laboratory notebooks. The presentation was followed by a re-iteration of the fantasy phase of the future workshop where the physicists were encouraged to imagine laboratory notebooks through ubiquitous instrumental interaction.

Ubiquitous instrumental interaction takes as its outset a fundamental critique of the way we currently create interactive software given the new technological landscape of multiple heterogeneous interactive devices whether being interactive walls or pocket sized multi-touch devices. It provides potentials for handling documents and objects across multiple heterogeneous devices, and provides flexibility for changing the way one interacts with objects. Hence we wished to present the physicists with a tool for thinking beyond their current perception of technology and beyond the potential limitations of current interactive software.

This methodological innovation has to strike a balance, well aware that one of the ideas with future workshops is not to force experts' solutions on the participants. The introduction of ubiquitous instrumental interaction could be thought of as a springboard in the terminology of Engeström: 'A springboard is a facilitative image, technique or socio-conversational constellation...misplaced or transplanted from some previous context into a new...' [16, chapter 4]. We avoided contextualising the concepts into the domain of laboratory notebooks exactly because we did not want to provide them with solutions.

Conceptual Framework

In this section, we present the theoretical framework used to structure interviews and analyze data. We also describe the scientific concepts we introduced to the practitioners in the future workshops.

Syntonic Seeds: An Activity Theoretical View on Lab Books

We structured our interview guide and analyzed the interview transcripts with a concept for analysis of inscription and collaboration, syntonic seeds [17]. 'Syntonic seed' is a concept informed by activity theory and associated approaches [16, 18, 19] suited for understanding development in activities characterised by collaborative inscription of objects which purpose is to sublate contradictions. The laboratory notebook can be seen in terms of collaborative inscription and the data can be analyzed in order to find what underlying contradictions that are resolved by using laboratory notebooks.

In order to give a proper definition of syntonic seeds it is first necessary to introduce two other activity theoretical concepts, namely activity systems and contradictions.

Engeström [16] elaborated on Leontiev's ideas of the basic constituents of activity by adding rules, community, and division of labour to Leontiev's subject, object

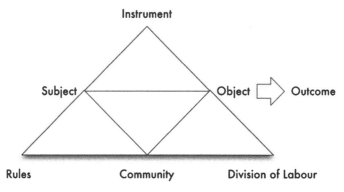

Fig. 1 Engeström's activity system [15, p. 37]

and instrument. Hereby Engeström introduced the iconic multi-triangle depiction of an activity system (Fig. 1). Engeström claimed that these six components are the minimal concepts needed for understanding human development.

In the model of general activity the subject refers to the individual or subgroup chosen as the point of view in analysis. The object refers to the raw material or problem space at which the activity is directed. It is not purely static and can have internal dynamics on its own, but has no agency. The object is transformed into an outcome with the help of physical and symbolic mediating instruments.

Engeström's concept of instrument is closely related to Vygotsky's 'mediating artefacts' but is applied also in settings that involve several individuals engaged in collective activity. The community consists of individuals and can include subgroups, which share the same general object and construct themselves as distinct from other communities in this context. The division of labour refers to both the horizontal division of tasks between the members of the community and to the vertical division of power and status. Finally, the rules refer to the explicit and implicit regulations, norms and conventions that constrain actions and interactions within the activity system.

The relationships of the constituents of an activity system show gradual transition, integration and disintegration. The subject is not a static entity affecting an object. At the same time as the subject transforms the object, the properties of the object and the properties of the relation between object and subject affect and gradually transform the subject as well. The same goes for all components and relations between components over time. Furthermore, the position of a component is not static. As the activity transforms, tools may become objects, subjects communities and so on [16].

All the components of an activity system can be part of many activities, and not necessarily having the same kind of role in the different activities they are part of. We refer to these activities that a given component is part of as it's web of activities [20].

Now to a second concept that is central to syntonic seeds, namely contradictions: A contradiction is an entity that is defined at a fundamental level of existence, i.e. not as something that is necessarily immediately and in an unproblematic manner presented to the senses. Activity theory insists that reality in the last instance is contradictory, not only in our perception of it, but also in reality itself [21, 22].

It is sometimes hidden; sometimes it shows at the surface. It is not metaphorical, i.e. as if we could 'see' something as a conflict/contradictory situation (see [23] for such a view). Of course we can do that, but this is not the sense in which the term is used here. The conflict situation is only the surface structure, which may be used to identify the contradiction. It is the form of the contradiction, not its substance. Bhaskar has eloquently nailed the difficult concept of contradiction in human activity as a 'situation, which permits the satisfaction of one end or more generally result only at the expense of another: that is, a bind or a constraint.' [12].

Syntonic seed is a concept informed by activity theory and constructed with the purpose of understanding development in activities characterised by collaborative inscription of objects which purpose is to *sublate contradictions*.

To sublate (from german: Aufhebung) a contradiction means that the contradiction is at the same time negated yet preserved [17]. For example using post-its as memory aids negates the contradiction between what should be remembered and what can be remembered, but preserves the indication of an insufficient memory.

Syntonic means that something is in harmony or synergy with its environment. A syntonic seed is an inscribed object that is pivotal in a web of activities, inscribed to bring relative harmony in the implied activities.

An example of syntonic seeds is architects' sketches. They are typically pivotal in a number of activities; they are used for negotiating ideas with colleagues, experimenting with own ideas, used as reference when making new design and added to a portfolio to further the architects career. The sketches sublate contradictions between the architect's mental capabilities and the requirements in an architectural activity, but they may also sublate contradictions between what other stakeholders in a project believe is possible to build and what the architect does [17].

More formally a syntonic seed is characterised by the following:

- It is persistently representing contradictions, and is inscribed to sublate these contradictions.
- It is simultaneously and/or sequentially a mediator in one or many activities and an object of one or many activities.
- It can at any given moment oscillate between being a mediator and object of activity.

Over time contradictions represented by the syntonic seed may change and so may the activities part of the syntonic seed's web of activities.

To return to the previous example; the architect sketches oscillate between being objects of the architect's drawing activity and being mediators of e.g. planning activities.

Springboard: Ubiquitous Instrumental Interaction

As described in "Method", we diverged from the classical use of future workshops by intervening with instruction of some concepts. In this section, we describe these concepts in somewhat detail, in order to provide a more concrete description of the activities in the laboratory notebook study.

Ubiquitous Instrumental Interaction [24] is a vision of an alternative way to interact with computers, a vision where the tools and objects the user interacts with are not bound to a specific computer, or type of computer, but can dynamically span multiple heterogeneous interactive devices.

The vision owes its heritage to Weiser's [25] famous ubiquitous computing vision of the late 1980s, however, Weiser's vision was mainly on computing – computing ubiquitously assisting us in our daily life, engrained in everyday objects creating smart environments adapting to their context. Weiser did not directly address whether e.g. the concept of applications were suitable for ubiquitous computing. Weiser envisioned that interactive computing devices would take different shapes and sizes, from wall-sized interactive displays to small matchbox sized tabs and paper sized tablets. Today we by and large have these heterogeneous interactive devices in our hands, however, as argued in [24], the way we interact with computers are still rests on an understanding shaped by personal computing, where the assumption is one user, one computer, on application at a time.

Ubiquitous instrumental interaction is a vision of an interaction paradigm that embraces the dynamism and heterogeneity of the landscape of interactive devices.

The central idea of ubiquitous instrumental interaction rests on a separation between interaction logic, or instruments, and domain objects. Instead of working with static applications for a specific work domain, the vision is that users can create dynamic configurations of instruments applicable across various objects and interactive devices. This is inspired by the way we use physical tools: A painter can freely add or remove brushes from his collection, pass them around, etc.; Brushes are not bound to paint on a canvas, they can also be used to paint on the wall or on the hand of the painter. Currently, computer applications do not support this level of flexibility: a brush in a drawing application can rarely be removed and used in another context, such as a text editor. Applications typically have a pre-defined set of tools that are difficult or impossible to adapt to one's needs or taste. This lack of flexibility limits the mobility, distribution and customizability of interfaces. It also typically results in complex monolithic applications, built for general-purpose personal computers, with dozens or even hundreds of tools to cover all possible needs [23].

In order to concretize the concept to the physicists we introduced them to a scenario that touches upon many of the main ideas of ubiquitous instrumental interaction (scenario paraphrased from [26]):

Grace is a graphics designer for a small advertisement bureau. She is currently designing a poster for a political campaign for an upcoming election and heading for a meeting with her client at a café downtown to discuss the poster proposal. To the meeting she brings along an A3 color-print of the poster. The client is quite pleased with the poster but asks whether it would be possible to create flyers matching the design. Grace thinks for a moment and reaches for her touch screen smart-phone in her purse. Connected to the wireless internet of the café Grace loads the poster object by navigating a list of recently edited objects. Grace already has a configuration of instruments ready for light graphics manipulation on the go. Meanwhile the client is watching and commenting on Grace rearranging, trimming and scaling of the poster into a flyer – the dimensions of which actually match the screen-size of the smart-phone quite well. Given the fast wireless network access of the café, features such as alignment of graphical elements can be computed externally – something the smart-phone does not have the computing capabilities to do without significant latency. Grace's move instrument exploits this and provides alignment feedback to her – Grace has, however, disabled automatic alignment in the instrument, she hates that. Grace and the client agree on a layout and Grace gives a finishing touch to the flyer at her home workstation in the evening. When she sits down at the workstation that evening she simply "picks up" the flyer from the smart-phone with a finger-gesture and "drops" it on the work- area of the workstation with a keyboard shortcut. In a similar manner she moves a color-palette with the poster's color-scheme to the smart-phone and places it on the left of her keyboard for easy access.

The vision moves beyond looking at interactive devices, such as a personal computer, as an isolated entity. Interactive devices are regarded as opportunities for interaction with one's digital objects – digital objects that are ubiquitously available to the user on whatever device. In principle the user should, as envisioned by Weiser, be able to pick up any interactive device and access her objects. The user interface can be adapted to the activities of the user, and to the devices available. Objects do not have a static type, like a text document, or a spreadsheet. This means that objects will change when new instruments are applied and new instruments can be added by the user when needs regarding the object change.

In [24] a software architecture, named VIGO (Views, Instruments, Objects, and Governors), is developed to realize ubiquitous instrumental interaction. Central to this architecture is a clear separation between interaction logic, objects or state, business or application logic, and visualization. In the paper they show how this architecture can facilitate implementation of use cases resembling those of the above scenario.

While we will not go into the technical details of the implementation of a VIGO based system, we mention it because it was presented to the physicists in the workshops. Given that all the physicists were computer literates and all had programming experience, we chose to present them to the technical terminology, and encouraged them to express their visions using that terminology.

The Laboratory Notebooks

The physicists were interviewed about the groups' use of lab books as the first step in the research process. In this section, we report the results, which lay ground for facilitation of the workshops. When the physicists were asked about the role of their laboratory notebook they responded:

- To ensure scientific probity
- To enable reproduction of experiments
- The keep track of what happens in the laboratory
- To log and structure experimental results
- To analyse intermediate results
- To document considerations for future experiments

- To document the mistakes of the past
- To act as a shared memory for the researchers in the lab

The books were all variants of regular A4 sized bound notebooks. All of these books were inscribed chronologically from left to right. The entries in the books consisted of a mix of written text, drawings, handmade tables and loose printouts of graphs and tables of data.

The most important piece of meta-information inscribed into an entry of all of the respondents' notebooks was timestamps. The timestamps were often coupled with a reference to a data file and sometimes the name of the author of the entry. It was not allowed to erase any data from the lab book after-the-fact, even though an experiment seemed meaningless.

Four out of five of the respondents used a laboratory notebook shared in a group. Three of the respondents furthermore used notebooks tied to a particular piece of equipment in the laboratory, e.g. for a certain laser. Such equipment notebooks could be inherited from the previous owners of the equipment. In two of the participants' laboratories both shared and personal laboratory notebooks were used, which sometimes were a source of conflict and confusion. The shared notebooks were used as means for communications more or less explicitly, e.g. for writing messages between researchers measuring in shifts.

One of the physicists explained that her laboratory notebook had three general types of inscriptions: At the right page of the bound notebook, the data and the instrument settings were noted (1). Sometimes this data were coupled with visualizations (2), e.g. printed or hand drawn graphs or drawings of the equipment. The left page was reserved to comments and analysis (3). This particular physicist navigated her book partly by judging if there were many entries on the left page – if so, that experiment probably was important.

The Lab Book in a Web of Activities and as a Syntonic Seed

The practice of the respondents' involving laboratory notebooks does not consist of one activity only. Rather, it consists of a web of activities, all causally interconnected and sometimes concurrently ongoing. Reading of the lab book for planning an experiment takes place concurrently with the reading required to perform maintenance of the lab, for instance. There are six main activities, which are distinctly different from each other in terms of e.g. object, their histories, rules and subjects but all involve the laboratory notebook:

- Experimentation
- Analysis
- Planning
- Lab maintenance
- Paper writing
- Documentation

There are also several types of educational activities going on in the lab: undergraduate, PhD student work and postdoctoral education.

The documentation activity and the educational activities stand out from the others. They are largely carried out in an unconscious and routinised manner, and is in an unconscious and co-ordinated state much of the time [27]. The experimentation activities are very different. They are often collectively co-ordinated and reflected upon. The same goes in less degree also for the other activities. The documentation for ensuring scientific probity is interesting in that it is the only activity where the inscribed notebook is the actual objective product of the activity.

The lab book is nonetheless referred to as a documentation device in our interviews, but in daily operation, that function is accomplished by routines rather than by conscious effort. The same goes for educational activities.

The lab book plays and important role in this web of activities. It is acting as an unfinished object in which data are inscribed in the experiment activity, and is at the same time used for reading explanations of results in the paper-writing activity. In several activities, it was found to oscillate between being an instrument and being a tool. For instance, a physicist may first enter some data into it, and then read in the lab book 1 h later in order to change the settings in some machinery. Another example of this is when the notebook frequently oscillates between being used from documentation, analysis and paper writing. Such oscillations are bound to take more time with paper – many such oscillations could be automated.

It becomes clear from the workshops with the physicists that inscribing a laboratory notebook does not transfer to a typical application as easy as e.g. writing a letter does. While letters and laboratory notebooks are both inscribed artefacts, the laboratory notebook appears to have distinct characteristics. The laboratory notebook is used by many people for many activities, and changes between being used to document and as a reference, and the inscriptions do not seem targeted towards creating a final product, like the inscriptions of a letter or a paper are.

In order to conceptualise the role laboratory notebook plays to the physicists we apply the concept of syntonic seeds [17] as a lens for understanding.

A central characteristic of syntonic seeds is that they are objects inscribed to sublate contradictions in activities. We identified four overall contradictions, which the paper-based laboratory notebook successfully sublates:

1. Contradictions *between two persons' plans of the experiment*, due to their different understandings. In a new experiment, the physicists come to the scene with different plans about prioritized things to investigate. These plans have to be negotiated, and the lab book is one of the important arenas for this.
2. Typically, the physicists deliberately try to make the data in the lab books stand in *productive opposition to previous knowledge* in their research community. They try to show that previous papers did not take important phenomena into account or that previous research cannot be corroborated by empirical data from the laboratory – in order to generate interesting research.
3. Doing physics research is a complex intellectual activity. It is not possible to remember each data result from an experiment; there may be extremely large data sets.

It is necessary with a *memory aid* in order to make the planned calculations and to construct connections between data. The innate memory skills clashes with the demands from the research community of doing physics at a contemporary level – and the lab book serves as memory aid and resolves the contradiction.

4. Experimental physics typically require a lot of instruments and equipment. These artefacts take time to master and at the same time the technological development is rapid. Therefore, no individual can master all instruments at the same time. The research community has solved this by *specializing* physicists and training technicians. Rarely a single individual understand all details in a specific experiment, but only their part. The lab book can hide the complexity each specialist brings to the experiment by letting them enter short configuration notes, understandable in a superficial way for other physicists. In short, it enables fragmented exchange [28].

The contradictions stated above are targeted by a number of inscriptions in the current practice. The key inscription is of course the physical lab book. Our observations and interviews reveal, however, that a large number of inscriptions are active and necessary constituents of the lab work. From an atemporal viewpoint, they are clearly distinct from each other, but in delineating the final outcome (a well-documented research process), all these inscriptions are parts of the unfinished documentation object in various stages (Table 1).

Given the analysis of above we can see that the praxis of inscribing a laboratory notebook differs from inscribing a letter. Writing a letter is an extremely product-oriented activity clearly oriented toward creating a finished product – which is in stark contrast to praxis of inscribing a syntonic seed, which is oriented to ongoing processes.

Table 1 Objects of inscription

Object of inscription	Elaboration
The laboratory notebooks	The main objects of inscription
Electronic files of data	Produced by the experimental equipment
The physical configuration of instruments	Everything is not kept in the notebook; during an experiment looking at the setup in the laboratory can support the researchers understanding
Software for data collection and analysis	Software is used to collect and analyse data. Comments appear both directly in the data and e.g. in the program code for performing analysis. Code which itself also acts as a meaning bearing inscription
Private notes	One physicist stated that he had co-workers who did not want to show their possibly *erroneous analysis*
Email correspondence	The physicists discuss interpretations with each other and collaborators
Whiteboards	Both in the researchers laboratories and offices there are whiteboards used for notices and analysis
Specialized lab books	In addition to the main lab book, some instruments have their own notebook, e.g. used for maintenance

Hence, building an information system for laboratory notebooks on the same premises as we create a word processor would not work.

From this analysis, we can learn that use of an ELN must be as smooth or smoother in the interplay with the other artefacts. Since the laboratories are physically large, it requires either full integration with all equipment, or mobile technologies.

Furthermore, an ELN must be able to successfully sublate the same contradictions as the paper-based lab book. It must allow for different conceptions of the experiment, allow production opposed to previous modes of scientific knowledge, act as memory aid, and allow for fragmented exchange between laboratory workers.

Findings from the Workshops

In this section we will present the findings from the two workshops. The first workshop went through all the three phases of future workshops, however, the most interesting findings were from the two first phases, and is what will be covered here.

In the second workshop the physicists were presented with the ubiquitous instrumental interaction vision and asked to re-iterate on the fantasy phase of the first workshop.

The visions and points of critique raised in the workshops are not all directly related to cooperation. In fact only a minor part deal explicitly with cooperation. However, it should be noted that the laboratory notebooks of the physicists are inherently cooperative artefacts. According to our interviews with the physicists cooperation happens both synchronously in the laboratory, when two or more colleagues work together on an experiment, or asynchronously when the researchers work in shifts. In the latter case, a newly arrived researcher creates overview of what happened in the previous shift through reading in the shared notebook. Writing in the laboratory notebook is in the general case not only for the writer, and therefore the design of laboratory notebook systems falls into a CSCW context.

First Workshop: Initial Critique and Visions

During the critique phase of the initial workshop, the physicists identified 15 problems in their use of their current paper-based laboratory notebooks.

A number of the problems were obvious problems with analogue, paper based documents: Hand written documents are hard to search through, not the least to find the notes of one's colleagues. Unique handwritten documents are vulnerable to fire, coffee spills, misplacement etc. The paper-based notebook is naturally restricted to being one place at a time which conflicts with it being part of many different activities at one time – but also non-collocated collaborative work on the notebook is naturally limited by the physicality of the laboratory notebook.

The physical properties of a bound notebook led to a series of problems as well. A notebook has finite space, both in the page area and number of pages, hence it was not unusual for the physicists to have dozens of old laboratory notebooks on the shelves, adding to the difficulty of finding old entries. Furthermore, a bound notebook enforces chronology (both for good and bad). Important notices can easily disappear and cannot, as one of the physicists stated, act like "stickies" on a web forum, meaning that they always would stay on top in the chronology. One physicist explained how an old warning about a setting on a laser in the laboratory notebook could have saved them for a setback of months – had they found it. Categorisation of entries in the notebook is also a cumbersome task, and requires third part objects, e.g. index pages or post-it notes.

The physicists listed a range of problems where the solutions did not necessarily have to be electronic. Namely that there was a lack of standardisation of what to document – a blank page gives no hints of what parameters should be documented. The physicists missed tool support for project management, and another (sometimes critical) issue was that the laboratory notebook in no regard enforced a proper handwriting.

One of the heavy weighing problems lay in what was *not* written in the laboratory notebook. The physicists argued that often they missed important readings (e.g. when they had to be manually read from a display) or didn't know until it was too late what to look for and inscribe in the book.

A final problem stated by the physicists was that all the different objects of inscription created, in their words, a broken work cycle: There was no technical integration between data collection, control of equipment and analysis in the way they worked now. They had to move between performing hand-written analysis in the notebook, to data analysis and equipment control on the computer and then again back to document results in the notebook e.g. with printouts of graphs (see Fig. 2).

In the second phase of the future workshop the physicists were asked how they envisioned a future electronic laboratory notebook system. This was *before* they had been introduced to the ubiquitous instrumental interaction vision.

The overall vision brought forth by the physicists was of a laboratory notebook system, that integrated documentation, equipment control and data analysis in the same user interface.

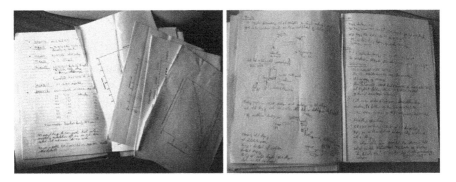

Fig. 2 Examples of the physicists' laboratory notebooks

The notebook should be configurable to document relevant information automatically and to support (or force) the researchers to document what had to be observed manually. They envisioned that through the automatic logging the system could help with error recognition through comparing with old entries in the notebook. Furthermore, automatic pre-analysis of the data could be configured, e.g. to produce intermediate graphs directly in the notebook.

As for the organization of the notebook, a structuring resembling a Wiki was suggested, where all data could be interlinked. One of the participants suggested abandoning the forced chronology of the bound notebooks and having something resembling a loose-leaf system. Both in terms of configuration and organization, the functions requested are more or less available on the market (see [29, 30]).

Regarding interaction with the notebook the physicists envisioned being able to access the notebook by multiple people from multiple devices – including mobile devices. They envisioned multi-modal interaction, and the support of interaction through handwriting e.g. on a tablet-PC. The ELN market is yet to provide these functions; state of the art by 2009 is a mobile client with a light-weight interface to the ELN application [29, 30]. It is worthy of note that the physicists did not raise the issue of inter-laboratory cooperation and sharing of result in the global community, as commonly envisioned in eScience [31], and that is why we have not focused much upon breakdowns in such workflows.

Second Workshop: Re-iterations Based on Ubiquitous Instrumental Interaction

A whole range of visions for a laboratory notebook system was catalyzed from the introduction to ubiquitous instrumental interaction. Some were a direct product of the physicists' introduction to the ubiquitous instrumental interaction vision, while others were probably a product of the participants being even further stimulated to be visionary.

The overarching vision, and the vision with the highest number of votes, continued to be a fusion between documentation, control and analysis. Hence creating not just a laboratory notebook for documentation, but also an integrated laboratory system to remedy the broken work cycle, is a consequence of using the paper-based laboratory notebook together with computer applications for data collection and analysis. They did not merely suggest a unified experimentation and writing application off-the-shelf, of the kind emerging on the ELN market [30]. They talked about a system that is iteratively constructed and reconfigured due to changing needs in their activities.

The physicists were introduced to the proposed software architectural model for ubiquitous instrumental interaction, the VIGO model. In some instances they used the terminology of the model explicitly to formulate the vision: The physicists envisioned an environment where instruments and governors (interaction logic and application logic respectively) could easily be programmed and shared.

One physicist suggested that she wanted to be able to easily write an instrument that could multiply selected settings with a given constant. This should be enabled through a dynamic scripting language or a visual programming language. They imagined that the challenge of collecting and processing data in the laboratory notebook could be handled in a LabView-like (http://www.ni.com/labview/) data-flow programming fashion, or even integrated with this product. Their point was that it should be possible to continuously work from configuring data collection and data analysis to configuring e.g. governors to translate the data into publication quality figures and graphs in the documentation part of the notebook environment.

In the software architecture to realise ubiquitous instrumental interaction that was introduced to the physicists, there are no clean distinction between objects for documentation (e.g. text and graphics) and objects for control (e.g. a widget). Inspired by this fact, one physicist imagined a laboratory notebook environment where it was possible to document e.g. the angle of a laser simply by copying the control widget into the documentation part of laboratory notebook – and potentially use these objects to reload settings (Fig. 3).

The physicists envisioned having the possibility to bring parts of the laboratory notebook's user interface to mobile devices. For instance support for loading a page on a tablet-PC to give the feeling of a notebook or to move a control object or readout of data to a PDA to support mobility in the laboratory. As one participant remarked, he sometimes had to do rather dangerous acrobatics to read a meter on the screen in the other end of the lab while climbing his pressure chamber to control a valve.

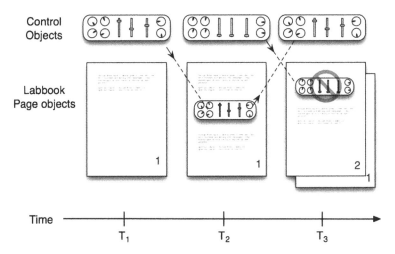

Fig. 3 In the envisioned laboratory notebook there is no distinction between objects for documentation and objects for control. Documenting the position of a laser at a given time involves copying the object that acts as a control to a page in the notebook. Later this control can be reloaded to restore the setting. In the figure a copy of a control pane is stored on a page in the notebook. The controls are changed but reverted back to the original by using the copy stored in the book. The intermediate parameters are documented in the notebook as well and annotated as non-working

Loading parts of the laboratory notebook to mobile devices could also facilitate remote monitoring of the activity in the laboratory.

The physicists furthermore had a number of visions that were not directly associated with the ubiquitous instrumental interaction vision, however, compatible with it. One participant suggested that the system should support the, either manual or automatic, generation of summary pages that could be loaded on an interactive whiteboard in a meeting room. It should be possible to structure and categorise entries in the laboratory notebooks in multiple ways. For example, sorted by activity, chronology, or particular piece of equipment, but doing away with the forced chronology of the bound notebooks.

One participant imagined that the system supported personal versions of entries to the laboratory notebook, where notes and annotations could be made that were not intended to be read by others – but could be made public through interaction with a simple instrument.

It should be possible to generate templates both comprising fields and layout for documentation, comments etc. but templates could also encompass controls relevant for a given experiment.

The physicists also elaborated on that it should be possible to browse editing history, but without cluttering the interface, and that it should be backed-up in a secure way. They also envisioned various hypermedia ways of clicking content to see associated data and controls. Many of such functions already exist in present applications [2, 30], and we do not dwell further with these aspects.

Discussion

From the critique and visions brought forth by the physicists it is clear that integration between the different aspects of their activities in the laboratories is one of the key aspects missing in their current use of laboratory notebooks.

Central for the respondents' activities is that they are in constant development – physics research is rarely routine work. This is apparent when browsing through one of their laboratory notebooks. The inscriptions change over time given changing requirements due to changing understanding, equipment, people and experimental foci. However, the documentation environment, the bound notebook, does *not* change.

The bound notebook is extremely flexible; it embodies only very low-level assumptions of the activity it is part of. You can write whatever you like wherever you like it with whatever type of pen you like. The bound notebook is easily extendable with printouts of digital graphs, objects that did not exist when the first bound notebook was created. But it has some fundamental limitations as brought forth by the physicists.

This flexibility of paper makes it possible to maintain a division of labor and specialization without getting dragged down in inscription-technical problems when work is reorganized. For example, when a new laser arrives in the laboratory, no setup is required in order to write down its settings in the laboratory notebook. This was one of the primary contradictions that paper managed to solve. We identified these in "The Laboratory Notebooks".

Joining one type of document with another in the digital world requires either that one format can be imported into the other, or that some meta-tool can incorporate and display both (e.g. a tagging tool which can also show .jpg, .doc, and every other format used in the laboratory). Because new formats, and needs to manipulate these in new ways, appear all the time, the applications will always be less flexible than paper; they can not perform given actions until the application vendor has incorporated tools to do so. Sometimes plug-ins can alleviate the situation, but it is only work-around, not a solution. Contrary to applications, in the environment the physicists envisioned one could interact with the laboratory notebook in ways not necessarily intended or expected by the software-developer.

It is interesting to compare the suggestions from the participants in our study with the suggestions from e.g. [8]. The latter we take to be a representative of design-oriented research into electronic laboratory notebooks, working under the assumptions of IT as packaged into applications [8] propose a knowledge management solution, which makes knowledge explicit and suggests it at the right time to lab workers. For such a system to be efficient, it is required that most inscriptions are integrated with the knowledge management system.

Our participants suggested completely other types of functions. What one physicist suggested was not necessarily relevant to every laboratory, e.g. a function that can multiply a set of control settings. Such suggestions witness a wide variety in needs.

What is difficult to convey with the idea of ubiquitous instrumental interaction is that in theory almost all functions in application-centric systems can be created and used within this paradigm as well once they are configured and appropriated by the user. Likewise, many of the functionalities envisioned in our future workshops could in many cases be implemented through applications. The novelty of ubiquitous instrumental interaction would first be seen in a process of adapting to new equipment, experiment or new colleagues, or to change a situation for the "better". The implication for design, then, is to give the users a more prominent role in the integration of instruments, and even in the building of instruments. Of course this can be paired with possibilities to package the results and distribute them afterwards to other users that have similar needs, *but nevertheless they are a small subset of the total ELN user group*. We wish to stress that classical application-like systems [8] ought to co-exist with highly configurable interaction paradigms, such as ubiquitous instrumental interaction.

Since this study does not have data from an ELN-using laboratory, we cannot report breakdowns resulting from neglect of the contingencies of needs in laboratories. Furthermore, a large part of ELN use is carried out in the pharmaceutical and biotechnology sectors, and these areas are relatively highly regulated by governmental actors, such as FDA and intellectual property legislators. These regulations may streamline laboratory work to a larger extent, and our findings may not be possible to generalize to that domain.

It is also important to remember that the workshop did not touch on certain advantages of paper that are not directly related to technology. Paper is still cheap and ubiquitous, for instance. Furthermore, the tremendous advantage paper has given, that researchers goes through an educational practice and possibly several other jobs that are paper-based, should not be under-estimated. Neither should other normative pressures such as IP legislation, et cetera, be forgotten.

Conclusion

With the introduction to the ubiquitous instrumental interaction paradigm the physicists were able to conceptualise their view of an IT solution that approaches the advantages of flexibility that paper has. The physicists envisioned how a ubiquitous instrumental interaction-inspired implementation could support objects shifting between having the role of a widget to being a piece of documentation. For example, by letting a copy of a control object both document and store settings for future re-uses *in ways not foreseen by the system developers*. This is a quite radically different way than how we typically work with computer applications today, and it illustrates that if one is to re-invent laboratory notebooks there seems to be a need to rethink some of the fundamentals in the way we build interactive software.

Our experience was that a general vision like ubiquitous instrumental interaction, serves well as a springboard for envisioning an expansive solution to a complex practical problem.

The theoretical framework and the modified version of future workshops were developed recently, and therefore new to the otherwise relatively well-studied domain of laboratory notebooks. Through our approach we have touched upon some new implications for design of ELNs:

- It is important that the contradictions that paper actually manages to resolve should not be discarded in an IT solution. This encompasses sublation of the contradictions between different plans of the experiment, to relate it to previous knowledge, memory aid, and specialization (see our syntonic seed analysis in "The Laboratory Notebooks").
- The needed functionality varies greatly even within a department and needs changes over time.
- Mobility is needed.
- There is a need for breaking down the artificial barriers between e.g. documentation and control.
- There is a need for dynamically adaptable templates for documentation.

Realising the kind of system with the features envisioned by the physicists is a major development task. The design and construction of application-based systems can lean on toolkits that have been refined over the last 20 years or more. Ubiquitous instrumental interaction tinkers with the underlying assumptions that these toolkits are built upon. Hence, they potentially have to be rethought and reconstructed. The sum of the visions brought forth by the physicists in this study would require extensive research, design and implementation – research on the technical realisation and of course comprehensive work-place studies and longitudinal participatory design.

However, the study in this paper has indicated that in order to create an electronic laboratory notebook system that maintains some of the qualities of the paper-based notebook, some rethinking of the traditional ways of building information systems is required. There is a special need for level of flexibility which is currently absent from both desktop and web applications in general.

Acknowledgements We thank the participating physicists for their willingness to contribute some of their time to this study. We thank Susanne Bødker and Olav Bertelsen for insightful comments on earlier drafts of the paper. Wendy Mackay and Aurélien Tabard are thanked for inspiring us to do the study in the first place. We thank Nikolaj Gandrup Borchorst, Marianne Dammand Iversen, and Ann Eg Mølhave for improving the written language of the paper.

References

1. Butler, D.: Electronic Notebooks: A New Leaf. Nature, 436, 20–21 (2005)
2. Polonsky, A.: Semantic Laboratory Notebook: Managing Biomedical Research Notes and Experimental Data. In CEUR Workshop proceedings vol. 194 (2006)
3. Mackay, W. E., Pothier, G., Letondal, C., Bøegh, K., and Sørensen, H. E. The missing link: augmenting biology laboratory notebooks. In Proceedings of UIST'02 (Paris, France, October 27–30, 2002). ACM, New York, (2002)
4. Sellen, A. J., Harper, R.: The Myth of the Paperless Office. MIT Press, Cambridge, MA (2002)
5. Mackay, W.: More than just a Communication System: Diversity in the Use of Electronic Mail. ACM Transactions of Office Information Systems 6(4), 380–397 (1989)
6. Bondarenko, O., Janssen, R.: Documents at Hand: Learning from Paper to Improve Digital Technologies. In the proceedings of CHI'05, pp.121–130. ACM Press, New York (2005)
7. Tabard, A., Mackay, W. E., and Eastmond, E. (2008). From individual to collaborative: the evolution of prism, a hybrid laboratory notebook. In Proc. of the ACM 2008 Conference on Computer Supported Cooperative Work. CSCW '08. ACM, New York, pp. 569–578
8. Sarini, M., E. Blanzieri, et al. From Actions to Suggestions: Supporting the Work of Biologists through Laboratory Notebooks. In the Proceedings of COOP'04, pp. 131–147. IOS Press, Amsterdam, The Netherlands (2004)
9. Taylor, K.: The Status of Electronic Laboratory Notebooks for Chemistry and Biology. Current opinion in Drug Discovery and Development 9(3), 348–353 (2006)
10. Kvale, S.: Interviews: An Introduction to Qualitative Research Interviewing. Thousand Oaks, Calif., Sage (1996)
11. Pawson, R., Tilley. N.: Realistic Evaluation. London, Sage. (1997)
12. Bhaskar, R.: Dialectic: The Pulse of Freedom. London, Verso. (1993)
13. Carlsson, S.: A Critical Realist Perspective on IS Evaluation Research. In the Proceedings of ECIS 2005 (2005)
14. Jungk, R., Müllert, N. R.: Håndbog i Fremtidsværksteder, Politisk Revy (1984)
15. Kensing, F., Madsen K. H.: Generating Visions: Future Workshops and Metaphorical Design. In J. Greenbaum & M. Kyng (eds). Design at Work. Cooperative Design of Computer Systems. Lawrence Erlbaum: Hillsdale, NJ, pp. 155–168 (1991)
16. Engeström, Y.: Learning by expanding: An Activity-theoretical Approach to Developmental Research. Helsinki, Orienta-Konsultit (1987)

17. Zander, P.-O.: Collaborative Process Change by Inscription. Lund, KFS i Lund AB (2007)
18. Bødker, S.: Through the Interface: A Human Activity Approach to User Interface Design. Hillsdale, NJ: Lawrence Erlbaum Associates Publishers (1991)
19. Leontiev, A. N.: Activity, Consciousness, and Personality. Hillsdale, NJ, Prentice-Hall (1978)
20. Bertelsen, O. W. & Bødker S.: Activity Theory. In Caroll, J. M. (ed) HCI Models, Theories, and Frameworks: Toward a Multidisciplinary Science, Amsterdam: Morgan Kaufmann, pp. 291–324 (2003)
21. Ilyenkov, E. V.: The Dialectics of the Abstract and the Concrete in Marx's Capital. Moscow, Progress Publishers (1982)
22. Marx, K.: Grundrisse: Foundations of the Critique of Political Economy. London: Penguin books Ltd in cooperation with New Left Review. (1968/1973)
23. Bjerknes, G.: Motsigelsesbegrepet – et Redskap for å Forstå Situasjoner i Systemutvikling. Institutt for informatikk. Oslo, Universitetet i Oslo: 125 (1989)
24. Klokmose, C. N., Beaudouin-Lafon, M.: VIGO: Instrumental Interaction in Multi-surface Environments. In the Proceedings of CHI '09. New York, NY, ACM Press. pp. 869–878 (2009)
25. Weiser, M.: The Computer for the 21st Century. Scientific American 265(3), 66–75 (1991)
26. Klokmose, C. N.: On Human-computer Interaction in Complex Artefact Ecologies. PhD Dissertation, Department of Computer Science, Aarhus University, Denmark (2009)
27. Wehner, T., Raithel, A., Clases, C., Endres. E.: Von der Mühe und den Wegen der Zusammenarbeit. Theorie und Empirie eines arbeitspsychologischen Kooperationsmodells. Zwischenbetriebliche Kooperation. In E. Endres and T. Wehner. Die Gestaltung von Lieferbeziehungen. Weinheim, Psychologische Verlags Union (1996)
28. Clement, A., Wagner. I.: Fragmented Exchange: Disarticulation and the Need for Regionalized Communication Spaces. In the proceedings of ECSCW'95, Kluwer, Stockholm, pp. 33–50 (1995)
29. Segelsted, S. H.: Which LIMS is Best? Scientific Computing 26(3), 6–8 (2009)
30. Elliott, M.: What You Should Know before Selecting an ELN. Scietific Computing 26(3): E11–E13 (2009)
31. Frey, J. G., De Roure, D., Schraefel, M. C., Mills, H., Fu, H., Peppe, S., Hughes, G., Smith, G. and Payne, T. R. (2003) Context Slicing the Chemical Aether. In: First International Workshop on Hypermedia and the Semantic Web, August 30, Nottingham, UK

Supporting Reflection in Software Development with Everyday Working Tools

Birgit Krogstie and Monica Divitini

Abstract Through their day-to-day usage collaboration tools collect data on the work process. These data can be used to aid participants' retrospective reflection on the process. The paper shows how this can be done in software development project work. Through a case study we demonstrate how retrospective reflection was conducted by use of an industry approach to project retrospectives combined with the examination of historical data in Trac, an issue tracker. The data helped the team reconstruct the project trajectory by aiding the recall of significant events, leading to a shift in the team's perspective on the project. The success of the tool-aided retrospective reflection is attributed to its organization as well as the type of historical data examined through the tool and the tool features for navigating the data. These insights can be used to help project teams determine the potential of their tools to aid retrospective reflection.

Introduction

Software development (SD) is highly cooperative work which has received considerable attention in CSCW [1–3]. In SD, mistakes are common as well as costly [4], and learning from experience is essential [5].

In SD organizations using large integrated systems to support and coordinate work, efforts to have the organization learn from experience may be integrated into predefined work processes and supported by tool functionality for collecting and providing experience data. The idea of experience factories [6] reflects a similar idea. In other settings, as in agile software development [7], learning from experience may be more informal and deferred to face-to-face project meetings and retrospective

B. Krogstie (✉) and M. Divitini
Norwegian University of Science and Technology, Sem Sælands vei 7-9, NO-7491,
Trondheim, Norway
e-mail: birgitkr@idi.ntnu.no; divitini@idi.ntnu.no

M. Lewkowicz et al. (eds.), *Proceedings of COOP 2010*,
DOI 10.1007/978-1-84996-211-7_9, © Springer-Verlag London Limited 2010

reflection sessions. *Project retrospectives* [8, 9] in agile SD are an example of what is known in the project management literature as project debriefings [10], which cover various methods for recording experiences from projects. Project retrospectives are conducted at the end of project phases or when projects are terminated. The major resources are participants' memory and collaborative effort to reconstruct the project, and various facilitation techniques exist (e.g. [11]). In this paper we generically refer to *retrospective reflection* to indicate activities conducted at the end of a project phase to rethink the working process with the goal of learning from experience. *Retrospective reflection* can be seen as an aspect of reflective practice [12] comprising reflection-on-action in context of the project.

One challenge, found to be among the reasons why many organizations choose *not* to conduct retrospective reflection [13], is the lack of adequate data to help participants reconstruct the process. Human memory is fallible in recalling a process of weeks or months. For other data sources to be useful in practice, however, they should provide access to data with an appropriate level of detail and enough context to help avoid oversimplification and examination of unimportant details [13].

The objective of this paper is to investigate the potential to support project teams' retrospective reflection by the use of historical data in *lightweight collaboration tools* [14]. These are tools typically providing basic functionality for collaborative activity without imposing much structure on the process. This allows flexible incorporation of the tool into the specific process. Taking lightweight collaboration tools into use requires little resources (e.g. acquisition cost, time for training) on part of users and organizations. Lightweight tools are in use in a large number of SD projects, some of which have very limited resources for organizing retrospective reflection sessions. Lightweight tools may be the choice of small organizations, teams doing cross-organizational work, teams basing their selection of tools and methodologies on local needs and preferences, or teams in organizations running 'lean' processes. As a side-effect of day-to-day work, the lightweight collaboration tools collect data originating in the work process. Such historical data may have the appropriate detail and context to aid participants' retrospective reconstruction of the process.

The CSCW literature has addressed the use of lightweight cooperation technology to support day-to-day project work, e.g. in software development [15–17]. Also, there is research on the use of data captured in collaboration tools to gain insights about collaborative work activity, as will be elaborated in the Background section. The potential to aid retrospective reflection on an entire project process by use of historical data in the various lightweight collaboration tools supporting that process was identified in [18].

For a project team to be able to determine the potential of their collaboration tools to aid retrospective reflection, they need knowledge about *what it is that makes a tool useful* for such a purpose. Such knowledge is also of value to collaboration tool designers who might want to extend the area of application of their tools to retrospective reflection.

Research contributions in this area should include empirical investigation of tool use as it unfolds in the context of retrospective reflection. This paper provides such a contribution by going into detail on how retrospective reflection is aided by the use of historical data in a collaboration tool in a SD project followed in an in-depth case study.

In the background section we outline relevant theory and related work from the CSCW field. The case section describes the SD project of our study and the project management tool used in that project. The research method section includes a description of the organization of the team's reflection workshop. Findings from the workshop are next described, followed by a section on discussion and implications, a section outlining a set of guiding questions regarding the potential of collaboration tools to support reflection in SD work, and finally our conclusion.

Background

In this section we briefly provide a background on distributed cognition as a way of understanding SD work and on the reconstruction of the process trajectory as important to retrospective reflection. We also address how the day-to-day use of collaboration technology results in the creation and storage of historical data.

In the analysis we have used distributed cognition [19, 20] to theoretically frame the problem. Distributed cognition is a perspective which has been used to understand learning [21], software development [22, 23], and cooperative work more generally [24]. Cooperative work can be seen as distributed across the people involved in the activity, through coordination of the processes between internal and external representations, and through time in such a way that results of earlier activity can transform later activity. Individual participants' mental representations [25] of the project process mediate day-to-day project work as well as reflection on the work. Strauss [26] argues that when people make sense of a process, they think of it as a *trajectory*. On this basis, retrospective reflection can be seen to involve the individual and collective reconstruction of the process trajectory, which includes identifying its significant events. The trajectory can have an internal or external representation (e.g. a diagram or a textual description). In sum, distributed cognition is a particularly useful framework for analyzing and designing for retrospective reflection because it helps shed light on the role of representations that mediate the reflective process, being used and transformed by participants individually and collaboratively.

In the day-to-day project activity shaping the project trajectory, cooperative work entails coordination, access to artifacts in a shared workspace, and formal as well as informal communication – aspects of work typically supported by cooperation technology. Formal communication, for which archiving is important, may for instance be conducted over email [27] and informal communication, e.g. about ongoing work, by synchronous [16, 28] and asynchronous chat. A shared workspace to hold artifacts under development must be provided, as well as ways of providing co-workers with workspace awareness [29–31], including social awareness [32]. Coordination of complex work, e.g. its planning, monitoring and re-planning, requires coordination artifacts [1, 33], computerized tools ranging from simple to-do-lists and bulletin boards to advanced enterprise solutions. Among the tools used to aid the coordination of work are issue trackers [34, 35] used in Software Development.

As a consequence of the activity along the trajectory, data get stored. Depending on the usage of each tool, its data will reflect different aspects of the SD work, e.g. development and bug-fixing, stakeholder collaboration [36], and team-internal, informal communication [37, 38]. From a distributed cognition perspective, the data are external representations originating in there-and-then distributed cognition. The data may have the form of logs (events, communication), versions of project artifacts (e.g. code, documentation), and plans and status reports. Data are generally recorded in repositories that are accessible through the tools. The idea of capturing information relevant to a work process from tools and artifacts already used to support that work process has been explored in several ways in the context of SD. Some approaches involve the deliberate tagging of information relevant to others [39, 40]. The use of logs from a code management system to support coordination in a SD team has been proposed [41]: An event notification system and a tickertape tool for CVS messages was integrated with the code management system, improving communication in the team. The project memory tool Hipikat is designed to help new members of a distributed SD team learn from more experienced colleagues [42]. The memory contains the artifacts produced during development and is built by the tool with little or no changes to the existing work practices. The SEURAT system [43] is designed to capture design rationale in software development and was originally intended to support software maintenance. The system can also trace requirements and decisions [44] in the project. Aranda and Venolia [45] found that for purposes of coordinating SD work, data repositories from the development process (bug databases and email repositories) could provide some information about the bug fixing 'stories', as reconstructed by the researchers having access to all the repository data, but the data in the repositories were incomplete and sometimes erroneous. The study showed that the reconstruction of the stories, including the social, organizational and technical knowledge, required the participants in the bug fixing process to account for the stories. Aranda and Venolia also found that among the most problematic types of missing data in the repositories were missing links from the bug records to the source code involved.

In [18] it was argued that data collected in various collaboration tools in daily use in a project may be systematically utilized to aid retrospective reflection in the project team. From a distributed cognition perspective, the historical data in the tools can be considered external representations of the project process. Together with team members' internal representations of the project process and external representations constructed in the team's collaborative reflection effort, the historical data in the tools are a potential resource in the reconstruction of, and reflection on, the project process. The outcome of the reflection (i.e. lessons learned, manifest in internal and external representations) subsequently informs the work practice, including the use of the collaboration tools from which the historical data were drawn. In the paper, a lightweight project management tool in the form of an issue tracker (Trac [46]) was used as an example of a tool with a potential to support retrospective reflection.

The aim of this paper is to demonstrate in detail how retrospective reflection can be aided by the use of historical data in Trac. Outlining how the historical data are utilized as an integral part of a systematic retrospective reflection approach with individual and collective steps, we stress how the collaboration tool plays a role in *knowledge building* as well as which *tool features* are particularly useful to support retrospective reflection in the team.

Case

Our case is a SD student team in an undergraduate, capstone project course. The projects have external customers, require a high level of independence in terms of choice of process, technology and solution, and are designed to provide a work setting as close to industry SD as possible. Meeting customer requirements is a primary goal, along with meeting the university's requirements for certain project deliveries, most notably a project report to be delivered in a preliminary, mid-term and final version. There are three to five students in the teams. The project takes up half the workload in the final (sixth) semester of a Bachelor of IT program.

As part of the course, a retrospective reflection workshop is arranged for each team at the end of the project based on a technique drawn from industry SD practice [8, 9]. With this technique, participants individually and collectively construct a timeline of project events. Opinions and feelings about what is positive and negative are added, e.g. by use of post-it notes in different colours or by use of curves indicating the 'ups and downs' of the process. The final steps of the workshop are directed at determining future action based on the analyzed experience. In the workshop of our course, we use the following main steps: the participants draw a timeline of their project, adding events considered significant. First, timelines are drawn individually and next a shared one is collectively constructed. The emotional aspects of the process are addressed by having participants draw curves (that we call 'satisfaction curves') along the timeline, indicating their satisfaction with the project at different times. Next follows a discussion of issues related to lessons learned. It was shown in a study that the workshops can help the teams share knowledge and reach new insights about their projects [47].

The project of our study had five team members (Fig. 1). Their task was to develop an application allowing people to use their mobile phone to keep track of the geographical location of their friends and engage in textual chat with them. The required solution was technically advanced, including a server, an administration client and a mobile client and the use of services from a provider of geographical positioning data.

Fig. 1 The project team of the case study: snapshots from everyday project work

To support the management of their development work, the team chose to use an issue tracking tool called Trac (http://trac.edgewall.org/). Trac is a web application that supports the organization of work into tasks and phases with milestones, and is lightweight in the sense that it contains only the basic features necessary to manage SD work and requires little resources to be taken into use. Tasks are defined by *tickets* that are assigned to the users, e.g. team members. Trac also contains a wiki, allowing for any contents to be flexibly added. Trac provides a set of views into the files managed by an underlying file versioning system (SVN) containing e.g. source code and project documents. When a team member uploads (i.e. *commits*) new or modified files to the file management system, e.g. from the development environment in which source code is produced and tested, it can be seen in Trac as a new *changeset*. Usually, the user adds a comment on what the changeset is about. All versions of all files that have been committed to SVN, as well as the differences between file versions, can be viewed through Trac.

The Trac timeline (see Fig. 2, screenshot (a)) contains an item for each changeset (and its comment), wiki update, ticket update, and milestone completion. Each item has a date and time of the update; an identifier linking to the particular version of the project artifact(s) affected; and the name of the user doing the update. In Fig. 2a, for example, the comment associated with changeset [86] reflects an update of source code to the SVN server made by Matthew on 13 February. Apart from conveying status updates, comments are sometimes used more directly for coordination, as in "be sure to update before doing any changes" (comment made by Justin on 5 May). The timeline is thus central to the coordination of SD work in the project, particularly when team members are not collocated. It provides an instant overview of state-of-affairs as well as an entry point to the project artifacts.

Research Method

The research reported in this paper is interpretive [48]. The main source of data is a retrospective reflection workshop conducted with the selected SD project team in a usability lab over a period of two and a half days at the end of their project. In addition, a longitudinal study of the team's work had been conducted throughout the project (one semester), including 45 h of non-participant observation of meetings

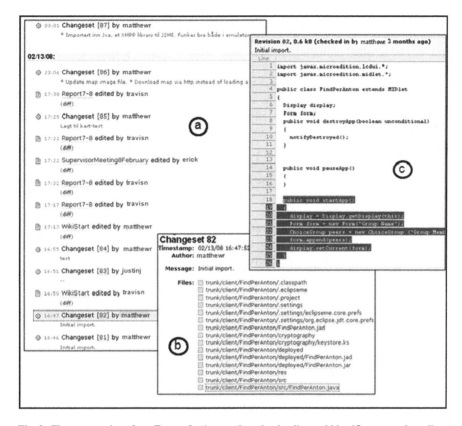

Fig. 2 Three screenshots from Trac as Justin examines the timeline and identifies pre-study coding

and work in the computer lab and frequent examination of project artifacts (including the contents of Trac) as well as the team's internal and external email communication. The study provided knowledge important to our interpretation of data from the workshop. Selection of the project was based on a combination of the technically complex project task and the team's decision to use Trac.

The workshop steps were based on the timeline and satisfaction curve approach described in the Case section. Compared to the short retrospective workshops conducted with the other teams in the course, the design incorporated an extra step of using historical data in Trac to aid recall. Further, individual timeline construction was done in a sequence of individual sessions (rather than in parallel) to allow the collection of rich data about each team member's timeline construction and explore how the use of historical data in Trac might be helpful in different ways or to different degrees among the team members. The lab was equipped like a small meeting room with a whiteboard and a PC. Several movable cameras were installed in the ceiling, and all sessions were videotaped. The use of Trac was recorded with screen capture and synchronized with the video recording. Photos were taken of the whiteboard.

In line with the principle of considering multiple interpretations [38], individual follow-up interviews were made 5 months after the workshop, i.e. when analysis of the data had resulted in findings to be presented to the participants and discussed in light of their interpretation.

Two questions guided our focus in the workshop and the subsequent data analysis. First, we looked for indications that the retrospective use of Trac benefited reflection, e.g. helped the team return to experience, re-evaluate it and create new perspectives. More specifically, we looked for events recalled *only by some team members*, events recalled *only after use of Trac* and, among those, events *of general importance in later discussion*, e.g. addressing lessons learned. Second, we wanted to know more about *how* Trac was used by the team members to aid their recall and reflection, i.e. what particular functionality and data in the tool seemed relevant and useful. In the data analysis we systematically examined the individual timelines and the shared timeline and the recordings of the sessions in which they were made, making a table of all events that were mentioned, noting who had mentioned them and whether they were mentioned before or after examination of the data in Trac. We picked *one* event, namely pre-study coding, based on the following criteria: the event was recalled only after use of Trac, it was recalled by some team members only, and it was important in the team's final discussion of lessons learned, The selection of an event guided further analysis, including close examination of all workshop data relating to the event with the aim of to providing a coherent account of how the event was elaborated in, and impacting on, the reflection process in the team, Data were transcribed and translated into English at need. In the presentation, names (including user names in screenshots) are made anonymous.

Our study can be seen as a "fine-grained, field-based empirical study" useful for designing systems and understanding the nuances of practice [24]. Even though the reflection workshop in our case was organized with a clear research agenda, impacting e.g. on its duration, the participants did real reflection on their SD project.

There are two main limitations to the study. First, it was conducted in the context of SD education. The project was however close to industry practice, e.g. with a customer and requirements for a working software product, and the team had some members who were relatively experienced as developers. Second, a single case study limits the possibilities to generalize from results. However, our purpose was to understand the details of a team's reflection on their project and investigate the potential to support reflection through certain steps and with certain resources.

Findings

In this section we draw on our workshop data and describe the project team's recall of and reflection on 'pre-study coding', an example of a project event recalled only through the aid of historical data in the collaboration tool. To provide some context, we start by describing the team's project process on basis of the longitudinal study.

The Process and Organization of the Case Project

The members were generally satisfied with their team and the assigned task. The relationship with supervisor and customer worked well throughout the project. Requirements for the product were more or less clear after the second customer meeting. Prior to midterm report delivery, time in the project was spent partially on trying out technology, later to be characterized by the team as 'pre-study coding', partially on writing the project report. After four iterations, the team delivered a product with which both they and their customer were satisfied.

The team had decided on a flat organization, formally with Eric as project manager. In practice, Justin had that role, taking main responsibility e.g. for deliveries and meeting minutes. Matthew was seen as the technical expert, taking responsibility for the server application and the overall design. Justin was in charge of the client application, and Travis for the map functionality implemented late in the project. All five team members actively participated in programming and report writing. Figure 3 (created by the authors processing information from the Trac timeline) shows that all team members participated and that Matthew and Justin did the most ticket updates.

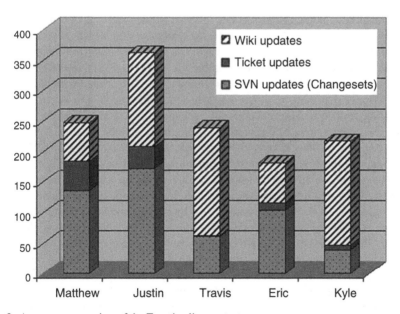

Fig. 3 A summary overview of the Trac timeline contents

Pre-study Coding in the Individual, Memory-Based Accounts

The five individual whiteboard timelines created on the basis of memory alone (workshop Step 1, see Table 1) vary in terms of the selection of events and the shape of the satisfaction curves. The events remembered to some extent reflect the roles in the project. For instance, Matthew is the only one who remembers choices of certain server technology. In comparison, a cancelled feature freeze that had a high impact on the entire team, is remembered by four out of five members. The onset of pre-study coding is not mentioned as important by anyone at this point. The onset of 'coding' is however mentioned by Matthew and Justin. Matthew refers to a couple of events involving the choice of technology in the project before midterm, but says nothing explicitly about coding in this period. He places 'coding startup' right after midterm. Justin places 'code start' on his timeline just before midterm. "Before that we had only been working with report, and then we actually started writing code." When accounting for the impact of a necessary change of framework some time after midterm, Justin explains that most of the coding of the final product took place during a short period towards the end of the project.

Pre-study Coding Emerging Through Examination of Trac

With the help of Trac in Step 2, all team members identify new events. In addition, there are some modifications of names of existing ones and changes of their time-line position. Justin and Matthew are the team members for which the examination of the timeline brings up most new events. As they chronologically examine the timeline, Justin and Matthew both examine the changesets [81] and [82] made by Matthew on 13 February. The comment 'Initial import' associated with both change-sets indicates that they are about the inclusion of files needed to start producing and testing Java code. Figure 2 shows the sequence of screenshots as Justin inves-tigates the timeline item of changeset [82]. Starting from the timeline view (a), he clicks [82]. The window (b) now displays what has been changed; a list of files. As a programmer Justin knows that the coding done by Matthew is in FindPerAnton. java, the rest of the files being files necessary to set up a running program and included for the first time in the initial import. He clicks the filename, and the win-dow changes to show the file contents (c). Examining the code, Justin exclaims: "Oh yes, it was only, kind of 'Hello world' on the mobile" and returns to the time-line (a). 'Pre-study coding' is then added to the whiteboard timeline (see Fig. 4).

Matthew, on examining the same item during his timeline construction, says: "Right there, we have started coding. It was probably pre-study coding." He suggests that the event be placed in the first half of the pre-midterm project period (see Fig. 4). As a consequence, 'startup coding', already on Matthew's timeline just after midterm, is changed to 'startup coding according to requirements spec (start iterations)'.

Table 1 Organization of the reflection workshop

Session type	Step	Explanation
Individual sessions (Days 1–2, each session 1.5–2 h) *The whiteboard was photo-graphed after these sessions*	(1) Reconstructing the project trajectory by memory	The team member was given a sheet of paper with a timeline containing a few fixed project events (e.g. delivery deadlines) and was asked to add important events. Next, for each of these events, the researcher added it to a similar timeline on the whiteboard and asked the team member to explain the importance of the event. Next, the team member was asked to draw on the paper sheet a curve showing how he had felt about working in the project. Finally he was asked to draw the curve along the whiteboard timeline, explaining its shape.
	(2) Using collaboration tool history to aid further reconstruction	The team member was asked to use the laptop and Trac to freely explain the project. When general browsing and explanation appeared exhaustive, the team member was asked to do a chronological walkthrough of the Trac timeline, exploring links at need. As new events deemed important to the project were identified, they were added to the whiteboard timeline by the interviewer, who took care to add events based on what *the team member* considered important.
Common session (Day 3, half day)	(3) Reconstructing the project trajectory using collaboration tool at need	The project timeline was reconstructed again, the researcher writing down events on the whiteboard as the team members listed them in a round-robin fashion. A PC with access to Trac was available to the team members, the screen projected onto the wall next to the whiteboard. When no more events were suggested, the team members came to the whiteboard one by one to draw their satisfaction curve and comment on it.
	(4) Discussion of tasks, lessons learned, roles	There was a common session addressing questions of project roles, tasks and lessons learned, each question answered by all team members in turn. Discussion was allowed and encouraged.

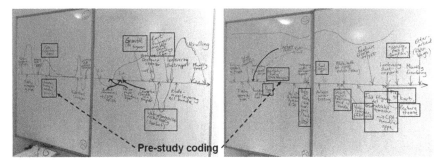

Fig. 4 Justin's and Matthew's timelines. Frames/emphasis of *arrows* show additions/modifications after examination of Trac

Pre-study Coding in the Co-constructed Account

In the collective session of Step 3, most events from the individual timelines were included in the shared timeline. Occasionally, the team on their own initiative looked into Trac to check details, typically the timing of events. The issue of pre-study coding was explicitly addressed. Justin early on repeated his statement that coding did not start until midterm, and this was not questioned by anyone. This can be interpreted as a shared understanding in the team that 'coding' (as a standalone term) meant 'coding in accordance with requirements specification'. As part of the round-robin provision of events, 'pre-study coding' was mentioned by Justin and added to the timeline. Eric suggested another name for the same event: "Unofficial coding". This received no further comments. In the later step of drawing satisfaction curves along the whiteboard, Justin explicitly referred to pre-study coding as he made an upward curve bend early in the project, explaining that he enjoyed the pre-study coding because they got things working then.

Pre-study Coding in Reflections on Lessons Learned

The topic of pre-study coding was recurrent in the discussion in Step 4, particularly when the team addressed lessons learned. Justin suggested that they might have overrated their own capabilities by starting coding as late as midterm. Matthew said that more pre-study coding might have helped the team avoid the extra work of learning a new framework, because they would have known better the limitations of the technology. Overall in the discussion, pre-study coding was given a central role in the account of what happened in the project and in conceptions of how to ideally run a similar project. The considerations on pre-study coding were made by Justin and Matthew. There seemed to be full agreement in the team that pre-study coding is necessary to reach the technical competence needed for producing design and code when a development task requires use of technology new to the team.

Insights from the Follow-Up Interviews

In the follow-up interviews with the team members, they were presented with the researcher's interpretation that the workshop had lead to a shift in the team's attention to pre-study coding and conception of its significance to the project. All team members expressed that this finding is in line with their own interpretation of what happened in the workshop. The interviews with Eric, Travis and Kyle however revealed some viewpoints that had not been brought into the team's discussion. When Eric during the collective reconstruction of the timeline had used the term 'unofficial coding' about the pre-study coding, he did not refer to the fact that the team de-emphasized this activity but to the fact that pre-study coding had been conducted by some team members only. In Eric's opinion, the project would have gained from a more distributed effort, making the entire team more competent with the technology at an earlier point. Travis and Kyle expressed similar views. While these viewpoints might have matured in the period after the reflection workshop, the workshop recordings indicate that the views were there during the workshop but had never properly entered the discussion.

Discussion and Implications

The example in the Findings illustrates how collaboration technology supporting day-to-day work practice in a SD project contained data that could be utilized by team members in a systematic and collaborative effort to reconstruct and reflect upon the project process.

The event called 'pre-study coding' was *identified only through the aid of collaboration tool history* and *only by two of the five team members* during the individual timeline construction. The event was later brought into the team's shared timeline, was referred to by a team member as impacting on his personal experience of the project, and was central in the team's reflections on lessons learned. Comparing the team members' original accounts of the project at the outset of the workshop with the final discussion, there was a clear difference: the significance of pre-study coding, in this project in particular and in SD projects in general, had become clearer. We see this as an example of knowledge relevant to the SD practice being created through retrospective reflection.

In this section we address why the tool-aided retrospective reflection was successful. We do this by considering the work practice, including the retrospective reflection effort itself, as a case of distributed cognition [18], and by looking into the type of historical data available in the tool, the tool features used to retrieve the data in the reflection workshop, and the organization of the workshop.

Historical Data in the Collaboration Tool

Cognition involved in a work practice is distributed over participants and the artifacts involved. Accordingly, it will typically be necessary to examine different data sources to make sense of an issue or event associated with that practice. In our case, what made Justin recognize that coding had happened in the project, was an item in the Trac timeline (see Fig. 2). The *type* of timeline item (a change to a file in the underlying file versioning system) and the *comment* following the change (i.e. the comment explicitly added by the user making the change, for purposes of day-to-day coordination) made it possible for him to quickly infer what this was about. Following the link, he recognized the element of interest in the list of files, and selecting the file in its there-and-then version, he could see what the piece of code was actually doing. The combination of the data and Justin's background (as a programmer, Trac user, and co-creator of the data in front of him), enabled him to reconstruct the state of the project and identify the event.

The type of data involved included (1) data used for day-to-day *coordination of project work*, reflecting ongoing tasks (e.g. timeline items with comments, made by different team members; the list of artifacts to which the selected timeline update applies) (2) data describing the *state of an artifact in the project workspace* (e.g. the there-and-then version of the source code file). Different aspects of the development work (e.g. project management, coding) being distributed in accordance with team roles, the data used to identify pre-study coding reflects a *social distribution* of the cognitive processes involved in the onset of pre-study coding.

The combination of data originating in coordination and data from the development workspace is useful for identifying events associated with development. A type of data less relevant for the identification of pre-study coding, but that frequently evoked team members' recall and reaction in the workshop of our study, are timeline comments addressing the social/emotional side of work and thus providing *social awareness* in day-to-day work.

Comparing the data examined in the workshop sequence illustrated in Fig. 2 with the aggregate data on the project process shown in Fig. 3, we note that the aggregate data could not have been used to provide context for single events. The diagram, though a useful resource, provides only a partial overview of the process. In our case, the aggregate diagram shows that all team members participated. What *cannot* be seen from the diagram is the exact type and amount of work done by each team member. For instance, we knew from observation of the team that Matthew tended to make updates in large increments, uploading new code to the shared server after working on it locally on his own machine for long, sometimes for days. While the diagram thus seems to indicate that Matthew and Eric did a similar amount of coding in the project, Matthew in reality did more coding than Eric. Another example is that when two team members were working in pairs, one of them tended to be in charge of the keyboard.

In sum, the aggregate timeline data provides an additional overview. To get adequately detailed and contextualized historical data from Trac for the recall of specific project events, however, an examination of individual timeline items is necessary. It should also be noticed that the fact that project work was sometimes conducted in pairs is not reflected *anywhere* in Trac. The day-to-day usage of the tool provides it with potential to be used in shedding light on some aspects of the project process – but not all.

Navigating the Historical Data in the Collaboration Tool

It was through chronological *traversal* of the timeline events that Justin identified the first uploading of source code to the shared workspace. Also, the timeline provided a condensed *overview*, including the possibility – unexploited in this case – to filter the type of events displayed. From the timeline item of interest, it took just a click to get more detailed, but still overview level information about the change, e.g. which files had been changed. The usefulness of this feature fits with the point made in [45] that missing links from bug records to source code is highly problematic for the reconstruction of the bug fixing process. Going *up and down between different levels of detail* thus proved important. From the overview, there was direct access to the *state* of the artifact (e.g. the selected file) at the time of the change. *Switching* between the modes of traversal, overview, and exploring the state of the artifact was easily achieved. The ease with which several months' work can thus be navigated in Trac by participants contrasts with the effort needed to examine less structured data on collaborative work, e.g. video recorded meetings [49].

While the data in the tool reflects socially distributed cognition, the timeline reflects the temporal distribution of cognition and is a starting point for identifying significant events. Another aspect of the temporarily distributed cognition is that when the tool is used retrospectively to make sense of data, familiarity with the tool provides context for the user. Justin had been using the Trac timeline daily throughout the project to get an overview of current project status. Justin's experience and skills in *how to make sense of the process through the collaboration tool* mediated his retrospective reflection.

Appropriately Organizing the Process of Retrospective Reflection

Essential to the success of the reflection workshop was its *organization*. The example in Fig. 2 shows *individual* use of Trac to reconstruct a timeline, but as a whole, our study shows how historical data successfully plays a role in supporting *cooperative* work. A core idea in the approach [8, 9] on which the workshop was based is that individual perspectives should be utilized in the construction of a shared understanding. In the study, individual timelines mediated individual recall and reflection as well as collective timeline construction.

From a distributed cognition perspective, the individual and shared timelines can be seen as external representations of the project trajectory, and the steps of the workshop as a process of coordinating the cognitive processing between internal and external representational states. In our study, we looked at a collaboration tool as a resource for the cognitive processing between internal and external representational states. This happens in three ways, as illustrated in Fig. 5. The day-to-day work, seen as a process trajectory along which there are multiple points of action and interaction, leaves a trace of external representations of the distributed cognition involved, in the form of historical data in the tool. This is a result of Trac's role in *supporting the day-to-day cooperative project work* (1). In the process of retrospective reflection, Trac is used as an aid to *individuals' recall of project events* (2), resulting in the creation of the individual timelines, which are also external representations of the project trajectory. The individual timelines are next used as a resource when the team collaboratively creates another external representation of the project trajectory: the shared timeline. To aid the alignment of the individual timelines, Trac is used collaboratively by the team as an aid to *clarify details* in the construction of a shared representation of the project (3), e.g. exact dates and times

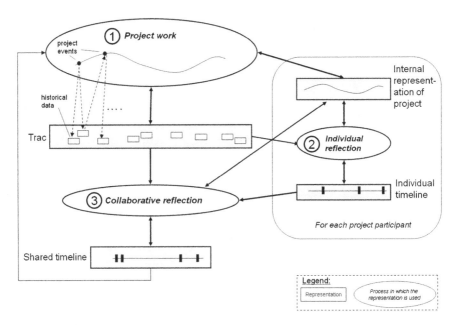

Fig. 5 Trac in a dual role as a collaboration tool in a project: supporting day-to-day work *and* retrospective reflection on that work (Adapted from [18])

of specific events. Figure 5 is an instantiation of the more generic model of retrospective reflection outlined in [18].

Used in retrospective reflection on day-to-day development work the collaboration tool serves as a boundary object between that practice and retrospective reflection [50]. Developers' awareness that the tool will be used retrospectively may affect their day-to-day work practice [24]. For instance, software developers may start providing more informative comments about their updates to make it easier to understand them retrospectively. This is likely to benefit day-to-day coordination. A change with potentially negative effects is if developers, to make a good retrospective impression of their work, start hiding information. For instance, mistakes in intermediate stages of work can be hidden by making less frequent updates or by avoiding commenting about error corrections (a type of comment common in the Trac timeline in our study). This could adversely affect day-to-day workspace awareness as well as the possibility to get a realistic picture of the development process from the Trac timeline.

Our findings indicated that the team in our study through the tool-aided retrospective reflection succeeded in creating new knowledge about their software development practice. However, the individual differences in respect of how helpful Trac was in the recall of events, point to challenges of uneven power distribution in the team. The benefit of using a development-oriented collaboration tool to aid reflection appeared greater for those dominating the development work. Strong involvement in the activity from which the data originated provided them with context for recognizing the data as connected to project events. Having *identified* the pre-study coding event, the two lead programmers seemed to retain ownership of the event in the team's discussion, which can explain why alternative viewpoints on pre-study coding among some team members were never properly disclosed.

The Potential of Collaboration Tools to Support Reflection in SD Work: A Set of Guiding Questions

The previous sections outlined how certain tool features as well as the type of data stored in the tools and the organization of the reflection activity were important when historical data in Trac was used to aid the reconstruction of the project trajectory in retrospective reflection. In this chapter we ask: in what way are these findings useful from a perspective of supporting reflection on SD work more generally?

Our answer is twofold. First, we believe that the results hold promise for the use of *tools like Trac* to assume a dual role of supporting daily work as well as retrospective reflection in SD projects. It was relatively unproblematic in our study to include steps of investigating collaboration tool history into an existing approach to organizing retrospective reflection. To make the tool-aided version of the approach integral to SD practice, the workshop organization must be adjusted to feasible schedule, i.e. one that can be followed under resource constraints in real projects.

Second, we believe that the findings can be generalized to the use of collaboration tools in retrospective reflection in SD work, answering the intent to provide empirically grounded insights to project teams and tool designers about what makes collaboration tools useful for such a purpose. In Section Discussion and Implications, we structured the findings into some issues that seem crucial to the success of the selected collaborative tool to aid retrospective reflection. Based on this understanding, we outline questions that point to essential aspects of how a collaboration tool and its historical data can support retrospective reflection. The objective is not to find the 'best' tool for the support of reflection but to help users and designers identify, or modify, strengths and weaknesses of the tools for such use. To illustrate how the answers may differ for various lightweight collaborative tools, we refer to the research literature on some tools often used in project work: project wikis, instant messaging, and email.

What aspects of the project process are reflected in the historical data in the tool? Which SD challenges worth reflecting upon have been addressed by use of this tool? An issue tracker contains data that may be used to aid reconstruction of the development process, with a focus on its technical and formal aspects. The *informal* communication is likely to be reflected in other tools, e.g. instant messaging tools [28, 51]. Other lightweight project management tools, e.g. project wikis [52], might reflect more of the informal collaboration in the team than what is documented in the historical data of an issue tracker. Stakeholder collaboration, a frequently challenging SD issue [36], may partially be reflected in email logs.

Does the tool provide features for getting a chronological overview of aspects of the project process? As seen in our study, the traversal of a chronological overview can be used to structure the process of examining historical data. Chronological overviews are essential in project management and thus provided by project management tools such as Trac. A project wiki, by being a wiki, contains functionality for getting an overview of the revisions of each page [52]. The disadvantage of browsing through numerous revisions of a wiki page is that changes may be small and uninteresting. Conversely, increments reflecting the process *as it unfolded* may shed light on the process in a way complementing more formal overviews. An email application allows for the filtering of email messages to be displayed in a mailbox, enabling for instance rapid overview of all email sent to the project customer or all messages with a particular keyword in its title (e.g. 'status report'). IM tools generally provide poor overview information, but the log contents are chronological and time-stamped.

Does the tool provide features for accessing the project artifacts in their there-and-then versions? One of the strengths of Trac as a SD tool is the way task organization links to project artifacts, stressing the close connection between process and product in SD work, the complexity of the process depending on the complexity of the product [1]. A project wiki may provide direct access to some project artifacts [17], but is not likely to provide read access to the entire development-related workspace with its artifacts in their there-and-then versions, as does Trac. Email frequently includes relevant project artifacts as attachments. Instant messaging logs might contain elements of project artifacts (e.g. source code excerpts) [51].

Does the tool provide features for easy navigation between overview and detail? The possibility to go into detail on a specific project event helped the participants in our study recognize it as an event worth including in their project timeline. Looking at project wikis, they provide reasonably good support for this e.g. through the page history overviews with links to each specific page [52]. Navigation in an email reader can be more cumbersome, but typically allows e.g. the use of different windows for the mailboxes and the contents of individual messages. Instant messaging logs mainly allow navigation on a detailed level of project interaction only.

With respect to overviews and navigation, limited features in the collaboration tools used to create the data may be amended by the use of other lightweight tools (e.g. search tools) to navigate the data. However, this comes at the loss of the contextualization of the data in the work (tool) environment from which it originated, a loss which may negatively affect participants' sense-making of the data.

Are the historical data subject to privacy issues? While the study reported in this paper considered data that were regarded as shared within the team, these characteristics do not apply to all data from project collaboration. IM logs, for instance, may be considered by their owners as too private to be shared [18]. Their potential to support *individual* reflection on the project process may be considered.

How will the use of historical data from the tool be integrated into a structured reflection activity with individual and/or collaborative sense making enabling participants to return to experience, reconstruct the stories [45] and draw lessons learned from the data? The organization of the activity can for instance be based on SD best practice for project retrospectives [8, 9]. An issue which is not the main focus in this paper, but which is nevertheless essential and should be considered as part of the organization of retrospective reflection, is how to subsequently draw upon the lessons learned in the work practice, within and/or across projects and teams.

For a project team considering the potential of one or more of their collaboration tools to support their reflection on, and learning from, their project process, it may be a good start to consider what aspects and challenges of their project work they would like to shed light on, and next consider what are the candidate tools to contain relevant data.

Finally, it should be stressed that when considering the potential of using a certain tool to aid retrospective reflection *in a specific case*, a general framework is only a useful starting point. The functionality of the specific tool will have to be considered along with the usage of the tool in the specific project, which heavily impacts on what historical data is being stored through everyday use of the tool.

Conclusion

By investigating a case of retrospective reflection in a software development project aided by historical data in an issue tracker (Trac), we have shown in detail how a collaboration tool in daily use in a project can be used to help participants learn from the project experience. We have demonstrated how certain types of data and certain features for retrieving them proved particularly valuable to aid participants' recall and reflection, aiding the reconstruction of the project trajectory.

Based on the findings we identified a set of questions that may be asked by a project team or a collaboration tool designer when considering the potential to use specific collaboration tools in retrospective reflection. The questions can serve as a starting point for the development of a more general framework outlining issues that should be addressed. To gain insight on the potential of different types of collaboration tools to aid retrospective reflection, more empirical studies are however needed. By unveiling project teams' use of specific tools in retrospective reflection we may identify ways of utilizing the tools that significantly differ from the way Trac was used in our study. This is an area of further research.

Another issue to be addressed in further research is how a project team's knowledge of the future use of a collaboration tool in retrospective reflection affects their daily use of the tool.

Finally, we will examine how the retrospective use of Trac can be integrated into retrospective reflection workshops within a time schedule feasible for real SD projects. We will do this by trying out the approach in SD projects on a larger scale.

References

1. Carstensen, P.H. and K. Schmidt, Computer Supported Cooperative Work: New Challenges to Systems Design, in Handbook of Human Factors/Ergonomics, K. Itoh, Editor. 2002 (1999), Asakura: Tokyo.
2. Grinter, R. Doing Software Development: Occasions for Automation and Formalisation. in ECSCW'97. 1997. Lancaster, UK: Springer.
3. Herbsleb, J.D., et al. Distance, dependencies, and delay in a global collaboration. in CSCW'00. 2000. Philadelphia, PA: ACM.
4. Keil, M., J. Mann, and A. Rai, Why Software Projects Escalate: An Empirical Analysis and Test of Four Theoretical Models. MIS Quarterly, 2000. 24(4), pp. 631–664.
5. Lyytinen, K. and D. Robey, Learning failure in information systems development. Information Systems Journal, 1999. 9: p. 17.
6. Basili, V.R. and G. Caldiera, Improving Software Quality by Reusing Knowledge and Experience. Sloan Management Review, 1995, pp. 55–64. Fall 1995.
7. Dybå, T. and T. Dingsøyr, Empirical studies of agile software development: A systematic review. Information and Software Technology, 2008. 2008(50): pp. 833–859.
8. Derby, E., D. Larsen, and K. Schwaber, Agile Retrospectives. Making Good Teams Great. 2006: Pragmatic Bookshelf. Raleigh, North Carolina.
9. Kerth, N., Project Retrospectives: A Handbook for Team Reviews 2001: Dorset House, New York.
10. Schindler, M. and M.J. Eppler, Harvesting project knowledge: a review of project learning methods and success factors. International Journal of Project Management, 2003. 21: p. 10.
11. Bjørnson, F.O., A.I. Wang, and E. Arisholm, Improving the effectiveness of root cause analysis in post mortem analysis: A controlled experiment. Information and Software Technology, 2009. 51: pp. 150–161.
12. Schön, D., The Reflective Practitioner. 1983: Basic Books, New York.
13. Kasi, V., et al., The post mortem paradox: a Delphi study of IT specialist perceptions. European Journal of Information Systems, 2008. 17: pp. 62–78.
14. Churchill, E.F. and S. Bly. It's all in the words: Supporting work activities with lightweight tools. in GROUP '99. 1999. Phoenix, AZ: ACM.

15. Gutwin, C., R. Penner, and K. Schneider. Knowledge sharing in software engineering: Group awareness in distributed software development in CSCW'04. 2004. Chicago, IL: ACM Press.
16. Handel, M. and J.D. Herbsleb. What is Chat Doing in the Workplace? in CSCW'02. 2002. New Orleans, LA: ACM.
17. Krogstie, B.R. The wiki as an integrative tool in project work. in COOP. 2008. Carry-le-Rouet, Provence, France: Institut d'Etudes Politiques d'Aix-en-Provence.
18. Krogstie, B.R. A model of retrospective reflection in project based learning utilizing historical data in collaborative tools. in EC-TEL 2009. 2009. Nice, France: Springer.
19. Hutchins, E., Cognition in the Wild. 1995, Cambridge, MA: MIT Press.
20. Rogers, Y. and J. Ellis, Distributed Cognition: an alternative framework for analyzing and explaining collaborative working. Journal of Information Technology, 1994. 9: pp. 119–128.
21. Daradoumis, T. and M. Marques, Distributed Cognition in the Context of Virtual Collaborative Learning. Journal of Interactive Learning Research, 2002. 13(1/2): pp. 135–148.
22. Flor, N.V. and E.L. Hutchins. Analyzing Distributed Cognition in Software Teams: A Case Study of Team Programming during Perfective Software Maintenance. in Empirical Studies of Programmers: Fourth Workshop. 1991: Ablex Publishing, Norwood, NJ.
23. Sharp, H. and H. Robinson, Collaboration and co-ordination in mature eXtreme programming teams. International Journal of Human-Computer Studies, 2008. 66(7): pp. 506–518.
24. Ackerman, M.S. and C. Halverson, Organizational Memory as Objects, Process, and Trajectories: An Examination of Organizational Memory in Use. Computer Supported Cooperative Work, 2004. 13(2): pp. 155–189.
25. Salomon, G., No distribution without individuals' cognition, in Distributed Cognitions. Psychological and educational considerations, G. Salomon, Editor. 1993, Cambridge University Press, Cambridge.
26. Strauss, A., Continual permutations of action. 1993, New York: Aldine de Gruyter.
27. Grudin, J. and T. Lovejoy. Messaging and Formality: Will IM Follow in the Footsteps of Email. in INTERACT 2003. 2003. Zurich: IOS Press.
28. Isaacs, E., et al. The Character, Functions, and Styles of Instant Messaging in the Workplace. in CSCW'02. 2002. New Orleans, LA: ACM.
29. Dourish, P. and V. Bellotti. Awareness and coordination in shared workspaces. in ACM CSCW. 1992. Toronto, Ontario, Canada: ACM Press.
30. Gutwin, C. and S. Greenberg, A Descriptive Framework of Workspace Awareness for Real-Time Groupware. Computer Supported Cooperative Work 2002. 11(3–4): pp. 411–446.
31. Gutwin, C., R. Penner, and K. Schneider. Group Awareness in Distributed Software Development. in CSCW'04. 2004. Chicago, IL: ACM.
32. Bødker, S. and E. Christiansen, Computer Support for Social Awareness in Flexible Work. Computer Supported Cooperative Work, 2006. 15: pp. 1–28.
33. Schmidt, K. and C. Simone, Coordination Mechanisms: Towards a Conceptual Foundation of CSCW Systems Design. Computer Supported Cooperative Work, 1996. 5: pp. 155–200.
34. Johnson, J.N. and P.F. Dubois, Issue Tracking. Computing in Science and Engineering, 2003(November/December): pp. 71–77.
35. Prause, C.R., et al. Managing the Iterative Requirements Process in a Multi-National Project using an Issue Tracker. in IEEE International Conference on Global Software Engineering. 2008. Bangalore, India: IEEE.
36. Poole, W.G. The Softer Side of Custom Software Development: Working with the Other Players. in Conference on Software Engineering Education and Training. 2003. Madrid, Spain: IEEE.
37. Kraut, R.E. and L.A. Streeter, Coordination in Software Development. Communications of the ACM, 1995. 38(3), pp. 69–81.
38. Whittaker, S., D. Frohlich, and D.-J. Owen. Informal Workplace Communication: What Is It Like and How Might We Support It? in Human Factors in Computing Systems. 1994. Boston, MA: ACM Press.
39. Dekel, U. and J.D. Herbsleb. Pushing Relevant Artifact Annotationsin Collaborative Software Development. in CSCW'08. 2008. San Diego, CA: ACM.
40. Storey, M.-A., et al. Shared waypoints and social tagging to support collaboration in software development. in CSCW'06. 2006. Banff, Alberta, Canada: ACM.

41. Fitzpatrick, G., P. Marshall, and A. Phillips. CVS integration with notification and chat: lightweight software team collaboration. in CSCW'06. 2006. Banff, Alberta, Canada: ACM.
42. Cubranic, D., et al. Learning from project history: a case study for software development. in CSCW '04. 2004. Chicago, IL: ACM.
43. Burge, J. and D.C. Brown. SEURAT: integrated rationale management. in ICSE'08. 2008. Leipzig, Germany: ACM.
44. Burge, J. and J. Kiper. Capturing Collaborative Design Decisions and Rationale. in Design, Computing, and Cognition. 2008. Atlanta, GA, USA.
45. Aranda, J. and G. Venolia. The Secret Life Of Bugs: Going Past the Errors and Omssions in Software Repositories in International Conference on Software Engineering (ICSE'09). 2009. Vancouver, Canada: IEEE.
46. Trac home page, http://trac.edgewall.org/, Last accessed 10 September 2009.
47. Krogstie, B.R. and M. Divitini. Shared timeline and individual experience: Supporting retrospective reflection in student software engineering teams. in CSEE&T 2009. 2009. Hyderabad, India: IEEE Computer Society.
48. Klein, H.K. and M.M. Myers, A Set of Principles for Conducting and Evaluating Interpretive Field Studies in Information Systems. MIS Quarterly, 1999. 23(1): pp. 67–94.
49. Wolf, C.G., J.R. Rhyne, and L.K. Briggs. Communication and Information Retrieval with a Pen-based Meeting Support Tool. In: CSCW 1992, Toronto, Canada, ACM.
50. Star, S.L., The Structure of Ill-Structured Solutions: Boundary Objects and Heterogeneous Distributed Problem Solving, in Distributed Artificial Intelligence, M. Huhns and L. Gasser, Editors. 1990, Morgan Kaufmann, Menlo Park, CA. pp. 37–54.
51. Krogstie, B.R. Do's and dont's of instant messaging in students' project work. in NOKOBIT 2009. 2009. Trondheim, Norway: Tapir.
52. Krogstie, B.R. Using Project Wiki History to Reflect on the Project Process in 42nd Hawaii International Conference on System Sciences. 2009. Big Island, HI: IEEE Computer Society.

Collocated Social Practices Surrounding Photo Usage in Archaeology

Marco P. Locatelli, Carla Simone, and Viviana Ardesia

Abstract A domain where photographs are a necessary part is archaeology: here they are used in different phases of the archaeological work for many purposes, some of which are common to other domains or to home usage (e.g., archiving). We concentrate our attention one of the initial phases of the archaeological process, namely excavation, since the related activities use photographs in a very peculiar way and under the constraints of a very demanding physical setting. Moreover, in this phase the advent of digitalized photographs is recent and their adoption is still interestingly combined with the usage of photographs printed on paper.

Paper presents the results of a study performed at an archaeological site in the south of Italy: we report the observed collocated collaborative practices surrounding photos and discuss these practices to identify some functionality of a supportive technology.

Introduction

The practices surrounding the management of photographs have been observed and studied mainly in the home where they are the objects of individual and collaborative activities [1–3]. These activities are aimed on the one hand at building a record of meaningful events, people, places, and on the other hand at retrieving this record and sharing it with relatives and friends both in co-located and distributed settings.

M.P. Locatelli (✉) and C. Simone
Department of Informatics, Systems and Communication, University of Milano–Bicocca, viale Sarca 336, U14 building, 20126 Milano, Italy
e-mail: locatelli@disco.unimib.it; simone@disco.unimib.it

V. Ardesia
Department of Archaeology, University of Bologna, Via Zamboni 33, 40126 Bologna, Italy
e-mail: viviana.ardesia@disco.unimib.it

M. Lewkowicz et al. (eds.), *Proceedings of COOP 2010*,
DOI 10.1007/978-1-84996-211-7_10, © Springer-Verlag London Limited 2010

This paper looks at photographs as artifacts supporting cooperation [4] as for example, in healthcare where X-ray films typically support diagnosis [5]; or in architecture where photographs support the design of buildings by documenting achievements or opportunities for the selection of some architectural detail [6]. This different perspective may change the actions performed on photographs: in any case it contextualizes both traditional actions (like archiving, searching, browsing, sharing that are typical of home photography) and the ones peculiar to the target domain in the framework of a broader goal and set of constraints. These goals and constraints define a framework against which actions have to be confronted to evaluate their effectiveness and their results. This is not the case of home photography: here the main goal is entertainment and social enjoyment [7].

A domain where photographs are integral to practices is archaeology: here they are used in different phases of the archaeological work for many purposes. We concentrate our attention on one of the initial phases of the archaeological process, namely excavation, since the related activities use photographs in an intensive way and under the constraints of a very demanding physical setting. Moreover, in this phase the advent of digitalized photographs is recent and their adoption is still interestingly combined with the usage of photographs printed on paper.

The paper presents the results of an ethnographic study performed on an archaeological site in the south of Italy. This study is part of a longer term project whose aim is to investigate the role of ICT in archaeology beyond the more traditional support of cataloging or setting up virtual exhibitions of various kinds of (material) cultural resources. In this joint investigation we had the opportunity to interact with archaeologists acting in the so called excavation campaign; that is, an activity aimed at starting or more often continuing an excavation that had to be suspended the year before because of adverse seasonal weather conditions. During these interactions, we collaboratively identified the main steps of the workflow defining the archaeological activities and the artifacts, tools and technology supporting them. Among others, photographs, their elaboration and management emerged as a basic support to construct and maintain the memory of what constitutes or has been found in the current excavation layer, before it is destroyed to access the layer below. The destructive and irreversible nature of excavation assigns to documentation, and specifically to photographs, a central role during both the campaign and the interpretation effort following it. The study was motivated by a question raised by the director of the excavation campaign: "how can ICT make our life easier in managing and exploiting the every day documentation we produce?" The question was challenging since the excavation work shows a serendipitous nature which has to follow some explicit and tacit rules in order to avoid the irreparable loss of relevant pieces of information. Moreover, the involved actors are not used to saying how they work, why they behave in specific ways, how they deal with unanticipated circumstances; in addition, archaeology provides only manuals describing very high level procedures that have to be instantiated in the current context (archaeological period, type of excavation, type of settlement, and so on). These considerations led us to start an empirical investigation based on observations and interviews to shed light on this unexplored domain. The next section describes the main aspects of archaeological work during the excavation campaign. Then, the work setting and the method adopted during the empirical investigation is described. The role of photographs in the observed practices is the focus of the subsequent section. A discussion of the empirical findings and its implications on the design of a supportive technology conclude the paper.

Archaeological Work

Archaeology is a discipline where photographs are an important tool supporting all archaeological activities since they require the documentation of disparate entities at different levels of detail: from the representation of the excavation area up to the memorization of information concerning the single material find. With the advent of the digital photos the use of the photography in archaeology has grown to integrate and, within some work teams, to replace more traditional methods of documentation that are based on hand-made drawings. These are based on observations and measures performed directly on the field with various (measurements) tools, and are completed manually by taking advantage of the artistic capabilities of the individual drawer.

To observe how the use of digital photography influences the practices characterizing archaeological work we studied the archaeological excavation of a bronze-age settlement in Mursia (Pantelleria, Italy): the excavation was directed by a professor from the University of Bologna. For several years, the Mursia archaeological setting has been a training field for students earning a degree in archeology. They are requested to perform the typical work in charge of "experienced" archaeologists, with the supervision of the more experienced colleagues. Since the latter are few in number, students actually work by themselves and ask for help only in specific circumstances: this reflects the labor division characterizing the archaeological work in almost all non-training situations as a consequence to the endemic scarcity of available resources. On the other hand, the activities going on there are also targeted to scientific investigations concerning methodological issues: then the practices reflect an experimental but rigorous attitude to new approaches and techniques. At the time of our observations (see Fig. 1), the *graphic survey* of the excavation area (that is, the representation of all its most remarkable parts) was no longer constituted of hand-made drawings: since the drawings have a strong component of subjectivity and formal simplification [8][1] the excavation director decided to introduce the usage of digital photographs. After this innovation, the survey is based on the so called *photomosaic*, that is a rectified and geo-referenced composition of zenithal photographs (that is, perpendicular photographs in relation to the target object). The survey obtained with this technique is called *photographic survey*.

The interviews with the excavation director highlighted that the use of the photographic survey offers important advantages in terms of informative content,

---

[1]This is one of the reference manuals that is adopted for the training of the students.

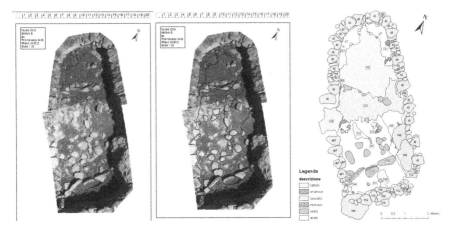

Fig. 1 The (digital) photomosaic on the *left*, the (digital) photomosaic with the graphic survey, and the final excavation map on the *right*

rapidity of execution and accuracy of the resulting measures. In fact, the use of digital photographs (1) allows the recording of more information (e.g., real colors and details, more accurate perception of the 3D view); (2) asks only for the time necessary to set and take the photo, whereas hand-made drawing would stop other excavation activities in the same part of the area; (3) if equipped with metric references, allows the computation of precise dimensional data of the photographed objects. However, the director emphasized that hand-made drawings are still used when the entity to be reproduced and its surrounding context is worth the subjective interpretation implied by the drawing: in this case the latter is very accurate; or when the environmental conditions make photographs of too low level quality: in this case the representation can be a very rough sketch of the real entity.

Photographic elaboration was performed partly at the excavation area and partly in the laboratory (Fig. 2), according to the following practice:

1. The zenithal digital photographs of the area were taken in the field; then they were elaborated and assembled into a rectified and geo-referenced photomosaic by dedicated software applications available in the laboratory where the photomosaic was printed using a large plotter.
2. The printed digital photomosaic was brought to the field to play the role of the reference map of the pertinent excavation area.
3. The digital photomosaic was further elaborated in the laboratory to become the reference artifact on which the relevant entities of the current layer (e.g., ceramic objects, fireplaces, tools) were put in evidence by drawing an irregular perimeter around them, this way obtaining what is formally called the *digital graphic survey*.

The senior archaeologists told us that at the end of every archaeological campaign all the digital graphic surveys produced have to be collected in a folder, named according to a naming convention, integrating location, year and the keyword "fotomosaici" (e.g., Mursia-2005-Fotomosaici). The relevance of this convention

Fig. 2 The setting at the excavation area and at the laboratory

was motivated by the fact that the collection of the elaborated photomosaics produced during the excavation, both in its digital and paper format, is usually searched and browsed at different points of the archaeological workflow. The *searching* activity is particularly intense during the planning of the archaeological mission: to this aim it is necessary to collect all the existing documentation concerning the areas in which the archaeologic activities will be performed, in order to check their state after the past campaign.

On the other hand, the *browsing activity* generally occurs during the post-campaign data elaboration in order to control the consistency and completeness of the collected documentation: to this aim, the browsing of all directories allows one to verify that everything was checked and appropriately organized. However, we observed that the browsing and searching of the printed photomosaics collection also occurred during the excavation: the archaeologists systematically checked the recently constructed photomosaics to analyze them against the physical changes produced by the excavation and then planned the next excavation phases accordingly.

Method

To uncover and understand archaeologist's practices we conducted a qualitative study of the archaeologists' work to identify the activities they perform, the strategies they adopt to coordinate their work, and finally the tools they use.

The data about the archaeological practices surrounding the usage of photographs during the excavation campaign was collected in two stages: the first one in summer 2006 and the second one in summer 2008. The study performed during the second stage was more systematic since it could build on top of some preliminary results obtained in the first stage. The qualitative study is based on the data collected in the 2 week observation of the work done by the archaeologists, both at the excavation site and when they work at the laboratory. Each day after the observation session, we discussed the observed practices with the team members to check and complete the collected information. In addition, we also reviewed our observation with the field director and one area manager when we were back from the campaign.

The professor who was the main responsible of the excavation campaign informed the people involved in the study about the presence of an observer: he clearly told them that the role of the observer was not about assessing the quality of their work, rather to "help them becoming more aware of what they were doing". In fact, the main goal was that their best practices could become part of the teaching/learning activities targeted to students involved in the next excavation campaigns. This perhaps unusual situation was made possible due to the presence of a really unique trust relationship between senior archaeologists and their young collaborators. This trust was generated by the behavior of the field director in all the excavation activities, and specifically, by way of turning all possibly critical or even mistaken situations into a positive learning experiences where the acquisition of knowledge was achieved by both sides. In fact, according to the experimental mood of the team, questions, critiques and innovations were welcomed and stimulated. Consequently, the observer was immediately accepted and perceived as just another kind of "strange young archaeologist" who had to learn something about their work. In this positive relationship, when a particular behavior was observed, the observer could ask the archaeologists for clarifications and motivations, irrespective of their level of experience and role in the excavation activities: the resulting interaction showed a high degree of mutual empathy. All this information was carefully annotated and constituted a precious source of data. The archaeological work is characterized by time slots where a lot of activities "chaotically" occur (typically in the morning when they have to organize their work or when something unexpected happens) followed by quite periods where the often prevalent manual work allows for relaxed conversations among archaeologists, and what is important in our study, between them and the observer.

The observer shared the living experience with the archaeologists in an almost isolated and not very comfortable location where the archaeologist lived (beside the very pleasant experience to enjoy the Mediterranean Sea): this full time presence was very important to observe archaeologist's activities and conversations because their work very often continues after the organized work periods, such as the morning activities at the excavation site before the temperature becomes to hot and at the laboratory in the afternoon. In fact, they also work in the evening and in many cases till late night, to perform activities that they cannot do or do not have time to do during the day: in particular they prepare all the necessary material for the day after, e.g. the new photomosaic. This situation made the apparently short stay at Mursia a very demanding experience and favored rich data collection.

At the time of our study in 2008 the team was composed of 16 persons, playing the following roles (some persons play more than one role): one field director; four area managers; one topographer; one laboratory manager; 11 junior archaeologists (students and graduates).

Fig. 3 Some uses of the photomosaic. An archaeologist and the field director (*left*); a group of archaeologists (*center*); two archaeologists working both with the digital and the printed photomosaic (*right*)

As alluded earlier, the environmental conditions at the excavation site were very critical. The hot temperature and especially the dust produced by the excavation activities and the wind in an area close to the sea, together with the lack of communication coverage, made it difficult to really use ICT technologies to their full potential. Data transfer was made manually by using different devices. The hardware equipment used at Mursia was composed of:

- An Electronic Total Station to take geo-referenced coordinates in the field
- Two digital cameras endowed with remote control to take pictures both of the excavation site and of the most relevant finds
- A USB hard disk on which both the source photos and the resulting photomosaics are downloaded
- Four notebook pcs where the photos were elaborated
- A color inkjet printer to printout the photomosaics (Fig. 3)

The two digital cameras were also jointly used to take stereo photographs to build 3D models of the excavation site; in fact, during the 2008 campaign in Mursia, archaeologists evaluated on one hand, the efficiency and effectiveness of the 3D-creation process (from taking pictures to 3D model creation) and on the other hand, if and how the obtained 3D model might be useful for the documentation and the study of the excavation findings. However this was only a potential innovation at that time and was not exploited in a meaningful way for our study.

The Collaboration Surrounding Photographs

Collaboration and coordination around photographs were affected by both environmental constraints and some needs intrinsic to their usage and management. The difficult environmental conditions (recall, hot temperature, dust and lack of stable network connections) reduced the availability of typical ICT supports that would have been taken for granted in other application domains. For example, at the excavation site there was a single PC available that was not easily reachable by the people performing the excavation, since it had to be positioned in a very protected location. It was used only exceptionally to upload data, collected using other less delicate instruments (like the Electronic Total Station) or photos when the memory of the camera was accidentally full; or to access some information that was not available on paper (e.g., if it had been forgotten in the laboratory or not printed at all by mistake). The uniqueness of another resource used in the laboratory, namely the USB hard disk, was due to the need to avoid distributed collection of the basic information to be organized in the official documentation of the excavation campaign. The lack of stable connections made this device a shared physical object that had to be used in competition whit other team members. This overhead of coordination was preferred rather than the possibility to lose or obtain unaligned information if it had been retrieved from the various PCs. Consequently, especially in the second case where the usage in the laboratory was continuous, a lot of conversations were about the most appropriate way to guarantee optimal access for all members in order to allow them to download the data on the PCs and to solve emergent information needs when the device was owned by one person.

On the other hand, the handling of the photographs raised the need to collaborate and coordinate actions among the members, although each single operation could appear as executable by a single person. In the following the main involved activities are considered.

Creating the Digital Photomosaic

The creation of the photomosaic, the most important artifact based on photographs, entails the selection of the source photos, their composition and the final archival in the hard-disk for shared usage. Each day a member of the team is in charge of this activity. Both for contingent reasons (like, the senior archaeologists are involved in another aspect) and pedagogical ones, the job can be assigned to junior archaeologists. In this case, the collaboration arises from the need to get advice and direction on how to do the job. However, collaboration is required also among more experienced members since the person in charge has a limited knowledge of each single photograph and of the conditions under which it was taken: for example, the time it was taken could affect the direction and intensity of the sunlight, the presence of a special configuration of the land could generate shadowed areas, the presence of strong wind could have made the zenithal photograph imprecise or somehow distorted, and the like. In fact, as said before, the typical division of labor is based on a regular partition of the excavation area in small squares that are each assigned to a single person every day. These areas can be quite for apart one from the other: so keeping awareness of others activities is not easy and not actually necessary for accomplishing one's own local activities. The selection of the photos from which the photomosaic will be built with the help of the specialized software requires the interpretation of their contents primarily on their borders since these

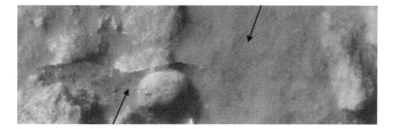

Fig. 4 Photomosaic composed by two images

should properly match to obtain a faithful composition. To this aim sometimes the photos have to be manipulated to improve the match: typically the geometry of the border has to be modified or a photograph is only partially used to complete the coverage (Fig. 4).

To understand this aspect better here is part of a dialogue between a student and an area manager from to two different areas of excavation.

Student: Sorry, can I ask you some advice?

Senior: Of course

Student: In your opinion is the area that I have delimited for the rectification all right?

Senior: well, here you could perhaps include the whole perimeter wall, rather than divide in half, while at this point I would pass the border over or under this stone instead whether of cutting it in two. Do you have to match other photos to this?

Student: Yes

Senior: Remember, it is better that the prominent elements are inclusive completely in one of the photos that composes the photomosaic because if you divide them, the border among two photos is particularly evident, while if you delimit the photos along the layers, the border among two photos is almost invisible.

As it is deduced by the dialogue and is clarified in Fig. 3, this activity, called rectification, has to be done carefully, so that the border between two or more photos is almost invisible, and at the same time, important details are not lost when the operator cuts the area of interest.

During this activity besides there have often been discussions related to the interpretation of the photos, particularly of the geometrical properties and sometimes of the "signs" contained in each photograph: e.g. is a dark shape the shadow of a stone or the sign of the presence of a relevant find? Here is another fragment of dialogue that illustrates what we described:

Senior1: But do these stones come from a fireplace?

Student: yes, we begun digging it this morning.

Senior1: look how well you can see the remains of ashes from the structure!

Student: What, this gray stain? But isn't a shadow?

Senior1: No, look how it follows the borders! And the shape of the deposit. It is clearly the remains of ashes from the fireplace. Remember to be careful when you outline it during the digitalizing! (he calls the other area manager).

Senior1: Senior2, come. Have you seen this beautiful stain of ashes?

Senior2: Yes, I noticed it while we were cleaning the area to take the photo. But in this photo it is better than what we can see here!

Naturally the experience supports the correct reading of the photographed elements, often allowing to observe particular that in the field are sometimes hardly visible, for many reasons like the different perspective, or the strong and direct light.

In the second case, some additional documents could solve the problem but usually there is no time to look for them and having a direct answer from someone who might know and help is easier and more effective. To sort out the problem some people gather around the computer reproducing the photograph and the discussions help them to reach a consensus and to socialize the direct experience acquired at the excavation site.

The Use of the Printed Photomosaic

Once the digital photomosaic has been created, archaeologists use the information it contains during the excavation to support many activities, namely those devoted to organizing their work, to performing the excavation and to validating the completeness of the collected documentation.

First of all, the photomosaic was used to do a very practical operation: the setting of the physical grid on the excavation area. In fact, a grid was printed on the photomosaic to support the identification of the square areas at the excavation site. Archaeologists set up a physical grid based on the one printed with the photomosaic to organize their work: in fact, every day square areas were occupied by a single archaeologist who could change area the day after. Moreover, due to the highly distributed work organized in small areas, archaeologists preferred to bring several printed versions of the digital photomosaic constructed the day before to the excavation site. Depending on individual preferences, they printed the photomosaic on a single A4 page or as a poster. Whichever the format of the printed photomosaic is, the switch from the digital to the printed version of this artifact makes it easier for the team to use it. In fact, on the one hand each individual or small groups of people digging could have her own version and manage it as they like. This artifact guided the excavation performed on the current day since the director, or a senior archaeologist on his behalf, indicating where to start the new dig in each small square assigned to the various juniors on the basis of the situation at the end of the day before it is recorded in the photomosaic. For this reason each individual copy of this artifact supports the "visual" memorization of the sequence of subareas to be considered within the square and also the motivations behind this digging strategy. When a relevant find is identified during the excavation, e.g., a piece of ceramics, an indication of the next underlying level or of a new architectural evidence, etc., the archaeological practice requires that the pertinent area is marked with a thick pencil and annotated with some codified information that will allow them to identify the entity during future interpretation The action of surrounding the relevant find was usually followed by the check of the presence of a sufficiently complete documentation of this find, especially when it had to be removed (typically, a tool, or a pot or even larger objects like a millstone) to proceed with the excavation. During the excavation, collaboration and coordination mainly occurred when the dig involved the borders of the individual digging area: in this case, the work going on in the close areas had to be suspended to allow the taking of photographs of the find, so that no dust was generated in the meantime, or to coordinate and agree upon a uniform inscription concerning the same find in all the involved copies of the photomosaic. Moreover, if the find is of special interest or relevance or it is difficult to evaluate its nature and value, then the digger calls the attention of more expert archaeologists and discusses what to do with it.

The graphic survey is created at the excavation site because only direct observation allows archaeologists to perceive different materials (in particular ceramic) and annotate their location in the graphic survey. During this activity we observed the occurrence of serendipitous collaboration and coordination with the topographer if very precise spatial coordinates were needed to localize relevant finds. On the other hand, the pressure to proceed with the excavation often forced the diggers to make rough highlights and annotations on the photomosaic. This partial information was completed in the afternoon work at the laboratory when the same data were reported, very carefully, on the digital photomosaic in order to obtain the digital graphic survey and derive the excavation map from it that organizes the findings according to each single excavation layer, as shown in Fig. 1 on the right.

Creating the Digital Graphic Survey

Once archaeologists are back to the laboratory with the graphic survey created at the excavation, they redraw the same survey over the digital photomosaic by means of the ArcGIS software application. In many cases during this activity archaeologists drew new graphic surveys that they deliberately left out at the excavation due to time constraints.

This activity is necessary because the digital graphic survey is used both to create the excavation map and to study the stratigraphic evolution. In particular, the last is made easier by the digital graphic survey because the ArcGIS software application allows one to superimpose different graphic surveys and select the entities belonging to the same stratigraphic layer.

There was one person, possibly different each day, in charge of the digital graphic survey: the appointed archaeologist collected the printed graphic surveys made at the excavation site and transferred the annotated information by using the graphic interface of the software application.

During the creation of the digital graphic survey, when all team members shared the same physical space in the laboratory, they discussed and commented what happened at the excavation site. Hence, this activity was by no means a mere transcription: on the contrary, it is when the richest exchange of information and awareness of all aspects of the excavation activities took place. Regarding this issue a dialogue took place among people digging in the same area.

Student1: I'm not sure, do you think the border that I drew is correct?

Senior: Yes, it's pretty good. Have you seen from the photo how clear the alignment that constitutes the partition wall is? (he calls the other students of his area). Look how well you can see the partition wall.

Student2: Yes, you're right, now I can see it well too. Then the hut was divided in two zones?

Senior: Probably, it would not be the first time that we find a structure with internal divisions.

Student1: But did the zones communicate through a door?

Senior: We cannot know with certainty. Look here (he shows the paper photomosaic of another area): in this hut we have found some large stones like for a doorstep from a side of the partition wall, for which it is presumed that there was an opening between the two rooms, but in other cases it is difficult to be certain. Tomorrow we will try to make a test along the wall to see if we can also identify a sort of doorstep.

In fact, we observed the usage of guiding people and speaking aloud to attract the attention of other potentially interested people as observed in [9].

Management of Photos

In archaeological work documentation, and specifically photographs, plays a fundamental role since it constitutes the unique memory of what is progressively, layer after layer, destroyed by the excavation. Actually, we observed all the three modes of recording reported in [10]. In fact, the photos might contain cues that allowed the archaeologists to remember or recollect past events: for example, the photo of a special find (an almost undamaged little amphora) was the trigger of a detailed narrative of where and how it was found and by whom during the past campaign, as well as all the actions that followed this rare event (its restoration and exhibition in the museum close to the laboratory). This narrative let the archaeologists not involved in this event know about it and hope to have a chance to experience the same emotion. Unlike the experiments described in [10], remembering of past situation triggered by the photos were a collective action and the narrative was the collage of each participants' small piece of experience. The same thing happened in less emotional situations where the cues were contained in the photomosaics: here the memory was more about the procedures used to manage the excavation of the specific represented layer and the problems that had to be dealt with in this professional activity.

Photographical documentation is quite complex, since it concerns synthetic information like the digital photomosaic instances and analytic information like the reproduction of a single find. To manage the photographical documentation archaeologists organized photos in directories, one directory for each day, and renamed photos' filenames to the date of the current day followed by an incremental number and stored all the photos in the *unique* USB hard disk. In addition, they stored some meta information (e.g., the excavation area, the stratigraphic layer) related to the photos and a link to the photo's files in a database that was created for future use (e.g., when they will study the excavation outcomes once back in their offices at the university) but it was not used during the campaign.

From the point of view of the sharing practices the availability of a unique USB hard disk caused the following main drawbacks: not more than one person could access the shared photos simultaneously, unless they were replicated to the laptop of each interested person; and more importantly from the cooperation point of view, it was not easy to know who was doing what with these photos.

On the other hand, photos-sharing did not require the concurrent elaboration of the same photos: in fact, photowork activities were well organized and coordinated in a way that avoided the concurrent elaboration of the same photos.

Related Work and New Findings

In this section we discuss the results of the analysis of the data we collected in the field and in subsequent meetings with some senior archaeologists who were particularly interested in the definition of innovative, at least for them, (technological) supports to make their work easier and to promote their "excavation school" and practices within a broader community of archaeologists.

Home Versus Professional Usage of Photographs

As anticipated in the introduction, in the literature empirical observations and design implications concerning photograph usage are mainly focused on home photography, where three main actions have been identified: photo-talk, photo-work and end-use. These terms support an analytical distinction between conversations and elaborations that might imply photograph manipulation or a simple action on them (e.g., display), respectively. On the contrary, this paper takes the point of view of professional usage, specifically within the archaeological domain: this fact allows one to identify both similarities and differences in the two distinct kinds of usages. In home settings [11, 12], practices surrounding photograph management entail many photo-work activities that can be both solitary and collaborative. The same holds for the case of archaeologists where the interplay of solitary and collaborative photo-work is a prevailing common practice. Frohlich et al. [12] identified collaborative photo-work by observing the emergence of photo-talk during photo-work activities. The practices that we observed in our field study confirm what has been observed at home: for example, when archaeologists work at the rectification of a photomosaic, their talks are focused on it, as we described in Section "Creating the Digital Photomosaic".

On the other hand, going deeper in to the analysis of the dialogues, we recognized that when people talk about the photo they are elaborating, they used lexical cues and voice intonation to separate the discussion about the photo's properties/characteristics from the discussion about the photo's content, i.e. what is depicted by the photo. For example, when two archaeologists work at the rectification of a photomosaic, they talk about how much to rotate/translate the photos constituting the mosaic, i.e. how to change a property of the photo, in relation to the represented excavation area as a whole, and in the general case not about its detailed contents. Photograph content, instead, is the unique topic of conversations following the strict elaboration phase (photo-work), when for example the goal is to plan the next day's activities (end-use).

The different nature of the talk contents has been already identified in [2], in particular with regard to storytelling and reminiscing. However, the proposed definition of photo-talk does not explicitly take into account the talks about the properties of the photos, which instead characterizes professional collaborative photo-work, since it often requires their digital composition. Since conversations about the properties of the photos are important during collaborative photowork, and in particular in archaeological work, this is important for its implication in design, as we shall see in Section "Implications for Design"; we would adapt the proposed photo-talk definition accordingly: photo-talk is the "naturally occurring conversations *about either the properties or the content of the photograph* in which photograph sharing takes place".

Here we notice that talking about photograph properties has the goal to better organize and articulate the ongoing collaborative photowork. In fact, the latter involves not only technical aspects, but also a form of creativity to identify the better manipulation strategy for the given situation: therefore, collaborative photowork cannot be based only on predefined steps but has to be articulated and negotiated to be both efficient and effective. Instead, talking about photograph content entails the articulation of future activities that belong to the workflow, organizing a broader process: of course, this process incorporates photograph elaboration as one specific activity, but it is oriented to the true goal of the archaeological work, that is, the collection and interpretation of the archaeological findings and their dissemination within the archaeological community.

Two Forms of Socialization

Archaeological work, in general and specifically the implied usage of photographs, is both collaborative and knowledge intensive. For this reason, "socialization of archaeological issues", as they call a relevant part of their work, assumes two distinct connotations, accordingly. These aspects were discussed with the archaeologists during both the field work and in subsequent meetings organized during our long term joint project. Our interlocutors used the term "socialization" after an early meeting where we discussed the various facets of knowledge work and mentioned the model proposed in [13]. Their use of this term was not fully coherent with its original definition, but we did not force any change of terminology since their interpretation, being based on the central role of experience, was altogether compatible with the model itself. Actually, the model associates socialization primarily with learning by doing/imitation, a concept that is closer to the phenomena that will be described in the next paragraph.

From the collaborative point of view, socialization was interpreted by archaeologists as the need to become more aware of what is going on during the excavation campaign. The desired awareness concerns the perception of how the produced documentation is growing, as a consequence of the ongoing excavation and the activities that are performed at the excavation site and in the laboratory by groups that are distributed in time and in space. The core artifacts gluing all these activities are the photomosaics and some predefined forms containing information about the excavation layers and their alignment according to what they call time phases. All actions refer to, and all discussions speak about, these artifacts and their connections. The current documentation is very fragmented and the connections between the artifacts constituting it are in the heads of the archaeologists, although these connections carry a very well defined and shared semantics. This fragmentation makes it difficult to share the experiential knowledge about time, space and context that governs their collaboration and is implicitly incorporated in the documentation beyond the pure data it contains.

From the point of view of the knowledge dimension, socialization was interpreted by archaeologists as the need to share and access excavation experiences and outcomes. This domain lacks from the predominant view of sharing and accessing knowledge as the availability of huge data sets where findings are collected and cataloged: they liked to describe this as "creating electronic dust instead of the real thing". The new archaeology school (to which our interlocutors belong to) tries to go beyond this narrow view (that is unfortunately common to many approaches to knowledge management) and looks for new forms of data aggregation and presentation that for the considerations made in the previous sections, cannot avoid being rooted in work practices and thus considers photographs and the results of their elaborations as a starting point.

Archaeological work showed socialization practices surrounding photographs similar to the ones that have been observed in home photography [2]: namely storytelling and reminiscing of what was going on at the time the picture was taken. Beside this, a similar form of socialization happened inside situations. Excavation teams, in general, are mainly constituted of young people since the excavation work is demanding in terms of physical effort: this was obviously the case of the observed team. According to young people's habits, the team took a lot of pictures of people at the excavation site or in the place where they lived together, by using their private cameras. They shared these pictures (sometimes through the facilities by which they elaborated the official excavation photographs), they kept them from one campaign to another, they showed and shared them with the newcomers and told a lot of (funny) stories around these photographs in order to receive them in the community or to recall meaningful or simply amusing situations with old friends. Although this aspect was foreseen, its relevance became more substantial than expected: actually, this specific kind and usage of photographs was in the heads of the observed archaeologists, a relevant part of the documentation of the excavation campaign itself. The above practices were socially very relevant. In fact, they were not only tolerated but also promoted by the senior archaeologists, since they naturally helped to build the social ties that make the hard and tiring archaeological work tolerable and less prone to the rise of conflicting behaviors in front of breakdowns.

Managing Control During the Usage of Photographs

During the collaborative usage of photographs we observed situations where the archaeologists had to manage the control of the related actions performed both at the excavation when the graphic survey is involved (Section "The use of the Printed Photomosaic") and at the laboratory in all the elaborations of the photomosaics (Sections "Creating the Digital Photomosaic" and "Creating the Digital Graphic Survey). The first situation is more about photograph sharing and is similar to the case discussed [7] where they investigated the effects of equality of control in photograph sharing: in this case, participants enjoyed equality of control because they "found photograph sharing to be more fun, less constrained and more natural" and that "roles were more flexible, that everyone was involved more, and that the conversation flowed better".

In the situation at the laboratory it is important to note that the control device (in this case, the mouse plugged into the laptop) was acquired not only to get control over the photo display, but also to get control over its elaboration. Although the observed group was not based on a hierarchical structure, we noticed some asymmetry in the behavior of the archaeologists engaged in the collaborative elaboration of the photos. Actually, when a junior archaeologist interacted with a more skilled one, it was not easy for her to take back the control of the mouse when the other archaeologist got it. This switch happened usually only when the latter had completed her photowork activity. Although this practice did not raise great conflicts due to the learning nature of the setting, however, in some cases the less skilled archaeologists told us that they would like to show how they had liked to do the same activity, maybe in a different way.

We discussed issue of equality of control with the senior archaeologists in relation to the possibility to stimulate autonomous if not original ways of solving problems, a necessary aspect also in professional excavation. To find a way to facilitate equality of control was appreciated as a possible approach to support learning by doing; in particular, it may be a way to support learning by imitation, i.e. when actors re-do the same actions that more skilled colleagues have done [13].

Implications for Design

From the practices we have observed and from the previous considerations, we can derive implications for the design of a photoware that at least can support the archaeological work rooted in photograph management. In so doing, we are well aware that the introduction of even a very light technology in domains like archaeology may have deep and sometimes unanticipated effects, as in fact, happened with the introduction of digital photography. However, the following with implications for design received a preliminary consensus from the archaeologists observed when we identified them during our joint discussions: this consensus was combined with the strong requirement that whatever the resulting functionalities could be, they should be easy to use by not only technology experts but especially by laymen, since information technology is not yet appropriated by the professionals working in the archaeology domain.

A first set of functionalities strictly concerns photowork. For example, the technology should support the management of the duplication of a photograph, the various (partial) elaborations performed on the copies and then their possible reconciliation in a single photograph to be stored for future use. At the same time, an easy way to manage the link of a photograph with its elaborations (without reconciliation) would also be appreciated. Moreover, additional functionalities could support the recording of the sequences of actions that led to high quality results when constructing photomosaics. As already mentioned, this is a creative activity that requires the solution of unanticipated problems: e.g., depending on the nature of the soil, the presence of geologic configurations, the low quality of some photographs, and so on. This kind of photo-work is often based on a try and error approach that would be more productive if the technology could help in handling the sequence of the performed actions and their outcomes, e.g., by supporting backtracking and the recording of productive sequences. The latter could be organized to become a more reactive and useful support by pointing to best practices and appropriate warnings in specific phases of the elaboration. Finally, in agreement with the experimental nature of archaeological collaborative photowork and in support of learning by doing/imitation, the issues about equality of control discussed in Section "Management of Photos" suggest the opportunity of multiple accesses to the instruments (i.e., multiple controllers) used to elaborate, specifically, the photomosaic and the digital graphic survey. In the case of the technological setting like the current one in Pantelleria this means installing two (or possibly more) mouses plugged into the same laptop in order to put both archaeologists on equal footing, allowing multi-pointer interactions such as in (and possibly by means of) MPX [14]. This way the skilled archaeologist could draw the digital graphic survey of a problematic area of the photomosaic and the student archaeologist could replicate the same drawing, or draw the graphic survey in his own way, and then compare the results.

By taking into consideration the socialization involving collaboration that we described in Section "Related Work and New Findings", the technology should provide a framework where photographs can be easily associated to other artifacts constituting the documentation of the excavation campaign. This way this documentation can be seen as "a web of artifacts" having photomosaics as privileged nodes (archaeologists liked this metaphor that we borrowed from the healthcare domain [15, 16]): in fact, the web evokes both strength and scalability, and at the same time, flexibility of the connections among the artifacts that the web makes explicit. On this web, awareness of new events (like, updates, completion of tasks, the creation of new nodes and connections, and so on) could be propagated according to disparate criteria (semantic proximity, role played by the user, etc.) by using different notification and awareness models [17]. This proactive behavior was considered as an adequate way to convey awareness of activities distributed in time and space that in archaeology (like in healthcare [18]) leave traces on the collected data in multiple ways.

The form of socialization based on the knowledge dimension requires a support to search and browse that is driven by the documentation contents: specifically, searching by similarity was mentioned as a functionality that could support many of the practices described in Section "The Colloboration Surrounding Photographs". This very simple and obvious requirement was, however, the source of a lively debate on its implications. In the experience of our interlocutors, the search based on keywords was too poor for their needs; on the other hand, the typical semantic search based on a predefined ontology was problematic. In fact, although the domain already generated models and languages for this, they are still unreconciled and too related to specific archaeological approaches: consequently, the definition of a really usable universal domain ontology was not deemed as realistic, and in any case too general purpose, to be used in specific situations. The alternative solution to maintain a locally defined ontology was deemed as an unsustainable effort. Moreover, as is often the case, the question to be answered by the search is not always well defined and often transforms the search in a browsing activity. This mixed functionality was described as a support of journeys that traverses the webs of artifacts that have been constructed in different campaigns: the same metaphor has been later proposed in [19]. In this uncertain process, similarity cannot also be defined on static and predefined parameters. From the archaeologist's point of view, a typical path starts from a find and the photographs containing it, it reaches the documentation of similar finds, then passes through the forms that incorporate their interpretation, from which it reaches a photomosaic indicating the finds and soon. In this process, existing consolidated taxonomies (e.g., characterizing the shape of ceramic artifacts) and metadata capturing locally defined semantics can be reasonably used to proactively identify alternative next steps of the investigation, up to the point that they do not undermine the flexibility required by this qualitative mix of searching and browsing.

Conclusion and Future Work

This paper described the setting and the outcomes of a field study aimed at identifying the practices surrounding the use and management of photographs as part of the archaeological work performed during an excavation campaign, both at the excavation site and in the laboratory where post excavation elaborations were performed. Beside practices that have been uncovered in home photography, professional usage of photographs shows additional practices that are motivated by the features and goals of the specific domain that make these artifacts a different kind in relation to forms and templates that have been considered up to now.

Since we will have the opportunity to continue this empirical research during the next campaigns, we are planning some short term activities to start the experimentation of initial technological solutions along with the ones mentioned in Section "Implications for Design". We distinguish between technologies to be used at the excavation site and those that can be used in the laboratory.

For what concerns the first kind, we plan to provide the archaeologists with small devices (like e-paper based iLiad or palmtop) in order to let them directly produce the digital graphical survey, thus avoiding the necessary passage via the paper based version. This solution does not prevent having the printed version of the previous photomosaics and the related digital graphical survey available at the excavation site: it allows instead the combination of the two media in order to have a more readable version of the excavation area reproduction, and at the same time, to avoid useless duplication of effort to produce the next survey, Moreover, this solution would allow them to construct on the fly links to interesting information (photographs, interpretations, structure of the excavation layers): this is a first step toward the construction of the web of artifacts that constitutes the archaeological documentation. To this aim, we plan to integrate open source technologies that augment photographs with "hot spots" to which multimedia information can be flexibly and easily associated.

For what concerns the technology to be experimented in the laboratory, our effort is oriented to support the management of the photographs that are used to build the photomosaic. Currently this management is based on the different extensions of the files that are produced by the cameras and are required by the integration software (jpeg and bpm, respectively). This is clearly not enough to manage the multiple versions of each photomosaic and their rich semantic links as discussed in Section "Implications for Design. For what concerns the collaborative work on the same photomosaic, we plan to experiment technologies like Google-docs, to be specialized for the collaborative elaboration of the same version of the shared photograph. This solution is preferred by archaeologists more than duplication/reconciliation because they agree with the literature giving evidence that in cooperative work social control is a strong and by far more acceptable form of coordination than the one driven by sophisticated and possibly error prone computer (graphics, in our case) algorithms.

Our long term research agenda concerns the full development and implementation of a technology supporting the metaphor of the web of artifacts and the various forms of awareness that can be propagated through the related semantic links: this support was initially conceived for the healthcare domain but our investigations proved that it is applicable to the archaeological domain as well. In fact, the two domains show a similar mix of tacit and explicit conventions that govern collaboration in situations where wrong behaviors might produce unrecoverable outcomes.

References

1. Kirk, D., Sellen, A., Rother, C., Wood, K.: Understanding photowork. In: CHI '06: Proceedings of the SIGCHI conference on Human Factors in computing systems, New York, USA, ACM (2006), pp. 761–770

2. Frohlich, D., Kuchinsky, A., Pering, C., Don, A., Ariss, S.: Requirements for photoware. In: CSCW '02: Proceedings of the 2002 ACM conference on Computer supported cooperative work, New York, USA, ACM (2002), pp. 166–175

3. Crabtree, A., Rodden, T., Mariani, J.: Collaborating around collections: informing the continued development of photoware. In: CSCW '04: Proceedings of the 2004 ACM conference on Computer supported cooperative work, New York, USA, ACM (2004), pp. 396–405

4. Bannon, L.J., Bodker, S.: Beyond the interface: encountering artifacts in use. In: John M. Caroll (Ed.), Designing interaction: psychology at the human-computer interface. Cambridge University Press, New York (1991), pp. 227–253

5. Hartswood, M., Procter, R., Slack, R., Soutter, J., Voss, A., Rouncefield, M.: 'Repairing' the machine: A case study of evaluating computer-aided detection tools in breast screening. In: ECSCW'03: Proceedings of the Eight European Conference on Computer Supported Cooperative Work (ECSCW), Helsinki, Finland, 14–18 September, Kluwer (September 2003), pp. 375–394

6. Schmidt, K., Wagner, I.: Ordering systems: Coordinative practices and artifacts in architectural design and planning. Computer Supported Cooperative Work (CSCW) **13**(5) (Dec. 2004) 349–408

7. Lindley, S.E., Monk, A.F.: Social enjoyment with electronic photograph displays: Awareness and control. International Journal of Human-Computer Studies **66**(8) (2008) 587–604

8. Fiorini, A.: Esperienze di fotomodellazione e stereofotogrammetria archeologica. In: Workshop Digitalizzare la pesantezza. L'Informatica e il metodo della stratigrafia. Foggia, 6–7 giugno. (2008)

9. Christian Heath, Marina Jirotka, P.L., Hindmarsh, J.: Unpacking collaboration: the interactional organization of trading in a city dealing room. Computer Supported Cooperative Work (CSCW) **3**(2) (June 1994) 147–165

10. Sellen, A.J., Fogg, A., Aitken, M., Hodges, S., Rother, C., Wood, K.: Do life-logging technologies support memory for the past?: an experimental study using sensecam. In: CHI '07: Proceedings of the SIGCHI conference on Human factors in computing systems, New York, USA, ACM (2007), pp. 81–90

11. Taylor, A., Swan, L., Durrant, A.: Designing family photo displays. In: ECSCW 2007. Springer, London (2007), pp. 79–98

12. Frohlich, D.M., Wall, S.A., Kiddle, G.: Collaborative photowork: Challenging the boundaries between photowork and phototalk. In Lindley, S., Durrant, A., Kirk, D., Taylor, A., eds.: Collocated Social Practices Surrounding Photos, CHI 2008 Workshop. (2008)

13. Nonaka, I., Takeuchi, H.: The Knowledge-Creating Company: How Japanese Companies Create the Dynamics of Innovation. Oxford University Press, New York (1995)

14. Hutterer, P., Thomas, B.H.: Groupware support in the windowing system. In: AUIC '07: Proceedings of the eight Australasian conference on User interface, Darlinghurst, Australia, Australia, Australian Computer Society, Inc. (2007), pp. 39–46

15. Bardram, J.E., Bossen, C.: A web of coordinative artifacts: collaborative work at a hospital ward. In: GROUP '05: Proceedings of the 2005 international ACM SIGGROUP conference on Supporting group work, New York, USA, ACM (2005), pp. 168–176

16. Cabitza, F., Simone, C.: "…and do it the usual way": fostering awareness of work conventions in document-mediated collaboration. In: ECSCW'07: Proceedings of the Tenth European Conference on Computer Supported Cooperative Work (ECSCW), Limerick, Ireland, 24–28 September, Springer (September 2007), pp. 119–138

17. Schmidt, K., Heath, C., Rodden, T.: Preface. Computer Supported Cooperative Work (CSCW) **11**(3) (Sept 2002) 3–4

18. Cabitza, F., Sarini, M., Simone, C.: Providing awareness through situated process maps: the hospital care case. In: GROUP '07: Proceedings of the 2007 international ACM conference on Supporting group work, New York, USA, ACM (2007), pp. 41–50

19. Benford, S., Giannachi, G., Koleva, B., Rodden, T.: From interaction to trajectories: designing coherent journeys through user experiences. In: CHI '09: Proceedings of the 27th international conference on Human factors in computing systems, New York, USA, ACM (2009), pp. 709–718

Direct Deliberative Governance and the Web: The Collaborative Work of Democratic Decision-Making Mediated by an Online Social Environment

Rean van der Merwe and Anthony Meehan

Abstract Direct deliberative democracy presents a conceptually attractive model of civic governance – particularly relevant at local scale. We outline the 'work' of direct deliberative democracy by considering its underlying principles and objectives, and discuss four fundamental challenges that are commonly proposed: the difficulty of coordinating direct participation, the expertise required of participants, the often underestimated dynamics of power in direct action, and that deliberation is not necessarily the sole, ideal mode of participation. At hand of a case study of an online "community of interest", the paper investigates the potential role of social media to facilitate this work, and to mitigate the challenges cited.

Introduction

Direct deliberative democracy (DDD) presents a conceptually attractive model of civic governance – particularly relevant at local scale – where stakeholders engage directly in cooperative decision making. This paper investigates the role of an online social environment in mediating the collaborative work of democratic local decision-making viewed as DDD. We consider the 'work' of direct governance by referring to the underlying principles and objectives of DDD. The literature further proposes four fundamental challenges: the difficulty of coordinating direct participation [1], the expertise required of participants [2], the often underestimated dynamics of power in both deliberation and direct action, and that deliberation is not necessarily the sole, ideal mode of contributing to decision making [3].

At hand of a case study of an online "community of interest" [4], the paper investigates the potential role of social media to facilitate this work, in particular relating to the challenges cited. We develop a typology of the acts which contribute to the work

R. van der Merwe (✉) and A. Meehan
Center for Research in Computing, The Open University, Walton Hall, Milton Keynes, MK7 6AA, UK
e-mail: r.vandermerwe@open.ac.uk; a.s.meehan@open.ac.uk

M. Lewkowicz et al. (eds.), *Proceedings of COOP 2010*,
DOI 10.1007/978-1-84996-211-7_11, © Springer-Verlag London Limited 2010

of DDD in the online community, and consider these in terms of their level of empowerment. We consider also how acts are expressed in terms of the social network structure of the online community by developing a network model of interactions. This shows how initiative is distributed and suggests further dynamics of action. A synthesis of these two dimensions, of action and structure, leads to clearer understanding of how the online social space mediated direct governance in the context of the case study, and potentially addressed aspects of the four challenges above.

The following section of the paper considers the theoretical background to our study, outlining the principles and challenges of DDD, before investigating a number of threads in the literature of cooperative work that potentially relate. This is followed by a brief case description, after which we describe the methodology and results each of the two analytical stages – an investigation of acts and of network structure.

Theoretical Background

A Description of the Work, the Principles of Direct Deliberative Democracy

To provide context for the discussion, we briefly outline our use of, as well as the theoretical contributions of the notions of 'civic governance' and 'direct deliberative democracy'.

While research frequently focuses on the role of social media to engage citizens with formal institutions of government, we use the concept of *'civic governance'* to denote a broader process. Isin [5] proposes that the traditional notion of what it means to be a citizen, of the relationship of subjects with a state, has recently evolved to encompass a much wider range of actions and contexts. 'Activist citizenship', as he frames it, implies diverse forms of involvement, in issues that may not fit the remit of traditional government in any number of ways – for example because they are too local, not yet 'on the agenda', or even outside of its constitution [6]. Our concern then is with a notion of governance which, much as it acknowledges the significant role of the formal institutions we call government, more broadly considers the role of citizens in governing the world they are part of. This paper investigates this process particularly at local scale.

By associating civic governance with the principles *democracy*, we imply a mode of governance that shares the democratic fundamental of "rule by the people" [1]. Dahl proposes that this principle follows from two fundamental values: intrinsic equality – that all are equally fit to contribute to decisions that affect the general welfare; and personal autonomy – that all have the right to be self determining, in other words to contribute to decisions that affect them to the maximum extent possible. There is long standing debate whether these objectives are best served in systems where people contribute to decisions directly, referred to as *direct democracy*, or in systems where an elected government and its officials conduct the business of governance, referred to as representative democracy. While the complex reality of participative decision-making quickly dispels notions of an ideal process [3], and there are compelling arguments for both direct and representative forms of decision making, Manin [7] points out that in practice a strict theoretical division is artificial, since neither implies an absolute form and the practical implementation of 'directness' has multiple dimensions. Barber [8], a strong supporter of direct democracy, proposes the intention is not so much to advocate one mode at the expense of the other, as to supplement representative forms "with a critical overlay of participatory institutions." While we accordingly do not labour the distinction, this paper focuses on more direct forms of democratic decision making, which we argue are particularly relevant at local scale.

As a final point of definition – the introduction refers to direct *deliberative* democracy. Bohman [9] provides an idealized characterisation of deliberative democracy: that legitimate, broadly acceptable decisions are the result of a process organised around the ideal of political justification, and which requires free public reasoning of equal citizens. In principle then, all forms of democratic governance are deliberative to the extent that they rely on reasoned evidence to support choices – much as their mechanisms may be more or less participatory, and more or less transparent. While Saward [3] points to the pitfalls of uncritically advocating deliberative decision making based on comparing such an idealized notion to the reality of its alternatives, Gutmann and Thompson [2] propose that its core value lies in the 'reason giving'. Decisions based on reasons (which have been made broadly accessible), rather than simply based on a position, are more open to be engaged and evaluated against their justification.

To operationalise the notion of direct deliberative democracy at local scale, Cohen [10] proposes that "[b]ecause of the numerosity and diversity of sites, we want a structure of decision-making that does not require uniform solutions … because of the complexity of problems, we want a structure that fosters inter-local comparisons of solutions." Cohen presents the basis for a form of localism [11], where citizens can make collective decisions through public deliberation, while their choices are examined in the light of relevant deliberations in comparable situations. This potentially combines the advantages of self-government and local learning with wider processes of social learning and heightened political accountability.

Civic governance, as we have framed it in terms of direct deliberative democracy, potentially relies on technologically mediated collaboration:

- To support processes of governance that do not necessarily have traditional government or any particular political party at their centre, and which are expressed in diverse contexts and across multiple networks.
- To facilitate decision-making which respects the democratic principles of intrinsic equality and personal autonomy.
- To allow exchanges between actors that focus on directly solving local problems, "where it matters" in terms of potential impact and their personal interest.
- To provide an accessible deliberative space where decisions are potentially subject to reasoned debate.

Specific Critiques of Direct Deliberative Democracy

While direct deliberative democracy offers an appealing model of governance, this next section confronts four challenges that are frequently raised. As we outlined in the introduction, these are the difficulty of coordinating direct participation [1], the expertise required of participants [2], the often underestimated dynamics of power in deliberation [12], and that deliberation is not necessarily the sole, ideal mode of participation [3].

Dahl [1] considers that large scale direct participation is not realistic considering the size and complexity of the modern nation state. Citizens have limited time to be involved, and do not have the specialist skills or expertise provided by a representative administration. Indeed, Dahl proposes that representative forms of decision-making evolved in part to overcome these two challenges. Gutmann and Thompson [2] similarly consider both practical and ethical concerns with direct forms of *deliberative* democracy. Particularly targeted at the national level, they essentially recast the objections raised by Dahl in terms of deliberative process: It is not practical to include everyone in deliberation, and the public are not all skilled (equal) deliberators – they may not give the best reasons, nor make the most astute decisions. Authors further question the accessibility of deliberation as a political process, where public opinion is largely formed in a "media space" [13] that is not equally accessible to all. We would argue that, in the local decision making context targeted by our research, these criticism are somewhat mitigated. The knowledge and commitment of participants is harder to question where they are most familiar with the contingency of local situations, and also most directly affected. The number of potential participants in any given decision is also significantly lower and channels of communication relatively accessible.

Related to the role of power in DDD, Foucault [14] notably criticized the ideal of dialogue "that circulates freely without coercion or distortion," as utopian. Though the comments were most directly addressed at Habermas' notion of communicative action [15], Foucault's point was essentially that power strongly influences what is considered true, and so that dialogue is inextricably linked to power. Though fundamentally supportive of deliberative democracy, Gutmann and Thompson [2] acknowledge that deliberation can be used cynically, as cover for power politics. They propose however that in such instances, the "giving of reasons" is its own best defense. Even in absence of overt conflict or coercion, power might however control the agenda – by determining what is "on the table" for discussion, or more subtly by framing what role players consider in their interest [12]. While such use of power is often framed in terms of control by institutions of government, Saward [16] proposes that where citizens participate directly there are no less "claims of representation." In other words, participants claim to represent the interests of a constituency they effectively "create" to support their argument. We cite these notions not to suggest that direct deliberative governance is more sensitive to the effects of power than for example representative democracy, they do however point to potential dynamics that cannot be ignored in a grounded analysis.

The fourth criticism is not so much that people do not have the ability, but that proponents discriminate against preferences that are not stated deliberatively [3] by proposing that only deliberative claims are legitimate. Cohen [10] acknowledges that deliberation typically relies on a particular discursive style – formal, rational, deductive and generalized – and so potentially excludes people who have a different style of communication (e.g. emotive or narrative) and also the information conveyed by these styles. Saward argues more broadly that deliberation is democratically secondary, a component in the larger process of enacting democratic governance. He points out that deliberative process typically relies on aggregative mechanisms such as a vote as soon as there is not perfect consensus. We agree that deliberation has shortcomings as sole mode of participation, and that a much broader range of acts do (and should) contribute to the process of civic governance, but propose that at local scale, where a small number of people directly cooperate to solve an issue, it has a central role.

The Potential Role of Social Technologies

We have outlined a specific model and context of governance, as well as some of the challenges frequently attributed to it. This section now briefly considers literature that informs our approach to the role of social technologies in this domain, particularly related to the aforementioned challenges.

Related to the notion that direct participation presents logistical problems in larger groups, Shirky [17] and Benkler [18] propose that online social media substantially reduce the co-ordination cost associated with collaborative action. They contextualise earlier work by Coase, who proposes that organisational forms are the result of attempting to institutionally minimise the extraneous costs associated with transacting. Because of changes in co-ordination cost brought about by the web, Benkler argues, collective governance and flat organisational hierarchy are becoming increasingly dominant forms of social organisation. Shirky claims that loosely co-ordinated online groups are supporting "… serious, complex work, taken on without institutional direction." Castells [13] similarly describes the development of a new communication sphere as the result of efficiencies in networked organisation. He refers to "mass self communication" with cautious optimism, where communication is self-produced as much as self directed in consumption, yet has the potential to connect a mass audience. We would point to the work of Cordella [19], who investigates the impact of introducing ICT within and between organisations, and reports that while some co-ordination costs are indeed reduced, new costs such as information overload are introduced in what is a complex web of interaction. While social media undeniably has potential to facilitate the group action required of direct governance, it would be unwise to oversimplify the mediation.

The mention of information overload raises the second challenge of DDD – which relates both to information and skill. Cohen [10] proposes that deliberation has the advantage that it potentially aggregates the reasons for decisions, information which might also inform future decisions in comparable jurisdictions. Undeniably digital conversations leave a record, such as the archive of a discussion forum – however research on decision support systems and automated argument summary [20] shows that these records are not always easy to mine and interpret. Presenting the information in digested form invites questions of bias, whether deliberate or simply by omission, though admittedly this is not specific to the digital domain. Accepting the information literacy and technical skills required of participants in the new domain, one might nonetheless argue that social technologies have the potential to empower participation in governance. While research frequently high-lights the challenges associated with the reduced information bandwidth [21] of online social interaction, one might conversely make the argument that it is a less intimidating environment within which to engage than for example to make a public speech, and that the relative anonymity overcomes differences in social status. The asynchronous nature of online deliberation further allows a considered style of input – while at the same time the medium is dynamic in that it affords direct feedback and the ability to edit, append or qualify.

A number of the points raised above relate also to the discussion of power – particularly Castell's notion of 'mass self communication' [13], which implies the deliberative process is more accessible within the "networked" public sphere com-posed of social media. His analysis acknowledges however that technology, used in this sense to refer to a socio technical system, is not neutral. In network terms, nodes are privileged to do only that which "[the network] is programmed to do", and conversely, the network discriminates against anything not considered a node, or not a member [22]. In other words, both in terms of technical and social programming, social technologies potentially mediate participation by their affordances, by what they are programmed to accept as legitimate behavior, but also by what and who they exclude. One of the key objectives of our study is to understand the balance of opportunities and challenges in the context of the case study, how the system might have empowered and who were afforded relative control over the governance agenda.

Further indication of how interrelated the aspects of interaction are, our discus-sion of the problem of expertise has already touched on the fourth challenge by referring to the nature of deliberation online. Deuze et al. [23] propose that, in the context of blogs and online journalism, digital culture is characterised by blurring of the distinction between the producers and consumers of media. The audience have an expectation to be able to participate in the process of meaning making. If deliberation is characterized in the broadest sense as a process of meaning mak-ing, online media afford participants significant diversity in the mode, style and scale of their contribution – from comments on articles, to video blogs, social bookmarking or even developing an independent online community to name but a few. Hindman [24] however proposes that this process of meaning making is highly unequal online. His research shows a power law distribution both of traffic and contribution – very few sites get most of the attention and so have a disproportionate influence on public opinion. What is not clear however, is the extent to which social media, potentially a single community of interest such as targeted in this paper, contributes to or mediates deliberative governance at very local scale – in particular where participants set out not to influence broader opinion, but make direct contributions to governance.

Case Study Description and Context

This paper draws on research into an initiative, launched in 2002 to promote information sharing and collective action between coastal stakeholders in southern Africa. In this section we describe the case study, but we also provide contextual interpretation that, we hope, enables the reader to better assess our later analysis.

The project donors hoped to incubate a community of interest [4] focussed specifically on sustainable development and environmental governance. A central project team was established, with both permanent and temporary employees to act as administrators and facilitators of the community. The team implemented a web enabled approach to participation and governance focused not only on socially inclusive interaction of citizens with government, but also, significantly, on citizen to citizen networking, capacity building and knowledge sharing. They aimed for governance to be as much driven from the bottom up, as from the top down.

The objectives of the initiative have clear parallels with key proposed attributes of direct deliberative governance [10] in that it seeks to support pluralistic, locally relevant solutions through collective decision making, while providing opportunity for social learning through inter-local comparison of solutions. In other words, while the scope of the overall initiative was regional, and it encouraged sharing solutions between countries even, its goal was to support pragmatic, local governance action. There were established environmental and development governance initiatives in the target region, but they acted in fragmented networks with little co-ordination between organisations. This resulted in the diffusion of effort and relatively little success against large, co-ordinated opponents such as local primary industry. The project aimed to provide a "meta network" to connect these fragmented initiatives. In the process of connecting stakeholder groups, the initiative sought also to reconfigure local networks to particularly afford disempowered communities increased voice or agency. This steered the points of engagement it sought.

In the 18 months prior to our study the online community platform had served 103,677 page views and recorded 2,200 unique monthly visitors – of these 57% were from within the region. More significantly, there were 650 registered members who had made 1,855 message posts to the discussion list. These statistics substantially exceeded the expectations of the project initiators given the relatively specialised focus, in a sparsely populated region with low level of technical development. The archive of discussion contributions further indicates that the community facilitated participation from across traditional organisational and geographic networks – members of civil society and NGO's, academics, the business sector, donor organisations, as well as local and regional government.

Discussion focussed on practical issues of governance. In some cases the deliberation was mainly opinion forming, or of "inter-local comparison of solutions" as Cohen [10] put it. There was e.g. an extended discussion of the impact of commercial firewood collection on the environment, and another providing advice about how to best deal with (protected) wildlife damaging farmers' crops. In other cases discussion lead to, or supported direct, local action. In three instances the online community had e.g. contributed to taking inequitable property development to task – cases where decision makers had distorted the mandated process, potentially blocking common access to natural resources. The online network provided opportunity for participants to raise issues when they arose, and though response was not guaranteed, to engage both like minded and the opposed in dialogue. In this sense, the social media created an accessible interface to the "media space" [13] – at least for anyone with access to the technology. The initial discussion of property rights had been started by a community member who found that, with local authorities abusing their position of authority, attempts to engage those responsible were simply ignored. Once the issue had however been published online, members of the online community rallied to the cause and attracted the interest of regional newspapers. The local authorities were ultimately forced to change their approach, and the development was interrupted until proper protocol had been observed – in that case resulting in a ruling against the developer.

By providing a library of locally relevant materials, from research reports to media articles, as well as aggregating information from burning discussion issues in topic pages and newsletters, the community platform further made it easier for participants to contribute in an informed manner. The property discussion was augmented by an accessible summary of the relevant laws and protocols by a member who was an expert in the subject. This proved to be a useful resource in subsequent cases also. Similar summaries were developed for, amongst others, coastal tourism, aqua culture and marine litter. Where a discussion touched on local issues, often there would be a reply from someone within the affected community, providing contextual information which a broader process would have missed. In the discussion relating to wood collection, it emerged that while policy targeted local communities collecting the wood for fuel, the resource was in fact being commercially exploited to supplement local income. A local stakeholder was able to give detailed account of the problem, the conflict of use, but also the complexity of organisational relationships that made the issue complex to truly resolve fairly and sustainably.

As the community grew, representing members across diverse sectors, so its potential as a space of governance deliberation grew, providing not only an audience, but also resources through its network as we have presented. However, to not gloss over limitations, the 650 dispersed members of the online community were not a sufficiently representative group to make legitimate, democratic decisions on many of the governance issues raised. To be fair, as we have described this was also not its intended purpose. For this reason then, aggregative mechanisms such as voting or polling were entirely absent from the interaction. None the less the dialogue facilitated within the community was in some cases sufficient to move along or resolve an issue – for example by involving stakeholders from previously excluded sectors, by creating awareness which then spread through related networks, or providing a member with information and social support.

This preliminary review proposes there are strong elements of direct deliberative governance to the community interaction, and broadly supports optimistic views expressed of the role of social media in literature. However, in order to more clearly account for the dynamics of interaction in terms of the principles and challenges discussed in "Theoretical Background", we investigate the online community in a more systematic manner in the following sections of analysis.

Analysis

Investigation of Acts that Contribute to the Process

As first step to investigating the range of contributions, we compiled a list of individual acts, in the context of the case platform, which might contribute to processes of governance. This was done by referring to affordances of the community web platform as well as reviewing project activity reports and previous case study material. In the introduction we referred to online participative governance driven by multiple types of action. De Cindio, Di Loreto et al. [25] similarly refer to "modes" of public participation in a socio-technical system, which proposes that participation in governance may be more diverse than purely deliberative action. If the community is analysed as a socio-technical interaction network [26], there is complex interaction between a range of actions – online and offline, from direct participation to informing others and moderating discussion, even externally orientated actions such as recruiting new members or promoting the initiative in the press. We considered the actions of various roles in the community – the agency supplying funding, the project team supporting the network, its users at different levels of engagement. The objective was to capture as much diversity as the case community offered, rather than trying to be literally complete. Each action was captured at approximately the same level of description [27, 28] in order to facilitate further analysis. The unstructured list of acts was subsequently synthesised through a series of open, "all in one" card sorts [27] Rather than setting specific criteria for the sorts, only a general framing "facet" was provided – in this instance it was to group cards in clusters of "overall similarity" in the context of types of governance action. Rugg reports this a useful method where a large number of items (42 in this case) are to be explored by a domain expert aiming to identify underlying factors.

Six groups of actions emerged after several rounds of sorting. Further reflection on the underlying factor, or organising principle to emerge from the sort suggested the groups might be characterised by "what a person might achieve with respect to their aims and values" – what might otherwise be interpreted as "level of empowerment" [29], or degrees of "agency freedom" [30]. In other words, organising the six groups of acts from relatively high levels of empowerment, to the lowest (in the context of this online community), gave the following typology:

- Animating
- Facilitating
- Filtering
- Creating
- Contributing
- Observing

We briefly discuss the acts in each group:

Animating indicates the ability to start or animate an independent initiative. This implies direct involvement in, or control over each of the other steps and also constitutes the opportunity to define a new network. The donors and key members of the project team were essentially the animators of the case project. They developed the initial project design, recruited members to the community from their own networks and provided much of the initial drive.

Facilitating refers to the process of shaping or steering the communication and actions of others. While a skilled (impartial) facilitator might e.g. attempt to ensure that everyone is given fair opportunity in discourse, this process is often strongly influenced by personal capacity and point of view, as well as a defined deliverable of the process of facilitation. The case community included discussion moderators who "seeded" conversation, posted provoking articles and were required to make judgements on inflammatory posts, or which contributions were considered "off topic". The project management functions relevant to our typology were also considered facilitating actions.

Filtering/editing actions shape or interpret the information visible to others a priori. These actions typically have influence on much larger scale than the filtering implicit in the creation of a single document. It also occurs in the background – filtering is not often exposed, or even explicitly considered in terms of its impact on shaping a governance agenda. In the case community filtering would refer to, for example, deciding what stories are reported in a newsletter, how images should be categorised in the reference library, or what constitutes a body of subject knowledge in a course.

Creating actions might have included developing subject briefings, writing a course module, or uploading documents to a central repository as group assets. This presents more than just a personal statement in an informal discussion. The act positions the creator as an expert, and contributes to community in more deliberate manner than through automated aggregation of informal actions.

Contributing actions differed from creating actions in both scope and nature – they include communicating in the online discussion groups or setting up a personal profile – in other words giving some form of input. At this level a participant potentially takes an active role in multi directional communication, much as they communicate largely in their own capacity.

Observing includes generic acts such as 'presence' and 'information seeking' – relatively passive engagement with the online resource. Also referred to as "lurkers" [31] in the context of online forums, people who mainly observe none the less contribute to the governance process: They provide an audience for those who contribute more directly, helping provide critical mass [32] and their actions further constitute an implicit vote – what they pay attention to is interpreted as important, their presence considered a measure of relevance.

While we needed to do further investigation to understand how these groups of acts might have been representative of segments of the online user community, a preliminary investigation indicated that while there were 650 "observing" members, only 163 had "contributed" by making message posts to the forum. Far fewer still, 20 depending on exact definition, had been involved explicitly in "creating" or "filtering" actions, while as few as three members had been involved in "animating" the online community itself. While absolute numbers are a matter of interpretation, there was strong indication that few users had acted at the highest level of empowerment, and that there was an overall decline in participant numbers from "observing" though the hierarchy to "animating". While this creates the further impression that initiative lay with a small relatively cohesive group, what Wenger [4] might have called the core of a community of interest, our subsequent investigation shows this would be an incorrect conclusion.

Investigation of Network Structure

To better understand the questions posed by our previous analysis, we conducted a follow on study to consider how groups of acts were expressed in terms of the social network structure of the online community. The objective was to understand how initiative was distributed and to suggest more detailed dynamics of action.

The structure of the network was derived from the community discussion system, which provided a record of all online communications archived by discussion thread. In the 42 months between October 2005 and March 2009 there were 145 "conversations" – threads with at least one reply – involving 163 unique users and 850 individual messages. Each participant was recorded as a "node" in the network diagram, and reciprocal links ("ties") recorded between all those present in any given conversation. The number of shared conversations determined the strength of the link between any two nodes. Huberman & Adamic [33] successfully used a similar approach in several studies to develop a network description based on email conversations. For the purpose of this analysis, members who did not participate in at least a two way exchange of communication were not included, as we were unable to infer their relationship to any of the active nodes.

This method developed a network model comparable to the dynamic characterisation of networked social organisation proposed by Wellman [34, 35], with ties defined by actions rather than by a description of static relations between nodes. We acknowledge that this analysis maps relations between only 163 of 650 registered users, based on only one aspect of their interaction. It does not consider relations that may have pre-existed the community, nor relations which are expressed in ways other than through online discussion – for example by users who were very active in "offline" activities of the community. Cautions considered, relevant features could none the less be discerned from the model. By being able to identify nodes as well as the content of interactions, the features that emerged could further be grounded in a detailed case history that had been developed over several years of study (Figs. 1 and 2).

The figures above show the resulting network diagram for 2 consecutive years. Squares represent "nodes" (participants) in the network, and have been scaled to reflect their degree of connectedness to make the diagram easier to read. Lines connect any nodes who have shared three or more conversations during the year. Each of the 163 nodes, or participants, were assigned an identifying number in order of them joining the community.

The two diagrams show similar characteristics of organization, but significantly share relatively few nodes – in other words, the more active participants change from 1 year to the next. One feature that is however evident in both diagrams is what network theorists refer to as a star [37] or "hub and spoke". These are characterized by a central "hub" (for example the larger nodes 6 and 8 in Fig. 1), with "spokes" connecting to other nodes who are themselves mostly not interconnected. The hub effectively mediates the connection between a number of nodes. There are by comparison no distinct groups of well connected nodes with only limited ties to the rest of the network. In other words, the network appears to consist significantly of "weak ties" [38], mediated by a few active hubs – rather than to consist of distinct, tightly interconnected subgroups bound by strong, homogenous ties. These hubs also change from 1 year to the next. This suggests a highly dynamic environment with perhaps less in common with the relatively stable models of community proposed by Wenger [4], than the loosely structured network models described by Wellman [34] and Castells [36].

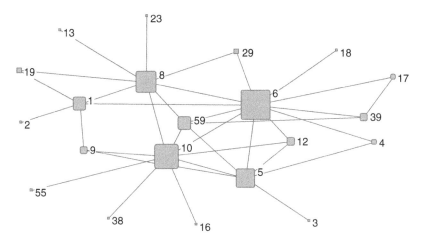

Fig. 1 Nodes connected by ≥3 relations during 2006

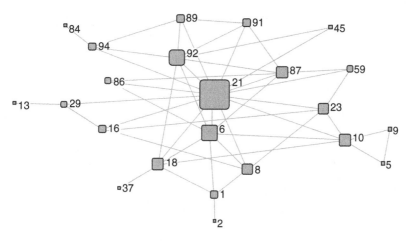

Fig. 2 Nodes connected ≥3 relations during 2007

Analysis of the discussion data indicates that while in some cases hubs were community administrators who interacted relatively frequently as part of their duty, in most cases they were normal participants. In the diagram for 2006, there are six nodes with four or more ties – three are normal participants. In 2007, of 13 nodes with four or more ties, nine are participants. The case history further indicates that most of these "participant hubs" acted in a way that was significantly embedded in a local community. They had strong personal interest in resolving or mediating specific local issues and were frequently animators in their local (offline) communities, with significant ability to facilitate or initiate action and significant "social capital" [40]. To refer back to the discussion of property development in our case description, the initial contributor temporarily became a "hub" of interaction online after using the online community to extend their reach. They however already had significant local support and were acting as informal community representative.

One possible interpretation of the turnover in hubs then relates to the issue driven nature of interaction, that participants interact as they are motivated by issues at hand, and disengage when discourse moves to topics that concern them less. This would fit the observation also that very active users, the "hubs", most frequently maintain their level of input for a year at most. In other cases interaction was however also driven by the professional role a participant occupied in the offline world – for example being employed as community development worker gave incentive to contribute broadly as a perceived civic responsibility. When their roles or situations change, participants appeared to again adapt their level of engagement. The two patterns of contribution are evident in discussion analysis also, where community activists typically make multiple contributions each to a small number of threads. In the latter case, a hub typically makes single contributions to a broad range of discussion threads.

Discussion

How the Typology of Acts Relates to Direct Deliberative Governance

The diversity of acts captured under our typology further supports the earlier claim that the online environment offered opportunity, at least in principle, for diverse forms of input to governance. Participants might deliberate an issue directly, provide emotional or technical support, signal preference or affiliation through their profile, contribute information or learning materials, simply provide an audience by being present, and so on. By contributing to the existence of the community in any substantive way, participants were effectively supporting or directing a broad process of governance. This proposes a broader view of deliberative governance, at least in this particular context, than assumed by critics who question the bias toward a single form of contribution.

In terms of the typology, the act of deliberation might be characterised as either a 'contributing' or 'creating' act, though either of these categories include other types of interaction. The broader deliberative governance process, as we have defined it a process of collective meaning making [23], encompasses all the categories of action. It is significant that the act of deliberation falls relatively low in the hierarchy of empowerment of our typology. In contrast, by creating and filtering content, a participant affords themselves greater capacity to determine "what is on the agenda" [12]. Setting up a community such as our case subject offers even more potential to have a significant impact on directing the larger discourse. This raises the question of who is empowered in this case – in terms of the principles of direct democracy, do the observed patterns of interaction violate the objectives of intrinsic equality and personal autonomy?

Progressing from observing to animating, power and the potential to influence or exert control over others increases, but we have also reported that case study data shows that

• The number of actors reduce as we ascend the hierarchy.
• And the ratio of project administrators to regular members increases.

We use the term 'administrators' to refer to members of the project team who were employed on part time basis to facilitate community affairs. It is then somewhat unsurprising that they were significantly visible in our visualisation of interactions. Their contributions were however not so much motivated by the content of governance deliberation, as to impartially facilitate and maintain the community itself in accordance with their responsibility to donors, as well as to the community members. We discuss their role and its implications in more detail in the following section.

In principle, the platform offered indiscriminate opportunity for members to act with high level of empowerment – we indicated the project further explicitly sought to solicit contribution by those who might have been discriminated against as "un-equal." In absence of coercion, the distribution of actors may simply reflect the economic reality that it requires much less effort to 'observe', than to 'facilitate' a group discussion or 'create' an article. While we have argued that these costs [19] are reduced as a result of the affordances of social media, there are costs associated with more empowered forms of action all the same. Unless a participant had good reason, they would be unlikely to engage the cost of coordinating, risking unfriendly response, associating significantly with an issue and so on. While in reality not all chose to act at highest level, or were able to make use of the affordance, one might conversely argue that the online environment provided opportunity for a significant number of people, even those who mainly contributed with their attention or presence, to behave in a way that was more significantly empowered than they might have done in its absence.

This does further raise the issue of agenda – that the goal orientation [39] of the community is potentially provided through acts at higher level in the hierarchy, so directing other contributions. While all the acts in the typology contribute to the process of deliberation, individual acts are not coordinated towards an overall goal as such. Participants respond to an issue, or in many cases narrower still, they respond to the previous contribution. This creates the assumed need for 'animators' or 'facilitators' to provide some form of overall direction – e.g. to broadly keep discussion "on topic", to stimulate new threads, and to provide supporting information. However, while the project design of our case implied goals for the community, there was no formal agenda for deliberation. Threads of discussion arose bottom up, from the issues that concerned members of the community, and were sustained only by their participation. The dynamic and interactive nature of online participation meant that the community were by no means a captive audience.

To forestall making premature conclusions – the investigation of the network structure gave further insight to the patterns of interaction.

The Network Structure

Our analysis of the network structure first remarked on its dynamism – how both dominant actors and network configuration changed year on year. We consider that the dynamic structure potentially indicates the absence of long term power dynamics within the community. We noted the absence of clusters of nodes in the network diagrams. No one person or group appeared to be significantly steering the community, rather it seemed responsive to issues as they arose. This would support for example Wellman's [35] dynamic characterization of networked social organisation, where participants act in multiple, overlapping networks each specialised to a need. In Granovetter's terms [38], the community mobilised 'weak links' to provide input or support to governance. This may be an artifact of a governance environment where, though intended action is local, the participants are geographically spread out. In other words, any network in the offline world was only very partially represented in the online network, and so members have only the relatively fleeting and limited association of individual governance issues to link to one another. This might be considered a shortcoming in terms of direct deliberative process – in that any given constituency has very limited representation in this particular environment. On the other hand, given the explicit goal for the community to act as meta-network, to develop links *between* networks, it may exactly strengthen one aspect of governance. Either way, this is a reality that must be confronted when social media is deployed in this context.

A further significant feature of network analysis was the hubs as mediators of links – that a relatively small number of people contribute the bulk of communication and have a proportionately large impact on the apparent "sharedness" of conversation. While this is certainly not unique to this instance [32], it presents a challenge in terms of the principles of direct democracy, which would expect broad ranging participation. It is somewhat mitigated by the range of acts which potentially contribute to deliberation online, we have proposed that even 'presence' has an impact on the process, but the principles of direct democracy none the less propose the imperative to design so that these contributions are made sufficiently visible. On one hand, the system has the imperative to support those who choose to strongly engage with issues, participants who may have had no access to the deliberative process in absence of the social media – on the other the needs of inclusiveness and diversity demands we encourage also the quiet voices. This highlights a challenge of deliberative democracy, where more contribution equates to increased visibility, and the potential for one person to dominate an issue. Aggregative mechanisms such as voting naturally allocate decision resources more evenly.

Acts Considered in Terms of Network Structure

If we consider a synthesis of the two stages of analysis, of acts and network structure, the network diagrams present a more diverse picture of the impetus in the community than initially imagined. Where previously the acts of hubs might have been simply aggregated to a community core, the network models show instead a distributed system of star patterns [37], a community with what appears to be multiple, temporary cores that arise from bottom up, ad hoc interactions. This might be interpreted as more fundamentally democratic – that all are considered intrinsically equal to contribute and further have the autonomy to decide what is 'on the agenda'. We have argued that the hubs might be said to act with relatively high level of agency in terms of the hierarchy we proposed. While we have presented that relatively few participants engaged at this level of activity in the online community, dismissing this as undemocratic would be a narrow view. It potentially affords a number of people the opportunity to directly contribute to governance they might otherwise have been excluded from. To refer to the theoretical introduction – we do not consider direct democracy in exclusion to other processes [8], and similarly acknowledge the role of this online community as supplementary to other online and offline networks.

Network analysis did further show that administrators play a significant role in the network – as mediators of links, as well as contributors of content. While we have chosen to interpret the role as neutral, we acknowledge the potential for such institutionalized mandate to dramatically impact the discourse, e.g.

- By steering discussion toward topics that they understood, considered sufficiently relevant and further that they were comfortable with
- By mediating interaction with potential new hubs in terms of their own views and relationships
- By implicitly presenting an "identity" of the community through their visible interaction

We do not attach normative value to these acts – their impact may variously have been positive or negative in terms of the community. The principles of democracy do however consider that such 'filtering', 'facilitating' and 'animating' actions need to represent diverse interests for equitable direct deliberative governance. While this presents a duty of care and careful consideration of the administration role, it also relates to the broader institutional arrangements that animate an online community. The socio-technical system in this case not only provided a context for stakeholder dialogue, but also a context for donors to promote a particular agenda through project design and subsequent governance arrangements. However benign, this part of the system was largely invisible to regular participants, who could not provide input to its development, nor later steer its course directly.

Conclusion

The analysis appears to support our contention that the online community, through social media, provided a context for diverse role players to engage in civic governance which in some instances met the ideals of direct deliberative governance. In sympathy with Cohen's characterization [10], it allowed participants to engage directly in local decision making, while affording inter-local comparison of solutions. Participants were afforded multiple ways of contributing to a process which did not have traditional, representative government at its centre. At the same time, it must be acknowledged that the system represented only fragments of any given constituency, and so was limited in its ability to facilitate broadly democratic processes of decision making. It arguably afforded all its participants at very least an additional channel through which to engage in governance, at best empowered a number to act with significantly increased agency.

While the discussion engaged both the principles and challenges of direct deliberative democracy outlined in the theoretical overview, the notion of power is perhaps most complex, both in its interrelation with other challenges, and how it is expressed in social interaction at multiple levels. Network analysis shows that while the case community was not dominated by closed groups of 'strong ties' [38], there were users who acted in ways that afforded them more control over the deliberative agenda than others. The hierarchy of actions implies that all forms of online contribution are not equal in their potential to impact decisions. In this sense, while the online environment potentially provides plurality, it does not fundamental overcome a key challenge of deliberative decision making when compared to aggregative mechanisms. We also touched on the notion that setting up the community itself was a form of 'animating' action, a way of steering discourse, which potentially affords its proponents a stronger position in the discourse. However, to not take a narrow view, this community is but one mechanism in the larger landscape of civic governance. Its pragmatic influence can only be evaluated in the context of how it is embedded in broader networks, where it appears to have empowered a number of community members to engage directly in decision making on local issues. This interface, between the online network and those that exist offline, is perhaps the least understood aspect of our research objective – to understand how globally or regionally distributed online networks pragmatically remediate the influence of power at the local level.

It is a shortcoming of the methodology of this study that it was largely "blind" to actions that happened beyond the online network, both in terms of how the online overlapped with networks of action in the offline world, and to understand the dynamics "behind the scenes" of the community. It also had limited capacity to explain directly how technology influences the process and balance of power – much as we had briefly touched on the notion of transaction cost [19] as a mechanism to frame this. For these reasons we propose to do a follow up study using Kling's [26] 'socio-technical interaction network' methodology. It has the advantage that it views technology not as neutral medium, but a vector of influence. It further affords the modeling of heterogeneous networks, in terms both of components and their relations, allowing a closer investigation of the questions raised by this study.

References

1. Dahl, R.: Democracy and Its Critics. Yale University Press, New Haven, CT (1991)
2. Gutmann, A., Thompson, D.F.: Why deliberative democracy? Princeton University Press, Princeton, NJ (2004)
3. Saward, M.: Less than meets the eye: Democratic legitimacy and deliberative theory. In: Saward, M. (ed.): Democratic Innovation: Deliberation, Representation and Association. Routledge, London/New York (2000), pp. 66–77
4. Wenger, E.: Communities of practice: Learning, meaning, and identity. Cambridge University Press, Cambridge (1998)
5. Isin, Engin F.: Theorizing acts of Citizenship. In: Isin, Engin F. and Nielsen, Greg M. eds. Acts of Citizenship. London, UK: Palgrave Macmillan (2008), pp. 15–43.
6. Lessig, L.: Code is Law. Basic Books, New York (2006)
7. Manin, B.: The principles of representative government. Cambridge University Press, Cambridge (1997)
8. Barber, B.R.: Strong democracy: participatory politics for a new age. University of California Press, Berkeley, CA (2004)
9. Bohman, J.: Survey Article: The Coming of Age of Deliberative Democracy. Journal of Political Philosophy 6 (1998) 400
10. Cohen, J., Sabel, C.: Directly Deliberative Polyarchy. European Law Journal 3 (1997) 313–340

11. Schumacher, E.F.: Small is Beautiful. Blond & Briggs, London (1973)
12. Lukes, S.: Power: a radical view. Macmillan, London (1974)
13. Castells, M.: Communication, Power and Counter-power in the Network Society. International Journal of Communication **1** (2007) 238–266
14. Willcocks, L.P.: Foucault, Power/Knowledge and Information Systems: reconstructing the present. In: Mingers, J., Willcocks, L.P. (eds.): Social theory and philosophy for Information Systems. Wiley, Chichester (2004), pp. 238–296
15. Klein, H.K., Huynh, Q.H.: The critical social theory of Jürgen Habermas and its implications for IS research. In: Mingers, J., Willcocks, L.P. (eds.): Social Theory and Philosophy for Information Systems. Wiley, Chichester (2004), pp. 157–237
16. Saward, M.: The Representative Claim. Contemporary Political Theory **5** (2006) 297–318
17. Shirky, C.: Here comes everybody. Penguin Books, London (2008)
18. Benkler, Y.: Coase's Penguin, or, Linux and "The Nature of the Firm". The Yale Law Journal **112** (2002) 369–446
19. Cordella, A.: Transaction costs and information systems: does IT add up? Journal of Information Technology **21** (2006) 195–202
20. Buckingham Shum, S., Okada, A.: Knowledge Cartography for Open Sensemaking Communities. Journal of Interactive Media in Education **10** (2008)
21. Riegelsberger, J., Sasse, M.A., McCarthy, J.D.: The mechanics of trust: A framework for research and design. International Journal of Human-Computer Studies **62** (2005) 381–422
22. Mejias, U.: The tyranny of nodes: Towards a critique of social network theories. Vol. 2009 (2006)
23. Deuze, M.: Participation, Remediation, Bricolage: COnsidering principal components of a digital culture. The Information Society **22** (2006) 63–75
24. Hindman, M.: The Myth of Digital Democracy. Princeton University Press, Princeton, NJ (2008)
25. De Cindio, F., Di Loreto, I., Peraboni, C.A.: Moments and Modes for Triggering Civic Participation at the Urban Level. In: Foth, M. (ed.): Handbook of research on urban informatics: the practice and promise of the real-time city. Information Science Reference, IGI Global, Hershey, PA (2008), pp. 97–114
26. Kling, R., McKim, G., King, A.: A Bit More to It: Scholarly Communication Forums as Socio-Technical Interaction Networks. Journal of the American Society for Information Science & Technology **54** (2003) 47–67
27. Rugg, G., McGeorge, P.: The sorting techniques: a tutorial paper on card sorts, picture sorts and item sorts. Expert Systems **14** (1997) 80–93
28. Upchurch, L., Rugg, G., Kitchenham, B.: Using card sorts to elicit web page quality attributes. IEEE Software **18** (2001) 84–89
29. Zimmerman, M.A.: Psychological empowerment: Issues and illustrations. American Journal of Community Psychology **23** (1995) 581–599
30. Barnbeck, S.: Freedom and Capacity: Implications of Sen's Capability Approach. Rerum Causae **1** (2006), pp. 10–16.
31. Preece, J., Abras, C., Maloney-Krichmar, D.: Designing and evaluating online communities: research speaks to emerging practice. International Journal of Web Based Communities **1** (2004) 2–18
32. Butler, B.S.: Membership size, communication activity, and sustainability: A resource-based model of online social structures. Information Systems Research **12** (2001) 346–362
33. Huberman, B., Adamic, L.: Information Dynamics in the Networked World. Working Papers. HP Laboratories, Palo Alto (2005)
34. Wellman, B.: Community: from neighborhood to network. Commun. ACM **48** (2005) 53–55
35. Wellman, B.: Little boxes, glocalization, and networked individualism. Springer, Berlin, Germany (2002) pp. 10–25
36. Castells, M.: Toward a Sociology of the Network Society. Contemporary Sociology **29** (2000) 693–699
37. Freeman, L.C.: Centrality in social networks conceptual clarification. Social Networks **1** (1978) 215–239

38. Granovetter, M.S.: The Strength of Weak Ties. The American Journal of Sociology **78** (1973) 1360–1380
39. Ciborra, C., Olson, M.H.: Encountering electronic work groups: a transaction costs perspective. Proceedings of the 1988 ACM conference on Computer-supported cooperative work. ACM, Portland, Oregon, United States (1988)
40. Coleman, J.: Social capital in the creation of human capital. In: Dasgupta, P. (ed.): Social capital: a multi faceted perspective. The international bank for reconstruction, Washington, DC (2000), pp. 13–39

How Creative Groups Structure Tasks Through Negotiating Resources

Christopher Paul Middup, Tim Coughlan, and Peter Johnson

Abstract Creative collaborations are a complex, yet common phenomenon. In this paper we introduce a model that describes the development of a creative outcome by a group, based on its efforts to structure the task through the exploration and adoption of concepts and artefacts. We use our model as a basis to analyse a collaborative filmmaking study. Through this, we show how the model is an effective tool for describing the actions of the group as its members work towards producing an outcome. We conclude that the model could be utilised as a tool for recognising patterns in creative collaborations, for understanding support needs, and for comparing instances of these tasks.

Introduction

This paper describes a model of the development towards an outcome in creative collaborations, through the exploration and adoption of artefacts that add structure, bounding the space of possible actions. This can be utilized as a method for understanding and comparing the nature of instances of a creative task. In this paper we define the model, and apply it to the analysis of instances of creative collaboration, in which two separate groups devised and produced short films.

The model focuses on the introduction, adoption and dismissal of resources by creative groups, which structures the path towards producing a creative outcome. In the development of this structure, a spectrum of types of resources exists: From tangible artefacts such as physical objects or software tools, that enforce processes, structure and direction on the group, to adopted concepts such as goals that lack definition or shared understanding. The model presented here reflects the effects of

C.P. Middup (✉), T. Coughlan, and P. Johnson
HCI Group, Department of Computer Science, University of Bath, Bath, BA2 7AY, UK
e-mail: c.p.middup@bath.ac.uk; t.coughlan@bath.ac.uk; p.johnson@bath.ac.uk

M. Lewkowicz et al. (eds.), *Proceedings of COOP 2010*,
DOI 10.1007/978-1-84996-211-7_12, © Springer-Verlag London Limited 2010

the characteristics of these resources on a group's creative process. This includes the need to explore the possibilities inherent in tangible artefacts, to develop shared understanding of novel concepts, and to connect the two together to produce creative outcomes that are both feasible and in line with goals.

In this paper we use the model to analyse examples of interaction with these artefacts in the instances of the filmmaking study, and how this affects the progression of the groups towards an outcome (in this case a short film). Through these examples we discuss how the model provides a useful means to consider how artefacts relate to the effectiveness and efficiency of the group, and how the model can be useful in understanding support needs for group creativity, both in terms of the structuring effects of providing specific artefacts, and the structuring processes that occur within creative groups.

Background

Researchers including Boden [2] and Schön [15] have described creative tasks as inherently ill structured, with no single, clear path to producing an outcome, as they aim at a combination of novelty and value [4]. Sawyer [14] argues that collaboration in creative tasks is common, as complex creative outcomes often require, or are improved by, the knowledge, skills and labour of more than one person. Creative collaborations therefore represent a complex but important phenomena, for which an ability to model and understand the processes involved would be valuable across a range of disciplines and purposes.

Rittel and Webber [12] describe these unique and ill-structured tasks as *wicked problems*. According to Ritchey [11], two of the criteria for wicked problems are that they have no definite formulation and that they have no stopping rules. The absence of a definite formulation of the task and its solution means that the perceived steps for the task at any given stage are tied to the current understanding of the solution; in order to fully formulate the problem, all possible solutions for it would need to be known at the outset.

The absence of stopping rules does not imply that projects involving wicked problems never reach a conclusion. What it does mean is that the best or most complete solution for a problem can never be said to have been met. With creative tasks this is particularly true, as any solution will have an element of novelty that cannot be compared directly with possible alternatives.

Central to the completion of ill-structured tasks is the adoption or development of a structure that affords and constrains the space of possible actions. Stokes [17] describes creativity as requiring strategies for the adoption of constraints that provide a structure through which a goal can be defined and creative outcomes can be progressed towards.

Progression towards an outcome in a creative task is rarely linear: Perez y Perez and Sharples [10] find that distinct phases could be identified in creative writing processes of engagement in the production of ideas, and reflection on the structures that constrain engagement. Similarly, Baer [1] and Gabora [5] explore how creativity involves periods of both divergent and convergent thinking, related to explorative and analytical modes of thought. The exploration of concepts and artefacts that may lead to novel ideas is balanced by the evaluation of concepts and artefacts that are considered for adoption. Whilst these processes have been identified and studied with respect to individuals, they are poorly understood with respect to creative groups. Whilst collaboration brings added complexity, it is essential to many creative tasks [14].

The characteristics of the various forms of structure affect the progress of the creative collaboration in different ways. The structures we consider range from tangible tools and artefacts that enforce behaviour, affording and bounding the space of possible actions, or novel, ill-defined concepts that the group develop as a basis for producing novel solutions. Norman [9] argues that the *perceived affordances* of objects are essential to how they are used. These artefacts, when adopted by a creative group, add a tangible structure, supporting a set of actions that can be performed. In contrast, Sarmiento and Stahl [13] develop Sawyer's argument that *indexicals* play a central role in creative groups – that is the shared development of symbols representative of novel concepts. These concepts form a structure of abstract goals, constraints and methods through which concrete ideas can be discussed, produced and evaluated.

Central to the understanding presented in this paper is the logic that creative collaborations negotiate the adoption and development of these various forms of structure, in response to the ill-structured nature of the tasks they undertake. Our previous work has considered both how the adoption of artefacts is negotiated [8] and how collaborators develop individual and shared structures in a software environment [3]. We have found evidence that supporting the shared end-user development of interfaces can aid co-ordination and negotiation by creative groups. In this paper we relate these pieces of work together, building a theoretical model that could inform both systems development, and the evaluation of instances of group tasks, by highlighting differences in group performance and process.

Issues with Creative Task Completion

Creative group tasks require a number of people to collaborate in a way that leads to a satisfactory outcome. Because creative tasks do not begin with a clear structure, the outcome of the task is unlikely to be obvious to the group members at the start of the task. They are likely to have some general conception of what this outcome may be – some of which is held only by individuals, some of which may be shared – but a collaborative process needs to be pursued so that the gaps in this conception can be filled.

Two types of structure that are routinely introduced by group members in order to make progress in collaborative tasks are concepts and tangible artefacts. In this paper we use the term *concept* to represent mental constructs and ungrounded ideas that group members introduce in the building of their conception of the outcome, and the term *tangible artefact* to represent things that have defined affordances, such as physical objects and software.

The introduction of new concepts into a group enables them to make steps that could lead towards a better understanding of and/or solution to the task. By contrast, the introduction of tangible artefacts could lead towards the implementation of those steps, also enabling progress towards the task solution. In this paper we suggest that the balance between these two approaches is important in maintaining effective task progress. This balance can be lost in two ways: Firstly, the generation of too many ungrounded concepts can leave the group with too much malleability in their ideas. Secondly, the introduction of too many tangible artefacts, or inappropriate ones, can leave the group poorly constrained and unable to produce an effective outcome.

In the development or deployment of technological support for creative collaborations, tangible artefacts – or means through which to find or develop these – need to be provided in order that groups can produce an outcome. It is also likely that functionality for mediating the introduction and negotiation of concepts by the group will be needed, such as shared representations or communication channels. The rest of this section elaborates on concepts that can be used to understand these needs in instances of creative collaboration. Firstly, the notions of *efficiency* and *effectiveness* are considered as measures of the success of creative groups. The notion of a *conception of the outcome* is then discussed, followed by the introduction of two important phenomena that occur in the process of creative collaborations: *concept mismatches* and *artefact mismatches*.

Efficiency and Effectiveness

The notion of *success* in a creative group is complex and multi-faceted, but it is important to define some aspects of this as a basis for understanding what groups are attempting to achieve.

We define *efficient* group collaboration as all group members doing what is required by the group to complete the task in the most expedient way at any given time. In complex or unstructured problem-solving tasks, determining whether someone, or the group as a whole, is performing an activity that will ultimately be relevant to the production of the outcome is difficult. It may be that on reviewing a project after it is completed, a group would not do many of the activities that they undertook along the way, or perhaps they would do them differently, or in a different order. However, that does not necessarily mean that a group, or its members, was not being efficient at the time. In many cases, such activities are necessary to make the group decide how not to proceed, leading to structure that further defines a conception of the outcome.

It is necessary to make the distinction between achievable efficiency and optimal efficiency. An achievable efficiency for a person is if someone is making the maximum use of their knowledge and capabilities, even if they are less optimal than they could be with practice, or even if they are less than somebody else's capabilities. An achievable efficiency within a group is slightly more complex, as it is also affected by the differing capabilities of its members, i.e. the most capable person for an activity within a group must be the one attempting it for the group to be efficient (although it is important to note that capability to attempt an activity includes availability, so if the most able person for an activity is not available, then they do not have the capability to attempt it). By comparison, an optimal efficiency is a theoretical 'best attempt' at a task, in which the best-known people were attempting the task in the best-known way. With even the slightest complexity or novelty in a task, the optimal efficiency will not be understood until after the task has been completed, and perhaps not even then.

If the collaborative effort of a group has been *effective*, then to an outside observer the outcome of the task would be judged to be a success. Therefore, a measure of the effectiveness of group collaboration has to be a measure of the quality of the group's output. González et al. [6] describe 'group effectiveness' as the aggregation to group level of the effect of the group's members' behavioural performances or actions; when these behavioural performances or actions all relate to a specific collaborative task, then this is a good definition for *effective group collaboration*.

As with efficiency, there has to be some distinction made between an achievable level of effectiveness within the group and an optimal level of effectiveness with respect to the task. A group would meet an achievable level of effectiveness if it were possible to answer in the affirmative *has this group achieved the best solution it was capable of for this task?* Whereas, the group would have reached the optimal level of effectiveness if it were possible to answer in the affirmative *is this the best possible solution for this task?* Sundstrom et al. [18] make the link between group development and effectiveness, suggesting that the group's capability to be effective increases as it builds through the phases of development; also supported is the argument that this capability for effectiveness increases because during a group's development they need to allocate less time to teamwork activities and can therefore spend more on taskwork activities.

Another way of looking at group effectiveness is to apply Simon's [16] rule of *satisficing*. In this case, instead of looking for the best possible solution for a task, either with or without respect to the group's members' capabilities, a satisficing solution would answer *is this a good enough solution for the task set?* To answer this, the assessor would have to understand the requirements of any sponsors of the task, rather than those of the group members contributing to the solution.

In creative group collaborations efficiency and effectiveness are important measures of the group's success, so understanding the patterns of creative collaboration that occur when groups of people work towards a shared goal is important when looking for ways to better support the process.

Conception of the Outcome

A group collaborating on a creative task move from an initial conception of the outcome, to a more refined conception as they work towards their goal, to a realised outcome when the task is completed. Initial conceptions of the outcome are likely to differ across the individuals in a group. A shared conception is developed through the actions that occur when the group works together. These actions, such as externalising and evaluating ideas or concepts, or exploring the use of tangible artefacts, can constitute progress towards the goal, or alternatively lead to a realisation that their previous conception of the outcome was inadequate or unachievable through adopted tangible artefacts.

The conceptual space in which the outcome could exist can therefore *shrink* in response to the actions performed, and the conception of the outcome held by group members also *shifts*, in response to negotiation and the improved understanding of the task built through the actions of group members.

Concept Mismatch

We use the term *concept mismatch* to describe a point where the group has too much malleability in its work to be effective. This occurs through a build-up of concepts that are not grounded in the tangible artefacts that can be applied to the task, or are incompatible with each other. Without grounding the group loses the focus that is necessary in order to make progress towards some sort of task outcome.

When a concept mismatch occurs in creative group work, there are two possible ways that this can be rectified. The first of these is for the group to choose some of their shared concepts and begin to apply them by negotiating the use of tangible artefacts that can apply or instantiate the concepts. Instantiation of a concept might involve selecting a technology that can be used to produce a concrete idea that reflects the concept, but equally it could be something as simple as one of the group members detailing this idea more explicitly with pen and paper.

The second way that a concept mismatch can be rectified is for the group to agree that their understanding of the final outcome has changed to something less constrained. In these situations, realigning the new understanding of the task outcome to the current level of malleability allows the group to proceed without grounding their concepts further. The result of this choice is that either they will go through another realignment process later to direct themselves towards a more structured outcome, or they will achieve a final outcome that is not well structured. The nature of an individual task will determine which of these is most appropriate for any given task.

Artefact Mismatch

We use the term *artefact mismatch* to describe a point where the group is too constrained by its chosen artefacts to be effective. This occurs when the artefacts that the group has chosen (or those that it has to use because of external direction) forces the group to work in a particular way that no longer allows it to achieve its current conception of the outcome.

In a similar way to the concept mismatch, there are two ways that an artefact mismatch can be rectified. The first of these is for the group to develop their use of their chosen artefacts. This may occur through exploration of tangible artefacts that leads to the discovery of further functionality, or by introducing new concepts that support the artefact's use.

The second way that an artefact mismatch can be rectified is for the group to agree that their conception of the final outcome has changed to something more constrained. In these situations, the group members will come to the conclusion that what they can achieve with the artefacts that they have is an acceptable solution for the task and agree a new goal that is based upon these constraints.

Directing a Shared Creative Task

If we use compass points to describe the progress made through a task, then it is possible to say that the start point is in the west and some form of optimal solution for that task is a straight line to a completion point due east of the start. The movement from the start point to the outcome represents a notion of task progress, the rate of which could be considered as the groups' efficiency. If all the movement is directly from the start to the outcome, then all of the group members' work has a direct and positive influence on the completion of their task. This would therefore represent a very trivial task, where the outcome and the steps required to achieving that outcome are well defined. Figure 1 illustrates such a task, showing that when all activities performed in the pursuit of a task achieve movement towards the desired outcome, this can be represented as linear task progress.

Lacking a specified structure for their completion at the outset, non-trivial tasks are less deterministic, and require elements of trial-and-error, learning and failure to achieve an outcome. Progression is not linear, as some activities do not achieve movement towards the outcome. Therefore, extending the compass metaphor, we can assert that any movement east of the start point is *progression* towards the completed goal; any movement west towards the start point is *regression* away from the completed goal; and so, any movement north or south represents a *digression* from this west-east optimal line.

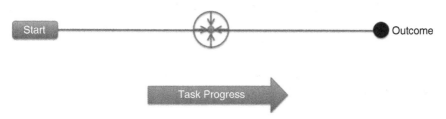

Fig. 1 Representation of a trivial task

As discussed in "Issues with Creative Task Completion", one perspective on the development of structure is the need for the group to balance and relate their use of concepts with their use of tangible artefacts. The introduction of either concepts or tangible artefacts into the group can be seen as a digression from the work towards task completion; it is only when they are accepted by the group as purposeful to the task in some way that they begin to contribute towards task progress. Therefore we have two types of digression: *concept digression* and *artefact digression*, caused by the introduction of concepts and tangible artefacts respectively.

Figure 2 shows how progression, regression and digression are forces that move the current state of a task around this plane. Progression is a force that moves the task towards an outcome; regression is a force that moves the task away from an outcome; and digressions over artefacts or concepts alter what the potential outcome might be.

As group members collaborate on a creative task, they generate forces that push the task in different directions, causing different combinations of progression, regression and digression to occur. Individual group members introduce all the concepts or artefacts used by the group, so these individuals generate the forces that cause digression. By comparison, the overall group reaction to the introduction of these concepts or artefacts determines whether they are adopted and lead to task progress, are rejected without them having any effect on the task, or whether they lead to a rethink over work completed so far, which can be seen as a regression from previous progress towards an outcome.

An individual who introduces a concept or artefact becomes its *sponsor* and they negotiate with the other group members to determine its purpose within the context of the task. This process of negotiation then determines the degree – if any – of task progress. Initially in a complex or ill-structured task there is a high degree of freedom over what is an acceptable final outcome, which means that the chance of concept or artefact mismatches occurring is lower in the initial stages of a task; as the understanding of the task's requirements becomes clearer to the group this freedom is reduced, meaning that the introduction of further concepts or artefacts is more likely to lead to a situation where these resources are mismatched to the perceived outcome.

In contrast to Fig. 1, Fig. 3 represents an example path between starting a task and its final outcome in a creative task. The start point and final outcome are not on a direct east-west line, such as that illustrated in Fig. 1, representing that the

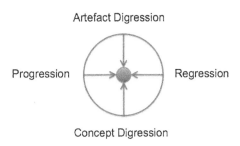

Fig. 2 Forces acting on the task

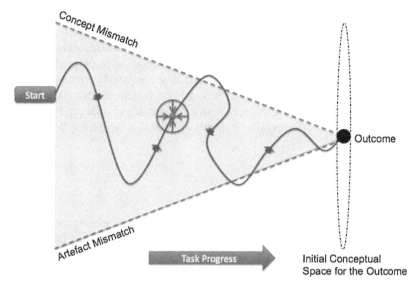

Fig. 3 Representation of a collaborative creative task

original conceptions of the outcome held by individuals at the start of the task have been modified and defined by the activities that have led to its completion by the group. Figure 3 also illustrates how the valid space for avoiding mismatches narrows as progress is made towards task completion.

A Study of Group Creativity

In the following sections we describe the filmmaking study, and then analyse vignettes that exemplify the progress of each group, using the model presented above. Three excerpts are taken from each group's process of completing the task, showing their chronological work towards the outcome and the characteristics of this at each stage through diagrams representing their path, and descriptions using the concepts presented.

Method

Two groups of four people took part in a creative task to produce one or more promotional videos to improve environmental awareness around a university campus. The groups were independent of each other and did not work concurrently. They were encouraged to have as many co-located meetings as necessary in order to complete this task within a 3-week timeframe.

The groups were provided with technologies that were expected to aid them in completing the task. This included a large touch screen display attached to a PC in the meeting room, and HP iPaq Smartphones for each individual. Video recording equipment was made available to the groups, but in the first instance the group used one of the member's own video camera, and in the second case combined clips recorded using the Smartphones. The groups were given assistance to transfer materials from the Smartphones on to the PC in the meeting room at the start of each meeting, but were told that they could use any other tools or artefacts they wished in completing the tasks.

Analysis of Group 1

Group 1 met four times over the 3-week period, including the opening meeting when the task was explained to them and a final meeting when they created their video to promote environmental consideration on campus. They envisaged a single 90-s video clip to be shown around campus and targeted making a production-quality version of this video, using a mixture of their own film and publicly available clips.

In Vignette 1, Group 1 are at an early stage in completing the task. They are involved in concept digression, leading to an artefact mismatch. This begins with A introducing ideas for the video that are supported by C. However, B reminds them that they have adopted the Movie Maker editing software, and the constraints

---

Vignette 1: Taken from Meeting 2 of Group 1

Group members discuss conceptual ideas, how they could be implemented, and the affordances of editing software in relation to these ideas. A has produced several concepts, including speeding up the film, that will require suitable technologies to perform. C is supportive of these ideas until B highlights that the software he was expecting to adopt is unlikely to be able to perform these functions.

A: So for reuse *(one of the adopted thematic concepts)* … the movie takes someone through the process of making paper, but funny, maybe Benny Hill-esq… We could intersperse ourselves with footage we can get… and so it could maybe be kind of speeded up as well."

C: "Yeah definitely"

A: "Cos it need to be short, and that would make it entertaining if it was sped up"…

B: "Windows Movie Maker, I've not found a way that it can speed up, or slow down, or reverse or anything like that… My theory would be that if we can come up with something without needing any gimmicky kind of effects, other than some editing, it would probably be better…

C: Yeah I mean, that's an idea, if it's easy we do it, if not… whatever.

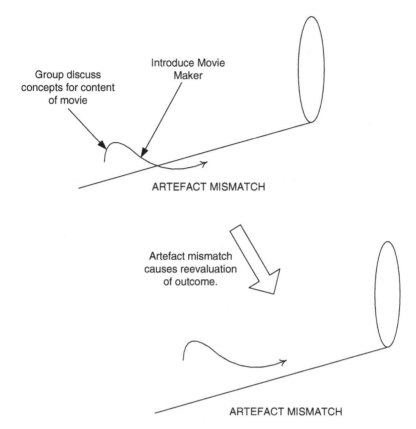

Group discuss concepts for content of movie

Introduce Movie Maker

ARTEFACT MISMATCH

Artefact mismatch causes reevaluation of outcome.

ARTEFACT MISMATCH

Fig. 4 Model representation of vignette 1

on this artefact means that they have a mismatch between their artefacts and their conception of the outcome at this stage of the task. The group members have a choice between changing their adopted artefacts to match their conception of outcome, or shifting their conception of the outcome to match the chosen artefacts. In this case, they choose the latter option and so Movie Maker remains within the group as before, but with the new understanding that whatever it does will be twisted to satisfy the task outcome.

Figure 4 represents this activity by showing an overall curve towards an outcome, shaped by digressions as group members introduce concepts and artefacts. The artefact mismatch boundary is crossed when we observe that the group has to re-evaluate its perceived outcome. In terms of providing technological support to creative groups, identification of points of transgression, such as this artefact mismatch, and instances where concept mismatches occur, could show where intervention is necessary in similar tasks so that the overall task work is either more efficient, more effective, or both. In this case, it would have been possible to improve the *efficiency*

Vignette 2: Taken from Meeting 2 of Group 1

The use of sound in the film is discussed, as C is interested in presenting some facts and advice to viewers. B and A are interested in how this may be done, and suggest the possibility of reading the facts out audibly. C then suggests that sound may not always be audible, and the group adopt the concept that the sound used in the film will only be complementary. C is explaining some of the advice he feels the film should get across.

B: How do you want to do that? I mean do you just want someone reading out these facts or some pictures...

C: No I have to admit I haven't worked on that.

A: I would think it could be pictures and then you reading the facts, which relate to the pictures...

C: Umm, I'm thinking if that is to be played in the Parade (*a bar*) or in the public streets, maybe sound is not an option.

A: That's true.

C: Or maybe we should have sound only as a complementary channel, and we should have the facts bring it out. So we have a quote displayed. You can have voice on top, but not dependent on it.

A: Yeah true.

C: We can have sketches that are without dialogue, and have some nice music on top, if its not being played its not necessary.

---

of the collaboration by constraining them to using Movie Maker from the outset of the task, as it would have restricted their discussions on content to only those things that are supported by Movie Maker. How the group's *effectiveness* would be affected by this intervention is less certain; the same artefact would ultimately shape the outcome, but the creative freedom that would be lost in the early phases of the task, although inefficient, may be necessary to help develop a 'better' solution. By not enforcing a choice of editing software during this study, the groups could consider a much wider space of initial possibilities and constrain themselves.

By the time this second meeting occurs, the group members have all completed some individual work on the task, based on activities identified in their first meeting. Vignette 2 represents a common pattern for this type of meeting, where ideas that have been formed by an individual prior to the meeting are introduced as concepts to the group, which are then discussed, modified and ultimately either accepted or rejected as the group members collaborate on these aspects of the task.

Figure 5 shows a representation of this vignette using the model. This particular vignette represents concept digression leading to progression, as the concept of making something that does not need to rely on sound is introduced by an individual and adopted by the group. Some narrowing and shifting of the space in which the outcome can fit also occurs, as the group have agreed to communicate their message visually. If the group members had been unable to agree on how to proceed, then the

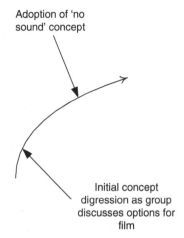

Adoption of 'no sound' concept

Initial concept digression as group discusses options for film

Fig. 5 Model representation of vignette 2

Vignette 3: Taken from Meeting 3 of Group 1

One of the group members – C – copies a video clip that he has prepared onto the desktop computer. It is suggested that he starts the meeting by showing this to the group. As the group members watch the video clip, they ask questions and offer suggestions on how C could develop this idea further.

A – Maybe C should start, cos you're doing the first bit

C – Yeah. *He takes the desktop mouse and starts the clip.*

They all watch the video for a few seconds, then B asks:

B – Do you have sound on this one?

C – No

B – Ok

They watch the remainder of the clip in silence; at the end, the discussion of it begins again.

D – That's good/A- Yes, very nice

B – I think we need a bit longer for the messages

A – I think the messages are ok, if it's playing on a loop

B – Some of them I didn't have time to read

A – I think we should … well *(he looks at C)* have you got any music to go with it?

C – No, I haven't

---

group could be described as regressing away from an outcome to their task, and this would be represented by the curve turning back away from the outcome.

In Vignette 3, the introduction of the video clip is an artefact digression that has arisen as a result of the introduction of concepts in a previous meeting. As he plays the video to other members of the group, this begins a negotiation process that will

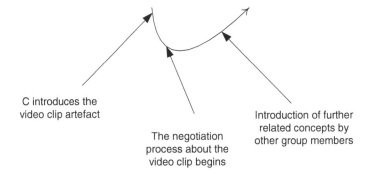

C introduces the
video clip artefact

The negotiation
process about the
video clip begins

Introduction of further
related concepts by
other group members

Fig. 6 Model representation of vignette 3

ultimately determine whether the artefact is adopted or rejected; whichever of these outcomes occurs, the group's shared understanding of the artefact will necessarily change as a result of the negotiation.

The negotiation process also adds a force to the group work that joins the artefact to some element of task progress. Depending upon how the negotiation develops, this may result in some form of progression or regression, towards or away from the solution, as well as digression. In this case, the video clip is received positively by the group, although there are some queries about whether there should be sound with the clip and whether some inserted messages were too quick to be read.

This process is represented in Fig. 6 as a strong digression initially as the concept is presented to the other group members. The curve then softens towards greater progress as the other group members become involved, before moving back towards concept digression as other group members begin to introduce related concepts. This illustrates what could be argued as one potential template for representing a useful level of achievable efficiency, whereby the negotiation process between the group members links the benefits of conceptual understanding with tangible artefacts to achieve overall task progress.

Analysis of Group 2

Group 2 met five times over an equivalent 3-week period, which were used for similar purposes to Group 1, but had two distinctions: first, in the third and fifth meetings, only two of the four group members were present – in both instances the two absentees were the same people; second, Group 2 needed two meetings (their fourth and fifth) to create their output for the task. Their interpretation of the task was slightly different to group 1: They envisaged a much grander set of 20 short videos to be played around campus, spoofing famous film roles, such as James Bond and Indiana Jones. However, they only aimed to use these meetings to create a few prototype videos to illustrate the environmental messages that they had scripted. This shows how the ill-structured nature of the same creative task leads to the adoption of different structures in each instance.

This shows early conceptual digression in a wide space of possibilities, which at the end of the vignette is found to be proceeding away from a suitable conception of what the outcome should be (it shouldn't irritate people). It is similar to Vignette 2 where Group 1 discusses the use of sound, although the outcome is different (showing that the problem space of the task is open to various solutions).

As the animal and noise concept is ultimately rejected, the progress that seemed to have been made is reversed, however the actions of the group are not without value – they have aided definition of the group's conception of the outcome, which has now been reduced in scope to disregard ideas that might irritate people through inappropriate use of sounds in a public space. Their conception now does include (and focuses on) possibilities for reminders that grab the attention of passers by, encouraging them to recycle.

Vignette 4: Taken from Meeting 1 of Group 2

The group are generating and discussing ideas for their film. The concept that the film is to be a reminder to people to recycle is suggested by A, and elaborated by A and B. A further concept of using animals is suggested, then – due to questioning from C – is elaborated to be animal noises that grab attention by A and B. D then interjects, noting that these noises may be irritating when in a public place.

A: Perhaps the film is just a reminder, I just forget to do it *(recycling)*

B: So you are talking about someone passing by?

A: Talking about someone passing by, I quite like this idea of reminders as you pass by.

B: OK you pass by and you see something, a message, just saying LOOK! This is the recycle bin...

A: Well I think the silly animal trick is quite funny sometimes...

C: How does that go?

B: Noise?

A: Well you just have an animal

B: Oh I see, you just have an animal... it grabs attention

A: you have that... people like animals it grabs attention.

C: So a cow?

A: Ducks... 'What's that duck doing there?'

B: OK that's interesting, you hear the sound of an animal, but it has nothing to do with animals. You hear the animal then you look at the screen and...

A: Its just a thought, it's a trick, you see it a lot in adverts on the tele*(vision)*.

D: Yeah, it's a good idea but if we're putting it somewhere where a lot of people are walking past...

A: It this going to make them fed up.

D: Its going to make them crazy...

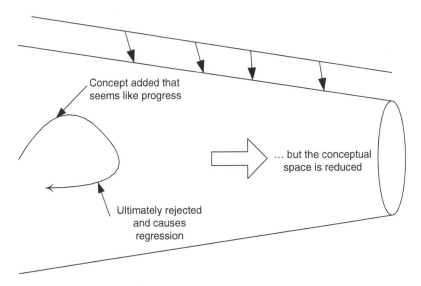

Fig. 7 Model representation of vignette 4

Later the group adopts a modified version of this idea, using film characters rather than animals, which would be less likely to "make them *(passers by)* fed up". This fitted better with their conception of the outcome – reminding people to recycle in a public space – but still contained much of the essence of the ideas presented here.

Figure 7 illustrates how this can be represented by the progress trail turning back on itself, showing that task progress has turned to regression and therefore the group ultimately are no nearer an outcome for their task. At the same time, it illustrates how the conceptual space for acceptable outcomes has been reduced through the negotiation process.

This instance demonstrates how support for creative collaborative tasks must take into consideration the tension between support for *effective* collaborations and support for *efficient* collaborations. In this case, an intervention could have been made to reduce the conceptual space earlier. If this were to be done, then the group's activity would be more efficient as their activities would be slightly more deterministic; however, reducing this space reduces the range of potential solutions, meaning that unless care is taken to understand the space in which effective outcomes exist, the group could be prevented from devising and producing the most effective outcome to their task.

Vignette 5 represents an artefact mismatch – the lack of a camera to film with, which is resolved by C suggesting the adoption of a new artefact to perform the filming. D agrees with C's adoption. The simplicity of the identification and rectification of this problem is due to the structure the group have adopted through their previous actions. The group had intended to film, and knew that they needed a camera to do this. Although A thought that the group would not film in the rain, C wants to follow this existing concept rather than change direction. As they have

Vignette 5: Taken from Meeting 4 of Group 2

The group have met with the intention of filming footage based on their ideas. A was expected to bring a camera but due to bad weather assumed it would not be needed. C suggests that filming is still possible and that a Smartphone (referred to as PDA by the group) can be used to record, the adoption of which is supported by D.

A – I've brought a bottle

A – 'My camera's in the car. I thought with this rain we wouldn't be bothering with much.'

C – 'we can film in the rain.'

B – 'Well, er, T just said...'

A – 'The camera's in the car'

C – 'We can film with the PDA'

D – 'Yeah, we can film with the PDA'

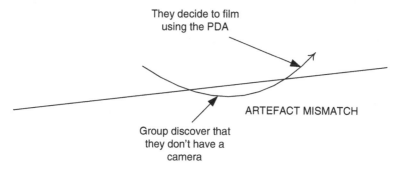

Fig. 8 Model representation of vignette 5

previously identified that the Smartphone could produce film, the rectification of the artefact mismatch is simple.

Figure 8 illustrates that in this instance the mismatch boundary remains the same. This means that the group has chosen to stay on track with their previously envisaged conception of the outcome, which at this stage remains broad, and modify how they will achieve it by introducing new concepts that are suitable to this outcome.

This shows how much more structured the activity has become by the time the group actually decide to produce the film. Concepts (shared understanding of the film idea, and that they are going to film footage now using the Smartphone) and artefacts (script, Smartphone as a camera) are in place, allowing A and B to define and share a detailed understanding of what will occur in filming.

Figure 9 illustrates that once the task (or part of it that is currently being undertaken) is well understood by the group, then it becomes trivial and can be represented in the same way as the abstract case shown in Fig. 1.

Vignette 6: Taken from Meeting 4 of Group 2

The group are getting ready to film a scene. B and A are looking at the produced script and checking that they share the same understanding of what will occur. A is to act the part of James Bond in the scene, so practises some of the required actions with B watching.

B – *(checking script with A)* So, is that ok?

A – Err.... *(he pauses)*

B – So what are you doing? Camera's there *(he gestures to an imaginary location)* You come in ... I mean, you have the bottle there. You come in. You recycle it.

A – Look at the camera...

B – and then, you turn to the camera *(he starts making gestures of adjusting an imaginary bow tie)*

A – ...and walk off

B – Bow tie, hair and you go out.

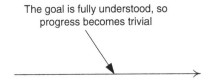

The goal is fully understood, so
progress becomes trivial

Fig. 9 Model representation of vignette 6

Conclusions

This paper has presented a theoretical model that describes the structuring of creative tasks undertaken by collaborative groups. In its current form, this can be valuable to the deployment of technologies to support collaborative creativity, by providing a basis with which to consider how providing tangible structures such as software environments will impact on the groups' efficiency and effectiveness. Perhaps more importantly, the model can aid in the development of technologies by describing the processes through which groups' members themselves need to develop structure in a task. This could be applied in the design of novel systems that support collaborative types of end-user development [7], or that support the shared development of novel concepts [13]. The model shows how both of these types of system could aid creative collaboration processes.

The model presented in this paper can be used to describe and analyse complex task progression in two ways. First, it provides a means of describing individual events in a collaborative activity and illustrating the effect of those events on the overall task progress. Second, it provides a means of joining these events to describe the collaborative task over its duration, thereby identifying more long-term patterns of task progress.

In future work, we expect to be able to identify particular recurring patterns that have consistent effects on the progress made in complex collaborative tasks. From descriptions of these patterns and their effects on the process of creative collaboration, design heuristics could be developed which would extend this model towards a useful prescriptive design tool for creative groupware. Of further interest would be the introduction of this model to participants involved in retrospection on tasks, to explore how they would describe their structuring behaviours and subjective experiences. The model could also be used for the comparative analysis of instances of collaborative creativity, providing scope to analyse the effects of interventions or variations between these instances.

References

1. Baer, J.: Evaluative Thinking, Creativity, and Task Specificity, In M. A. Runco (Ed.), Critical Creative Processes. Hampton Press, USA, pp. 129–151 (2003)
2. Boden, M. A.: The Creative Mind: Myths and Mechanisms. Abacus Books, London (1993).
3. Coughlan, T., Johnson P.: An Exploration of Constraints and End User Development in Environments for Creative Tasks, International Journal of Human Computer Interaction. Vol. 24, Issue 5. 444–459 (2008)
4. Coughlan, T., Johnson, P.: Interaction in creative tasks: Ideation, representation and evaluation in composition. Proceedings of the SIGCHI Conference on Human Factors in Computing Systems, Montreal, Canada, pp. 531–540 (2006)
5. Gabora, L: Cognitive mechanisms underlying the creative process. Proceedings of the Fourth International Conference on Creativity and Cognition. ACM Press, New York, pp. 126–133 (2002)
6. González, M.G., Burke, M.J., Santuzzi, A.M., Bradley, J.C.: The impact of group process variables on the effectiveness of distance collaboration groups, Computers in Human Behavior, Vol. 19, 629–648 (2003)
7. Lieberman, H., Paternò, F. & Wulf, V.: End User Development, Springer, Berlin (2006)
8. Middup, C.P., Johnson, P.: Modeling Group Artifact Adoption for Awareness in Activity-focused Co-located Meetings, Proc. 6th Int. Workshop on Tasks Models and Diagrams, Toulouse , France (2007)
9. Norman, D. A. The design of everyday things. Doubleday, New York (1990)
10. Pérez y Pérez, R., Sharples, M.: MEXICA: A computer model of a cognitive account of creative writing. Journal of Experimental & Theoretical Artificial Intelligence, 13(2), 119–139 (2001)
11. Ritchie T: http://www.swemorph.com/pdf/wp.pdf (2008)
12. Rittel, H.W.J., Webber, M.M.: Planning Problems are Wicked Problems, in Cross, N. (Ed.) Developments in Design Methodology, Wiley, New York, pp. 135–144. (1984)
13. Sarmiento, J. W., Stahl, G.: Group Creativity in Virtual Math Teams: Interaction Mechanisms for Referencing, Bridging and Remembering, Proc. Creativity and Cognition, ACM Press, New York, pp. 37–44 (2007)
14. Sawyer, R. K.: Group Creativity: Music, Theatre, Collaboration. Lawrence Erlbaum, Mahwah, NJ (2003)
15. Schön, D. A., Educating the Reflective Practitioner, Josey-Bass, San Francisco, CA (1987)
16. Simon, H.A.: Models of man - social and rational, Wiley, New York (1957)
17. Stokes, P.: Creativity from Constraints: The Psychology of Breakthrough, Springer, New York (2005)
18. Sundstrom, E., De Meuse, K.P., Futrell, D.: Work Teams: Applications and Effectiveness, American Psychologist, Vol. 45, Issue 2, 120–133 (1990)

The Role of Social Capital and Cooperation Infrastructures Within Microfinance

Rethinking the Example of the Grameen Bank

Simon Plogmann, Muhammad Adeel, Bernhard Nett, and Volker Wulf

Abstract Microfinance has become a most important instrument for rural development. In regard of its technology, there are two main positions: a static analysis points out that ICT does not play a central role in many of today's microfinance activities and, therefore, will not do so in future, whereas technological determinism assumes the technological path of microfinance to follow the one of established banking in the North. In this paper, in which the well-known Bangladesh Grameen Bank is analyzed as an example, we want to show that both assumptions are wrong. Instead CSCW foci may play a productive role in developing appropriate technology for microfinance.

Introduction

During the last development decade, microfinance has become one of four major instruments of the United Nations to fight extreme poverty. At the same time, research started to address the growing impact of microfinance for the poor. Microfinance institutions (MFI) need to deal with a large number of clients, small-size loans, and periodical transactions. Therefore, information and communication technology (ICT) is seen as a potential to render MFI more effective. But even if there is some research into what effectiveness means for MFI (it is not perfectly clear as there are very different activities related to microfinance), there is little research into the role of the actual infrastructure MFIs use for effectiveness.

In the context of microfinance, Social Capital [2,19] is discussed as a means to reduce overhead costs for lenders of micro-credits [11,16] and an important factor

S. Plogmann (✉), M. Adeel, B. Nett, and V. Wulf
Institut für Wirtschaftsinformatik und Neue Medien, FB5, Hölderlinstrasse 3,
D-57068 Siegen, Germany
e-mail: simonplogmann@gmx.de; adeel.Muhammad@uni-siegen.de; bernhard.nett@uni-siegen.de;
volker.wulf@uni-siegen.de

M. Lewkowicz et al. (eds.), *Proceedings of COOP 2010*,
DOI 10.1007/978-1-84996-211-7_13, © Springer-Verlag London Limited 2010

for credit-takers to succeed [1]. It generally seems to play a large role in the context of microfinance. As not every technological advance must be a step forward in the fight against poverty, we regard it as extremely important to understand the existing relation between practices of microfinance organizations, the cooperation infrastructures they use and the Social Capital in the formal and informal economy of the poor.

CSCW has not yet looked deeply into the banking/finance sector. Some exception is the work of Richard Harper et al. [9], which has been related to banking in the North. But microfinance in the South demands for new ideas and research. Micro finance in the South is not as established as finance in the North. Some conceptions and practices of microfinance in the South involve community building and poverty reduction, issues, in which CSCW has quite some experience, but this has not yet led to research into the question what a CSCW-focus could contribute to the field of micro finance.

The following article will, therefore, deal with the concrete case of the well-known Grameen Bank (GB), in particular, the existing relation between practices and infrastructure. The results are based upon a related ethnographic study which has recently been conducted by Simon Plogmann, one of the authors, at several levels of GB. The ethnography unveils that the practices of GB can hardly overcome the limitations on flexibility, but are used a means through which the bank reduces its dependency upon the technological infrastructure and thus makes it possible to reach the poor in areas, where such infrastructure is poor.

The paper starts with some general perspectives on microfinance and technology. Afterwards, the empirical research design of the ethnography at GB is presented. A somewhat detailed description of the organization of GB in terms of hierarchical levels and product-based relations to the customers follows. Typical problems are described, and practices of GB to overcome them. It turns out that GB replaced large technology investments by social capital formation in its relation to the clients. The discussion attempts to reflect upon opportunities and problems of GB's unique relation between practices and technology, which lead to the final conclusions.

Microfinance and Technical Infrastructure

In the field of development politics, microcredit and microfinance are relatively new instruments (although the conceptions had historical antecessors, see [10]). As a development instrument, they first came to prominence in the 1970s (see: [15]). Before (this is: from the 1950s through to the 1970s) the provision of financial services by donors or governments was mainly given in the form of subsidized rural credit programs. These often resulted in high loan defaults and did not reach poor rural households [20].

According to Otero ([15], p. 8), microfinance is "the provision of financial services to low-income poor and very poor self-employed people". [12] observed that such financial services generally include savings and credits, sometimes further financial services such as insurance and payment services. The existence of such services can reduce the dependency of extremely poor people, who often otherwise may have no alternatives to overcome crises than to suffer or become depend upon loan-sharks [7].

The majority of research on microfinance deals with its general financial functioning. In this context, Tamagaki [24] reports so-called "dual objectives of micro finance": a trade-off between sustainability and the outreach to the poor. He describes a low outreach to the poor as a result of sustainability: instead high administrative cost, low revenues and very high risks are attributed to broadened outreach. ICT is presented as the solution at stake. [18] when developing new, mobile-phone based microfinance architecture state that in "microfinance, where the cash value of individual transactions is very small, the only way to be profitable is to serve many clients efficiently. This is an important measure of efficiency in the industry". They emphasize the need to develop a technological infrastructure which is easy to use and allows serving more clients.

While such general demands for efficiency are rather easy to be made, it is a problem to identify changes, which are feasible under given conditions and appropriate technology. As the microfinance sector needs to grow in such places where the overall infrastructure is poor, the latter is somehow a problem and the solution, at the same time. This shows that it is an interesting research gap to look more detailed at the infrastructural side of microfinance.

However, to do so, one has to be aware that if there is a cultural and geographical distance between people in the anticipated field of application and the living environment of technical experts, the mutual understanding, even on what is infrastructure, can be a problem. For instance, the identification of banking with well-established and well-equipped services in rich countries can make it even difficult for ICT professionals to identify the services and infrastructures implemented in fully different societal contexts.

Furthermore, when reflecting about impacts of microfinance, one has to keep in mind that there generally is little related awareness among MFI. Their evaluation is often restricted to mere financial performance. Brochures and websites published by MFIs are often written in a sort of boulevard-journal style and only present achievements without describing the real practices at field level. [3] state: "The difficulty and cost inherent in assessing social impact are such that most MFIs do not try to assess social impact; nonetheless, donors and policymakers have a legitimate interest in assessing the social returns to their social investments. Some knowledge of social impact is therefore necessary for MFI management and other stakeholders (e.g., donors and policymakers) to assess overall program effectiveness. (Information on financial performance alone gives an incomplete picture of program performance)".

Quite some studies on microfinance, therefore, tackle the impact of microfinance upon the addressed strata, in particular, often gender issues. The Grameen Bank, for instance, has been studied in nine case studies, which study the impact of participation upon issues such as household income or family planning. The wide majority of these case studies are gender studies, whereas technology and Social Capital have not been the main foci of such studies [3].

Diniz et al. [6] noticed that ICT-based innovations allow banks to establish low-cost "electronic banking" media like internet banking and automated teller machines (ATMs), but that not all of these applications necessarily fit to the demand of microfinance in the South. While this shows lacking understanding among technical experts, similar problems do not have to be confined to them: MFI staff may, for instance, have problems to anticipate innovative infrastructures for their business without the help of mediators or examples. Technology adoption is strongly shaped and (also shaping) local markets: established technologies impact on social experience. Therefore, social, lingual and literacy standards have to be taken into account when analyzing technological situations [8,14].

The term "infrastructure" here describes available and used technologies and services, which strongly affect the possibilities which MFI have at their disposal. As already mentioned, studying the field of the socio-cultural factors may be influenced by certain perceptions. The reduction of "technology" to modern hard- and software is one example at stake. Instead it is important to study infrastructure in an unbiased way: e.g., the use of stones to mark properties makes the stones a part of the technological infrastructure, and may under certain circumstances make them a very appropriate one.

Infrastructure definitely is a big issue for MFIs in developing countries [17] concludes that "one of the biggest challenges facing microfinance service providers, particularly in rural areas of the developing world, is implementing a Management Information System (MIS) that can interface with a large number of clients across a region with unreliable physical infrastructure (communication, power, transport, etc.)". Instead of looking upon microfinance from the perspective of MFI service management, one can also look upon it from the bottom-up perspective of practices which allow operation under the given conditions of the existing "physical infrastructure".

A similar perspective has often been applied to economic cooperation using the concept of "articulation work", this is: the self-coordinating activities that make formal organizations work [21], which can be studied by ethnographic research when distinguishing between formal organization and informal practices [23]. This paper tries to apply related research upon the identified research gap: the interrelation of given and used infrastructure upon practices in MFI and Social Capital.

Therefore, the paper focuses on the mostly not yet computerized frontend activities. For this intent, the case study of GB will act as an example that is meant to help understand the existing role of technology in microfinance performance, and related demands on the development and implementation of supportive technology.

Research Methods

The basis of this article was an internship of Simon Plogmann, one author of this paper, at GB in Bangladesh. His internship allowed to study GB practices from "within" and to access the different members and locations. The internship started at April 12, 2009 and ended 1 month later. It allowed some first views upon many organizational elements of GB. In structural terms, information was gathered at the head office, in zonal, area offices and branch offices, as well as in the associated centers of the latter. In geographical terms, the head office is located in Dhaka, the other studies were done in the Feni district.

Data was collected about the local situation by means of observation, participation at operations, and by interviews, mostly with GB staff and clients. Talking to the borrowers themselves and getting an impression of the structure and hierarchy that expands between the very personal work in the fields and the administrative work in Dhaka was a most important research experience. The local situation was documented on field notes and on a few hundred photos, as well. Further information was drawn from a literature analysis (micro finance literature, bank brochures etc.).

The close contact of Simon Plogmann to K.M. Tipu Sultan, a manager at Feni branch, has been very helpful. In particular, it allowed for ex-post interviews, which helped to clear the picture, whenever there were doubts or blind spots.

The Grameen Bank

The Formal Organization

Historical Development

Grameen Bank (GB) was established as a small project of the governmental banks on the initiative of Muhammad Yunus in 1976, 5 years after the independence of Bangladesh from Pakistan. In 1983, a special law was released, recognizing GB as a "specialized bank", still under the control of government. This special legislation made GB itself special. At that time, the government controlled 60% of the shares, while the borrowers held the other 40%. By now the borrowers hold 94% and their part is still increasing as it is compulsory for every new member to buy a share of the bank [25]. This is quite unusual among other MFIs too.

GB is usually referred to as a microcredit institution and, in fact, that is what it has always been. Only during the last years, the amount of savings has exceeded the amount of disbursed money. This change was probably caused by the change of GB's policy in 2002, when the government offered GB to discharge their activities from taxes under the condition that they would establish a so-called "rehabilitation fund" for natural disasters, and rise their own budget without accepting any foreign donor money any more.

At that point the bank introduced a variety of new saving products such as the Grameen Pension Fund and other Special Savings Accounts to ensure its liquidity would not get in danger. Studies have proven that MFIs that offer deposits to their customers are more shock resistant during times of financial crisis [13].

Clients

The law on GB describes it as a "specialized bank", related to its devotion to the poor. Ten criteria, known as the "ten indicators of poverty", have been defined by GB, and are employed to distinguish between those who are poor enough to join the bank and those who are not. They are also used to evaluate the process of poverty alleviation.

GB has some 18,000 employees, this is: around one employee per 426 customers. When giving loans, GB does not ask for any collateral. Nevertheless, GB's recovery rate is 98%. One reason for the bank's success is the so-called "group approach" and the very close relation between the bank and its customers (the related practices will be dealt with in the following chapters) [25]. Some more number: 97% of the borrowers at GB are women. Today, GB has more than 7,670,000 members; this is nearly 5% of Bangladesh's population. Some 20% of Bangladesh's households are related to GB in one way or another.

For any future members, there are strict criteria. First, candidates are not allowed to own more than a certain amount of square meters of land. This is the main criteria, apart from Indicators of Poverty. Second, all members have to be female. Male members can still be found, but only as relicts from older days, when criteria for acceptance were different. Third, only one woman per family can become a member of GB. No "blood relation" between members is allowed. Fourth, candidates have to come from the same area and need to have a similar level of education. At the best, they are of the same age. This is for the benefit of the borrowers themselves, as groups become more homogeneous and the ways shorter.

Data about a person that is stored is taken from the application form (including fathers name, mothers name, number of family members, their profession, etc.) and the national ID number. GB abandons contact data such as mobile phone numbers (Fig. 1).

Structure

Grameen consists of head, zonal, area and branch offices. The branch is usually responsible for around 60 centers. Centers are informal workplaces or offices where meetings take place. As their name says they form a sort of social centre, which is established and run by GB. Here is where branch employees meet with the clients – even before they become clients: As the clients generally are illiterate, they are taught what a contract is, and how they can sign one. Furthermore, the structure and policy of GB is explained to them such as a moral code for the members (Figs. 2 and 3).

Although a speaker for any group of borrowers is elected in the center, usually branch employees head the meetings in the centers discuss the matters and collect the money if necessary. The centers provide the service to the customers in their localities instead of traveling to the branch, which generally is further away from their homes. At the centers all borrowers gather once a week for 1 or 2 h to learn, discuss and pay back their installments. There are usually around seven groups, each with five to ten members, in a centre, this is, some 50 persons.

Fig. 1 Clients

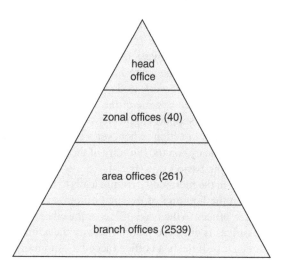

Fig. 2 GB Division

As mentioned, the branches are in steady contact with their centers. Therefore, a branch usually employs five to six employees including the branch manager. Each of them attends two meetings at the centers (often using a bicycle) every morning. This means that a branch generally is responsible for some hundreds of borrowers.

Fig. 3 Center near Dhaka

The area offices are the lowest computerized administration unit. An area office coordinates approximately ten branches and thus some thousands of loans. The area office employs six employees, of whom three are responsible for the transformation of the oral and written information that arrives from the branches into digital data. Usually every area office, and most of the zonal offices, too, rent services from GC.

GC sends three or four of its employees to every area office and supplies them with computers, printers and fax. The same happens with the zonal offices, even though they have less computerized work to do, you will find 2–3 GC employees in each of 27 out of 40 zonal offices. Aside of the 70 employees in the head office, there are 40 supervisors and 20 support engineers, who are stationed decentralized all over Bangladesh and come to action, whenever a problem occurs. It is also the area manager's task to have an eye on the liquidity of the branches and to judge over the proposals for some of the basic loans (Fig. 4).

The next step upwards in the hierarchy pyramid leads to the zonal offices. Again, they also have an eye on the liquidity of the area offices and forward information and money from the area offices to the head office, or the other way round. The staff working at the zonal offices is either collaborating with the administration division or with one of the three units of the head office (accounts, monitoring & evaluation, purchase & distribution).

On the top of this pyramid we find the head office with its 2,000 employees, located in Dhaka the capital of Bangladesh. The head quarter is located in a skyscraper, the Grameen Tower. The skyscraper has also become home to many of the sister companies within the Grameen family that were formed around Grameen Bank during the last decades.

Fig. 4 Different views of area office

A lot of GB's influence results from the individual and sometimes very personal performance of the branch managers. A rating system on the level of the branches has been introduced, awarding individual performance by stars in five different colors. Thus the upper management creates additional motivation for the branch staff to commit with the idea of GB.

Products

Grameen offers only a limited range of products. In respect of an investment scheme one finds the Grameen pension fund and a 7-year-contract in the Grameen Saving account. However, the core products are the loans: there are, among others, the basic loan, which is Any amount, approved by branch and area offices, usually between 3,000 Tk (31.6) and 10,000Tk (105), can be disbursed to a borrower for her business. Interest rate for this common loan is 20% on declining rate (which is equivalent to 9.5% normal interest rate in general banking), not taking into consideration the loan insurance of 3% per insured person and inflation. Housing loans are usually disbursed to construct houses. This loan has to be repaid with interest as well. Another type of loan is micro-enterprise loan. This loan works like a basic loan but covers larger sums of money.

One special kind of loan is to uplift social community. This is known as "Educational Loan". This loan gives financial support to students. There are many different types of educational loans. Some work with interest, some without and some need not be paid back at all. These products are designed in a highly standardized manner.

Standard Process of Crediting

Loans are usually disbursed at the branches. Therefore, a borrower has to annunciate her intention to take a loan at the centre meeting at least 1 week before, handing in a loan proposal that has been printed by the area office and must then be signed by the borrower himself and the branch manager. If the borrower gets the permission from the area or zonal office after satisfying the basic and further requirements (depending on the type of loan), she can come to the loan disbursement at the branch office, where the branch manager hands out the loan and makes a note in the borrower's book and in the books of the branch. Once a week this information is delivered on hard copy to the area offices.

The installments she starts paying in the following week are collected by each groups' chairwoman. During the centre meeting, the chairwoman hands the money over to the GB employee who is in charge of collecting the money. After the employee has visited two centre meetings, as he does every morning, he brings the money to the branch (Fig. 5).

A member who does not attend the centre meetings to pay back the installments in cash is not necessarily a defaulter as long as the amount can be taken from her savings account. After that, serious problems for the bank only occur if there are no special savings or pensions and insurances deposited by the borrower.

GB has developed two very sophisticated organizational strategies, which have become examples for other MFIs. First, the groups which meet in the centers create a social environment for the borrower that encourages her to comply with the rules she accepted, when becoming a member. A borrower's failure will have an effect on the other group members. This reduces the willingness to fall behind with repayments and, at the same time, makes sure that borrowers will help each other to comply with the bank's demands by lending small amounts of money from borrower to borrower or helping to find a solution for the business of somebody else. (While this is called "group approach", other MFIs rely on the so-called "family approach".)

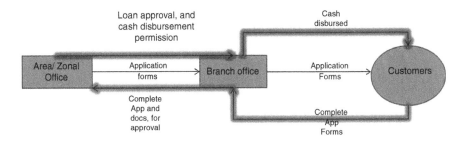

Fig. 5 Standard loan model

Second, the relationship between the operating branch manager and his borrowers is very close. As the bank claims to be "a bank that comes to the people" (and not the other way round, as it is usually the case), the regular meetings in the locally established centers, sometimes entail visits to families nearby. This creates a personal relationship between borrower and branch manager.

Whenever a borrower is impending to become a defaulter, the manager will, therefore, know about the situation of family and business. He is able to analyze what the problems are and tries to motivate and encourage the person and make some alternate business proposals, as he will feel responsible for that person. Additionally, it is a constructive routine with the aim to strengthen the borrower in her position follows.

In case of problems with a loan, first, the head of the centre, the elected representative among the borrowers, and two branch managers visit the defaulter at her home in order to motivate her and evaluate her situation. Although they are asked not to put any pressure on her, afterwards the area manager will visit, and the borrower will do all she can to avoid that embarrassing encounter.

Finally, as the last institutional step, the loan can be changed into a so-called flexible loan, meaning that the amount of weekly installments is decreased in agreement with the borrower without decreasing the total amount. The borrower does not lose her credibility within GB and can take a new, regular loan after she has paid back completely.

Practices Beyond Formal Organization

Media Used in GB

A huge amount of data has to be exchanged within Grameen Bank every day. As this can hardly be done without the help of computers, GB already relied on computerized work before 1995 [4]. Therefore, one finds a large variety of information and communication technology within GB. Already the lower levels of administration like the branches do not only use paper and other traditional means of communication, but mobile phones, as well. These mobiles are paid by GB up to a certain amount, depending on the status of the manager.

In 1997, GB launched a sister company, Grameen Communications (GC) in order to create technological solutions for GB. However, GC provides its services not only to GB, but also to other national microcredit institutions and international organizations (mainly located in other Asian countries). GC helped to computerize the higher units (starting from the area offices), which now use means of communication such as Fax and emails. Memory sticks and mobile phones are very common. We shall present some related practices later.

Together with the Kyushu University in Japan and the Swedish International Development Cooperation Agency, GC is already planning future projects such as the "electronic borrowers' passbook", the "village computer and internet program" or the "classmate pc", a device to facilitate GB's centre manager to collect and access information from borrowers. Some software has even been exported as a product. This export business is run by Grameen Solutions, another sister company. GC has developed the fifth version of the "Grameen Banker" and "Grameen Accounts", backbone software of GB and still under in use in the bank.

The Grameen organizations and their international relations are becoming more complex. In contrast to their dynamic performance, GB itself operates relatively smoothly. This is in line with GB's policy not to experiment with the money of the borrowers.

Drawing upon Existing Services

Not every branch always has a balanced in- and outflow of money. One finds loss-making branches, as well as branches with a surplus. Whenever a branch is facing low liquidity, a branch manager consults the area manager and asks for surplus from other branches. This happens very informally by mobile phone or text message. Area managers can give permissions to branch managers to send money to the "deficit" branch.

Transactions are documented on papers that will be stored in both branches and the area centre. Larger transactions (>100,000 Tk) are made with the help of private banks. Indeed every branch manager runs an account at the closest private bank that can be found in the surroundings of his branch. From this short-time account (only 3.5% interest) he manages most transactions.

Smaller transactions (<100,000 Tk) can also be handled by messengers who transport the money from one branch to another. It can also happen that surplus money of a branch is sent to the area office, then forwarded to the zonal office and then to the head office. But, while the branches can exchange their money directly between each other with permission of the area manager, the area offices have no permission to do so. The area is expected never to be in illiquid. If so, every transaction has to be done via the accounts unit of the zonal office.

The head office, after receiving money from the lower administration units, stores it in many different bank accounts, spread over more than 20 banks. GB emphasizes that they do not invest at any stock market. They do not want to "play with their customers' money", as they say (Fig. 6).

Locally Dealing with the Local

On the area level there is a strict accounting and a resource exchange in cases of problems. Here the maintenance of the average performance is controlled in a very strict way. The area is connected to the overall informational system of the bank. The area level is used to guarantee the bank's performance. On the branch level instead, GB abstains from full equilibrium and automatic control of payments. The branch employees who visit the groups at the local centers do not only know the

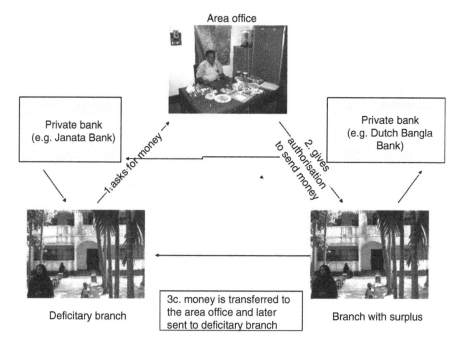

Fig. 6 Flow of funds, information at local level

local situation in most detail, they also have personal relations to the clients. Therefore, the assessment of the local situation is based upon them, such as the first reaction to crises. Only in case of remaining problems, higher levels of the organizational hierarchy are involved in the management of the individual cases.

This shows that GB combines two different infrastructural integration forms: the branches work on face-to-face basis with paper prints, whereas the area is the interface to an electronic data processing. Under the given situation, GB could neither operate without the ICT-based core nor without the paper-based periphery.

Accounting Practices on the Local Level

On the branch level, printouts are used for account statements which were produced on the area level before, that is: independent from the actual payments – which nevertheless are documented on them. The clients thus receive account statements, which are out-of-date already when been delivered, if there are no payments. Therefore, they are only handed out as is to the customers, if they pay the anticipated sum. In this case, theoretical and actual values of the account are identical.

If the customer does not pay, the branch officer will apply emergency practices. One is to communicate the non-performance of the loan to the area managers who have to correct the information system of the bank. Such information generally takes place by means of mobile phone (Fig. 7).

Fig. 7 Branch level, dealing and working

This is to say that the bank distributes account statements with hypothetical payments of the customers: at the time, when the branch officer brings these account statements to the centers, they only display the expected values of the accounts, not the actual ones. However, when the branch employee hands them out, he secures that statements are of the actual value. In the normal case, this is only done by getting the calculated money from the customer and giving the statement in reverse. Only in case of problems, the accounts are changed by annotations, which are reported straight to the area management (Figs. 8 and 9).

This practice allows GB to print account statements in advance and, therefore, independently from factual payments. The "simultaneity" between payments and the account is only secured ex-post by the branch employee at the group meeting in the center. Therefore, the account statements can be printed and distributed top-down like newspapers and do not need an electronic upward feed of information. The employees of the branch offices thus are the interface of an integrated data system (reaching down to the area level) and the clients. Nevertheless, the system would come into trouble if the rate of the non-performing loan would increase, as this could lead to an information bottleneck.

Innovation Attempts

At its start, GC launched some pilot projects in GB trying to computerize the branch level of the bank. However, they had to realize that it did not make sense to computerize the bank at the branch level for several reasons like: branches are very

Fig. 8 Monthly computerized Statements

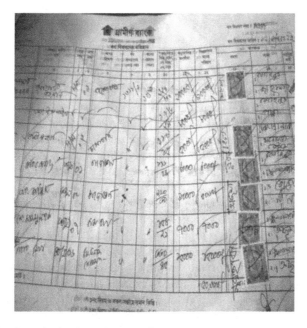

Fig. 9 Local cash received and payment record

small units, and there are a lot of them, especially in rural areas, branches are facing frequent electricity shortages, scarcity of local computer skills would demand the cost-intensive hiring of external experts for each branch. Costs for trouble shooting, electricity supply and matters of education were reasons for the computerization process to stop one step higher at the areas. The local level was considered to be problematic by GC (and GB as its customer), otherwise they would not have launched their pilot projects. However, the local level turned out to be less problematic the anticipated ICT solution.

Other claims for innovation came from demands of more customization of loans by groups that cannot comply with the repayment schedules offered by GB. As only very few borrowers have a regular income, expecting them to pay back in regular installments is not in line with their possibilities. In the best case, members overcome the hindrance with the help of other group members and lend each other very small amounts of money to adhere with the strict repayment schedules. While this practice turns every single borrower into a sort of one-person microfinance institution, it does not succeed, if all borrowers run short of resources, at the same time, for instance, farmers before the harvest. Farmers who take a loan to buy the seeds for the field and get in harvest two or three times a year need a shorter repayment period than 1 year and will not be able to pay installments during the month when plants are still growing on the fields. In such cases, borrowers even have to take loans at other MFIs to be able to pay back their loans at GB. GB reacts with limited differentiation of its standard products, but sticks to as much standardization, as possible.

Discussion

GB is an exceptional case due to its conception and self-image as a bank for the poor, which allowed the organization to see the clients as stakeholders of a common movement instead of alien forces to be centrally controlled. Attempts are made to combine credit-giving with education, mobilization and empowerment. Many other MFI do not share this orientation of GB, and could not exploit the related reduction of costs. Only to give one example: MFIs in Pakistan are much more stressed by their efforts to clear anomalies at the branch level, as their ties to the clients are only financially.

GB has developed its process model according to general social, economical and political values. GB has adopted community norms and values, and made them decisive for its organization. When Daniel et al. [5] state that Social Capital is "developed and fostered when individuals believe that their actions will be appropriately reciprocated, and that each member of a community will meet expected obligations and abide the available social norms", the GB groups experience the values incorporated in the mutual care of their participants for each other. So, one reason for GB's high rate of repayment is the Social Capital that it represents.

Some MFI try to copy this strategy to reduce information demands and support the payback rate, but do not focus as much as GB on supporting the establishment of trust between clients and bank staff. Community and institution building are both seen by GB as part of the empowerment of the poor, who otherwise remained in the informal sector in total [26]. For instance, only under the auspices of trained personal, the loans can be used by the clients in a so profitable manner, that repayment of loans becomes generally possible. This means that the time-intense contact of the branch employees with the borrowers may not only be seen as a little efficient way of organizing installments, but is a form of coaching, too.

For GB on the other hand, to organize the process according to the assumption that the borrowers perform well, allows for a lot easier handling of information. This way, there is no need for any bottom-up communication in the case of the standard customer. Only a one-way communication channel is needed for most of the transactions. The information upwards is given by the branch officer, and he can concentrate upon those clients who do not perform as expected. The branch officer adjusts the values of the accounts. The demanded trust is secured in GB through Social Capital and mutual dependencies.

By the distinction between standard customers (=> nearly no need of information exchange) and exceptional customers (=> high demand on information flows), it became possible to organize the core of the bank in a computerized way, but to organize the area as the interface to the non-computerized branch and center levels. As the upper management does not deal with problem borrowers or react upon them by developing modi operandi, it is also less important for them to be supplied with up-to-date information and actual values. Though the area level is remote from the operating branch or centre level, little problems occur.

Dealing with local problems locally, therefore, reduces the costs of transactions and data collecting at the same time. And using the areas as interfaces between two differently mediated sectors of the bank represents organizational intelligence, which is used by GB to avoid the necessity of too large investments in ICT. Trust based upon Social Capital allowed for the insight that it is enough to know about the performance of the clients' accounts only with some time lag, if some financial reserves and smooth operation are maintained.

As the factual status of the accounts is not needed in time, the bank can use the regular meetings with the clients to confront them with the expected state of their accounts, which can be printed out using a central computer with account data: only in case of problems, alterations have to be made. The default case for GB thus is a well-performing client. Therefore, one may say that GB substituted Social-Capital generation of the branch employees for infrastructural capital. What is the economic rationality of this infrastructural strategy? It is the avoidance of large infrastructural investments and the application of a labor-intensive strategy.

In technological terms, GB makes interactive use of paper, when using printouts, which can, at the same time, be read, annotated and corrected by hand. GB has generated an efficient mixture of paper and ICT, which enables it to reduce the investment on heavy infrastructure. At the same time, the account statements function as a boundary object [22]: the bank behaves within the established rules by using media, which are explained to the clients. This allows the clients to control the bank operation, and gives them a feeling of be a part of it.

On the other hand, if all communication and cooperation within the bank would only rely on labor-intensive, technologically un-mediated face-to-face communication, no accounting would be possible for the bank. Therefore, GB has to integrate paper-based and ICT-based work. In order to reduce related efforts, the other part of GB's technological strategy is the extreme standardization of products. Both elements (social capital of the field officers built upon ongoing intense communication and a most reduced central control of most standardized products) have been implemented by the invention of an accounting process, which abstained from full actuality of central control of the state of the borrower's accounts.

Standardization of the products generally is a typical mass production strategy. In the case of GB, it has not only been adopted to benefit from economies of scale, but due to the fact that technological alternative were not at hand, when the bank was established. The poor electrical and communication infrastructure given, any other strategy would have demanded for very large investments, which were not at hand.

However, the standardization of products, which allowed for the very establishment of GB's existence, is not without problems for further development. It seems to be for that reason that GB only offers four different types of loans and is not willing to accept any major changes according to the conditions of disbursement and repayment. Apart from the total amount, changes in duration, repayment method and interest can hardly be achieved. So branch employees have no large space for maneuver to negotiate with customers to individualize the loans.

One can understand the insisting on regular repayments as a sort of conditioning of the borrowers, which thus learn to accumulate a reserve in good times in order to have it for bad ones. However, some borrowers are that poor that they cannot afford to accumulate a necessary reserve: thus the demanded regularity of paybacks is a problem for them, and the material offers of GB for them (talking with them and offering them flexible loans) is only an exceptional alternative to the normal, fully inflexible regular loans.

The use of Social Capital, which is based upon members of the bank becoming part of the self-organization of its clients, is restricted by the standardization, which limits the opportunities at hand for the self-organization of the groups. However, under the limitations given, standardization is up to now the only way to deal with lacking physical infrastructure in rural areas. The example of GC attempting to computerize the branch level shows that GB is aware of the technological dualism within the organization, tried to delimitate it, but failed. However, the same business model (standardization) that enabled operation for GB may become a problem in the future, and for special types of borrowers.

The branch level of operation for the bank is organized in the form of visits of the branch employees to meetings of the borrowers, mostly women. They thus regularly bring them the new statements of their accounts, calculated by a computer on the area level under the assumption of orderly payback of the loans. In case of non-performing loans, these numbers, therefore, are wrong.

In this case, the field officer discusses future opportunities with the borrower, and corrects the wrong account statement by hand, immediately informing the area manager about the changed situation. Thus the need of feedback from the local to more central levels is reduced to the max. Furthermore, the branch manager may handle the case in "political" terms, this is: he can draw upon his situational knowledge when looking for solutions. On the other hand, the area managers are very restricted to a financial perspective.

If GB, when establishing new fields of operation, wants to benefit from its main assets, it has to involve, at least, the branch officers into related development processes. This would require an application of participatory design. Furthermore, it has to be kept in mind that there is no save electrical and informational infrastructure in the countryside in Bangladesh. In this context, the widespread use and functioning of mobile phones is an important aspect which could be used for future developments.

However, any technological strategy for GB as a microfinance institution has to keep in mind that the infrastructure of the bank has been implemented as an embodiment of organizational intelligence. GB's intense awareness of the borrowers' situation and the mutual trust and respect among GB field officers and the borrowers is one of its main assets, which to a large degree rests upon the transparency of the standardized products and the way how they are managed.

However, for instance, for the poorest and the most successful borrowers, the strict standardization of products, which forms the original basis of operation, may also become problem. As for the majority of borrowers this should not be the case, GB would surely prefer a diversification of its organizations according to business models to a shift of the original business model. The increasing number of daughter enterprises speaks for this assumption. Even if GB wanted, its infrastructure would hardly be changeable in technological terms without massive investments.

Conclusion

Access to financial services such as savings, loans, payment transactions and insurances may help poor people to make independent and lasting improvements to their living conditions. GB has developed financial service to the poor at a time when otherwise there was little interest into this issue worldwide. GB has reached the poor, because it has combined the provision of financial services with other services such as education and coaching. Activities that seem to be peripheral for many Northern banking experts thus have played a core role in the GB case. The result is even the more impressive, as the majority of borrowers consists of poor women, the most affected and peripheral strata of the Bangladesh society.

Within GB a lot of activities are performed in a synergic manner, integrated through the charismatic leading figure of Yunus. Strong differences exist among different MFIs: a solution that fits for one organization must not fit for another one. Even more: what makes one MFI more efficient may destroy sustainability for another one. The field of microfinance must neither be seen as a sort of banking like in the North – only more simple, nor as a domain of its own, the logic of which is already known.

On the contrary: what "microfinance ICTs" are, is in no way already clear, at that moment. Therefore, related product finding could benefit from the experiences of CSCW in participatory design, even the more, as Social Capital formation, trust, and learning issues play a central role. Success stories are of great importance.

It is striking that there is that little awareness of MFIs about their social impact. That may become a domain of certain "microfinance ICTs" of its own. Furthermore, the need to teach the mostly illiterate clients how to interact with a MFI could lead to the use of new media. As infrastructures of rural areas are changing, for example, through the availability of mobile phones, there is a lot of potential to analyze microfinance under a design-oriented CSCW focus.

References

1. Ajani, O.I.Y., Tijani, G.A.: The Role of Social Capital in Access to Micro Credit in Ekiti State, Nigeria. In: Pakistan Journal of Social Science, 6 (3), (2009) 125–132
2. Bourdieu, P.: Le capital social. Actes de la Recherche en Sciences Sociales 31 (1980), 2–3
3. Brau, J.C., Woller, G.M.: Microfinance: A Comprehensive Review of the Existing Literature. In: Journal of Entrepreneurial Finance and Business Ventures, Vol. 9, Issue 1 (2004) 1–26
4. Counts, A.: Small loans, big dreams. Wiley, Hoboken, NJ (2008) p. 255
5. Daniel, B., Schwier, R.A., & McCalla, G.: Social capital in virtual learning communities and distributed communities of practice. Canadian Journal of Learning and Technology (2003) 29(3)
6. Diniz, E.H., Pozzebon, M., Jayo, M.: The Role of ICT in Improving Microcredit: The Case of Correspondent Banking in Brazil (2008)
7. Friedman, J.: Empowerment. The Politics of Alternative Development, Blackwell, Oxford (1992)
8. De Angeli, A., Athavankar, U., Joshi, A., Coventry, L., Johnson, G.: Introducing ATMs in India: A contextual inquiry, Interacting with Computers, Special Issue Global Human-Computer Systems (2003)
9. Harper, R., Randall, D., Rouncefield, M.: Organizational Change and retail finance. Routledge International Studies in Money and Banking, London, UK (2000)
10. Hollis, A., Sweetman, A.: Microcredit – What can we learn from the past? World Development 26 (1998) 1875–1891
11. Karlan, D.S.: Social Capital and Group Banking. In: Economic Journal, Vol. 117, No. 517, February (2007), pp. F52–F84
12. Ledgerwood, J.: Microfinance Handbook: An Institutional and Financial Perspective. World Bank. Washington, DC (1999)
13. Littlefield, E., Kneiding, C.: The global financial crisis and its impact on microfinance. CGAP, Washington, DC (February 2009)
14. Medhi, I., Gautama, S. N. N., Toyama, K.: A Comparison of Mobile Money-Transfer UIs for Non-Literate and Semi-Literate Users. CHI 2009, (April 8th 2009) Boston, MA, USA
15. Otero, M.: Bringing Development back into Microfinance, paper based on a talk at the conference, "New Development Finance," held at the Goethe University in Frankfurt, September 1999 (1999) URL: http://www.accion.org/Document.Doc?id=64 (accessed 15.10.09)
16. Olomola, A.S.: Social Capital, Microfinance Group Performance and Poverty Implication in Nigeria, CSAE 2002 (2002), URL: (downloaded 08/08/09) http://www.csae.ox.ac.uk/conferences/2002-UPaGiSSA/papers/Olomola-csae2002.pdf

17. Parikh, T.S.: Rural microfinance service delivery: Gaps, inefficiencies and emerging solutions. ICTD 2006, abstract, (2006), URL: (accessed 10-10-2009) http://www.ischool.berkeley.edu/ictd2006/abstracts.html#CameraReady_152

18. Parikh, T., Javid, P., Sasikumar K., Ghosh, K.: Mobile Phones and Paper Documents: Evaluating A New Approach for Capturing Microfinance Data in Rural India. Proceedings of the SIGCHI 2006 Conference on Human Factors in computing systems, ACM, NY (2006), pp. 551–560

19. Putnam, R.D.: Making democracy work. Civic traditions in modern Italy. Princeton, NJ, Princeton University Press 1993

20. Robinson, M.: The Microfinance Revolution, Sustainable Finance for the Poor, World Bank, Washington, DC (2001)

21. Schmidt, K., Bannon, L.: Taking CSCW Seriously: Supporting Articulation Work. In Computer Supported Cooperative Work (CSCW): An international Journal 1 (1992) 7–40

22. Star, S.L.; Griesemer, J.R. (1989): Institutional Ecology, 'Translations' and Boundary Objects: Amateurs and Professionals in Berkeley's Museum of Vertebrate Zoology. In: Social Studies of Science, 19, pp. 387–420

23. Stevens, G., Nett, B.: Business Ethnography as a research method to support evolutionary design, in: Habscheid, S., Nett, B. (eds.): Schnitte durch das Hier und Jetzt, Qualitative Methoden medienwissenschaftlicher Gegenwartsforschung, Zeitschrift Navigationen, 2/2009, Schüren, Marburg (2009)

24. Tamagaki, K.: Effectiveness of ICTs on the Dual Objectives of Microfinance (2006) URL: www.waseda.jp/assoc-cioacademy/pdf/tamagaki.pdf

25. Yunus, M.; Khan, A. Hai; Wahab, Md. A.: Grameen Bank at a Glance, December 2008, in: Grameen Bank, Banking for the Poor, (2008), URL: (accessed 22.12.2008) http://www.grameen-info.org/index.php?option=com_content&task=view&id=26&Itemid=175

26. van Bastelaer, T.: "Imperfect Information, Social Capital and the Poor's Access to Credit." Working Paper No. 234. Center for Institutional Reform and the Informal Sector (IRIS), University of Maryland, College Park (2000)

Computer Enabled Social Movements? Usage of a Collaborative Web Platform within the European Social Forum

Saqib Saeed and Markus Rohde

Abstract Networks of social activists traditionally lack financial and human resources, resulting in low interest in employing sophisticated IT. There are not many studies describing the development and use of computer systems for networks of social activists. Especially with regard to web 2.0 applications, it is interesting to analyze how social activists appropriate social web platforms. In this paper we describe the usage of a collaborative platform called "OpenESF" by social activists taking part in the European Social Forum. The results of this study will provide us with an understanding of the needs of social activists for effective computer support and highlight directions for the redesign of OpenESF.

Introduction

IT appropriation in civil society organization is a socially highly relevant field of research. Most of these organizations lack financial and human resources to establish and maintain IT infrastructures and they are more or less dependent on volunteers for setting up IT resources which hampers IT sustainability [1]. There is not enough research that documents how this community benefits from new features of the social web like blogs, wikis, etc. In the absence of empirical studies it is a bit early to proclaim the advantages of these applications for this sector. Keeping this in focus we analyzed the interaction of the social activists with a computer supported collaborative applications called "OpenESF".

World Social Forum (WSF) is a regular event of anti-globalization movement involving international networks of NGOs, labor organizations, trade unions, social movements and other activists. The success of WSF resulted in many thematic,

S. Saeed (✉) and M. Rohde
University of Siegen, Hölderlin Str. 3, 57076 Siegen, Germany
e-mail: saqib.saeed@uni-siegen.de; markus.rohde@uni-siegen.de

M. Lewkowicz et al. (eds.), *Proceedings of COOP 2010*,
DOI 10.1007/978-1-84996-211-7_14, © Springer-Verlag London Limited 2010

regional, national and local forums having independent organizing processes. In this paper we focus on the European Social Forum (ESF) which attracts activists from all around Europe. Different organizations propose different activities for the event and these activities are merged with other various activities to keep the program manageable. Organizations and other interested activists participate in the workshops, seminars and discussions at the event and establish networking to do future actions. In order to make this event a success, large scale planning, organizing and mobilization efforts are required. This ultimately leads to extensive collaboration among the organizations and activists. The last ESF event was held in Malmo, Sweden in September 2008 and was attended by approximately 13,000 activists. We have been investigating the role, technology serves in this community. In our earlier paper [2] we analyzed the work practices and usage of IT in organizing the Malmo event and in this paper we looked at collaborative practices of activists and their interaction with the collaborative application "OpenESF" to highlight the design deficiencies. "OpenESF" was developed to prepare for ESF events as well as a continuous platform for communication in between the events. The fact that this community of social activists comprises of organizations and activists from different cultural backgrounds will enable us to better understand the computer supported collaborative needs of this community. In this study we are mainly interested in findings about how social activists are using this collaborative technology, how this technology is being setup and what the main problems are faced by them during the use and establishment of technology. The empirical findings highlight some insights for the future design of better web2.0 based collaborative systems for civil society networks.

The structure of remaining paper is as follows: Section Related Work describes related work. The third section focuses on the research methods applied in this study. Section Importance of Collaboration highlights the importance of collaboration for the social activists whereas Section Evolution of OpenESF describes the evolution of the OpenESF platform and Section Appropriation of "OpenESF" discusses how social activists interact with this system. Section Problems with OpenESF discusses problems faced by activists due to the system and Section Design Concepts presents a discussion of our findings and the last section focuses on conclusions with regard to further ICT development for CSOs and civil society networks.

Related Work

Many different studies have analyzed the use of traditional web applications and IT artifacts in different voluntary organizations in different geographical locations [cf. 3–11]. These studies have been carried out where intercultural and interorganizational differences were not so obvious. Similarly there have been participatory design efforts by some researchers for achieving technological appropriation in this community [cf. 12–14]. There have been similar efforts at Penn State University to empower regional volunteer organizations by involving them in design process [cf. 15–17]. Rohde applied participatory design methods to electronically network an Iranian NGO community [18] and Mclever worked on supporting collaborative legislative work among NGOs at the World Summit on the Information Society (WSIS) [19]. As anti-globalization movement is an important platform for voluntary organizations, there has been recent interest in the movement's use of new technologies. Aelst and Walgrave analyzed the Internet use in organizing protests in the anti-globalization movement [20]. Kavada investigated the use of email lists in the organizing process of the European Social Forum event of 2004 [21]. Fuster Morell has carried out a study to analyze the advantages and problems associated with the adoption of collaborative platforms for social forums [22,23]. In our earlier work we analyzed the organizing processes of ESF 2008 in Malmo, Sweden and also at the WSF 2006 event in Karachi, Pakistan to analyze the work practices and the use of IT in the organizing process [2,24]. Furthermore a study of knowledge transfer practices among different organizing committees managing the ESF is also carried out [25]. Despite these research efforts a design focus on collaboration processes in a multi cultural and heterogeneous organizational environment of non professional voluntary settings requires further exploration. So in our current study we are focusing on the use of a specific web 2.0 based collaborative application "OpenESF", which is currently available for use by the activists, and our intention is to improve the system design. This study will help in understanding the collaboration needs and practices of activists. The collaboration needs of this network differ from traditional organizations due to the multilingual and multicultural nature and the heterogeneity of participating activists/organizations coupled with weak organizational structure. The result of this work will help in improving the system design so that the interaction among social activists and "OpenESF" system could improve.

Research Design

In the organizing process of ESF there are two important actors, the first being the European Planning Assembly (EPA) and the other being the organizing committee. EPA is an open meeting and anyone could participate in this meeting and participate in discussions. This regular meeting of activists and organizations, interested in European Social forum activities takes place after every 3–4 months in a European city. This platform is responsible for political discussions, campaigns and future of the ESF. There are some self-constituted thematic groups established around specific themes like education, public services etc. to discuss campaigns and plan common actions around these specific themes. Normally a day before the EPA meeting these network meetings take place where organizations and activists interested in these themes participate and discuss future plans, which are further reported in EPA meeting, too. A local organizing committee is responsible to plan and carry out practical activities. The organizing committee can have further subgroups to better coordinate the work. Our study started in 2008 and as the ESF 2008 was scheduled for Malmo, Sweden and accordingly the local organizing committee was the Nordic Organizing Committee (NOC), though now it has changed to the Turkish Organizing Committee (TOC) since the next ESF in 2010 is taking place in Istanbul, Turkey.

The empirical data presented in this paper are part of an ongoing study and some of this data has been used in earlier papers [2,25], but in this contribution we have a different focus than earlier papers, a focus that is only limited to computer supported collaborative activities with the "OpenESF" platform. Moreover, the empirical data increase continuously. The empirical data are collected by using multiple methods such as participant observations, field studies, content analysis and semi-structured interviews. The participant observations were carried out during four field visits. These field visits helped to understand the work practices of the activists. The first visit was conducted in February 2008 during the European Preparatory Assembly meeting in Berlin whereas the second visit was at the European Social Forum event in the Malmo during September 2008. The third visit was carried out in March 2009 at the EPA meeting in Athens and fourth visit was at the EPA meeting in Vienna during June 2009. During this period the online activities were also observed to analyze the usage and content by joining different projects at the "OpenESF" system. As the activists come from all over Europe it is difficult to have only onsite interviews, so the interview data are a mix of onsite and telephonic interviews. All the interviews were recorded and transcribed with a recorded content of approximately 12 h from 22 different people. The semi-structured interviews consisted of questions concerning work practices, evolution of IT infrastructure, and the problems faced in their use of the IT systems.

Importance of Collaboration

In order to analyze the success of computer supported collaboration, it is important to understand whether social activists need to indulge in collaborative activities in their work practices. As the core objective of organizing a social forum is to learn from the experiences of other organizations/activists in anti-globalization campaign and to take part in joint activities (demonstrations, protests, etc.) for future, this makes collaboration an important activity for the activists participating in the process of ESF. Describing the objective of collaboration between the social activists, one of the interviewees described similar views:

> A national and international cooperation is very important for us. It is to exchange information, to share experiences and to do common actions.

Describing the importance of collaboration in the European social forum process, one Greek activist described as follows.

> The most important in the ESF is to collaborate with different organizations ...it was not so obvious before for a lot of organizations, to put themselves together with the other and try to find common solutions and to organize common activities.

During the start up process of an ESF event different organizations (trade unions, labor organizations, foundations, grass root movements etc.) propose to organize different activities (workshops, seminars, cultural activities etc.). Due to logistical problems it is not always possible for an organizing committee to schedule all those activities. In order to minimize the number of activities the organizing committee puts up different suggestions for organizations, proposing to merge different activities with each other. As a result of this complex negotiation process involving collaborative discussions, different activities are merged with each other and as a result single activity is normally hosted by multiple organizations. As an example of the magnitude of the number of activities there were almost 800 activities proposed for the last European social forum and the final program comprised of 272 activities. The moderators of each activity then collaborate with each other to prepare activities. Furthermore as the organizing committee of ESF keeps on changing so there is a need to transfer knowledge around organizing activities, which results in collaboration among the current and previous organizing committee members. There are also different thematic networks which are constituted by different activists around a specific theme like education, public services etc. to do common activities around its theme. One activist who carried out a workshop at the ESF 2008 in Malmo described the collaboration practice as following:

> We make new collaborations, especially with organizations we know; we have contacts in the movement I work, and we know a lot of international organizations, some we met and become connected in World Social Forum or in European Social Forum… and we have an exchange of information not only in the social forums but it (European Social Forum) is a (one) possibility to meet and to exchange experiences and planning.

It was also observed that *trust* is an important parameter before indulging into the collaboration activity. Describing the collaboration practices one French activist mentioned:

> This is the common use I won't get in touch with you without any recommendation; I am in France and interested to work in Pakistan for instance, for instance in women rights, but I don't know your organizations, though maybe you have a website. Ok, I can go to your website, but I don't know who are you? Which relationship you have with government etc. I don't know. So I only begin to work if some other organization which is already in my network says this is a good organization.

Evolution of OpenESF

After ESF 2003 in Paris a memory project was launched and as a subproject of this, a collaborative website was proposed. Since the merging (the process to decrease the number of proposed activities) is a complex process, the first idea of setting up collaborative space came to support this process. Describing the objective of the tool one French activists involved in this project described as following:

> We wanted to make a collaborative tool to help the merging process … It was the first point which decided that we need a collaborative tool. Because very quickly forums had lot of

demands, lot of activities that people wanted to make and we had logistical problems, not so many rooms for people to meet and not so many money so people must merge. This is one of the key points of the social forums' difficult thing to solve. And collaborative tool should help people to negotiate between them and try to make common activities around the issues.

The workspace was built using Plone content management system. This workspace allowed organizations to register themselves but this initiative was not very successful as the activists did not use it much during the organizing process of 2006 European Social Forum. One French activist working in the "webteam" described this in the following words:

When we decided to leave the first workspace and having this new one (openESF), it was first of all in Lisbon in March 2007. We showed the results of our work and tried direct evaluation with participants and the majority of the participants said we do not want it, it is not useful, it is too complex. So when we had EPA in Stockholm in September 2007, we officially decided within the web-team group to leave it, to abandon the workspace and to create a new tool from free software, small, simple and people feel it is more useful.

Another activist of "webteam" described the late launch of the website, another factor in the low response. He commented as following:

It was too late and it was not very well conceived, so people didn't use it at all.

The "webteam" is a group of volunteers who try to help European social forum in their personal capacity by advising which kind of IT infrastructure would be required. These are mainly a group of volunteers who have technical knowledge and they establish networks with other people and try to carry out their activities. This is mainly volunteer work and is derived on the personal motivation but some work is partly financed by the organizing committee. The Greek developer who developed the event website for ESF 2006 in Athens met some volunteers from WSF and the same application was cloned for the 2008 World Social Forum event. On the basis of his experience he proposed to use a new platform for ESF as there were many problems in this application. The main problem was that the website was based on an older version of Plone and, secondly, the workspace was modeled in UML by a tool "Gentleware Poseidon" and code from this model was generated by ArchGenXML tool. The code is extended by doing manual changes in code or by changing the model. Gentleware Poseidon was not open source and the people who developed the workspace used a free of charge version of the system, which expired in 2006. Furthermore the UML model cannot be exported by any other modeling tool from this proprietary software [26].

He established an initial website for free to give people an impression of the system. This website was based on the "OpenPlans" system, which is an open source system developed by the Open Planning Project [27]. The objective of this website was to support collaborative discussions in merging and other organizing processes and also serve as a communication platform in between the two events. As voluntary networks are mostly short on finances and try to employ cheap available alternatives, one activist of the "webgroup" sums up the evolution of this platform as following.

OpenESF was not developed, it was copied. It was copied from OpenCore because we do not have the capacity to develop anything.

Later he developed the full system and it was launched on 27 November 2007 and currently there are 197[1] projects and 946 registered users. This web system is to support the ESF but it is not the official website. The system is called "OpenESF". The server is Linux based and all of the software is open source. It is an open website where anybody could register themselves and register their projects. Every project could have multiple mailing lists, wikis, blogs and mapping tools to have collaborative maps. Every user had a profile page where he can give his basic information, picture and a list of all projects in which he is added. The page also shows the activities of that profile on the OpenESF system. The system also allows sending an email message to that profile once you are logged in. By opening any project page one could join the project, browse wiki pages, summary, mailing lists, task lists, list of members and contents. On the other hand the third button "Start a Project" allows you to start your own project. A snapshot of the system is shown in Fig. 1. The OpenESF was promoted through information on different mailing lists

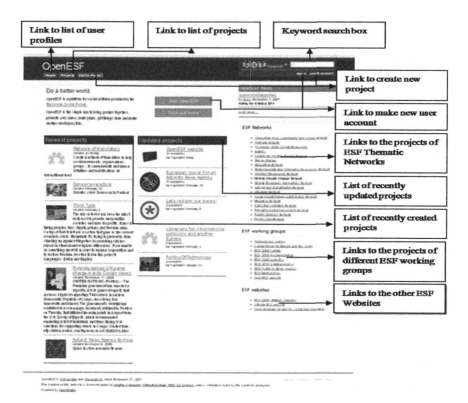

Fig. 1 Snapshot of OpenESF

---

[1] There are 30 private projects whose data is only visible to the administrator. So in our paper we will discuss the statistics of 167 projects.

of social activists and at the EPA meetings in Berlin and Kiev volunteers helped people to make their accounts and showed them how to use the system. It was also advised to describe a website for all the proposed activities at the Malmo forum to promote OpenESF but not many organizations used it effectively. Currently there are three volunteers who intend to work with Turkish organizing committee members to help them in using this system.

Appropriation of "OpenESF"

We were interested in analyzing how this collaborative system is being used by the activists as this platform is open for everyone to join, initiate and participate in discussion. A member of "webteam" described the OpenESF as following:

> OpenESF is a space which can be used by a lot of people; they can organize groups, they can organize discussions (and) they can organize meeting, so it is very important to use it.

Different European Thematic networks like antiwar, public services etc., which focus on specialized themes, have their projects on the website to describe their activities. One activist participating in "anti war" network described that they are using this platform as an information publishing tool, but sometimes due to the sensitivity of information it is not possible to write everything here. He cited that they organized discussions against war in Georgia during ESF but it was not possible to put all that information online. He described as following:

> There is some information about NATO stored there and we will try to provide [information about] the activities against NATO.... First of all we have to collect the information, especially the appeals and what is proposed in the European Preparatory Assembly meetings and then we can make documentation about this[at OpenESF].

As different thematic networks and working groups have created their projects on this website it provides information about their activities, which is quite helpful when one could not participate in all of the physical meetings. One activist from Turkey described the advantage of OpenESF as following:

> I found different networks and working groups over the website. I found it very good because I did not have the chance to join many of them; I can see what is going on in the working groups.

Different working groups of the Nordic Organizing committee opened their separate projects on OpenESF and used this platform to coordinate activities. The Voulanteer working group launched a project on the OpenESF where volunteers could socialize with each other before the forum so that they could work in a better and more coordinated way during the event. One member of the organizing committee of the 2008 event described the use of OpenESF during the merging process that was coordinated by Program working group.

What happened, which was really cool, when there were proposals about to be merged, they (the organizations) never met before and they started communicating well before the forum. They formed an OpenESF project and they already formed the network before the forum, which, I think, it what's really cool to see because we were off course. I mean one of the aims with ESF was to make new networks and contacts for future action and then if you already see this because of merging process.

Since most of the activities organized at the ESF were managed by more than one organization some activists used this platform to prepare for their seminars/workshops at the forum. They discussed the pattern and structure of their seminars. Seeing how the next European Social Forum is going to take place in Turkey, there are some spaces being used for planning and coordination for the next ESF and, in doing so, transferring previous knowledge to the Turkish organizers. There were also many projects opened on specialized political debates like Energy poverty and consumers' rights, Feminism and neo-liberalism, Eastern experience, financial crisis seminar etc. There are also different country chapters of social forums like the Hungarian Social Forum, London Social Forum, Romanian Social Forum, and these are processes that have a presence on OpenESF. These describe specific information related to their geographical location. One activist from the United Kingdom described that they are going to use this platform as a tool to coordinate the activities in their country.

We are planning to use OpenESF as a wiki now because we could develop and make a project on the OpenESF website and then put it on the other [official] website when it is finished. For example, when we have a meeting we can put the minutes on OpenESF, then people can edit the minutes and then after a certain amount of time it could go to official website.

As one of the objectives of setting up this space was to provide a platform for continuous discussion in between the social forums as well, it is interesting to monitor the activities of users over a period of time. In order to find out this aspect we analyzed the joining pattern of new members and the creation of content at OpenESF on the monthly basis. Table 1 describes the number of new members, projects and mailing lists created every month. As in September 2008 the European Social forum took place, the maximum number of new people joined the OpenESF platform also in the same time. There are not many people joining the forum and also there is not much activity in terms of creation of new content, presumable because there is some time left until the next forum which is scheduled to take place in July 2010.So these statistics show that the creation of new content still revolves around the physical event and its objective as a communication platform in between the event is somewhat lacking.

We further investigated the users who are already using this platform, how often they participate in discussions and activities, so at the end of each month the statistics were analyzed in three categories. Firstly there are active users, who have logged in at least once in the last month, whereas inactive members are those who never used their account after first 24 h. The third category was of dormant members who were active users at some point in time and later they become inactive. As the following graph shows that after the September 2008, when the ESF took place,

Table 1 Monthly statistics of OpenESF

Month	New members	New projects	New mailing lists
December 2007	80	11	14
January 2008	43	7	10
February 2008	84	28	28
March 2008	93	15	13
April 2008	70	21	24
May 2008	54	18	20
June 2008	88	23	23
July 2008	72	9	8
August 2008	90	9	10
September 2008	130	9	10
October 2008	58	7	6
November 2008	24	3	7
December 2008	15	4	4
January 2009	10	0	0
February 2009	13	2	2
March 2009	13	0	0
April 2009	9	1	1
Total	946	167	180

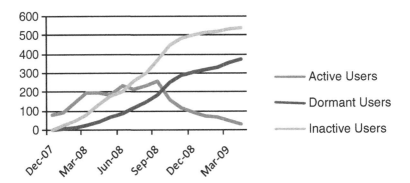

Fig. 2 Members statistics

the number of active user kept on decreasing and on the other hand a major number of users were inactive since the start so they made their accounts once and never returned back while in the case of dormant users, the curve is not so steep as is the case with inactive users (Fig. 2).

Our next point of investigation was to look at the presence of activity at OpenESF, as users may be interested in participating in pre-existing projects rather than creating new projects. So similarly projects were also divided in three categories, active being modified in last 1 month, Inactive being not updated after first 24 h of project creation, and the dormant category showing projects which remain active for some time but then turned into inactive. The graph in Fig. 3 again shows

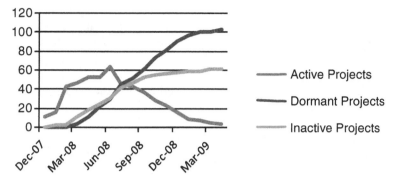

Fig. 3 Projects statistics

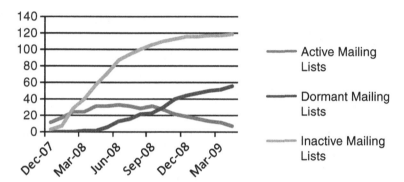

Fig. 4 Mailing lists statistics

that there were many active projects before the forum and June 2008 being the month where the maximum number of projects (64) were active and after the event collaboration, activity has turned to almost zero, despite the fact that regular EPA meetings take place every 3–4 months and the preparations of next ESF by Turkish the organizing committee are also under way.

During the empirical studies it was observed that activists are more accustomed to using the mailing lists and there were also instances where only the mailing lists were used instead of using other features like wiki pages, blogs etc. So we also monitored the activity on the mailing lists present on the platform. The following graph describes the status of mailing lists, which were again distributed in three categories. Active mailing lists being the ones having at least a single message in last 30 days and inactive being never used after first 24 h of creation and the dormant mailing lists are also shown. Here again the similar patters persisted and after the ESF 2008 not many active mailing lists exist (Fig. 4).

As the statistics point out the relatively low traffic on the platform and also the users who are using this system are in a somewhat inactive mode. Most of the initiatives taken by creating a user account or creating a project/mailing list could not really be followed up and ultimately never used beyond the 24 h after creation. Moreover, the relationship between the number of users who take part in the events and the use of this space is very weak. For example there were nearly 13,000 participants at the last ESF, but the number of people who actually used this platform is much lower. The Greek developer who developed this website associated the lack of activity with the lack of parallel physical activity, weaknesses in platform and the low skills of activists.

> There were last month (February 2009) probably 650 people who logged into the website and there are like 900 visits per day. So around 900 people visit website everyday and some of them actually use it but, yeah, there is not too much activity I guess but it has to do with the fact that there is not parallel activity.

He further said

> Most of the people involved in the ESF process are not used to such tools or haven't been using it. I think this is a cultural problem and of course there are some technical problems or bugs which can be discouraging to people and they have to be fixed. There is also a need for more new functionalities to be developed.

Problems with OpenESF

As the activists participating in ESF activities come from quite diverse cultural, political and organizational backgrounds, it was interesting to find out about their perceptions of technology. Some activists find the technological support for the ESF very important. One activist who is also participating in the "webgroup" described her views as follows:

> I think it is a good tool but is used underutilized – not everybody in the process is using this tool, not everybody knows how to do it and at the end of the day it is more that when we meet, we say things and not during the time when there is not an EPA.... People are afraid of using something like this or they don't know how to use it but we have done so many demonstrations. It's not very difficult to use. Now it's very open stuff and maybe it's at the end of the day, speaking is always better but as we are so far from each other we have to start using this kind of things.

Another French activist who is also participating in technological support commented in the following words:

> The technology can help us to simplify the necessary work the people want to do. So first you have to know what people want to do exactly and then you find the simplest technology because they don't want to be bored with technology. They only want to click, click and that's all.

On the other hand there are some activists who are skeptical about the role of technology in the ESF. One activist working in the Nordic organizing committee described his views about technology in the following way:

> I am a bit skeptical because with these organizations in NOC we have nothing in common. There is no basis for the Internet tools. Among them there are maybe a dozen who are really actively interested in the European Social forum. There is no need for anything else

other than this email list, that's perfect. It works perfectly and that's what people look at. More and more I see now that these kinds of grand Internet website things do not work and people go back to make email lists because everybody opens the email box but people don't go up to a website to find out things.

The similar concerns were raised by another Greek activist. He gave the example of this while they arranged an EPA meeting in March 2009.

Sometimes, even now, I receive phone calls from colleagues and friends and hear 'you didn't call me to inform me that European preparatory assembly is taking place' and when I said, 'but it's on the website,' they respond with 'but I don't see that; I was waiting for your phone call'.

Describing the reasons for this behavior one volunteer of the web group described following:

I think it is a generation gap. Here the people are quite old and they don't know how to use technologies. It is not that they don't want. I mean for example my mother; it is not that she does not want she does not have skills to use it.

In order to find the problems in the system we tried to find the experiences and problems faced by activists in their interaction with the system. One of the criticisms of the system was less content creation in the projects and most of the projects do not have meaningful, updated information after their start. One Swedish activist described this situation as follows:

There is a phenomenon with the Internet and I call it the wardrobe phenomenon. You never create large enough public space for people to be able to participate and it becomes sort of specialized in a very small corner. If you look through the OpenESF.net, you find that there is very, very little participation in the different projects.

As it becomes difficult to reach people when there is no response on the emails or discussion forums, he recalled his previous communication practices and said:

Before, immediately when something started, address lists with telephone numbers were immediately produced so everybody could reach each other; now only email lists are produced and it is very hard to get into contact with the people because telephone numbers are not reachable and you can't get direct contact with them. And they do it by these emails and with the emails you never know if they will respond or not because only a few respond, creating a very different kind of culture in terms of knowing what is going on and people are less interested in really preparing a meeting, deciding on a meeting and following up.

Another important factor contributing the low adoption of this platform is the digital divide among the activists. Activists, especially from eastern European countries, have low accessibility to computers and, furthermore, a significant number of activists have language problems while communicating in English and they prefer to initiate discussions in their native languages. As a result there are always translation arrangements at physical meetings of ESF. One activist from Turkey described his views in the following lines.

I personally use OpenESF but we are not using so much as a general social forum of Turkey.... You need to have very good connection with the Internet and the language, because OpenESF is in English but in Turkey (there are) not many people who can use English on the website.

The similar concerns were raised by another activist from Hungry while discussing the potentials of this platform.

> It [OpenESF] can improve [our working] but it is a slow process. It means people must learn foreign languages or another alternative is to have good translations, good people who are ready to translate Hungarian material into English and back and this is one point, and other point is people should use the Internet but people who are poor have no access to this fancy thing.

As the number of projects grows some activists reported difficulty in finding interesting projects, although at the main user interface the list of recently created and updated projects are shown. One German activist described the problem which she faced with the interaction with the OpenESF system as follows:

> In my view there is no comprehensible navigating system; the only way to find something is the function "search" and under the list of projects by alphabet letters ..... There is no real structure. It is like a big sum of information but it is very difficult to find the information and many organizations opened projects and there is nothing in the project and ... there is no visible and understandable structure. It is a summary of anything and everything.

The similar concerns were raised by another Swedish activist.

> I think it is difficult to find the spaces that I am interested in. What if I search a specific topic, specific region or specific country? It can be quite difficult to find. You have to search by index, by the first letter of the name of the space and there are also many spaces that are not active so that becomes discouraging in that not so much is going on. I think the front page could be much better; I think the explanation on how to use it could be better and more visible.

She further described her preferences for user interface as follows:

> I would like to have information on how to navigate the web pages, how to find what I am interested in and how to use it.... The spaces with more members or more active spaces should be on the first page.

Another activist described that she would like to see a list of projects in which her friends are collaborating, so on the basis of those suggestions she may choose to join them. The heterogeneous nature of the organizations and activists involved in the process has also implications on the acceptability of the system. One activist who has participated in IT initiatives described the reasons for not using the collaborative application as following:

> The problem in my opinion is cultural.... We have here big networks and they only exchange (information)by email and send documents etc. and sometimes they use phone, but the two mentors are meeting (Physical) and email, so they don't see what decent use we bring to them first. The second thing is that those tools are very useful for individuals and used by individuals, but here we have two logical (identities). We have one logical (identity), who is individual. How can I myself with my culture and my technological background and can I use the electronic tools? But on the other side I am not only an individual, I am also part of an organization and as part of the organization I cannot do what I want, i.e. put text in the wiki. I cannot, because my organization is behind me and you cannot combine the two logical (identities) ... and they cannot solve this problem and they leave it.

The similar concerns were raised by another Swedish activist.

> OpenESF is supposed to be a decentralized process where any person can participate, but if you are representing a trade union or an organization you can't just write what you want, you have to check with your organization.

On the one hand activists are interested in providing everyone equal chances to create and initiate a political discussion, but on the other hand some activists are skeptical and think that this is the main reason of the lack of interest of people in this platform. One French activist described this in following words:

> As an individual you have no legitimacy. I mean in a political sense you can be somebody whom I appreciate, I can like you. There is a difference in you as an individual and you as a member of an organization.

An activist involved in the NOC described his views about this as following:

> If you will look through it (OpenESF) there is an enormous amount of projects started by one, two, or even three people and nothing happens again, so the whole process seems to be fragmenting rather that creating/accumulating, because you never know if it is an individual saying something or if it is an organization saying something ... for me as a public movement person I am totally uninterested in starting individualistically nice and cute discussion forums myself because I know that this is not the way it works. So to start a discussion forum it has to be a lot of organization's interest in doing it, so then it could become some kind of general political debate.... They don't even understand the problem because they believe that every individual takes his initiative and then the question whether there will be a response on that or not has only to do with quality of the initiative, if it is good quality then it develops, otherwise it will disappear but this is a market concept; this is the newly created world market culture, which is totally against any kind of responsibility for the process, and it doesn't work. So that's also why you have this.... In terms of knowing how much effort is behind a certain initiative, then it becomes important to know what it is and what it is not.

Similar concerns were raised by another activist, too.

> The process of the social forum does not have to be this because the idea is that people come here, they discuss the things and they do things together, but there are still people who come here, who always talk with their organizations to understand what they have to do. This is not the spirit of the social forum, but yes, there are people here who think that it is very important. I think that we have to remind ourselves all the time of the real spirit of the forum.

As the majority of the activists in this community are not expert users of the computer systems, it is very important that the technology deployed should be simple and easy to use and that it have a clear objective. Some of the activists are not clear enough about the objective and the focus of transforming this space into a platform for continuous interaction among the European Social Forum events. One German activist described this in following words:

> After the ESF in Malmo, the OpenESF for the first lost all relevance. It is not a tool to organize activities or to give information. The OpenESF is not connected to the movements; therefore the movements filled in information before the ESF, but they don't use it as an information source and network tool and database. There is no input about the current activities against the NATO summit, the finance crisis or the G20 Summit or local activities connected to social forum movement. The OpenESF is in my view a tool that the Swedish organizers demanded to use, but it is not used by the movements. Activists are looking anywhere and everywhere to get information, but not in OpenESF.

Another activist described the reason for this behavior as a conflict between the social forums itself. She described that some people/organizations are not sure whether it is a continuous process or just an event which takes place after every 2 years.

Design Concepts

Appropriately designed technological systems could improve the technological usage in voluntary organizations [cf. 13–26]. So in order to reap the benefits of technology, there is a need to improve the system design. The empirical findings from the presented ethnographic case study seem to be quite useful in deriving some design requirements for technological support of the ESF process and the involved activists. As is the case with voluntary organizations there are many different IT projects undertaken in ESF as well. Some of them have been used at some point in time and some of them just faded away without being used by anyone. Since most of these initiatives are taken from different people at different points in time and with different motivations, there is need for appropriation efforts to make them more active. As in this contribution we have been focusing on collaborative website mainly we will focus only to the design appropriation of OpenESF website.

Improving User Interface

As most of the activists have limited IT skills it is important to optimize the user interface of ESF. As some of interviewees described that language barrier is resulting in low participation, user interface in major European languages could facilitate the activists in using OpenESF. Furthermore, some of the interviewees also reported problems in finding interesting projects. Instead of just displaying the lists of recently launched and updated projects on the main interface, a list of projects the user may find interesting based on his previous involvement in different projects could be helpful in locating interesting project spaces at OpenESF. As it is visible in the user interface snapshot that some of the user interface elements are redundant, multiple user interface elements point to same pages, and hence add confusion to the user. Furthermore, while browsing through some pages users could get lost as there is no way to navigate back stepwise, so you have to either use browser back button or skip to the main interface; thus, a redesign of user interface is required as well.

Designing for Multilingual Collaboration

As it was observed that majority of activists need native language support while communicating, a mere interface in multiple languages is not sufficient. There is need to carry out automatic translations of the contents so that the information could be localized and collaborative work could be carried out in multiple languages. Yamashita and Ishida [28] (2006) looked at the effects of machine translation on collaboration. While perfect machine translation is not available for practical and theoretical reasons, the functionality of existing online tools could be integrated into ESF. Computer supported back and forth translation could increase the quality of the translated items. The number of languages which need to be supported by the system is a complex issue, as the ESF focuses on activists all over Europe. Additionally, whenever ESF moves to a new location the participation of activists from host countries increases, the need for translation and that specific language becomes important. So as a first phase at least major European languages need to be supported by automated translation features.

Supporting Recommendation and Enhanced Searching

As the number of projects increases, it is difficult for the distributed actors to keep on top of the decision process. A major problem resulted from the complex structure and the limited search functionality of the www-site. The search capabilities could be enhanced by employing a tagging mechanism, so whenever a new project is created, it could be associated with different tags and also managed within a tag cloud. Furthermore when the search results are displayed a visual relative grading mechanism of the projects on the basis of their relevance could help in determining better keywords. Moreover, it could be helpful to have a recommending system which could give suggestions to join certain projects based on the personal network analysis of individuals. Email is the most commonly used tool among activists and they prefer to work with collaborators with whom they have (indirect) personal relationships. Therefore, a social networking tool linked to their email address book could be beneficial. It could be used, for instance, for recommending projects which most of their contact persons have joined.

Personal and Organizational Profiles

A further domain to explore technical support is making the institutional and personal background of the different activities more transparent. While organizational directories [cf. 29] and yellow page systems [cf. 30] have already been discussed, these functionalities need to be tailored to the specific needs of the ESF. In OpenESF there is not any mechanism to distinguish among organizational and personal content and this could be one of the reasons leading to low participation at the site. At some point it is important to understand whether certain content is initiated by an organization or an individual, so there is need for establishing organizational profiles as well in OpenESF. The individual profiles could map to these organizational profiles to show their affiliations and to deal with certain ambiguities between institutional and personal standpoints. Specifically in fluid structures, such as the ESF, organizations and the organizational personal background or actors may change; new actors will become part of the process and leave again. Therefore, techniques for semi-automatic profile generation need to be explored [cf. 31].

Conclusion

The recent interest in technological support for voluntary organization by different researchers has benefited this specialized sector in technological appropriation [cf. 20–22]. The characteristics of weak organizational structure, limited technical background of the volunteers and the shortage of financial and human resources to design and maintain IT infrastructures differentiate this sector from other traditional organizations. As these organizations become more diversified in their structure and functioning, ranging from grass roots organizations to professional transnational NGOs, it is very important to look deeply in their organizational structures and practices to achieve technological appropriation. In our current case these traditional weaknesses of voluntary organizations compounded by the heterogeneous nature of the participating organizations in ESF process makes it more interesting. The paper shows that the activists need to make collaborations to do their work in a more effective way, but the computer supported collaboration in this kind of heterogeneous network is a complex process. The empirical analysis highlights the benefits of using the OpenESF system by some activists, but the quantitative and qualitative data show that most of the projects were only created and there is no further discussion. Though this platform was also supposed to serve as a platform for continuous discussion, the data show that no new users are joining the system since the event held in September 2008 in Malmo and also the members who have already joined the forum become passive. Although there are regular EPA meetings, many different mobilizations initiatives and preparations for the next ESF by the Turkish organizing committee are going on, there is no active visibility of these initiatives at OpenESF. The problems faced by the activists in interacting with the system have highlighted some design deficiencies, which need to be improved to facilitate activists. Although there were some cases when the sensitivity of the information and lack of technical skills hindered the use of technology, some positive use of OpenESF advocates that if the design issues could be dealt with, this could act as a major discussion point for the ESF community. The empirical data suggests that distinction among organizational and personal identity is important for some activists while collaborating on the web. It is also important to find interesting projects joined by the people in one's email network that could provide suitable choices and tags associated with different projects thus helping in improving upon the search results. Furthermore, multilingual interfaces and automated content translation could attract a larger majority of activists in collaborating on the web.

References

1. Saeed, S., Rohde, M. and Wulf, V.: A framework towards IT appropriation in voluntary organizations, Int. J. Knowledge and Learning, 4(5), 438–451 (2008)
2. Saeed, S., Rohde, M. and Wulf, V. Technologies within Transnational social activist communities: An Ethnographic Study of World Social Forum In: 4th International conference on Communities and Technologies pp. 85–94, ACM Press, New York (2009)
3. O'Donnell, S.: Analysing the Internet and the Public Sphere: The Case of Womenslink, Javnost, 8(1), 39–58 (2001)
4. Cammaerts, B., Van Audenhove, L. ICT-Usage among Transnational Social Movements in the Networked Society: to organise, to mediate & to influence. ASCoR, Amsterdam Free University, Amsterdam (2003)
5. Pini, B., Brown, K., Previte, J. Politics and Identity in Cyberspace A Case Study of Australian Women in Agriculture online', In: W. van de Donk, B. D. Loader, P. G. Nixon, and D. Rucht (Ed.), Cyber Protest, New Media, Citizens and Social Movements, pp. 259–275, London: Routledge (2004)
6. O'Donnell, S. and Ramaioli, G.: Sustaining an Online Information Network for Non-Profit Organisations: The Case of Community Exchange. In: Community Informatics Research Network (CIRN) Conference (2004)
7. Cheta, R.: Dis@bled people, ICTs and a new age of activism A Portuguese accessibility special interest group study, In: W. van de *Donk*, B. D. Loader, P. G. Nixon, and D. Rucht (Ed.), Cyber Protest, New Media, Citizens and Social Movements, pp. 207–232, London: Routledge (2004)
8. Edwards, A.: The Dutch women's movement online Internet and the organizational infrastructure of a social movement, In: W. van de *Donk*, B. D. Loader, P. G. Nixon, and D. Rucht (Ed.), Cyber Protest, New Media, Citizens and Social Movements, pp. 183–206, London: Routledge (2004)
9. Cardoso, G., Neto, Pereira P. Mass media driven mobilization and online protest ICTs and the pro-East Timor movement in Portugal, In: W. van de Donk, B. D. Loader, P. G. Nixon, and D. Rucht (Ed.), Cyber Protest, New Media, Citizens and Social Movements, pp. 147–163, London: Routledge (2004)
10. O'Donnell, S., Perley, S., Walmark, B., Burton, K., Beaton, B. and Sark, A.: Community-based broadband organizations and video communications for remote and rural First Nations in Canada. In: Community Informatics Research Network (CIRN) Conference (2007)
11. Kavada, A.: Civil Society Organizations and the Internet: the Case of Amnesty International, Oxfam and the World Development Movement, In: W. de Jong, M. Shaw and N. Stammers (ed.), Global Activism, Global Media, pp. 208–222, University of Michigan Press (2005)
12. McPhail, B., Costantino, T., Bruckmann, D., Barclay, R., Clement, A.: CAVEAT Exemplar: Participatory Design in a Non-Profit Volunteer Organisation, Computer Supported Cooperative Work 7(3), 223–241 (1998)
13. Trigg, R., H.: From sand box to "fund box": Weaving Participatory Design into the Fabric of a Busy Non-profit. In: Participatory Design Conference, pp. 174–183. Palo Alto CA. (2000)
14. Pilemalm, S.: Information Technology for Non-Profit Organizations Extended Participatory Design of an Information System for Trade Union Shop Stewards. Ph.D. thesis Linköping University, Sweden (2002)
15. Merkel, C., B., Xiao, L., Farooq, U., Ganoe, C., H., Lee, R., Carroll, J., M., Rosson, M., B: Participatory Design in Community Computing Contexts: Tales from the Field. In: Participatory Design Conference, pp. 1–10. ACM Press, New York (2004)
16. Farooq, U.: Conceptual and Technical Scaffolds for End User Development: Using scenarios and wikis in community computing. In: IEEE Symposium on Visual Languages and Human-Centric Computing: Graduate Student Consortium on Toward Diversity in Information Access and Manipulation, pp. 329–330, IEEE Computer Society (2005)

17. Merkel, C., Clitherow, M., Farooq, U., Xiao, L., Carroll, J.M., Rosson, M.B.: Sustaining Computer Use and Learning in Community Computing Contexts: Making Technology Part of 'Who They Are and What They Do" The Journal of Community Informatics (online), 1(2), 158–174 (2005)

18. Rohde, M.: Find what binds. Building Social Capital in an Iranian NGO Community System. In: Huysman, M., Wulf, V. (eds.): Social Capital and Information Technology, Cambridge: pp. 75–112. MIT Press (2004)

19. McIver, W.: Tools for collaboration between transnational NGOs: multilingual, Legislative Drafting. In: International Colloquium on Communication and Democracy: Technology and Citizen Engagement (2004)

20. Aelst, P., V. and Walgrave, S. New media, new movements? The role of the internet in shaping the anti-globalization movement, In: W. van de *Donk*, B. D. Loader, P. G. Nixon, and D. Rucht (Ed.), Cyber Protest, New Media, Citizens and Social Movements, pp. 97–122, London: Routledge (2004)

21. Kavada, A.: The European Social Forum and the Internet: A Case Study of Communication Networks and Collective Action. Ph.D Thesis. University of Westminster, UK (2007)

22. Fuster Morell, M.: Social Forums and Technology: Hypothesis on why online communities promoted by Social Forums don't easily scale up In: Networked Politics and Technology seminar UC Berkeley (2008)

23. Fuster Morell, M.: Governance of Online Creation Communities: Provision of Platforms of participation for the building of digital commons Self Provision Model: Social Forums Case Study. In: European Conference on Political Research Postdam (2009)

24. Saeed, S., Rohde, M. and Wulf, V. Towards Understanding IT Needs of Social Activists: The Case of the World Social Forum 2006 Organizing Process In: 1st World Summit on Knowledge Society, Springer (2008)

25. Saeed, S., Pipek, V., Rohde, M. and Wulf, V. Managing Nomadic Knowledge: A Case Study of the European Social Forum *(In Submission)*

26. Moraitis Dimitirs Thoughts on the present and future of the workspace codebase

27. Open Plan Project http://topp.openplans.org/

28. Yamashita , N., Ishida, T.:. Effects of Machine Translation on Collaborative Work. In: International Conference on Computer Supported Cooperative Work (CSCW-06), pp. 515–523, ACM Press, New York (2006)

29. Prinz, W.: TOSCA Providing organisational information to CSCW applications, In: 3rd European Conference on Computer Supported Cooperative Work. pp. 147–161, Kluwer, Dordrecht, pp. 147–161 (1993)

30. Ehrlich, K. Locating Expertise: Design Issues for an Expertise Locator, in: Ackerman, M.; Pipek, V.; Wulf, V. (eds): Sharing expertise: beyond knowledge management. Cambridge, MA: MIT Press, 2003, pp. 137–158

31. Reichling, T.; Wulf, V.: Expert recommender systems in practice: evaluating semi-automatic profile generation. In: 27th ACM-CHI Conference on Human Factors in Computing, pp. 59–68, ACM Press, New York (2009)

'Keep Up the Good Work!': The Concept of 'Work' in CSCW

Kjeld Schmidt

Abstract The scope of CSCW has been a topic of sporadic debate for many years, but in a programmatic article from 2005, three esteemed CSCW researchers – Andy Crabtree, Tom Rodden, and Steve Benford – now forcefully argue that CSCW should 'move its focus away from work'. It is thus time to reconsider CSCW, to rethink what it is and why it might be important. This paper focuses on CSCW's scope: the rationale for its focus on ordinary work. It offers an analysis of the concept of 'work' (based on Ryle, Urmson, and Schutz), a critique of prevailing illusions about the realities of work in the contemporary world, and an attempt position CSCW in the context of technological development more broadly.

Introduction

It is hardly controversial to say that our understanding of work practices has become significantly more realistic and sophisticated over the last 2 decades or so. It is hardly controversial, either, to say that CSCW has been a major force in bringing this about. The intellectualist and mechanistic (or 'cognitivist') notions and theories of orderly activities that only 1 or 2 decades ago seemed unassailable and unquestionable have been upset and, by and large, overthrown. By virtue of its commitment to the development new classes of information technology, CSCW has succeeded in situating technology in the context of ordinary practical activities in material settings. In doing so, CSCW researchers have developed conceptual frameworks and investigative strategies and techniques that, however tentative they may be, enable us to hone in on the ways in which mundane artifacts and clusters of such artifacts are deployed and developed by practitioners and have set a new standards for rigorous analysis of actual work practices. And complementary to

K. Schmidt (✉)
Department of Organization, Copenhagen Business School, Denmark
e-mail: schmidt@cscw.dk

M. Lewkowicz et al. (eds.), *Proceedings of COOP 2010*,
DOI 10.1007/978-1-84996-211-7_15, © Springer-Verlag London Limited 2010

these achievements, CSCW has articulated (in outline, at least) a fundamental critique of fundamental assumptions and tenets in computing and has fostered multiple promising lines of technological development in areas such as 'awareness' mechanisms and flexible workflows.

However, these achievements are somewhat overshadowed by retrograde developments in the form of, for example, the increasing emphasis on studies of the use of well known 'collaborative' technologies with little or no relevance for the development of new technologies. At the same time, and related to this, doubts about the direction and scope of CSCW, especially the field's declared focus on 'work', have been simmering for years (witness various panel discussions at ECSCW 2003 and 2007). In the meantime, however, a programmatic article has moved the debate to the public forum. It is written by three distinguished CSCW researchers, namely, Andy Crabtree, Tom Rodden, and Steve Benford [7] who deserve credit for providing an occasion for taking the discussion to the public arena. *The horse is out of the barn.*

CSCW's program obviously needs clarification, but as Wittgenstein asks somewhere, Isn't a clarified concept a new concept? That is, in taking the challenge, I will not simply articulate what was previously taken for granted as common ground, for that is obviously no longer the case. It is time to reconsider CSCW, to rethink what it is and why it might be important. This paper will focus on CSCW's scope: the rationale for its focus on ordinary work.

Moving with the Times, or Blowing in the Wind?

Crabtree and his colleagues do not beat around the bush. Under the title 'Moving with the times', which is obviously meant to resonate Dylan's clarion call ('And the first one now/Will later be last/For the times they are a-changin'), the article states its message forcefully already in the abstract: "it is no mere accident that CSCW took work as its topic and resource – the historical nature of IT research from which the field emerged meant that for all practical purposes it could not be otherwise. Yet times change. IT research moves on. Today mobile, ambient, pervasive, ubiquitous, mixed reality and wearable computing, et cetera, are of fundamental concern to the contemporary computing research community. Furthermore, these developments are accompanied by a movement away from the workplace to focus on diverse settings in everyday life: homes, games, museums, photography, tourism, performances, indeed diverse bodies of people and pursuits that generally fall under the conceptual rubric of the 'ludic'. Accompanying this shift away from work is a call for new approaches and concepts that will enable researchers to better understand the ludic and inform design appropriately" [7, p. 217].

The prophetical rhetoric is obviously intended to convey a notion of ineluctable fate: 'times change' and 'IT research moves on' ('you better start swimmin'). Invoking 'The Development' and other forms of hype is very much like military March music and battle cries; it is meant to encourage the faint-hearted ('We'll be victorious!') and to intimidate the opposition ('Resistance is futile!'). New technologies, we are told, are emerging that are 'of fundamental concern to the [sic] contemporary computing research community'. And nothing less than 'a movement away from the workplace' is taking place, shifting the 'focus' from work to 'diverse settings in everyday life', and this 'shift away from work' is accompanied by 'a call for new approaches and concepts that will enable researchers to better understand the ludic'. In short, we are told, 'move with the times' ('or you'll sink like a stone').

Pipes and drums notwithstanding, the three authors are already slightly less confident in the last section of the article. Here CSCW no longer has to 'shift its focus away from work', nor does it have to 'radically reshape itself in order to tackle these new areas of interest' (p. 247). Rather, 'the horizon should be broadened' to 'incorporate' 'ludic pursuits'. But this is just a change in tone, not in substance. The basic argument is that new information technologies require the scope of CSCW to be altered significantly.

Their argument runs like this: 'Contemporary IT research agendas are concerned with the development of such technologies as mobile, mixed reality, ambient, pervasive, ubiquitous, and wearable computing systems, devices, applications, and architectures. Visions of these technologies often hinge on notions of ubiquitous or pervasive computing where technology is interleaved with our everyday activities, located in the places where we live, work and play. The need for these technologies to be situated in our everyday lives suggests that many of the lessons learned in CSCW about the sociality of work are salient to ongoing developments in these and other emerging areas of IT research. To explore the salience of CSCW in such contexts will require the field to extend its boundaries and broaden its horizons beyond the bounds of the workplace, however' [7, pp. 218 f.]. Accordingly, they argue, CSCW should shift its focus from work to "homes, games, museums, photography, tourism, performances, indeed diverse bodies of people and pursuits that generally fall under the conceptual rubric of the 'ludic'" (p. 217).[1] They elaborate this proposal: "while ludic pursuits may be essentially 'playful' in character they are nonetheless socially organized and it is this that makes them available to CSCW research. Furthermore, the need for new technologies to be situated within these diverse activities strongly aligns this research with the underpinning motivation of CSCW to develop technologies that are situated within real world activities and informed by our understanding of the socially organized nature of those activities" [7, pp. 219 f.].

The gist of what the authors are saying can be summarized in two arguments:

1. The first argument is that CSCW is to be demarcated in terms of certain technologies. Their argument, stated clearly and repeatedly, is that *because of* these new technologies CSCW should abandon or broaden its scope, 'shift away from work' (p. 218) or, less drastically, 'broaden' its horizon (p. 247). Condensed, the argument is this: (a) CSCW was and should remain 'thoroughly intertwined with

---

[1] It takes some stretch of 'sociological imagination' to extend the concept of the 'ludic' to include, of all things, domestic life.

IT research'; (b) IT research now 'moves out from the workplace to consider how IT may be situated in a broader range of social settings'; (c) *therefore* CSCW 'must also move with it' (p. 247).

2. The second argument, to which the bulk of their paper is devoted, is formulated as a reply to an objection to this program that was raised in 2001 by Bill Gaver who argued that 'ludic pursuits' are characterized by very different objectives, priorities, and criteria of validity compared to the world of ordinary work: 'There is a danger that as technology moves from the office into our homes, it will bring along with it workplace values such as efficiency and productivity at the expense of other possibilities. People do not just pursue tasks and solve problems, they also explore, wonder, love, worship, and waste time' [10]. Gaver restated and elaborated this argument in 2002: 'As collaborative technologies move out of the office and into the home or local community, new goals emerge, and thus new requirements for information and media. At home technologies could support emotional connections, providing access to other peoples' moods or attitudes, not simply their presence or availability. Within the community, technologies might help bridge different social groups, values and attitudes, to potentially mediate the communication of varied subcultures.' [11, p. 477].

In short, Gaver is warning that the concept of *working* and the concepts of exploration, wondering, loving, worshipping, and wasting time cannot simply be assimilated, as these different domains are characterized by different criteria, priorities, values, attitudes, and so on. Gaver could have said simply that we must be careful not to make 'the phenomenon disappear', to use a key expression from ethnomethod-ological studies of work [22].

Anyway, Crabtree et al. object that it is indeed possible to 'unpack the social characteristics of ludic pursuits using existing CSCW concepts' such as 'routines', 'constant interruption', 'distributed awareness', 'local knowledge', 'surreptitious monitoring' (p. 248). To support this, they present a study of a game and then show that such CSCW concepts can be applied to the data. They are indeed able to rec-ognize 'routines', 'constant interruption', 'distributed awareness', 'local knowl-edge', 'surreptitious monitoring' in the way the players go about doing the game. Indeed! They conclude from this that 'ludic pursuits' and other domains of activity beyond ordinary work settings are 'available to CSCW research' because they are 'socially organized'; that is, such activities also *rely on, exploit, and exhibit their sociality* as a condition of their intelligibility, meaningfulness and value' (pp. 219, 247). Hence, they argue, CSCW can shift or widen its focus to address 'socially organized activities' in all generality without confounding what we normally would consider quite different domains.

This argument is immediately and obviously absurd, for Gaver did not claim that such CSCW concepts *cannot* be applied beyond the domain of work. He argued that doing so would make the phenomenon disappear, namely, the phenomenon of playing games, of horsing around, of worshipping, etc. Doing so would not yield an adequate picture of the phenomenon, playing games, etc. And in fact, in presenting their study and in applying CSCW concepts to the case, Crabtree, Rodden, and Benford do not manage to give us an inkling as to whether the players were having fun! They do not seem to have realized that they would have to do *just that* to demonstrate that Gaver was unduly worried. As it is, then, Gaver's objection still stands.

My concern, on the other hand, is what it would do to CSCW if its scope is extended and broadened, as called for by Crabtree et al. My answer is that for CSCW too the phenomenon would disappear.

I will deal with these two sets of issues in turn.

Before we move on, however, it should be pointed out that the general argument advanced by Crabtree et al. seems to be shared by significant sections of the CSCW community. It is for example echoed by Barry Brown and Louise Barkhuus in their introduction to the special issue of the *CSCW Journal* on 'Leisure and CSCW': 'Our goal [...] has been [...] not simply to move CSCW into studying leisure, entertainment and pleasure but to explore the new contributions and outputs from our research' [5, p. 8]. Citing the article by Crabtree et al. they state: 'The interdependences between work and leisure cuts across many core concerns of CSCW: awareness, division of labour, collaboration, distribution of tasks, efficiency and even workflow. These exist in our leisure lives as much as [in] our work [...]. It is not that leisure is exactly like paid employment, but rather that many of the concepts of CSCW are concepts of *collaborative organization*. As such, leisure can depend upon this organization as much as work, giving CSCW leverage in understanding, and designing for, this domain of activity' [5, p. 3].[2]

However, Brown and Barkhuus are more circumspect in their discussion, in that they remain aware of the 'irony in how a field such as CSCW, and the concepts it has developed, have turned out to be of relevance when looking at leisure', and they caution that 'studying leisure demands that we consider aspects of practice, such as happiness and enjoyment, as much as effectiveness or efficiency' (p. 7). This leads them to suggest that the issue that should be explored is: 'How can our methods help develop enjoyable and not just effective systems? How can we explore enjoyment as a broad research goal?' (p. 8). If these questions are researchable questions at all (which I seriously doubt), are they issues that can be accommodated within a practice-oriented research program of CSCW without depriving the program of practical relevance and orientation? And at another level of abstraction, are we now, after all these years, supposed to again embrace the scientistic myth of a universal method?

Interdisciplinary Pitfalls

Early in their article, the Crabtree, Rodden, and Benford observe that CSCW was 'motivated and underpinned by advances in distributed computing and aligned with a number of technological research trajectories' (p. 218). This is not controversial

---

[2] It should be noted, also in passing, that it requires *more* than 'sociological imagination' to claim that 'awareness, division of labour, collaboration, distribution of tasks, efficiency and even workflow [...] exist in our leisure lives *as much as* [in] our work' (emphasis added).

at all; it is a historical fact. Without computers in networks, no CSCW. But the authors then begin modulate their language: 'Technological developments and research played a central role in establishing a nascent field of interdisciplinary inquiry at the centre of which was a concerted effort to develop systems from these emerging technologies that would resonate with the social character of work and organization' (ibid.). This is at first rather puzzling. Should this be read as implying that CSCW is about developing 'systems' (based on 'these emerging technologies') but has no role in developing 'technologies'? The difference is important. Do we have the requisite technologies and is the job simply restricted to configuring these technologies in the form of 'systems' for specific settings? If this reading is correct, how are the new technologies supposedly developed? Do the authors believe that they are and can be developed 'automatically' or 'spontaneously', that is, without a view to their potential application? Although not uncommon, this notion of a strictly unidirectional process of technological development, from mathematics to technologies in search of an application, is a fantasy. This reading is confirmed when the authors emphasize that "the historical context of interdisciplinary research, which underpinned the emergence and development of CSCW [...] was one motivated by the needs of IT researchers to understand the socially organized ('collaborative' or 'cooperative') *situations and settings in which developing systems would be deployed and used"* (p. 218, emphasis added).

This paints a strange picture of the roots of CSCW. It is a picture where 'technological development' and 'developing systems' were *going concerns* that simply happened to be in need of supplementary understanding of the settings 'in which developing systems would be deployed and used'. Were the then existing technologies adequate for 'designing systems' that 'resonate with the social character of work and organization'? Did CSCW just have to take the technologies and put them together?

This picture of the origins of CSCW is a gross misrepresentation. One example will suffice to show this. If we take the classic CSCW article by Rodden, Mariani, and Blair from 1992, we will see a completely different view:

'Cooperative applications which have started to emerge from CSCW research place new demands on the computer technology used to support them. These demands raise a number of fundamental questions about the way in which computing systems provide application support.' 'The majority of applications have been developed using existing and proven computer systems and technology. These supporting systems provide many of the services necessary to realise cooperative applications. However, the means by which these services are provided and the techniques used to present technological support to application developers incorporates an assumed model of use' [18, p. 41]. Calling for 'a re-consideration of the design decisions underpinning existing computer techniques', Rodden, Mariani, and Blair stated that: 'Many of these assumptions are challenged by the needs of cooperative applications which highlight a significant role for computer science research within CSCW and suggests that CSCW will have far reaching consequences for computing' (p. 42).

As this one example amply demonstrates, CSCW from the very beginning did not merely take existing technologies for granted (apart from *post-hoc* studies of the uses of 'groupware' and computer-mediated communications). On the contrary, progressive CSCW research questioned the 'assumed model of use'. What Crabtree, Rodden, and Benford now propose is a view of CSCW that is the diametrically opposite. On this view, CSCW is field defined by a certain family of technologies and its role is to assist technological researchers in developing systems based on these technologies; the 'assumed model of use' is not questioned.

Crabtree et al. are of course correct in emphasizing the potentials of new interaction technologies such as mobile, ambient, pervasive, ubiquitous, mixed reality and wearable computing, etc. What they refer to is a family of technologies that, in different configurations, may make it possible to build applications that are both embedded in ordinary artifacts, typically mobile devices (handheld, wearable, etc.), and at the same time reactive to the state of the material environment. This family of technologies includes positioning based on any kind of wireless networks (GPS, GSM, WiFi, Bluetooth, RFID), sensor and actuator technologies, multi-modal representations, and the like. By making it possible to build highly mobile and reactive devices these technologies may enable us to build applications that support 'mutual awareness' in ways that are far more effective and far less intrusive than previously [for fascinating examples, cf. 11]. After all, how much 'mutual awareness' can be obtained by means of a 17 in. screen, a keyboard, and a mouse? In short, these technologies are obviously quite relevant for ordinary cooperative work. They promise ways to facilitate 'mutual awareness' in settings in which the state of the physical environment and of actions in terms of location, movement, direction, velocity, temperature, etc. have practical significance for members: Where is part #36.87.6745? Has it been moved? Whereto? Will the next shipment of cylinder blocks arrive on time? When will this process be finished? Has this roll been exposed to humidity? Is Mike from Maintenance on his way? Has he already been here?

But this is not the message Crabtree et al. want to convey. The potential application of these technologies in ordinary cooperative work settings is not even mentioned in the article. Their message is the opposite: that CSCW must to shift the focus away from work or 'broaden' its horizon *in order to* accommodate these new interaction technologies. But this line of reasoning is a *non sequitur*. For the arrival of these technologies offer no reason whatsoever why CSCW should 'shift away from work'.

Unusually muddled thinking seems be at work in the call for shifting the focus of CSCW away from work. This becomes evident if we, just for a minute, consider other technologies than the ones mentioned by Crabtree, Rodden, and Benford. When we do so, we will easily realize that a vast variety of other technologies exists, in various stages of maturity, that (potentially) are of equal relevance to CSCW. Let me just point to high-level computational notations for 'business process modelling' (e.g., BPEL), computational 'ontologies', peer-to-peer protocols, 'service-oriented architectures' (SOA), robotics, space-based architectures ('data grid' technology), 'bigraphical reactive systems', 'XML spaces', and so on. In fact, no kind of information technology is, in principle, without actual or potential relevance to CSCW. Given the endless variety of technologies of potential interest to CSCW, it would be futile for CSCW to shift its focus in response to new technologies. In short, their argument for moving away from work is confused.

The Concept of 'Work'

When the scope of CSCW is discussed and the proposal is put forward to remove or ignore the 'W' in the acronym, the argument is often that 'work' is a term of many uses anyway and that CSCW. It is thus suggested that. since the term 'work' is being used in some sociological literature in a highly derived sense, the same loose usage is legitimate in deliberating the scope and focus of CSCW as well. But to argue that just because we use the word 'work' in many ways and for all sorts of phenomena, then all these phenomena are *of the same kind* and can be studied as more or less the same phenomenon – is the classical nominalist fallacy.

I will here present two arguments, one based on some remarks Ryle made rather tangentially, and another based on some remarks that Schutz developed as a centerpiece of his philosophy of sociology. I will then, thus supported, try to put these arguments to work.

'Work': A Rylean Argument

In his protracted effort to evict Cartesianism (and Behaviorism) from the philosophy and psychology of *thinking*, Gilbert Ryle introduced a series of auxiliary or meta-logical concepts and distinctions. They were all introduced in an ad hoc manner as useful tools for his analyses. One of his tools is a class of concepts he calls 'polymorphous concepts'.

To understand what Ryle is up to with this category, let us briefly follow his argumentation in a short paper on 'Thinking and language' from 1951. When theorizing about *thinking* we are, he notes, naturally inclined to say what thinking consists of and how these various elements are combined. Since processes like perspiring, digesting, counting, and singing can be broken down into elementary processes, we would expect the same of thinking. 'But this is a mistake', Ryle observes, adding: "There is no general answer to the question 'What does thinking consist of?'". Ryle then, to sustain his argument, switches to the concept of work:

> If asked "What does working consist of?" we should quickly object that there was no general answer. Some sorts of work are done with some sorts of tools, others with other sorts. But sometimes the same work might be done with alternative tools. Some work does not require tools at all. The dancer uses her limbs, but her limbs are not implements. A headmaster might do his work though deprived of the use of his arms, or his legs or his eyes. Some sorts of work are done with special materials, like string or Carrara marble. But the work might be done with different materials, and some work does not require materials at all. An artist's model need not even be attending to her work. She might be paid for sleeping or playing patience in the studio. There need be no action, inner or overt, performed by the policeman on his beat, which he may not also perform when strolling round the same streets when his work is over. Not all work is for pay; not all work is unpleasant; not all work is tiring. Nothing need be done, thought, or felt by the professional footballer at work that might not be done, thought or felt by the amateur at play. *Work* is a polymorphous concept. There is nothing which must be going on in one piece of work which need be

going on in another. Nothing answers to the general description "what work consists of". None the less, each specific job is describable. The workman can be told what he is to do. The concepts of *fighting*, *trading*, *playing*, *housekeeping* and *farming* are also polymorphous concepts, where the concepts of boxing and apple-picking are nearly enough non-polymorphous. [19, pp. 260 f.]

For Ryle the concept of work has now done its job and he can turn back to the job at hand: 'The concept of *thinking* is polymorphous' (p. 261). We leave his inquiry there, for what concerns us here is of course not Ryle's analysis of the concept of 'thinking' but his characterization, in a kind of adjunct line of argument, of the concept of 'working' as a polymorphous concept. Concepts like 'practicing' or 'obeying' are polymorphous in that none of these words indicate some specific activity. By contrast to concepts such as 'singing', the concept of 'working' is polymorphous in the sense that the application of the term 'working' does not imply the performance of any *specific* activity.

In the words of Alan White, in his concise account of Ryle's philosophy of mind, polymorphous concepts like 'practicing' or 'obeying' indicate the relationship of a given activity 'to its circumstances, and thereby signifies what, on this occasion, it is a form of' [25, p. 59]. What is implied, then, when we say of a man, for example, that 'he is now working again', or that 'he is working hard', or that 'he has not been working for quite some time', or that 'he is only pretending to be working'? James Urmson, another of Ryle's and Austin's younger colleagues at Oxford, has written a comment on these remarks by Ryle in which he makes some, for our purpose, very cogent remarks on the concept of working:

> Working has no strict opposite or contrary; but it is most typically contrasted with recreation and leisure pursuits. One of Ryle's leisure pursuits and recreations is gardening; I should never be surprised to hear that he has spent the afternoon working in his garden. But perhaps I ought to be surprised when I hear this, for if gardening is his recreation how can he be working when he is gardening? Yet in fact it does not ring at all oddly if somebody says that his favourite recreation is working in his garden. However, we should be surprised if a professional philosopher, filling in one of those tiresome statisticians' questionnaires, were to include his hours of gardening in his answer to a question about the number of hours he worked each week; we should be shocked if he were to refuse a legitimate professional call on his time on the ground that he had other pressing work to do, if it emerged that this other pressing work was lawn-mowing; if he can find much time for gardening over a certain period, then for that period he cannot have been very busy. It is clear that only for certain limited purposes can a professional philosopher's gardening be called work, and that for many important purposes it must be contrasted with his work. [24, pp. 260 f.]

That is, to categorize a given activity as work involves implicit references to motive and circumstance. Just like a man's writing his signature on a piece of paper may be described as his practicing his signature, authorizing a purchase order, or signing a peace treaty, depending on the situation at hand, a man's turning soil with a spade may be described as recreation or as working; it simply depends on the context. That is, without background information, one would not be able to tell from a short video snippet of an activity whether what it depicted was somebody engaged in work or recreation or something complete different (somebody imitating a gardener, say, for purposes of satire or ceremony). In short, the same activity may count for working in certain situations, or when referred to in certain discourses, whereas the same categorization of the same physical activity in another discourse would be considered flippant.

However, Urmson goes on, not *any* activity would qualify for the label *work*: 'It is also worthy of attention that not all recreation, however strenuously pursued, can be called work. It is all very well in the case of gardening, knitting, carpentry, and rug-making; these are most naturally categorized as working; it is perfectly reasonable to speak of somebody as working on his stamp-collection or on a painting. But we should require some special explanation if we were told that somebody was working on a game of ludo or a detective story, or that he was working at a country walk or a game of cricket. No doubt, if I am writing a detective story, even for fun, I may be said to be working at or on it, but not when I am sprawled in an armchair reading it' [24, p. 261].

It is evident that we, in our ordinary discourse, make an informal distinction between occupations which would be counted as 'work' in *all* standard contexts and those which would be called 'work' only for *some* purposes. Dubbing the first ones 'primary cases of work' and the others 'secondary cases of work', Urmson then goes on: 'The central among the primary cases of working are those in which one does something, whatever it consists of, because it is necessary or useful in a practical way. Since people typically have the duty to do such things and are frequently paid for doing them, we also extend the primary cases of working to include doing anything, whatever it consists of, if it is done as a matter of duty for pay. In this way the game-playing of the professional comes to be counted as a primary case of work. [...] In the case of primary work we thus have a slide, excluding action-content, from whatever is practically necessary or useful, to the same done as a matter of duty for pay, to anything which is done as a matter of duty for pay' [24, p. 263].

That is, central to the concept of work, *the primary cases of work* designate activities that are considered 'necessary or useful', either in terms of the concrete fruits of the labor (food, clothing, timber, tools, machines) or in terms of some other reward (recognition, salary). The point is practical necessity or usefulness. For an activity to count as working requires more than its unfolding in time and space. What counts is whether it is done and done well. In performing the activity the actor must deal with all sorts of constraints and requirements, and in the modern world, in the dense web of global division of labor, these are typically externally defined. Preparing a meal for others, perhaps even for paying clients, implies different constraints and requirements and hence different concerns, procedures, and techniques, than preparing a meal for oneself. After all, if you are cooking for yourself, no real harm is done if the sauce is too salty or the steak too 'rare'. It is not very serious. It may look the same but it is a different ballgame: the criteria are different, the requirements in terms of planning and skill are different.

The *secondary cases of work*, by contrast, can be considered work because they are *also* serious affairs in that they *too* require 'effort and concentration': 'Secondary cases of work are those which resemble reasonably closely in action-content typical and common forms of work. One of these, for example, is the cultivation of the soil, and thus the construction of an ornamental rockery for the pleasure of its construction comes to be counted as (secondary) work. Also, since central cases of work typically require effort and concentration, we are even prepared to say of an enthusiastic amateur game-player that he is working hard, though we are unlikely to say that he is working *simpliciter*. It would seem that we will not say that the solver of crossword puzzles is working because he is not doing anything sufficiently similar to what people commonly do in the way of primary work, though we can say that the amateur carpenter is working at his bench without any qualms' [24, p. 263].

In sum, the concept of work is used in ordinary language to highlight or emphasize that the given activity serves practical purposes, that it requires effort and concentration, and that it presumes mastery of all sorts technicalities. The concept of work implies that it is not mere pleasure but serious stuff: activities faced with serious complexities. It is because of this that one can say, as Marx does, that even 'really free working', such as composing music, 'is at the same time the most damned seriousness, the most intense exertion' [16, p. 499].

In other words, the meaning we impart to an activity by using the term 'working' was expressed succinctly by Johnny Cash in his introduction to the song 'There ain't no easy run', a salute to the work of truckers:

Sixteen forward gears, diesel smoke trailing in the wind.

Eighteen tires checked and singing on the pavement.

Five thousand miles to cover, three weeks away from home.

And it's work, Mister, it demands the best.

And whether your run is on Interstate 70 or hauling freight down the eastern seaboard,

If you're a gearjammer you know there ain't no easy runs.[3]

Work, as we know it, demands the best: it requires skill and training, stamina and effort, dedication and attention.

'Work': A Schutzian Argument

The everyday world of working plays a key role in the thinking of the founder of phenomenological sociology, Alfred Schutz, who discusses the concept of work in many key places. His purpose of these discussions are of course different from those of Ryle and Urmson, but his line of reasoning is nonetheless somewhat congenial with their argument. In view of the historical role Schutz played in the development of the sociology of ordinary practice (from Garfinkel [9] to Bourdieu [4]), it may be worthwhile to quickly summarize his view on 'work'.

'We begin with an analysis of the world of daily life which the wide-awake, grown-up man who acts in it and upon it amidst his fellow-men experiences within

---

[3] Johnny Cash: *The Johnny Cash Show*, Columbia Records, October 1970.

the natural attitude as a reality,' goes a typical beginning of a Schutzian argument. He then goes on to describe this natural attitude of a person engaged in his or her daily work: 'To [the natural attitude] the world is from the outset not the private world of the single individual but an intersubjective world, common to all of us, in which we have not a theoretical but an eminently practical interest. The world of everyday life is the scene and also the object of our actions and interactions. We have to dominate it and we have to change it in order to realize the purposes which we pursue within it among our fellow-men. We work and operate not only within but upon the world. Our bodily movements – kinaesthetic, locomotive, operative – gear, so to speak, into the world, modifying or changing its objects and their mutual relationships. On the other hand, these objects offer resistance to our acts which we have either to overcome or to which we have to yield. Thus, it may be correctly said that a pragmatic motive governs our natural attitude toward the world of daily life. World, in this sense, is something that we have to modify by our actions or that modifies our actions' [21, pp. 208 f.].

In this particular context, Schutz wants to contrast the world of work and its natural attitude with other regions of human experience. Taking his cue from some comments by William James in the latter's *Principles of Psychology* on different experiential 'sub-universes', such as the world of material things, the world of ideas, the worlds of mythology and religion, or the world of sheer madness, he wants to 'free this important insight from its psychologistic setting'. Schutz therefore proposes the term 'finite provinces of meaning', mentioning as examples, in addition to the world of working, 'the world of dreams, of imageries and phantasms, especially the world of art, the world of religious experiences, the world of scientific contemplation, the play world of the child, and the world of the insane' (pp. 229 f.). The major difference between the world of working and these 'finite provinces of meaning' is that 'the *epoché* of the natural attitude' of the world of working is replaced by 'other *epochés* which suspend belief in more and more layers of the reality of the daily life, putting them in brackets' (p. 233). 'The world of working in daily life is the archetype of our experience of reality. All the other provinces of meaning may be considered its modifications' (p. 233). For Schutz, that is, the world of working – the world of embodied socially situated material activities – stands out as 'paramount' because 'We have an eminently practical interest in it, caused by the necessity of complying with the basic requirements of our life' (p. 226 f.). In short, if we follow Schutz's train of thoughts, the distinction between the world of working and those other 'provinces of meaning' is critical to the project of phenomenological sociology, because without it the essential insight expressed in the concept of 'the natural attitude' is blowing in the wind, down the drain, gone.

But what is now being proposed is just that: to move or widen the scope of CSCW to include 'socially organized activities' of whatever 'finite province of meaning' ('ludic pursuits' like playing games, watching daytime TV, playing the Ancient World of Warcraft, but presumably also – why not? – daydreaming, courting, pillow talk, praying for redemption), without discrimination or ranking, on an equal footing with ordinary cooperative work.

'Work': Sociological Jargon and Ordinary Language

As noted by Urmson, the concept of 'work' is used in different ways, in the primary case used of serious and demanding activities that serve practical purposes; in the secondary case of activities that, in the effort and technical mastery required, resemble work of the primary category. We of course also use the term in even more derivative ways, tertiary and onwards, such as when we ask someone proposing a new technical term, 'What kind of work does it do for you?', meaning of course: is it of any *practical* use? does it make *a difference*? does it *do* anything? We use terms in such derivative meanings routinely, normally without getting into trouble.

Not surprisingly, the term 'work' has been appropriated by different disciplines to do, well, all kinds of 'work' for them. In physics, for instance, 'work' means the expenditure of energy required to cause a state change (a displacement of an object). An abstraction over the notion of work as mere toil, 'work' is here defined as 'force times distance'. Physicists and mechanical engineers normally have no difficultly in distinguishing this concept of work from the concept of the work in which they daily are engaged. They do not apply the mechanical or the thermo–mechanical concepts of work when they discuss whether a particular project is interesting work or hard work or boring work. Likewise Freud could talk about 'dream work' without falling into the trap of mistaking the work in 'dream work' for the work of those who manufactured his couches and cigars.

Now, the term is also used in sociology in a similarly derivative sense, for instance when ethnomethodologists use it to denote what members do to sustain social order [23, p. 11] or when Anselm Strauss in more or less the same sense talks about 'articulation work'. These phenomena are dubbed 'work' because they involve specifiable competencies. But nobody in his right mind mistakes, *or should mistake*, this derivative sense of 'work' for 'work' in the primary sense. The distinction is one that all workers apply and must apply, and they do that when they complain that they have too many meetings, that they are being interrupted in their work by phone calls, that some colleagues spend too much time drinking coffee or on Facebook. It is the distinction workers apply when they say, 'Enough talk, let's get to work!' It is a central concern to all work (in the primary sense). It is the basic tenet, also, of 'the natural attitude'.

We thus get into trouble if a term from ordinary language, like 'work', that has been appropriated by sociology to do some specialized job, is then re–imported into and imposed upon ordinary discourse. But the urge to do so is sometimes strong and it is perhaps not surprising that this stratagem is deployed in a later paper by Crabtree and colleagues [8] that argues that the ethnomethodologically informed ethnographic studies of work that have been published in CSCW are not really about work as we know it, and that most of the CSCW community thus must have got it all wrong. These studies were rather about 'the *interactional work* through which people organize a setting's activities' (p. 880 f.). Having thus emptied the concept of work of its ordinary meaning and retroactively made CSCW an esoteric outgrowth of the philosophy of sociology, the authors feel free to dismiss any idea that 'somehow or other the analytic practices of ethnography in the workplace are different to the analytic practices of ethnography in, for example, the home or the museum'. It is an old trick that has been played for centuries, sometimes to overawe the peasants, as when a enthusiastic student of nuclear physics on his first weekend back home tells his dumbfounded parents that the family's sturdy dining table is not solid at all: it's mostly empty space. Some would call it playing with words.

By going down the path suggested by Crabtree and his colleagues, i.e., the path of assimilating the dissimilar, we would not only be causing confusion; we would be losing our ability to *focus* on exactly those practices that we find in complex cooperative settings: the elaborate coordinative practices (skills, typifications, techniques, schemes, notations, etc.) that have been developed *to get the job done* and get it done efficiently, well, timely, dependably, etc. We would produce accounts of work in which what is specific about work – about cooperative work in modern settings – is bracketed out, and we would instead come up with something akin to the vacuous accounts produced by mainstream sociology.

In this regard, we have been duly warned by Sharrock and Anderson: 'The things that characterize ordinary activities for those engaged in them seem to disappear whenever sociological theories and methods are brought into play. Whenever sociologists talk about family life, work, leisure and the rest, they seem to change the subject and discuss things that we as ordinary people would not recognize. In fact, in order to decipher what is being discussed, even sociologists have to refer back to their ordinary knowledge and experience of social life.' [22, p. 15]. Only this time it seems as if ethnomethodology itself is being dressed up as yet another presumptively universal method that can be applied across the board, without alteration, irrespective of the specifics of the domain. Old habits certainly die hard.

'Work': A Reality Check

What are the criteria for demarcating CSCW's horizon? By arguing that CSCW has to move in the particular direction they are pointing to, Crabtree, Rodden, and Benford seem to employ an implicit criterion that we most definitely need to make explicit and discuss. A closer look at their argumentation will make it clear.

The article makes one *non sequitur* after another. This is very weird indeed. Why would Crabtree et al. argue that, since CSCW has lessons for, say, the computer games industry or for performance art, then its focus should be shifted away from work? Why abandon a line of research just because it has produced interesting and successful spin-offs? Why shift the focus away from work when this focus has produced insights – conceptually and technologically – that apparently are exceedingly valuable to other fields? Likewise, why should the arrival of interaction technologies of the contextual computing category, which are of obvious potential relevance to ordinary cooperative work settings and thus to CSCW, motivate CSCW to shift its focus away from those very same ordinary cooperative work settings? Why is their potential application in ordinary cooperative work settings not even considered by Crabtree and his colleagues? Why should CSCW move away from work when these new technologies are in fact highly relevant to CSCW? Why should CSCW move in precisely *this* direction? Why exactly *these* technologies? It would of course make sense for CSCW to move its focus away from work if its program have been completed and if the major problems that motivated the field in the first place have been solved. But CSCW has *not*, by any standard, solved the problems of supporting 'articulation work' in complex cooperative work settings. Why abandon a progressive research program that is important in its own right? This is perplexing.

Now, could it be because the authors believe that problems of cooperative work are no longer important problems? This seems confirmed by this passage: 'As research moves out from the workplace to consider how IT may be situated in a broader range of social settings, then CSCW must also move with it to consider how best to inform technological development within these contexts, *unless it is to run the risk of becoming a historical curiosity rather than a vibrant living research community*' [7, p. 247, emphasis added]. But how *could* CSCW possibly become 'a historical curiosity' *if and as long as* ordinary cooperative work is economically, demographically, socially important and *if and as long as* the conceptual and technical problems of developing adequate computational support for articulation work are large and generally unsolved? Because, I suggest, the authors presume ordinary work to be of ever diminishing importance (Brown and Barkhuus in fact argue along that exact line). This interpretation solves all the puzzles: it would explain the direction Crabtree et al. argue for CSCW to take: 'the ludic'; it would explain why the obvious relevance of the new interaction technologies for ordinary cooperative work settings is not considered at all; it would also explain why 'business process modelling' and other technologies destined for work settings would not be considered either; and it would explain the dramatic rhetoric and the fear of being left behind when 'the times' move, the fear of becoming a relic, a mere 'historical curiosity'.

If the authors believe that ordinary work is waning, they are not alone in doing so. It has, in different shapes and forms, been the gospel of business pundits and central bankers for quite some time. Epoch-changing transformations of human society are indeed proclaimed at a frequency that seems to match the business cycle perfectly. Social scientists are as gullible (or cunning) as technologists. The 'post-industrial' society that was proclaimed by Daniel Bell (in 1973) has been overtaken many times since – by the 'network society', the 'new economy', and the 'knowledge-based society'. The refrain of all these postulates is that ordinary industrial work is on the way out, to be replaced by 'service' work, if not by leisure *tout court*. We are all of us, or so we are told, already or soon to become, 'symbol analysts' or 'knowledge workers' who make our income in 'virtual organizations' and dwell in 'cyber-space', in the 'weightless world' of the 'digital economy', and because of the ever-increasing amount of time at our disposal for leisure, the 'experience industry' is destined to become the big thing of the future 'leisure society'. If this was even close to being realistic, it would certainly seem as if CSCW, with its focus on ordinary work practices, is indeed in risk of becoming 'a historical curiosity'. The problem with this, however, is that it has no foundation.

The Myth of the 'Leisure Society'

Let us take the issue of leisure first. Are we not moving into the leisure society or whatever it is called: an era where work plays a diminishing role in people's lives?

The first thing to note is that statistics about work and leisure are tricky. However, there are some serious and careful studies we can build on.

In the United States, working hours have been on the rise for decades. While US workers around the middle of the nineteenth century had put in about 70 h per week, the working week was gradually reduced to about 40 h by the time of the Second World War, at which point it stabilized. From 1948 to 1969 this level was maintained. However, according to the authoritative study by Schor [20, p. 79], the number of hours worked per adult per year 'rose modestly', whereas hours per labor force participant fell slightly (the difference largely reflecting the effect of women's increased participation in the work force). But then the trend shifts. 'After 1969, hours began to rise' (ibid.). During the 2 decades from 1969 to 1987, the hours worked by labor force participants increased from 1,786 per year to 1,949. Public perceptions notwithstanding, the conditions in 'Old Europe' are comparable. A survey study commissioned by the European Union from 1997 concludes that 'Overall Europeans work long hours'. Half of the employees work more than 40 h per week [3, pp. 140–147].

Now that we are considering the presumptive need to move the focus away from work, we should not omit the domestic or household work that has to be taken care of after paid work or in weekends: caring for children, shopping, cooking, cleaning, washing clothes, personal hygiene, and sleeping. In her study of the development in working hours in the US from 1969 to 1987, Schor shows that the total hours spent by US labor force participants on paid work together with household work rose from 2,675 to 2,837 h annually; that is, average time for leisure *fell* by 162 h per year. If one considers the entire population ('working age persons'), 'leisure time has fallen by 47 h a year' [20, pp. 35 f.]. Again this is not special to the US. In the industrialized countries members of the work force on average work about 80 h per week [12, 15].

Finally, for the sake of proportions, workers in East Asia are of course even less close to the 'leisure society' than workers in Europe and North America. China is the obvious example. According to Judith Banister, an authority on Chinese labor statistics, in many export-oriented factories in the Pearl River Delta, the new manufacturing center of the world, 'employees usually work 6 or 7 days a week, totaling 60–80 h per week in whatever period constitutes the peak season for that manufacturing sector. That season can last up to 8 months a year. Average yearly hours actually worked per employee might be as high as 4,000 h in some China manufacturing enterprises' [2, p. 31].

The leisure society is not imminent. Nor is there any necessity in its coming.[4] References to it coming are somewhat premature. That is, a change in the scope of

---

[4] The huge increases in productivity under the Industrial Revolution were accompanied by something in the magnitude of 100% increase of overall work time [20, Chapter 3]. The fact of the matter is that the development of technology does not in any way automatically translate into improved conditions of work and life.

CSCW cannot be motivated by references to the notion that work should play a diminishing part of people's lives.

The Myth of the 'Post-Industrial' Society

Proclamations that the 'industrial age' is behind us are usually buttressed by official occupational statistics that show that 'manufacturing' jobs and similar jobs in material production[5] are indeed dwindling and have long since been overtaken by jobs in the 'service' industries. True, in the developed countries, the OECD countries, the occupations categorized as 'services' have long since surpassed 'manufacturing' in numbers of people employed; they now employ approximately twice as many as 'manufacturing'. However, such statistics are useless when used as a basis for understanding structural developments and long-term trends.

However, as pointed out by many researchers, the concept of 'service' is confused [e.g., 14]. Or to say it as clearly as possible: 'The services category is a category totally devoid of scientific value' [3, p. 120]. This makes occupational statistics largely useless with respect to understanding major changes in the national and international economy. But even leaving aside the utter meaninglessness of the 'service' category itself, the debates over the issue of the relative size of 'manufacturing' versus 'services' in OECD countries is really quite absurd; or rather, provincial. The fact that factories can no longer be *seen, heard, and smelled* from the suburbs of the West, is no proof that they no longer exist. What has happened over the last 2 decades or so is that many industrial jobs have been moved from the West, especially from the US, to East and South Asia and Latin America. The percentage of jobs in manufacturing (as reflected in occupational statistics) has certainly declined in the West but, as pointed out by (even) Manuel Castells, the decline is more than offset by the increase in manufacturing in the Third World [6, p. 253]. In fact, he observes, 'While theorizing on postindustrialism we are experiencing [...] one of the largest waves of industrialization in history' (ibid., p. 113).

Today, more than 10 years later, that wave has not subsided one bit. If we again take China, the case in point, the official statistics showed 83 million manufacturing employees in 2002, but, adds Judith Banister, 'that figure is likely to be understated; the actual number was probably closer to 109 million' [1, p. 11]. To give an idea of the proportions, Banister adds that the major industrialized countries in the Group of Seven (G7) in 2002 had a total of 53 million manufacturing workers. And we have not even considered the growth of manufacturing in the other industrializing countries of Asia (India, Thailand, Vietnam, Philippines, Indonesia, etc.). As for China, there was a period, in the late 1990s through 2000, where the number of manufacturing workers in China was declining, caused by privatization of state- and

---

[5] The term 'material production' is here used as shorthand for 'production of material goods'. The term 'material work' should be understood in the same way. This usage should not be read as implying that 'immaterial production' is something out of this world.

collective-owned factories in cities and the ensuing massive layoffs and increase in productivity. However, 'China's manufacturing employment began to rise again after 2000, regaining the upward trend from 1980 to 1995' (ibid.).

We have not entered a 'post-industrial' age or a 'weightless world'. We live in the middle of an industrial revolution on a truly global scale, a massive transition from traditional agricultural work (and the domestic work and small-scale craft work that is connected with traditional agriculture) to industrial work.

What does that mean for CSCW? It means first of all that millions if not billions of people these years are moving from forms of work in domestic production, subsistence agriculture, and small-scale handicraft, which are only sporadically performed as cooperative work, to the generally systematic and increasingly complex cooperative work relations that characterize the industrial mode of production. More than that. The current process of industrialization in East Asia and elsewhere does not reiterate the forms the industrialization of England took two centuries ago. The historical *milieux* in which the current industrialization process unfolds is radically different from that of the original, of course. The process of industrialization unfolds within an already established world economy, with a global infrastructure of transportation, communication, banking, etc. Consequently, the millions of new industrial workers typically enter the world of industry in production sites that are part of global production networks, that is, they enter cooperative work relations of global scope.

In sum, focusing on ordinary work hardly makes CSCW 'a historical curiosity'. If somebody claims that CSCW's program, its focus on work, *has* to be changed, then it *cannot* be because work, including ordinary work in material production, has ceased to be economically, socially, or demographically important.

The Work of CSCW

Focusing on work is crucial for CSCW for these reasons. Work is the paradigm of the natural attitude. The worker has things to do, he or she is faced with things that have to be done in a certain way at a certain place at a certain time and that must meet requirements of all sorts. It is necessary activity, 'the realm of necessity', and resources are scarce. It is characterized by all sorts of technicalities that workers must master. It demands 'the best'. For those reasons, workers develop (or acquire or a trained in) sophisticated coordinative practices. Professional work of any kind poses the paradigm of sophisticated coordinative practices and hence of the natural attitude.

For CSCW ethnographic and other forms of in-depth workplace studies are of critical importance simply because understanding professional cooperative work practices that, as a rule, are alien to technologists, requires rigorous studies, in contrast to many other provinces of activity in which we all engage and generally master (domestic life, tourism, having fun, hanging out). Of course, *for sociology* all work domains and all kinds of work are of equal interest. The *chique boutique* in the city center offers instances of work that, to 'the sociological eye', are just as interesting as the work of assembling an airplane, performing heart surgery, or devising the proof of a mathematical theorem. But CSCW is not sociology, nor is it sociology of work; it is an interventionist enterprise, very much drawing on sociological competencies, of course, but committed to the *development of technologies* for – and their transformative integration in – cooperative work practices. This has implications for what is of *particular* interest to CSCW. And what is of particular interest to CSCW is, I submit, cooperative work practices in which coordination technologies serve, or may serve, as regulators of the interdependent activities of the members of the ensemble.

Let me flesh this out by very briefly attempting to position CSCW is the context of technological development. The machines of the Industrial Revolution – such as Robert's Self-Acting Mule spinning machine from 1825 – were mechanical in the sense that the transmission of power and the control of movement were physically integrated. Power was transferred to the tool or the work piece by means of belts, cogwheels, gear trains, camshafts, and so on, and those very same parts at the same time also regulated the movements of the tool (controlled the speed, direction, etc.). To construct and modify machines required significant skill and effort, and indeed, the cost of their construction and modification were such that the use of machinery was restricted to a few branches of industry, typically mass production [13].

This picture has changed radically with Turing's computer design: the stored program architecture. It makes it highly economical to construct control systems that are not physically integrated with the power supply. One can in fact consider the computer as a universal control system: it can be made to incarnate any control function, be it a spinning machine, a machining center, a typesetter, or a jukebox. Now, in view of the mythological notion of the digital as something non-material, it is necessary to point out that a software program that has been launched and resides in the computer's memory, in RAM, is a *machine* as much as the Self Acting Mule. It is just as material, it is just not *tangible*: one cannot touch it. However, a software machine is infinitely faster because the mass of the electron is many magnitudes smaller than a cogwheel, a camshaft, a crank, etc. (the difference in magnitude is about 10^{30}). It can move at a velocity close to the speed of light. What is equally important is that software machines can be constructed more or less automatically. When the blueprint has been designed, that is, the source code has been written and tested, the code can be compiled and executed automatically. The costs of modifying a software machine like a spreadsheet model of a budget are insignificant compared to the cost of modifying, say, the gearbox of a car. And as soon as the software machine has been built, it can be copied and distributed at an insignificant cost. And more than that, software machines can be linked: they can transfer data or code to between themselves, and one machine can trigger the execution of another, perhaps at another location. In this way, vast machine systems are being built. In fact, the Internet itself is a vast machine system that facilitates the construction and operation of other specialized machine systems. The economic, organizational, and social consequences of this radical reduction of the cost of producing and modifying machinery are enormous, to say the least: we live in the midst of the turmoil unleashed by this.

With electronic computers (with high-level programming languages and the rest) the construction of machinery has become immensely inexpensive compared to previous technologies. The same applies to the cost of modifying such machines. Whereas machinery, until a few decades ago, was rare outside of mass production industries, it now becoming ubiquitous: from CNC machines and CAD to CT scanners and GPS navigation. Moreover, due to the development of computer network technologies, it has, in the course of merely a couple of decades, become economically feasible to construct and deploy vast systems of interconnected and interoperating software machines. The 'industrial' modes of working that Marx characterized as working with and collaborating via 'machine systems' [17], are now no longer confined to classical mass-production industries, but are, in important ways, becoming characteristic of medical work, movie production, scientific laboratories. The post-industrial society is industrial, through-and-through.

And this is where CSCW enters both the story and the history. With networked computers it is technically and economically feasible to build machine systems specifically designed to regulate the coordination of cooperative work activities: workflow management systems, production control systems, scheduling systems and group calendar systems, project management systems, document management systems, configuration management systems (in software engineering), medical record systems, etc., just as it is technically and economically feasible to integrate such dedicated coordination technologies with the computational tools of the trade (CNC machines, CAD plans, etc.). More importantly, it is – in principle – technically and economically feasible for these coordination technologies to be designed in such a way that ordinary workers, of whatever profession, can devise, adopt, modify, and control the rules according to which their work is coordinated by machine systems.

These potentials have only been realized sporadically. Why? Because our understanding of cooperative work and its coordination is deficient, vague, patchy. This, I submit, is the task for CSCW.

References

1. Banister, Judith: 'Manufacturing employment in China', *Monthly Labor Review*, July 2005, pp. 11–29.
2. Banister, Judith: 'Manufacturing earnings and compensation in China', *Monthly Labor Review*, August 2005, pp. 22–39.
3. Basso, Pietro: *Modern Times, Ancient Hours: Working Lives in the Twenty-first Century*, Verso, London and New York, 2003. Transl. by G. Donis. Text ed. by G. Donis.
4. Bourdieu, Pierre: *Le sens pratique*, Les Éditions de Minuit, Paris, 1980. – English translation: *The Logic of Practice*, translated by Richard Nice, Polity Press, Cambridge, 1990.
5. Brown, Barry; and Louise Barkhuus: 'Leisure and CSCW: Introduction to Special Edition', *Computer Supported Cooperative Work (CSCW): The Journal of Collaborative Computing*, vol. 16, no. 1–2, April 2007, pp. 1–10.
6. Castells, Manuel: *The Rise of the Network Society*, vol. 1, Blackwell, Oxford, 1996.

7. Crabtree, Andy; Thomas A. Rodden; and Steven D. Benford: 'Moving with the times: IT research and the boundaries of CSCW', *Computer Supported Cooperative Work (CSCW): The Journal of Collaborative Computing*, vol. 14, 2005, pp. 217–251.

8. Crabtree, Andy, et al.: 'Ethnography considered harmful', in R. B. Arthur, et al. (eds.): *CHI 2009: Proceedings of the 27th international conference on Human factors in computing systems, Boston, MA, 4–9 April 2009*, ACM Press, New York, 2009, pp. 879–888.

9. Garfinkel, Harold: *Studies in Ethnomethodology*, Prentice-Hall, Englewood-Cliffs, NJ, 1967. Polity Press, Cambridge, 1987.

10. Gaver, William W.: 'Designing for ludic aspects of everyday life', *ERCIM News: Online edition*, no. 47, 2001. <http://www.ercim.org/publication/Ercim_News/enw47/gaver.html>

11. Gaver, William W.: 'Provocative awareness', *Computer Supported Cooperative Work (CSCW): The Journal of Collaborative Computing*, vol. 11, no. 3–4, 2002, pp. 475–493.

12. Goldschmidt-Clermont, Luisella; and Elisabetta Pagnossin-Aligisakis: *Measures of Unrecorded Economic Activities in Fourteen Countries*, United National Development Programme, New York, 31 January 1995. *Human Development Reports*. – Occasional Papers #20. <http://hdr.undp.org/publications/papers.cfm>

13. Hirschhorn, Larry: *Beyond Mechanization: Work and Technology in a Postindustrial Age*, MIT Press, Cambridge, MA/London, 1984.

14. Huws, Ursula: *The Making of a Cybertariat: Virtual Work in a Real World*, Monthly Review Press, New York, 2003.

15. Ironmonger, Duncan S.: 'Household production and the household economy', in N. J. Smelser and P. B. Baltes (eds.): *Encyclopedia of the Social & Behavioral Sciences*, Elsevier, Oxford, 2001.

16. Marx, Karl: *Grundrisse der Kritik der politischen Ökonomie* (Manuscript, 1857–58). Text ed. by V. K. Brušlinskij; L. R. Mis'kevič; and A. G. Syrov. In K. Marx and F. Engels: *Gesamtausgabe (MEGA②)*. Dietz Verlag, Berlin, 1976–1981, vol. II/1, pp. 47–747.

17. Marx, Karl: *Das Kapital. Kritik der politischen Ökonomie. Erster Band. Buch I: Der Produktionsprocess des Kapitals* (Hamburg, 1867). Text ed. by E. Kopf, et al. In K. Marx and F. Engels: *Gesamtausgabe (MEGA②)*. Dietz Verlag, Berlin, 1983, vol. II/5.

18. Rodden, Tom A.; John A. Mariani; and Gordon Blair: 'Supporting cooperative applications', *Computer Supported Cooperative Work (CSCW): An International Journal*, vol. 1, no. 1–2, 1992, pp. 41–68.

19. Ryle, Gilbert: 'Thinking and language' (*Proceedings of the Aristotelian Society*, 1951). In G. Ryle: *Collected Papers. Volume II: Collected Essays, 1929-1968*. Hutchinson, London, 1971, pp. 258–271.

20. Schor, Juliet B.: *The Overworked American: The Unexpected Decline of Leisure*, Basic Books, New York, 1992, 1993 (Paperback ed.).

21. Schütz, Alfred [A. Schutz]: 'On multiple realities' (*Philosophy and Phenomenological Research*, June 1945). Text ed. by M. Natanson. In A. Schutz: *Collected Papers. Vol. I. The Problem of Social Reality*. Martinus Nijhoff, The Hague, 1962, pp. 207–259.

22. Sharrock, Wes W.; and Robert J. Anderson: *The Ethnomethodologists*, Ellis Horwood, Chichester, 1986.

23. Turner, Roy (ed.): *Ethnomethodology: Selected Readings*, Penguin Books, Harmondsworth, England, 1974.

24. Urmson, James Opie: 'Polymorphous concepts', in O. P. Wood and G. Pitcher (eds.): *Ryle: A Collection of Critical Essays*, Doubleday, Garden City, NY, 1970, pp. 249–266. Macmillan, London, 1971.

25. White, Alan Richard: *The Philosophy of Mind*, Random House, New York, 1967.

Appropriation of the Eclipse Ecosystem: Local Integration of Global Network Production

Gunnar Stevens and Sebastian Draxler

Abstract Eclipse and Mozilla Firefox represent a new type of open software that can be supplemented by manifold extensions, being implemented by independent software vendors and open source projects. Research on such software ecosystems shows that collaboration patterns in the software industry evolve from value chains to value nets. An often ignored side-effect of this development is a vast extent of integration work that needs to be done by users. Taking a user point of view, this paper presents an empirical study on the practices of appropriating the Eclipse ecosystem as an example of radical tailorability, based on new opportunities given by the surrounding ecosystem. We show the practices users have developed to manage the antagonism of maintaining a stable and productive working environment, while simultaneously innovating it. Based on these results, we outline different opportunities to improve flexible software by supporting cooperation among the diverse actors involved, in a network of production and consumption.

Introduction

How do end users tailor and appropriate their computational working environments?

This question has been intensively investigated in HCI as well as CSCW research [inter alia 1, 2–6]. However, studying the tailoring of Eclipse as a daily working environment in an ethnographical manner, reveals a topic that is rarely discussed in literature – namely the fact that the tailoring work is 'shaped by' and 'part of' a software ecosystem.

The term software ecosystem was introduced by Messerschmitt and Szyperski [7]. It is semantically related to concepts such as production networks or network economies, but tries to integrate the economical and the technological point of view.

G. Stevens (✉) and S. Draxler
University of Siegen, Hölderlinstrasse 3, 57068 Siegen, Germany
e-mail: gunnar.stevens@uni-siegen.de; sebastian.draxler@uni-siegen.de

M. Lewkowicz et al. (eds.), *Proceedings of COOP 2010*,
DOI 10.1007/978-1-84996-211-7_16, © Springer-Verlag London Limited 2010

A Software ecosystem can be defined as a network of related actors, interacting with a shared market [8]. These relationships are frequently underpinned by a common technological platform or market and operate through the exchange of information, resources and artifacts.

Technologically, software production networks are related to McIlroy's vision of component-based software development [9]. As early as 1968, he saw future application development as plugging together different components bought on the free market. He envisaged the role of a general contractor offering application services similar to roles in the manufacturing industry. Since the 1990s, a large number of changes have been accomplished to make his vision real. Furthermore, we observe a tendency of supplementing major products in the different market segments by loosely coupled networks of Independent Software Vendors (ISVs) and open source projects, which provide extensions and services to the core product. Organizationally, software production networks are mainly studied with focus on coordination in globally distributed software engineering [10].

Existing research on production networks focused mainly the developer perspective, neglecting the user perspective. But it is the user's role that changed, because unlike McIlroy envisaged, there is no general contractor. Tailoring eclipse may hold as example here. The work of picking the right pieces from a loosely coupled network and integrating these into their local work context are 'outsourced' to the user's sphere of responsibility.

Even Grinter, as one of the few who studied both – global coordination in distributed software production [10] as well as local integration work [2] – missed to draw the connection between both views. We introduce a brief gedankenexperiment to raise the awareness of this topic (see also Fig. 1) and its implications. Assume a world1 where a developer A creates an UML tool extension for the Eclipse platform. Taking a bird eyes view on distributed software production, one can conclude that the work of developer A depends on the work of the Eclipse platform developers. In a world2 a developer B creates a Mobile phone extension for Eclipse, so that we conclude in an analogue manner that the work of B depends on the work of the Eclipse developers. The platform in world1 and world2 is the same, but it does not constitute a need for cooperation between A and B [see also 11].

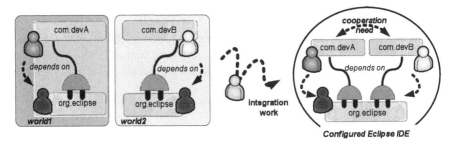

Fig. 1 Constituting new cooperation needs in the actor-network of a software ecosystem, through the integration work of the users

Now, what happens if a user C brings world1 and world2 together by downloading the extension A and B to use both together (e.g. because his project leader have told him that in the current mobile phone app project he should document the architecture concept with the help of UML diagrams). As mentioned by Grinter, user C has to carry out some integration work, which potentially confronts him with the problem of compatibility issues between A and B. In reflection of this anticipated breakdown, one might argue this problem arises because of missing cooperation work between the developers A, B and the Eclipse developers. This is true of course, but neglects the fact that the need to cooperate was introduced by the integration work of the user.

The argument illustrated by the example is that in software ecosystems cooperation is sometimes constituted by the integration work done by the users. In this article we do not investigate the consequences to study cooperation in distributed software development, but using this as a theoretical consideration that shapes our analytic lens in the following manner: Firstly the example explains why breakdowns are no accidental phenomena, but essentially connected to the freedom of choice provided by open software ecosystems. Therefore we need a profound understanding of the practices to integrate a loosely coupled network of components into the local context. Secondly, understanding integration work of the user as part of the distributed development in software ecosystems influences the framing of the design space and motivates to search for new solutions to support the cooperation in the actor network given by the software ecosystem. However, we give only an outlook on this new field of CSCW research, while our primary focus is to explore the practices of users appropriating the Eclipse ecosystem, while being under the pressure of getting their ordinary job done.[1]

Based on this focus, the paper is organized as follows: Section Bringing a Component Network into Practice gives an introduction into the research on designing and managing an adaptable software application. Further, Section Eclipse Workplaces as an Expression of a Global Ecosystem gives a brief introduction into the Eclipse ecosystem, illustrating, how the Eclipse ecosystem functions as a decentralized, open production network that gives users new opportunities to adapt their working environment to the local needs. However, the openness of ecosystems prevents that developers can fully anticipate all the side effects that emerged in the local context. Against this backdrop, Section Managing the Eclipse Ecosystem in Practice presents an empirical study on Eclipse tailoring practices, making use of the dynamical evolving market of Eclipse plugins. We close with an outlook of design options to support end users appropriating software ecosystems.

---

[1]Eclipse users are typically software developers. Despite the fact that this group does not present 'the' typical end user, we decided after discussing the pros and cons, to investigate the appropriation practices of Eclipse. The main reason is similar to a 'lead user'-approach as we can observe emerging strategies to make use of a widespread, dynamical and complex software ecosystem. It has millions of users, it realized a highly advanced technological concept of 'everything is a plug-in' [12] and its complex ecosystem offers one of the most advanced platforms to enable a network economy in the software industry.

Bringing a Component Network into Practice

The CSCW and HCI literature that has taken into account the user perspective, can roughly be divided into research on the creation of end user-oriented flexibility on the one hand, and research on the management of the flexibility of IT-infrastructures on the other.

Design for Flexibility

Tailorability is a concept that allows users to flexibly fit an application into their context of use. Tailorability is a general demand in the concept of End User Development [4]. On the background of Participatory Design, the aim of tailorability additionally is to support the democratization of the workplace [3, 4]. Tailoring takes place after the original design and implementation phase of an application [13]; it typically starts during, or right after the installation of the application in the field.

The scope of possible changes can consequently be rather broad. Henderson and Kyng [3] distinguish three levels of complexity: choosing between alternatives of anticipated behavior, constructing new behavior from existing pieces and altering the artifact (i.e. reprogramming). Several research prototypes have been implemented in the 'design for flexibility' approach. In particular the CSCW research systems have followed more or less a concept of component-based tailorability [14] similar to Eclipse and proposed highly tailorable groupware application frameworks.

Managing Flexibility

In spite of the great extend of research on making systems more flexible, there are only few studies tackling the management of related flexibility in practice [1].

Based on a field study, Bowers emphasizes the unanticipated work required to make flexible systems work [1]. He notes that there is a unique way to deal with this issue and that a significant burden is not always recognized as such in a working environment. Extra work can even be a reason for abandoning technologies or certain courses of action. On the other hand, sometimes "it might be regarded as 'a good job for a junior to do in order to find out what is going on here' and so on and so forth." [1].

Grinter et al.'s empirical studies point out that managing a home IT infrastructure is a collaborative issue, where an informal division of labor arises [2]. Typically, the party with the biggest technical competence gets the job to run and maintain the network. In their field study, Star and Ruhlender observe that 'signing on and hooking up' is a form of artful integration into a socio-technical infrastructure, in large scale as well as in situ. This integration reciprocally shapes the infrastructure [17].

In particular, 'infrastructuring' is a severe and complex issue, where "socio-material relations of multiple, heterogeneous elements and the collective, situated inter-weaving of people, artifacts and processes" [18] inter-relate. Pipek coins the term "shared infrastructure scenario" [16] to describe such a constellation. Balka and Wagner point out that the configuration of a technical infrastructure to make things work is part of the appropriation process [18].

Several empirical studies have demonstrated that tailoring is usually carried out collaboratively by end users, local experts, IT support or helpdesk staff, and takes place in social networks within organizations [15] or within user communities [16]. Based on these results, different authors have suggested cooperative solutions for customization [4]. However, these studies rely on the diffusion of adaptations, which has been created in the local context and not on the adoption of extensions, which are available within a worldwide community.

All these studies demonstrate that managing flexibility is more than simply assembling and configuring components, indicating that tailoring has to manage the complexity of integrating independent, but inter-dependent production processes.

Eclipse Workplaces as an Expression of a Global Ecosystem

The case of Eclipse is in several dimensions an example of a global software ecosystem in recent commercial software production. Each of them is worth being studied for its own sake. But we want to concentrate on three different facets of Eclipse that influence the socio-technical environment of Eclipse users.

Transformation of Eclipse into a Global Ecosystem

Eclipse, with all its historical contingencies can be described as the transformation of internal solutions of the problem of how to integrate a heterogeneous network of product development divisions into a global informational production ecosystem [cf. 19], where a distributed development process has to be coordinated [20].

IBM started the story of Eclipse in the 1990s as an answer to several internal and external challenges. In the mid-1990s, IBM shifted its strategy to a software- and service-oriented enterprise. IBM Software group had grown rapidly, also by the fact that IBM has acquired a large number of other software development companies. As a result, IBM's software portfolio was only loosely coordinated. This led to several problems of 'inter-usability' (e.g. tools did not have a common 'look and feel'), as well as of inter-operability (e.g. it was difficult to exchange data among the applications). IBM was also confronted with the problem that the applications had been independently developed from the beginning and could not share compo-nents in order to save costs. As a result of this organizational context, the idea of Eclipse as a common integration platform for several software tools was born.

It was planned as a coordination strategy [cf. 20] to manage the loosely coupled production and product network inside the firm. Extensibility was a critical design decision: IBM and its partners wanted to integrate different modules and applications seamlessly.

The next step in the history of Eclipse was related to IBM's middleware strategies, which consisted of three parts: the application – built by ISVs, the application-development tools (like IBM Visual Age, Sun's NetBeans or MS Visual Studio) and the server software (the cash cow in the strategy of IBM). In order to convince ISVs to adopt Eclipse and to send out a clear signal not to lock out developers on a proprietary platform, Eclipse was made an open–source product. An egalitarian Eclipse Consortium (now the Eclipse Foundation) was founded, were all members of the consortium should have equal decision rights: "*[W]e created this dual edged or bi-polar organization that on the one side would play by Open Source rules of engagement to develop the technology and of the other side was the eco-system side, or the commercialization of the technology.*" [19].

Today, Eclipse has become a multi-facetted brand with millions of users. Eclipse stands for example for a platform technology (e.g. the whole Lotus product line is based on Eclipse) that is available on multiple operating systems (including Mac, Windows, Linux and others), for the second most used IDE today, for an Open-Source project, for a standard-like consortium (organized in the Eclipse Foundation, supported by big players like IBM, SAP, Oracle, etc.), for a software ecosystem (where ISVs built more than 1,000 different extensions and applications on the top of the Eclipse platform) and/or for an ecosystem (where an Open-Source community co-exists with commercial players). In addition, commercial products like ondemand.yoxos.com or poweredbypulse.com are specialized in maintaining repositories of third party plug-ins for Eclipse and supporting organizations as well as end users to pick up plug-ins from these repositories in a safe manner.

"Everything Is a Plug-In": The Technological Fundament of an Ecosystem

Eclipse is a living software ecosystem that faces the problem of a consistent evolution of the heterogeneous network of producers and products. The strategy Eclipse realizes to provide consistency can mainly be studied from a structural and process perspective.

On the structural level, Eclipse applies an 'everything is a plug-in' philosophy [12] to address the requirements of flexible and extensible infrastructure. This means that Eclipse is decomposed into hundreds of components (so called "plug-ins"), which use features of other plug-ins themselves and provide extension points to be used by other plug-ins. Through this component architecture, an Eclipse installation is technically specified by the acyclic dependency graph between the plug-ins of the installation.

In the first version Eclipse implemented its own component model, but since version 3 it switched to the industry standard OSGi. OSGi defines a sophisticated component model supporting independent loading mechanisms, dependency resolving, versioning control, etc. This architecture is to protect components from corruption by others and to address the integration problem at the same time. In particular it manages situations where two components are used by a third component (but in a different version).

The component's architecture not only creates a dependency graph in a technical sense, but also in an organizational sense, i.e. between different actors in the Eclipse ecosystem. This means the component architecture is a technical as well as a social artifact. Therefore the component architecture also affects the power structure and negotiation processes inside the Eclipse ecosystem, as changes of plug-ins included in the core distribution have a greater effect than changing peripheral plug-ins, distributed by third parties: "You need someone who can be a strong advocate to protect the integrity of the platform; you need someone who has the strength to say: *'no we are not going to put that in the platform if it is only for your tool.'*" [19].

An interesting aspect from an End User Development research perspective is how Beck and Gamma translate the Eclipse plug-in philosophy into a discourse of empowerment that is based on the idea that designers should "[g]ive the users an empowering computing experience and provide learning environments as a path to greater power" [12].

Based on this idea, they argue that the plug-in concept constitutes a pyramid of increasing commitments and rewards, in which the committers of the Eclipse Foundation are at the top. In the middle of the pyramid are publisher and enablers, who contribute third-party plug-ins to the Eclipse Ecosystem without being part of the Eclipse core. End users are also part of the game, as they build the bottom of the pyramid. They can influence the design of Eclipse directly by configuring and extending an Eclipse installation. Since we take a CSCW and HCI perspective on Eclipse, the view of these end-users at the bottom of the pyramid, constitute our field for research.

The 'Eclipse Way': The Rhythm of Evolution

On the process level, Eclipse has to face the challenge of providing a stable and consistent network of plug-ins and innovating it simultaneously. One of the major problems in this process is that further development of one piece in the global plug-in network can lead to a crash in another part. The only secure method to prevent this is to stop any changes, but this also hinders innovation and reaction to dynamics in the environment. Unlike this draconic solution, the Eclipse strategy (sometimes called 'The Eclipse Way') is to create as much transparency as possible, and to establish a generally accepted evolution rhythm, so that independent production processes can be synchronized with each other. The transparency helps Eclipse core projects as well as third parties to stay aware of changes (e.g. through API or plug-in refactoring) and project progress. In addition, the transparency allows users to give feedback in early stages to influence further developments.

The heart of the Eclipse evolution is a specific development rhythm. It is structured as follows: 12 months pass between every major Eclipse release. This time is split into different phases: "warm-up" (1 month), several "milestone builds" (9 months) and "endgame" (1–2 months). The warm-up and milestone phase are innovation-oriented and allow for new features to be implemented. All milestone goals are released in form of a release plan at the Eclipse foundations website, as well as the resulting milestone builds themselves, which was announced with a 'news and noteworthy' description in order to foster community feedback. The endgame phase is stabilization-oriented and consists of continuous switches between integration, testing phases and bug fixing phases. In the endgame, different release candidates are published (like 3.2RC6). Each release candidate is more stable than its predecessor, ending in a new major release (like 3.2).

In addition, public nightly builds and integration builds are created. Their target groups are users and developers who are eager to figure out the quality of the integration of the components they use or develop and to detect integration problems. Supporting the integration work on the producer network side is important for global quality management.

Discussion

In summarizing the background of Eclipse, we can describe it as an evolving socio-technical network, where technical dependencies between individual plug-ins are negotiated between different actors in the environment of related socio-economic dependencies. The Eclipse Foundation – which is a non-homogenous organization, but a political institution of different interest groups – presents the centre of the network. Dealing with the problem of how to organize the global evolution and integration of an independently produced, but inter-dependently operating network of products, Eclipse applies innovative professional strategies: on the structural level, the plug-in concept helps to establish trust in the beneficial nature of the existing technology among the different stakeholders in the network. On the process level, the strict evolution rhythm with the transparency strategies helps to establish similar trust in the beneficial nature of its future technology among the different stakeholders in the network.

Managing the Eclipse Ecosystem in Practice

Our empirical study of (collaborative) appropriation practices of Eclipse users was part of a public founded research project (CoEUD), where we cooperated with four different software companies in Germany. Two companies, a groupware producer (company alpha) and a web-development specialist (company beta) started to experiment with Eclipse as their development environment. Both employ approximately ten people. The third enterprise (company gamma), also a web-development and IT-infrastructure specialist (approximately 250 employees), already used Eclipse as the standard working environment for quite some time. The fourth company (company delta) is part of a holding, while the participating group consists of roughly ten members. This group is specialized in executing eXtreme Programming projects and in providing this expertise to other companies. This company also builds domain specific applications on top of the Eclipse platform, though this was not the primary focus of our empirical study.

These four companies were selected as research partners for different reasons: First of all, they use Eclipse in their daily work practice, in addition, they represent typical enterprises of the German software industry. These are usually classified as Small and Medium Enterprises (SME). Additionally, there already exists a long and trustworthy relationship between the companies and the researchers, which was an important factor doing workplace studies as a part of participatory action research.

In its attempt to improve the flexibility of Eclipse from an end user perspective, the CoEUD project followed the *Business Ethnography (BE)* approach [21], where participatory design and ethnographical informed analysis are of equal importance. *BE* does not draw on direct implications of ethnography for design, but rather on the decomposition of projects into different reference frameworks of participants, based on their working practices and views. This decomposition can be used as a reflection method to support mutual learning and discourse processes between participants of the project. However, in this paper, we focus only on the findings of this empirical study and not on our intervention in the field.

In each company, we conducted at least two semi-structured interviews (altogether, we conducted ten interviews from August 2007 to September 2007). We interviewed four junior developers, four senior developers and two CIOs, all of them were using Eclipse for their daily work (except one CIO). The interviews took about 1 h and covered questions about role, tasks and responsibility of the interviewees in the enterprise. In addition, we asked questions about their experience regarding Eclipse as well as their update and learning strategies.

Additionally, we visited two SMEs (company beta and delta) for a defined period of time (3–5 days) for participatory observation. The observations were accomplished in the typical ambience of the developers, in order to get a detailed insight in their working activities. The participant observations were written down as field notes. Furthermore, we also cooperated intensively with company gamma, which had established a project to develop a prototypical solution to support a company-wide provisioning of Eclipse. In three design workshops with the project leader, we discussed requirements and implementation opportunities for a cooperative provisioning solution. As part of the participatory action research approach of *BE*, we actively participated in these workshops, discussing potential side effects of centralizing the administration of working environments.

All interviews and the workshop were recorded, partly transcribed, paraphrased and analyzed together with field notes and supplemented by personal experiences. In a second step we selected specific parts of the empirical data for a microscopic

examination using the 'Kunstlehre' of sequence analysis as suggested by
Oevermann [22]. Similar to Grounded Theory, the aim is to reconstruct the categories from the case instead of subsuming the case under pre-defined categories.
Similar to Conversation Analysis it is guided by some interpretation principles like
immanent, extensive and verbatim interpretation of record following the sequential
structure applying the principle of austerity.

With the help of our qualitative studies, it was possible to understand the work
practice and to uncover and document situational work practices and strategies in
respect to the appropriation of the Eclipse ecosystem. In order to triangulate our
findings we additionally conduct an quantitative oriented online survey from
February 2008 until April 2008 and analyze the Eclipse configuration used in practice following a 'mix method' approach [23].

The online survey consisted of a questionnaire, which additionally asked the
participants to add certain Eclipse configuration data. This allowed us to analyze
which plug-ins have been installed by the online study participants. It was
announced in different online forums, mailing lists, by our project partners and
two research institutes (however to protect the anonymity it was not possible to
determine which respond came from which context). We addressed several
different target groups of the Eclipse user community (computer science students,
software professionals, project leaders etc.). The survey aimed at the local context
and experiences regarding Eclipse, but also asked for information on the local
Eclipse configuration, which gave insights into the features and plug-ins the
users had locally installed. One hundred and thirty-eight persons participated in
the survey and 59 additionally sent us their Eclipse configuration, which we
analyzed in detail.

In the following we present the results of the online questionnaire analysis that
draws a first picture of appropriation practices of Eclipse users. Afterwards we
show the core findings of the interviews and participatory observations to point out
the user's motives and strategies in modifying Eclipse.

The Quantitative Side of Managing the Eclipse Ecosystem

Fifty-nine of 138 participants of our online survey sent us information about their
Eclipse configuration. Surprisingly we received 76 configurations for our analysis,
because some persons were using more than one configuration. This also means
that these users own more than one Eclipse installation on their computer (in our
workplace study presented in the next section, we found some reason for that
phenomenon).

As a first step, we were interested how many plug-ins are used in practice. This
should help us to answers several questions (1) how complex is the appropriation
task users are confronted with in their efforts to manage the Eclipse ecosystem, (2)
is the modification of Eclipse installations a common practice and (3) what do
Eclipse users usually modify.

We were surprised to find 2,428 different plug-ins within the collected sample (the number rises to 4,944 when we take the different versions into account. This means that on average each plug-in was installed in two different versions). The average number is 326 plug-ins per configuration.

Furthermore, we analyzed the so-called "features" of the captured Eclipse configuration data, as these are the basic elements of update management and configuration management in Eclipse.[2] The concept of features reduces the complexity of the plug-in network for the users. Instead of managing about 300 plug-ins, the user only has to manage around 40 features (cf. Table 1). The standard deviation of features $\sigma_f = 36.8$ is an indicator for the diversity individualizing Eclipse. Furthermore, we calculated the normalized average distance between two Eclipse configurations. The value of $\bar{u}_{feature} = 0.42$ confirms the findings of other empirical data, which stated that practically no Eclipse installation resembles another one.[3]

Regarding the integration of a heterogeneous network of producers, we tried to find out, if Eclipse is used as an off-shelf product or if third party plug-ins from independent ISVs are integrated into Eclipse installations. We focused therefore on features that are not delivered by the Eclipse foundation. One of these features is the support for the *Subversion* source-code version control system for Eclipse, which was by this time provided by two different independent open source projects. At the time of the survey, none of these tools were integrated into Eclipse by default; instead it is up to user to integrate this extension into the Eclipse installation if Subversion support is needed. In our sample 40% of the Eclipse configurations included Subversion plug-ins, which is a strong indicator that the users make use of the global market of Eclipse extensions.

Table 1 Amount of plug-ins found in Eclipse installations (with $n = 76$ Eclipse installations)

Overall number of features (no versions counted)	418
Overall number of features found (version sensitive)	865
Min. number of features in an Eclipse installation	3
Max. number of features in an Eclipse installation	196
Average number of features per Eclipse installation	42
Standard deviation σ_f	36.8

---

[2]A feature in Eclipse defines a set of plug-ins and sub features which must be installed when the feature is installed.

[3]We calculated the distance of two configurations with the set of features Ci and Cj as follows: $u_{feature}(Ci,Cj) = (|Ci \backslash Cj| + |Cj \backslash Ci|)/(|Ci| + |Cj|)$. Based on this calculated the average distance: $\bar{u}feature(C1,..., Cn) = 1/n*(n-1)*\Sigma_{0 \le i < j \le n} U_{feature} (Ci,Cj)$. A value of $\bar{u}$ near 0 means that the different Eclipse installations are almost identical; a value near 1 means that the installations are most different.

In order to learn how the evolution of Eclipse is reflected in the configuration data, we took a closer look at the version number of the core feature *org.eclipse.platform* (which is part of every Eclipse installation). In our data, we found 11 different versions. Sixty configurations are of the 3.3.X release (published June 2007), 12 cases of the 3.2.X release (published June 2006) and three cases of the 3.1.X release (published June 2005). We did not find a configuration based on one of the Eclipse 3.4 milestone builds, released a few weeks before the survey (which we expected after our workplace study). Within the range of 3.3.X releases, 36 cases were not older than 2 months. On average, a version in use is approximately half a year old.

In addition the online survey asks several questions on the practices to integrate the global plug-in network into the local context. In a first step, we were interested if the adaptation of Eclipse is a common and regularly practice. Therefore we asked: *"How often do you adapt your Eclipse (installation and update of plug-ins, or configuration settings)?"*. Almost all of the participants (92.66%) declared they adapt their installation to their needs (7.34% never, 14.71% right after the installation, 77.21% sometimes, 0.74% daily). This result corresponds with the analysis of the configuration data. In addition, it shows that adapting the working environment is not only a singular, but in most cases a regular activity.

We are also interested in strategies to inform oneself about activities of the Eclipse ecosystem, the role of collaboration and configuration sharing practices. In particular, we are interested, if a local network of Eclipse users exists. Therefore we asked: *"How many of your colleagues also use Eclipse?"* The majority (71.32%) explains that in local environments also other persons use Eclipse (only 4.41% say no other person use Eclipse, 24.27% give no answer to that question). This confirmed our workplace observation that in most cases a local social network of Eclipse users exists.

We also asked: *"How do you inform yourself about new plug-ins?"* The most frequent answer was the Internet with 78.48%, colleagues were mentioned by 54.43%, 21.52% use magazines and 6.33% use special online plug-in marketplaces (multiple answers were possible). This demonstrated that the Internet as a global resource is the most used source for information, but it also demonstrated that local social networks play an important role.

The question *"Do you have ever received plug-ins from colleagues?"* also addresses the aspect of collaboration, but directly focuses on the diffusion of plug-ins. The answers also indicate that local social networks play an important role in the appropriation of the global network of plug-ins (65.44% of the participants stated 'yes', 17.65% stated never and 16.91% gave no answer).

We were also interested in the channels used for diffusion of plug-ins, therefore we asked: *"Which ways did you use to receive these plug-ins?"*. Figure 2 gives an overview on the answers (it was possible to choose multiple answers). The answers demonstrate that there is not just one way used for plug-in diffusion. However, 69.41% of the Eclipse user state that they receive plug-ins via personal communication and 32.94% say that in some cases they have used a file copy strategy to get the plug-in on the desktop. Both answers are a strong indication that local networks also play an important role by the diffusion of plug-ins, although this was not anticipated by Eclipse designers and it is not well supported by Eclipse.

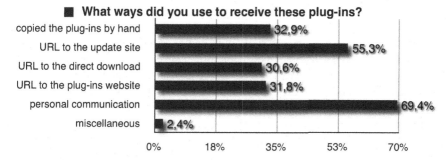

Fig. 2 Channels used to receive plug-ins and plug-in information[4]

The analysis of the online survey shows that the dynamics of the global Eclipse evolution and the heterogeneity of the Eclipse plug-in universe are reflected at the micro-level of Eclipse configuration. It also demonstrates that local social networks play an important role in the appropriation of global Eclipse network of loosely coupled components.

Doing Integration Work

In our workplace study we focused on practices and motives of integrating Eclipse as part of the daily work. Similar to the quantitative data, our observation shows a huge diversity and a highly dynamic evolution of Eclipse installations and the importance of local social networks in appropriating the global Eclipse ecosystem.

From our ethnographic point of view, we identified one reason for the diversity of Eclipse configurations. There are no strict regulations for tool configuration in the observed companies. Furthermore, software development is organized in projects, which are highly dynamic and diverse by themselves. E.g. the company gamma mainly implemented individual non-standard software for their clients' work with project durations ranging from 1 week up to 1 year or longer.

One of the key competences of this company was its knowledge about current technology trends and its competence in building an individual integration solution on the top of heterogeneous IT-infrastructure of their clients. In most projects special tools like PHP or XSLT editors or environments for testing purposes, like databases or application servers are needed. Logically they belong to project-specific

---

[4]The other way round *"Did you ever share plug-ins with colleagues?"* and *"Which way did you use to share these plug-ins?"* provide a nearly identical pictures.

working environments, but technically they cannot be well integrated into the management of the Eclipse working environment.

Typically, a project at gamma starts with one or two developers, but during its lifetime the core team sometimes calls upon further developers as experts for specific technologies or tasks (e.g. an expert on a particular database or an UI designer). As a consequence, the consulted experts have to synchronize their working environment with the one of their colleagues in order to cooperate with each other.

This means, that the project context and progress triggers the modification of Eclipse, but nevertheless leaves room for negotiation and individual exceptions from project norms if this is needed to get the work done. In addition, the individual appropriation of new Eclipse plug-ins can also become the source of grass root innovation, where one picks up a new feature that then diffuses into the whole organization through local social networks e.g. through the shared working context of project team. This is very similar to Mackay's observations [15].

This way projects establish the context of implicit-knowledge sharing which goes along with the sharing of Eclipse configuration. E.g. the following transcript demonstrates this practice as part of a cooperative appropriation strategy: *"If a new colleague starts to work here, I would advise him to begin with the standard IDE, and as a starting point for further exploration, I would show him which plug-ins... I did integrate in my Eclipse installation... could be of interest for his job (based on his experience)." (Interview transcript with a senior developer at gamma).*[5]

Through the specific characteristics of Eclipse, it is also possible (nevertheless cumbersome) to share best practices through *Copy and Adapt*-installation. Mackay describes a similar phenomenon in the case of customizations [15]. Applied on this case it means, one user sets up and adapts an Eclipse installation and afterwards shares it with his or her colleague(s) in the project: *"I did configure Eclipse a few times. Or rather we did this more or less together. For example [within the project] we use the CheckStyle component and some other plug-ins, of which I forgot the names, because in fact my colleague did set up the original configuration. And I eventually copied the whole configuration over to my workstation." (Interview transcript with a junior developer at company delta).*

Another important aspect is related to the *habitus* of software professionals, who usually consider their own work to be a craftsmanship rather then assembly-line work as Strübing [24] describes his observations. In our study we found that sophisticated knowledge about tools and an *always be up to date* attitude knowing the current technology trends seems to be a core element of this *habitus*. This is similar to the result of Day, who has analyzed the failure of the tayloristic CASE tool paradigm in practice: "Each user [of a CASE tool] has his or her professional

---

[5]This citation also shows how subtle the balance between autonomy and cooperative integration is constructed: The seasoned developer submits an individualized offer, but respecting the autonomy and the tool competence of the other, even if he is a novice. Below, we discuss this topic in more detail.

perspective regarding appropriate models and procedures for software development. Many feel that their trade is as much an art as a science and resist the application of constraints." [25].

Although tool autonomy is an important issue for software professionals, whether something is disrupting the own autonomy depends on the perceived rationality, an often quite subtle issue:

E: Which Eclipse version do you use?

I2: Mhhh, if it were up to me, I would probably change my Eclipse at least every half a year. Because there ...err ... happen a lot of things. Though I can also understand when my company says that it is of course a little risky ... err ...as if bugs show up or incompatibilities ... err ... Look, I once even wanted to install Eclipse 3.2 here. (laughs) ... err ... they said the same about Eclipse 3.1. [not to change too often], think that I can really understand. (Interview transcript with a senior developer at gamma)

We can interpret this passage in two different ways. First, we can argue that the developer was bent by the power of the company leading to an alienation from his production means, but this related to the issue that the developer accepts the rules of the game, because he understands the need for the rules of this social context. Regarding the related actor network, the user draws a connection between his company and Eclipse (treating developer and artifact as a unit) and tailoring his working environment is related to manage the conflict in the two different innovation rhythms of this both actors.

Beyond this outline of some triggers for workbench modification, the analysis exposes also particular fears concerning tool modification like a decrease of efficiency or a complete failure of the tools being used. This leads to the antagonism of stabilization versus innovation (or informally spoken "never change a running system" versus "being up-to-date"). This antagonism reproduces the general characteristics of the evolution of Eclipse, where stability of the environment is very important, but in the area of software development everything is oriented towards innovation, which means that if you don't move forward you go backwards.

As a result, Software developers are aware of new technologies and trends. For example, the field study at company beta shows that the tracking of technology trends was as much a common habit like reading newspaper:

9:00 a.m. the developer C sit at his PC workplace, organizes his daily work, e.g. checking his mailbox. During these activities he takes time for visiting bookmarked web pages to read news and trends related to the Eclipse IDE. When asked, the developer explained: '... from time to time I go through the web to see what is new.' (Observation diary beta p. 38).

Also software professionals communicate and discuss new trends and new tools they found on the Internet. This discussion can be a trigger not only to speak about the new tools, but also to try them out.

On the other hand, each modification has to be appropriate and might cause trouble for the working routine. This means that it is not to be taken for granted that every modification is a step forward. Therefore, the developer has to balance the antagonism by taking different aspects into account. For example:

E: Did you always use the newest Eclipse Version?

II: Well, most of the time only up to the release version, err to the real one[6]

E: err.

II: Except when there is something special, such as – for example the web tool platform ...
err ... which contains so many features one needs. That it is a real benefit, to really use
some release candidates or former versions. Something that's still more or less stable,
otherwise the risk is just so high that you could lose half a day or something like that, just
because you still somehow... some function, yet again... or something that is still too error-
prone (Interview transcript with a senior developer at beta)

Another case demonstrates that the balancing of the antagonism is not an up-front
and fixed decision, but can be changed, based on the actual experience of adapting
the workbench:

Software developer C tried to integrate a new component into eclipse. During this activity
a mistake suddenly occurred, so the system showed a message box including a hint for a
version conflict. The developer cancelled the installation with the quotation: 'That's too
hazardous... afterwards something might get broken.' (Observation diary beta p. 70)

One can see that in the practice of tool modification the antagonism between "never
change a running system" and "being up-to-date" cannot be conciliated for once
and for all, but the reasons for one or the other have to be balanced constantly
according to the specific context.

Aspects in Managing a Working Environment

In this section we want to describe the tasks of managing an Eclipse working
environment in more detail. In particular, we observed that users have developed
their own strategies to deal with this issue. For example, a senior Java developer at
alpha, who was continuously looking for new features and technologies, created his
own strategy for dealing with the antagonism of stabilization and innovation. In the
past, he spontaneously integrated new components into Eclipse, which sometimes
led to annoying damages and total breakdowns of his working environment. Based
on these experiences, he changed this practice. Now he uses different Eclipse installations: Before he changes his working environment, he creates a backup copy to

---

[6]At first glance the expression "the real one" sounds strange. But a fine-grained analysis showed
that he applies a conservative release policy (in respect to his colleague) using only major releases.
His colleagues also use the innovation-oriented milestone builds, but as they are not that stable,
they are "unreal". We could validate this interpretation by using other interview passages. The
case shows that Eclipse is updated quite often, which confirms the quantitative data (although the
quantitative data also indicates a more 'conservative' or 'rational' update behavior, as we found
no milestone build configuration in any of the 75 cases).

generate a fallback system.[7] After an adequate period of testing, he copies the fallback system to a folder containing older installations, which are out-dated, and then uses the testing environment as his new productive system.

Through a careful analysis of the empirical data we found three different aspects of appropriation work, that are related to each other and that we want to show in more detail:

Keeping Workbenches Up-to-Date

This aspect includes all technical issues of installation, updating, configuration and disposing components or component sets. Eclipse addresses different aspects of workbench modification by different user interfaces. The functionality is split into the *"Search for updates ..."* dialog for updating existing tools, the *"Search for new features ..."* dialog to enhance the workbench and the *"Product-Configuration"* dialog to inspect, update or dispose existing features. A user eager to inspect his workbench environment at the plug-in level has to use another user's interface. If he wants to dispose a specific plug-in, he has to jump to the file system.

So, even if it makes sense to separate these different aspects analytically, the separation on the user interface level leads to several usability problems. The fact that the user can only inspect his environment at the feature level and not at the plug-in level is also problematic, if system malfunctions appear. Also an appropriate support configuration sharing in the local context facing the issue of autonomy and cooperative integration is missing in Eclipse.

Keeping Tool Competence Up-to-Date

Installing a tool is one thing. Being aware of the tool and evaluating it with respect to the own working practices is another. And learning how to use the tool efficiently is a third one. In addition, from an analytical perspective one should separate the aspects of switching to another version from integrating a new tool. The integration of new components or, more specifically, switching to a new release is motivated by the ambition of being up-to-date. In relation to Eclipse, this has two different meanings. On the one hand, the developers in our study always used the newest version of installed components. Concerning the aspect of tool competency, switching to another version of an existing tool is mainly done to refresh one's knowledge. Quite another task is to integrate and try out special third-party components in the Eclipse framework. Here, the modification serves as 'enhancing tool competency'.

---

[7] Here, the qualitative data explain what the quantitative study suggested, namely that some participants have more than one Eclipse configuration. Another reason is that developers sometimes working in several projects, where a different set of tools are needed.

Disposing Workbenches

It seems a surprising fact that 'removing software' has to be taken into account as an own activity, because nothing seems to be easier than to delete a file or a folder. But from a work-practice perspective, the case is not that simple. This is due to two different reasons: This first reason is that some developers are always skeptical about the reliability of the workbench. Therefore they do not just remove outdated installations, but keep different old versions. E.g. in context of Eclipse, the *"Configuration Manager"* feature is responsible for the support of such kinds of functionality. But we observed that users developed their own strategies to deal with this problem. This might be an indicator for the functionality and/or the usability of the solution to be insufficient. The second reason is that the dynamics of projects have to be considered: as each project uses its own specific workbench with tools and tool versions, even if it is finished, it could be opened again, e.g. to fix a bug.

Appropriation as a Collaborative Effort

Another interesting aspect that is already well described in the literature could also be found in this setting. Users collaborated by acting as experts (by sharing knowledge and giving advice) as well as by sharing appropriation artifacts (e.g. components or preference settings) when modifications were necessary. We could especially observe collaboration to introduce experienced Eclipse users into a new team or novice Eclipse users into the Eclipse technology. We could find people acting as source of innovation for the whole team, by being its connection to the global community.

The complexity of the Eclipse technology as well as the complex integration of local user-groups into the huge Eclipse community resulted in regular collaborative appropriation efforts. This differs from existing research through the integration of the group into the global community or Eclipse ecosystem.

Discussion

Eclipse is one of the most advanced technologies and software ecosystems today. It allows end users to create an integrated working environment by assembling components from different vendors. Through shifting this work from the manufacturer to the end user, the integration work becomes an important piece in distributed software production.

Our case study demonstrates that this is not just a theoretically given option. The qualitative as well as the quantitative findings demonstrate that users started to appropriate the new opportunities given by the Eclipse ecosystem and take advantage of an open market of Eclipse components. However, our study also demonstrates that following the market of extensions and integrating components from different manufactures into the local working environment is a complex task – even for very experienced users as in our study, who also, as part of their job, take care of the tools themselves. So, we have to conclude that the openness of software ecosystems in practice is two-edged: While it introduces a new freedom, it also comes with new burdens as the user has to ensure the quality and compatibility of components himself. We should not misinterpret this as a necessity to step backwards to a time, when the integration work was fully done by the producer. Instead, different observations tend to ask for techniques and tools to support this kind of integration work.

In order to explore and systematize the diverse design opportunities, we pick up the train of thought of the introduction. As mentioned, the integration work constitutes new relationships in the actor network of a software ecosystem. Breakdown situations while tailoring Eclipse often reveal an absence of cooperation among the actors involved in the situation, but also create a ground for future cooperation among them. Regarding the opportunities of computer support to manage the evolving cooperation needs and cooperation conflicts, we can distinguish a micro, meso and macro level.

The *micro level computer support focuses* on supporting the individual users to manage their working environment, making use of an open component market. Eclipse already includes some advanced concepts to support the user. First of all, Eclipse implements a software ecosystem friendly component-based architecture. In addition the update and configuration manager (see also Section Keeping Tool Competence Up-to-Date) provide a built-in mechanism to download and install components and to manage the environments configuration. Moreover, the update mechanism does not just install new versions as they get available, it also links the personal software evolution rhythm to the evolution rhythm of other actors in the network, raising the need synchronize these rhythms (see Section The 'Eclipse Way': The Rhythm of Evolution as well as related view of users on this topic described in Section Doing Integration Work). Although Eclipse already includes support mechanisms, the observed workarounds (realizing e.g. backup strategies, work with multiple configuration etc., see Section Managing the Eclipse Ecosystem in Practice) indicate room for improvements.

The *meso level computer support* focuses on groups and organizations, taken into account that tailoring is a social activity where actors rely on their local social network. In the case of plugin sharing we found similar patterns as Mackay [5] described in a study on sharing of customizations. With one important difference: Mackay's customizations where created and shared within a group or organization, while Eclipse plugins usually are created by people outside the local network. We observed that the diffusion or sharing is often rooted in personal contacts, project teams, work groups or maybe even a whole organization (as observed in some of the SME). Furthermore, we observed that such meso level cooperation can even cross organizational boundaries, where project teams with e.g. external consultants become innovation drivers. One important result of our qualitative study was to reveal the connection between plugin integration and specific software engineering expertise (like Test Driven Development) and related to this, the co-diffusion of tailoring/use expertise and the tailored working environment. We observed a lack of tool awareness is correlated to a lack of local expertise awareness. Taken our empirical results into account, to respect the individual tool autonomy, but support the cooperation in team, we developed a first prototype called Peerclipse [26]. It is integrated into the working environment and establishes a local peer-to-peer network. It retrieves the Eclipse configurations and uses this information to support awareness of available components among the members of an organization. Furthermore it adds a component sharing tool to use the local network as group repository and visualizes (usage) expertise.

The *macro level computer support* focuses on the software ecosystem as a whole, taking into account that tailoring is an integral aspect of the distributed software development. Apart from a few exceptions, like Dittrich [27], existing research on tailoring mainly focuses on individual persons or group collaboration. However, our case study demonstrates that several problems keeping work environments up-to-date are linked to the macro level of open software ecosystems. Therefore the macro level presents a new and relevant dimension in designing support systems.

Through this new dimension the micro and meso level do not become obsolete. Instead, we need good design concepts to connect and integrate the different levels. Although we are just beginning to explore design concepts on this level, we assume that online market places will be a highly relevant space to mediate cooperation needs among the diverse actors of the ecosystem. In particular, products like yoxos.com or poweredbypulse.com started to integrate public market places into Eclipse configuration tools. This is a first indicator of a transformation of the traditional function to mediate between an open network of producers and users, providing additional services like reducing complexity in offering products and finding producers. Beyond this, combining configuration support and mediation functions, allows the mentioned solutions to support the integration work by giving e.g. feedback if the selected components are compatible to each other. Moreover, exploiting the new opportunities of the Internet as a collaboration infrastructure and distribution infrastructure for digital goods, such platforms might play an important role in visualizing implicit or latent cooperation needs, opportunities and in mediating between the integration work made by the users and the further development work of the producers.

However, the role of these agents to enable new forms of collaboration in software ecosystems just in the beginning and further research and development is needed to synthesize the different level of computer support in an appropriate manner.

Conclusion

In this paper we studied the appropriation of the Eclipse software ecosystem, which is constituted by heterogeneous networks of independent but interdependent components and related stakeholders. We should be careful in generalizing our results, not just because of the fact that software developers are trained to solve technical problems, but also it is part of their habitus to follow technological trends.

However, we assume that tailoring applications by making use of software ecosystems will become an important issue in general. Therefore, we should explore in detail the practices to cope with the antagonism of stabilization and innovation. Also in this open and loosely coupled software production, the role of users who establish (collaboration) relations between different actors has to be further explored. In this paper we identified opportunities to support these activities at different levels. However, these opportunities have to be further elaborated in future. Also a more elaborated concept of cooperation is needed that capture the fluid cooperation constellations in software ecosystems given by the dialectic of production and consumption. This underlines the need to rethink software development in terms of Marx *"Just as consumption gave the product its finish as product, so does production give finish to consumption"*.

Acknowledgements We thank the participants for their time, Volker Wulf and Bernhard Nett for discussing earlier Versions of this paper and Thomas von Rekowski for his help preparing this document. The CoEUD project was funded by the German Ministry for Education and Research.

References

1. Bowers, J. *The Work to Make a Network Work: Studying CSCW in Action.* in *Proc. of CSCW '94.* 1994: ACM Press, New York.
2. Grinter, R., et al. *The Work to Make a Home Network Work.* in *Proc. of the ECSCW'05.* 2005.
3. Henderson, A. and M. Kyng, *There's no place like home: Continuing Design in Use*, in J. Greenbaum and M. Kyng (eds.), *Design at work.* 1991, Erlbaum, Hillsdale, NJ. pp. 219–240.
4. Lieberman, H., F. Paternò, and V. Wulf, eds. *End-User Development*, 2006, Springer, Dordrecht.
5. Mackay, W. *Patterns of Sharing Customizable Software.* in *Proc. of CSCW'90.* 1990.
6. MacLean, A., et al. *User-Tailorable Systems: Pressing the Issues with Buttons.* in *Proc. of CHI 90.* 1990: ACM Press, New York.
7. Messerschmitt, D. and C. Szyperski, *Software Ecosystem.* MIT Press, Cambridge, MA, 2003.
8. Vasilis, B., J. Slinger, and B. Sjaak, *Formalizing software ecosystem modeling*, in *Proc. of 1st international workshop on Open component ecosystems.* 2009.
9. McIlroy, M.D. *Mass produced software components.* in *Software Engineering - NATO Science Committee Report.* 1968. Garmisch, Germany.
10. Herbsleb, J.D. and R.E. Grinter. *Splitting the organization and integrating the code: Conway's Law revisited.* in *Proc. of ICSE'99.* 1999.
11. Schmidt, K. and L. Bannon, *Taking CSCW seriously.* JCSCW, 1992. 1(1): pp. 7–40.
12. Beck, K. and E. Gamma, *Contributing to Eclipse: Principles, Patterns and Plugins.* 2003, Addison-Wesley, Boston, MA.
13. Muller, M.J., J. Haslwanter, and T. Dayton, *Participatory Practices in the Software Lifecycle*, in M. Helander, T. Landauer, and P. Prabhu (Ed.), *Handbook of HCI.* 1997, Elsevier, Amsterdam. pp. 255–313.
14. Mørch, A., et al., *Component-based technologies for end-user development.* Communication of the ACM, 2004. **47**(9): pp. 59–62.
15. Mackay, W. and L. Angeles. *Patterns of Sharing Customizable Software.* in *Proc. Of Conference on Computer-Supported Cooperative Work.* 1990.
16. Pipek, V., *From tailoring to appropriation support: Negotiating groupware usage.* 2005, University of Oulu: Oulu.
17. Star, S.L. and K. Ruhleder, *Steps toward an ecology of infrastructure: Design and access for large information spaces.* ISJ, 1996. **7**: pp. 111–134.
18. Balka, E. and I. Wagner. *Making Things Work: Dimensions of Configurability as Appropriation Work.* in *Proc. of CSCW 2006.* 2006: ACM Press, New York.

19. O'Mahony, S., F.C. Diaz, and E. Mamas, *IBM and Eclipse* 2005. Boston, Harvard Business School Press, pp. 906–1007.
20. Grinter, R.E., J.D. Herbsleb, and D.E. Perry. *The geography of coordination: dealing with distance in R&D work.* in *Proc. of GROUP '99.* 1999.
21. Stevens, G. and B. Nett, *Business Ethnography as a research method to support evolutionary design.* Navigatoren, 2009. **9**(2).
22. Oevermann, U., et al., *Structures of meaning and objective Hermeneutics*, in Meja, V., Misgeld, D. and Stehr, N. (Eds.), *Modern German sociology*, 1987, Columbia University Press, New York. pp. 436–447.
23. Tashakkori, A. and C. Teddle, eds. *Handbook of Mixed Methods in Social and Behavioral Research.* 2003, Sage Publications, Thousand Oaks, CA.
24. Strübing, J., *Arbeitsstil und Habitus – zur Bedeutung kultureller Phänomene in der Programmierarbeit.* 1992, Universität Kassel, Germany.
25. Day, D., *Behavioral and perceptual responses to constraint management in computer-mediated design activities.* EJC/REC, 1993. **3**(2).
26. Draxler, S., H. Sander, P. Jain, A. Jung, and G. Stevens, *Peerclipse: Tool Awareness in Local Communities.* In Supplementary Proceedings of the 11th European Conference on Computer Supported Cooperative Work. Vienna, Austria, 2009. p.19.
27. Dittrich, Y., S. Vaucouleur, and S. Giff, *ERP Customization as Software Engineering.* IEEE SOFTWARE, 2009. **26**(6): pp. 41–47.

Practices Analysis and Digital Platform Design: An Interdisciplinary Study of Social Support

Matthieu Tixier, Myriam Lewkowicz, Michel Marcoccia, Hassan Atifi, Aurélien Bénel, Gérald Gaglio, and Nadia Gauducheau

Abstract People are turning increasingly to the Internet to find support and share their experience and feelings when they are undergoing hardships such as medical problems. The aim of our ongoing research project is to design innovative online social support services. In order to pave the way for this complex undertaking, several interdisciplinary studies were conducted in this framework: discourse analysis was carried out on online discussions focusing on social support, observers attended support group meetings attended by family caregivers, and interviews were conducted with these caregivers. The application of our findings to our design project is discussed.

Introduction

Social support involves giving advice, information, and emotional, psychological, or material support to people undergoing difficult situations (disease, stress, loss of work, etc.). Social support is often provided by relatives, friends, the family, or trained professionals (such as psychologists or social workers). However, a new trend has been developing on the Internet during the last few years: social support is now being provided by peers, who are neither relatives nor professionals, mostly on Internet forums. There now exist many medical websites where people with medical problems can exchange information (more than eight million connections[1] were made in June 2008 with the French web site Doctissimo), forums dedicated to pregnant women, weight problems, bringing up children, etc.

---

[1] Nielsen Net Ratings – Doctissimo – http://www.doctissimo.fr

M. Tixier (✉), M. Lewkowicz, M. Marcoccia, H. Atifi, A. Bénel, G. Gaglio, and N. Gauducheau
Troyes University of Technology (UTT), ICD/Tech-CICO, 12 Rue Marie Curie – BP2060, 10010 Troyes Cedex, France
e-mail: matthieu.tixier@utt.fr; myriam.lewkowicz@utt.fr; michel.marcoccia@utt.fr; hassan.atifi@utt.fr; aurélien.bénel@utt.fr; gérald.gaglio@utt.fr; nadia.gauducheau@utt.fr

M. Lewkowicz et al. (eds.), *Proceedings of COOP 2010*,
DOI 10.1007/978-1-84996-211-7_17, © Springer-Verlag London Limited 2010

In view of this emerging trend, it was proposed to define and apply new principles for developing innovative online services to meet the current social demand which has arisen for the following reasons: traditional social links have been loosened (people tend to live in large cities, far from their families), self-administered medical care is on the increase, and traditional medical systems are finding it hard to provide all the needs of patients with serious diseases.

Although the aim was initially to set up general online social support services rather than services focusing on a specific type of problem, we started off by analyzing the specific needs of a group of people, which is allowing us to be familiar with the social support activity. These people are the family caregivers of patients with memory disorders (Alzheimer's disease in most cases) in the Aube region (N-E of France), where a dedicated healthcare network named "Réseau Pôle Mémoire" (RPM) was launched in 2001.

Serious neurodegenerative diseases such as Alzheimer's disease (AD) greatly reduce the patients' autonomy as their cognitive abilities gradually decline. Patients' relatives find it hard to cope with playing the role of caregivers, for which they have not been prepared. As shown by several surveys on French caregivers' situation [1, 2], apart from the financial cost of the disease (due to patients' need for assistance with housework, adapting the home, etc.), it makes heavy demands on the supporting spouse or relative in terms of their time and attention. The assistance these caregivers provide takes up a large part of their time and energy and leaves them little opportunity of escaping and taking care of themselves.

Caregivers express the need for help, apart from the need for financial assistance, which is generally felt to be the responsibility of social institutions. They clearly lack means of expressing their distress, finding a hearing and discussing their problems in order to obtain information and comfort [1]. Some of the best candidates for providing this hearing are other caregivers who are facing similar problems. The only means available so far for obtaining support of this kind are the support groups run by associations. To make up for this lack, some caregivers are turning to Internet forums and discussing their problems online with people in similar situations.

Due to caregivers' lack of time, providing a web-based system available at all times seems to be a particularly relevant response, since it gives them a space where they can share social support with peers. In addition, receiving social support on a daily basis enables people to talk about their problems immediately rather than letting worries accumulate for a long time before they find a hearing. This aspect is in line with the idea that the benefits of social support provided by peers are mainly short-term benefits [3]. The anonymous communications mediated via the Internet with people living elsewhere might motivate people who are reluctant to participate in face-to-face support groups or unable to do so for various reasons [4]. Online services of this kind would usefully complement the services already proposed by medical healthcare networks, as they would improve caregivers' access to information and help them cope with their distressing situation.

The challenge here is to succeed in understanding and implementing an activity (social support) which it is difficult to describe. It was therefore proposed to design a tool for family caregivers which would be as intuitive as possible. It was assumed that the more we keep in mind actual social support practices in designing our platform, the more intuitive and user-friendly it will be for caregivers.

For this purpose, we therefore carried out an "action-research" project in which several disciplines (sociology, conversational analysis and psychology) were combined with computer science. This project was based on analyses of several kinds, the aims of which were as follows: (1) understanding computer-mediated social support activities, (2) understanding the specific needs of the set of family caregivers for whom we are designing the platform, and (3), developing the platform.

This paper was written in line with these three objectives: after explaining our definition of social support and deploring the lack of previous studies on online social support (Section State of the Art), the present approach to online social support practices is described in Section Understanding Online Social Support Practices. This approach is based on a functional analysis of existing online services dedicated to social support, completed by an analysis of online social support exchanges on the internet, focusing on the issues involved in running online discussions in order to achieve successful social support. Section Social Support Among Family Caregivers is devoted to the specific needs of the group of family caregivers for whom we are designing the platform, based on the observation of the social practices of family caregivers attending support group meetings and the semi-directive interviews which were carried out with some of these caregivers in order to define their day to day practices and determine their needs in terms of social support. The contribution of these descriptions and analyses to our design project is clearly stated at the end of each section. The findings obtained are presented and the implications for our design project are discussed in Section Implications for Design and Discussion.

State of the Art

Defining Social Support and What It Involves

Barnes and Duck [5] have defined social support as an exchange of verbal and non verbal messages, which transmit emotion or information in order to reduce people's uncertainty or stress. Lending somebody social support either directly or indirectly implies recognizing the value of this support. Even if social support is of a purely informational nature, it is based on a spirit of affection/sympathy, which makes it comforting [6]. The authors of several studies on social support have proposed a typology of the different kinds of support:

- Emotional support (providing comfort, friendship, love, and sympathy [7]) which is a basic component of social support
- Informational support (providing information, advice, opinions, judgments [8]) which help people to assess and understand their problems [9]
- Tangible support (providing instrumental or material help, such as goods or services)

As mentioned above, the present research project involves *computer-mediated* social support, which has attracted considerable attention in the literature since the early 1990s.

Studies on Computer-Mediated Social Support

Most studies on computer-mediated social support come under the heading of social or experimental psychology, medicine, computer-mediated communications, and computer science. Fewer studies have addressed this topic in the field of management science, HCI, or CSCW. The situations observed in these studies have mostly had a medical context, and deal with the social support provided to ailing people, their relatives or the healthcare staff involved. Several studies have dealt with the benefits and drawbacks of computer-mediated social support. The benefits described include the accessibility of the media [10–12], the availability of the participants [13], the abolition of geographical distances and frontiers, the asynchrony (which makes it possible for people to log in whenever it suits them), the disinhibitory effects of anonymity [6, 13], etc. The drawbacks mentioned include the need to have a computer which is connected to the Internet, the decontextualization of the information dispensed, which can lead to misunderstandings, and the doubtful authority of some would-be helpers.

We have identified several gaps in these studies. First we noted some methodological weaknesses in the way social support situations are analysed. Many previous authors have analysed patterns of communication using various methods such as content analysis, interviews and questionnaires [8, 14, 15]. Some of the analyses presented in the literature are not sufficiently fine-grained or are not sufficiently pragmatic, since no attention is paid to the sequential pattern of organization of social support exchanges, for instance. Secondly, at the instrumental level, there are some weaknesses in the design processes, which have not usually been based on analyses of real-life social support activities. Besides, as we will see in the next section, most of the tools used so far are very generic, and include very few functions specifically designed to deal with at least one of the aspects of social support.

Understanding Online Social Support Practices

Functional Analysis of Existing Online Social Support Services

Thirteen websites providing information and communication services contributing to social support practices were selected on the basis of their representativity and analyzed. The aim was to identify the functionalities proposed by these websites. It was attempted to include an equal number of research projects (Hutchworld [16],

Krebsgemeinshaft [17], CHESS [10]), classical discussion forums (five), and web2.0 generation platforms (five) showing features typical of most social networking systems. These platforms were selected either because they explicitly claim to provide social support or because their focus (healthcare, social problems, etc.), their contents and the communication facilities they provide are relevant to developing social support practices.

Whenever possible (we were able to have access to some research projects only via the authors' publications), a user account was created on these sites It was thus possible to test normal users' experience of the functionalities, contents and presentation of most of these sites. The data collection phase was conducted from March to September 2008. It is necessary to specify the date because the presentation and functionalities of some platforms are constantly being updated.

We started by assuming that online social support services (leaving aside the question of the underlying models) consist essentially of eliciting interactions between users. On this basis, we drew up a two-dimensional analytical grid giving the functionalities used to directly or indirectly mediate communication and interactions versus the way in which these functionalities and the content in general are presented on the platform.

To sum-up,[2] 27 functional components were identified that were common to most of the platforms studied. Some functional components can be part of larger functional entities that serve more specific goals. In these groups of functionalities which are common to several platforms, a general trend was observed: several functionalities tend to be combined in order to provide more specific situations than those available on classical discussion forums. Some platforms allow users not only to exchange messages, for example, but also to ask and answer questions, to give and receive advice and to share experience.

An interesting result obtained in terms of the platform design was that the innovations observed on these platforms are not based on novel technical solutions (3-D and video contents were quite rarely encountered on the platforms we studied, for instance). In other words, these platforms are based on similar text fields and checkboxes to those initially used when the Internet was launched. The systems studied rely on combinations of components (e.g., an asynchronous communication system combined with assessment functionalities is used to obtain an advice-sharing functionality) giving functionalities which encourage the users to take part in the online communication situations just as they do in the usual face-to-face situations.

As the result of our analysis, the kind of innovation we are aiming at in this project is more a question of combining well known web components to obtain relevant functionalities than applying the latest technological advances.

---

[2] The complete results, the list of websites analysed and the data set on which this study was based are available at the following URL: http://www.orkidees.com/missWiki.See also [18] for detailed results and analysis.

In order to complete our survey of current online social support practices, it is now proposed to complete this review by analysing the interactions which take place on web-based forums focusing on social support.

Analysis of Online Social Support Exchanges

In order to determine exactly how social support is provided on a forum, the exchanges taking place on three different French-speaking discussion forums were analysed. The corpus taken from the two first forums contributed to define patterns of interaction within online social support. The analysis of the third forum helped us to focus on the role of information seeking in the online social support activity.

Defining Patterns of Interaction. The first of the two forums was part of an extremely popular French website dedicated to health information, Doctissimo [19]. The first ten messages in 12 discussion threads were analyzed. The topics of these threads were various and representative (diet, blood pressure problems, etc.). The second forum selected was edp ("enseignants du primaire" – primary school teachers) which promotes mutual assistance between French primary school teachers. The first ten messages in eight representative discussion threads on this website were also analyzed. The topics were again quite varied and representative (the choice of textbooks, doubts about teachers' own competence, etc.).

A two-step process was adopted here: first we used a persistent observation method adapted to CMC research by Herring [20]. This method consisted in regularly consulting social support forums and gathering samples for a long period. The next step consisted in performing discourse analysis and pragmatic analysis on samples. Discourse analysis on conversational exchanges makes it possible to define how social support sequences are organized. Pragmatic analysis consists in identifying the speech acts which constitute each episode in the sequence.

The following findings were obtained on how a social support sequence is organized:

First, as in the case of question-and-answer exchanges, most of the exchanges analyzed were ternary exchanges: this means that an initial message (posted by participant 1) is followed by one or several reactive support messages. These reactions/responses are followed by a final message of assessment (a feedback message) from participant 1. With this message of assessment – when it is positive – participant 1 closes the exchange and states that he or she has found the support helpful. The macro-illocutionary act which is performed in this message of assessment is a gesture of thanks. Sequences of this kind constitute successful exchanges.

Some exchanges are binary: the request for support is followed simply by one or several reactive support messages. When a pattern of this kind occurs, it is not possible to determine whether or not the exchange was successful, because the author of the first message does not confirm whether the response received was helpful.

These exchanges sometimes include a sub-sequence of negotiations between the participants, when Participant 1 is asked to reformulate his/her request, for example.

A pattern of this kind can be said to be a mutual adjustment mechanism, which is introduced in order to achieve a satisfactory social support exchange.

Lastly, some exchanges are not completed because the questions put forward receive no answers. This can occur, for instance, when a message contains too many questions. Messages of this kind do not trigger any answers because they require too much effort.

We now complete these results by presenting those of the pragmatic analyses we conducted. The social support exchanges analysed using this approach were found to contain messages of various kinds consisting of several micro speech acts.

Messages of request, whatever the kind of support requested, were found to generally contain the following micro-acts:

- Greetings: nearly all the requests (73%) opened with greetings ("hello" or "hi").
- Presenting the problem (82%): the participant who is asking for support devotes a part of his/her message (generally the beginning) to the description ("I am suffering from baldness....") or the narration ("after taking several kinds of drugs", etc.) of his/her problem.
- Presentation of the negative consequences of the problem: the participant describes how the problem affects his/her life. The consequences can be physiological ("It has made me hoarse") or psychological ("I'm afraid that the girls I like will not like me any longer").
- Statement of the request: generally (54.5%), the participant who is asking for support explains or describes (more or less explicitly) the support he/she is looking for ("I would like to hear about other people's experience if possible"). People seeking for informational support often ask the canonical question ("is there a risk of heredity for my son?").

Messages of support are generally composed of the following micro-acts:

- Greetings, as in the messages of request.
- Providing support is both the macro-illocutionary act which constitutes the message itself, and the main micro-illocutionary act contained in the message (85%). Support can be given in several ways:

    - By expressing wishes and encouragement ("don't give up") which is a canonical way of providing emotional support.
    - By contributing information (for example, by describing a similar experience to that of the applicant), which is obviously the expected response to a request for informational support.
    - By summing up the situation: the seriousness of the situation is questioned and the fact that other people encounter the same problem is mentioned ("your situation is not so very exceptional").

- Anticipating the success of the support. It is surprising to see how often the providers of support express their conviction that the person who is asking for support will find it on the forum ("there are a lot of nice people here who can help you if you need").
- Closing terms or friendly expressions ("love").

Messages of assessment generally contain:

- Thanks: This was certainly the most frequent micro-act encountered in messages of assessment (58%).
- A description of the support and its effects: participants asking for support show that they are satisfied with the support provided and sometimes state that it belongs to the expected category of support ("a warm welcome", "helpful advice and experience").
- A description of the situation or the person's psychological state or their state of health: usually (67%), when assessing the support provided, the participant gives some information about the result ("I feel a little bit better now").

By following this pattern, participants intuitively obey a set of rules which have to be followed in order to achieve a successful social support exchange. This pattern is in fact a norm for achieving social support, and each participant expects the others to comply with this norm. This normative dimension is confirmed by the negotiations which occur when the rules are not obeyed. For example, when an initial message does not contain a clearly expressed request, the act of request is not ratified by the other participants: for example, Participant 1 writes: *I TAKE glucophage eight-hundred and fifty milligrams all the time. I am tired. my blood sugar level is one.thirty I put aspartam sweeteners in my coffee, thanks for your answers.* Participant 2 answers: *and so what??? What is your question?*

To conclude, the micro-acts underlying these patterns of interaction set up the psycho-social conditions required for social support to be provided. Micro-acts set the conditions for successful online social support. In face-to-face social support, these conditions are generally determined by the context (the relationships between the participants, knowledge about the participants' situation, etc.). In computer-mediated communications, where the context is not really known, the pragmatic aspects of the messages exchanged makes for a kind of re-contextualisation. For example, greetings are often exchanged, as between people in a close face-to-face social support relationship (support between intimates [21]). The final message of thanks can be said to be a way of achieving reciprocity, which favours social support in face-to-face situations; receiving support increases the likelihood of providing support [22].

The Importance of Information Seeking in the Online Social Support Activity. The third forum, named Bladi.net, is dedicated to the Moroccan Diaspora. About a hundred of messages from the "mutual aid" section were analyzed [23].

This corpus highlights the importance of information seeking. We observe two different aims of this activity; the first one is basic; people ask for information. The second one is an assessment, people ask for an opinion to decide between X and Y.

In the first case, people use forums as they would do for search engines. They ask for instance further information on how to do paper-work (e.g. for a visa). In the second case, they are also waiting their pairs to assess the information. Thus, they ask to the other users to judge, to evaluate, to settle the services, products, companies or professionals. Here, forums operate as assessment websites.

Contribution to Design

The results of the above functional analysis of existing online services dedicated to social support led us to design our social support platform based on mundane functionalities. By mundane functionalities, we mean those quite unremarkable functionalities which have come to seem quite intuitive and ordinary. They are often simple, minimalistic and loosely defined, and yet they mediate richly layered social interactions because of their high-level of adoption. We can for instance quote chatting, "questions and answers", uploading a document, commenting.

More specifically, understanding the factors making social support exchanges work yields new insights for designing an online social support platform. This platform will have to provide suitable conditions for mediating successful social support exchanges.

Based on our analysis of efficient patterns of interaction, it is now possible to define the main episodes of which online social support exchanges should consist, along with the corresponding functionalities, which will form the core of the platform. For instance, the initial results of the conversational analysis presented above suggest that "asking a question" and "sharing experience" are important components.

These results also showed that reciprocity is a key to successful in online social support exchanges. It was therefore concluded that this factor should be implemented on our platform, in other words, that reciprocity between users should be encouraged, by providing "alert" features which could help users to easily keep up with new contributions, for instance.

This analysis of online social support also pointed out that information seeking and the assessment of this information is an important feature, which has then to be implemented on our platform. From our point of view, this is reinforcing the importance of the component: "asking a question". The need for assessment can be fulfilled by a section where "official" documents (as procedures or institutional websites for instances) could be share.

In addition to this generic knowledge about online social support practices, we needed to obtain detailed information about the actual social support practices and the expectations of the group for whom we were designing the first version of our platform. These practices and expectations are described in the following section.

Social Support Among Family Caregivers

The main aim of the "Réseau Pôle Mémoire" (RPM) launched in 2001 by a group of healthcare professionals in response to the many problems arising in the diagnosis and management of Alzheimer's disease (AD) patients in the Aube region (N-E France) is to coordinate the work of the many professionals (neurologists, general practitioners, social workers, psychologists, etc.) involved in the care and support of these patients. Secondly, it dispenses care by performing neuropsychological screening activities (cognitive tests and diagnosis) and follow-up with patients and their caregivers. The network is also responsible for informing professionals and the public about memory disorders and their treatment: it organizes training sessions for professionals and family caregivers and medical symposia for professionals, and publishes documents (such as booklets and website information) targeting various audiences.

Observation of Face-to-Face Social Practices Among Family Caregivers

The RPM runs monthly support groups for spouses and children who act as caregivers in order to provide them with a space where they can talk about their experience and discuss their problems. The training courses run by the RPM for caregivers also provide an opportunity of meeting other people in similar situations. At each session in these training courses, representatives of all the health professions (physiotherapists, speech therapists, occupational therapists, neurologists, and psychologists) involved in the care and support process explain how they work and give practical advice about how to deal with patients and solve caregivers' everyday problems.

Here we describe the situation of two typical family caregivers:

- In the first case, the caregiver is the spouse, who spends a great deal of time caring for the patient, since patients and their spouses generally live together (70% of the spouses who are caregivers devote more than 6 h a day to their partner). These caregivers are 71 years old on average [2] and the patient they care for is approximately the same age. Despite the existence of specialized centers that can take care of patients for a day or half a day per week, caregivers have a heavy load to carry. They have to be available day and night and it is difficult for them to leave their spouse alone. Their children often live and work far away and cannot easily help them. In any case, spouses who are caregivers all say they want to protect their children from the burden of care giving.
- In the second case, the caregiver is the patient's son or daughter. These people provide care of various kinds, depending on whether the spouse, who is the main caregiver, is able to cope with the situation. Children who are caregivers can take care of their ailing parent during the holidays, assist their mother or father with their everyday care, visit the parent at the nursing home, or share the daily assistance with other brothers and sisters. But this situation is also difficult, whether or not they have to provide regular support (which they often do on a weekly basis), because it adds to the many other responsibilities they already have to carry at their age (the children in the above survey were 52 years old on average [2]), such as their work, their own family, and their children and grandchildren.

Two support groups exist for these two kinds of family caregivers; the spouse caregivers' support group, which has been in existence for about a year, mainly includes caregivers who have attended at least one session of RPM training at which health professionals explained how they contributed to the care and support of AD patients. The children caregivers' support group has been in existence for over 2 years and closer relationships have been formed among its members, although the assistance with which they provide their parents is of various kinds and the burden they carry differs from one person to another. The existence of two separate groups corresponds to common practices [3].

The two care-giving situations and the relationship with the recipient of the care are very different (in terms of whether the caregivers live with the patient, their age, whether or not they have a job, etc.). The members of the two support groups have no contact with each other, although there are no hard and fast rules about this point. Each group consists of about 15 members, who attend some or all of the regular support group meetings held on the first Friday of every month. The afternoon session is intended for spouses who are caregivers and the evening session, for children who are caregivers. The way these support group sessions are organized is roughly the same each time: the caregivers meet around a table at the RPM office, where they are served with cakes and drinks, which are sometimes provided by the caregivers themselves. The ensuing discussions are led by the network coordinator, who is a psychologist. She gives everybody an opportunity to speak in turn and dispenses accurate medical information.

The two RPM caregivers' groups, which include about 30 persons in all, correspond to only a small proportion of the 600 patients currently catered for by the RPM. Some of the support group members occasionally call each other between group meetings, but most of them have no direct or indirect contacts apart from their monthly meeting at the RPM office.

The caregivers have a lot to say about their experience with their ailing spouse or parent and about their daily care practices, and they often give each other advice. They express their opinions about institutional issues (nursing homes, insurance policies, etc.) and medical practitioners. Spouses who are caregivers often refer to the training they underwent at the RPM. They mention the knowledge and the benefits of the insights thus gained about their spouse's disease. The treatment available and the latest scientific knowledge about these diseases are frequently discussed during the meetings chaired by the RPM coordinator, who is an authority on the subject.

Although the experiences and events they talk about are sometimes emotionally quite intense, the level of mutual listening was not found to be very high in the spouse caregivers' group. The fact that it includes fairly elderly people who may have hearing problems may partly explain the lack of interest they were found to show in their peers' stories. However, according to the psychologist who is the RPM coordinator, from the psychoanalytical point of view, this also reflects the difficulty spouse caregivers have in accepting their husband's or wife's disease. However, we do not have enough clinical knowledge to discuss this aspect in greater detail. At the practical level, the many digressions which tend to occur oblige the coordinator to intervene frequently and to manage the caregivers' interventions more than with the other group. The children caregivers' support group seems to be a much more closely knit group. They discuss the crises and upsetting episodes they have experienced with the other members of the group. They also talk about the friendly events they have enjoyed together (such as the New Year party, members' birthdays, etc.) at their monthly meetings at the RPM office.

To supplement these findings and ideas, we conducted semi-directive interviews with caregivers participating in the RPM support groups. Interviewing family caregivers helps to understand their day-to-day practices outside the monthly support group meetings. Their description of the way they are coping with their ailing relatives and the burden they often feel is a key to understanding their needs, which can be either clearly expressed or more latent.

Semi-Directive Interviews with Family Caregivers

Interviews were conducted both inside and outside the RPM with caregivers (including persons whose parents were suffering from other diseases such as cancer, and caregivers who use existing forums to help them manage their situation). We focus here on five interviews with spouses acting as caregivers inside the RPM.

These spouses knew we were working with the RPM network in order to design web-based information and communication services. However, the questions they asked generally focused on the caregivers' experience and not only on their use of ICT and what they thought about it. Most of the caregivers were not very familiar with the use of computers and therefore had few expectations about how ICT might help them, and designers therefore have to bring their needs to light.

The interviews in question consisted of four parts:

- An account of the onset of the disease, its development and how the caregivers are coping with this hardship
- A description of the care with which they are providing their relative, what help they are given, and what additional support they would like to have
- A description of the caregivers' relationships with the patients' doctors and health professionals in general
- Their use of information technology, the Internet, existing online social support, and their needs in this respect

A detailed review of these interviews, with a description of the day-to-day care practices and an attempt to define the kind of collective the caregivers are forming can be found in [24]. We are focusing here on the expressed and latent needs of the family caregivers we met.

First, what are spouses who are caregivers looking for at the support group? The following two points emerged here:

- First, caregivers come to the support group to talk with other people but also to talk about themselves. The group is therefore not an end in itself but a means of feeling better, as far as possible.
- Secondly, they come to learn, to understand Alzheimer's disease more clearly, and to acquire useful information helping them to anticipate difficult situations with their ailing husband or wife and to deal with their patient more effectively in the future.

Few of their needs were clearly expressed. They encounter many difficulties but they cope with them as best they can day after day. Since spouses who are caregivers experience many difficulties in their everyday life from which it is hard to escape, one specific need emerged from the interviews: the need for a respite care service for caregivers, whereby the spouses of Alzheimer patients could be replaced occasionally at home by somebody who will look after them and occupy them (by playing with Lego?, puzzles, or cubes, for example, as proposed by one of the caregivers interviewed). This service would not have to be provided by a specialized institution, and could be used for just a few hours (not necessarily for a whole day each time). The aim would be to give caregivers a chance to "breathe", to go out to a cinema or the theatre with friends, for instance. This result refers to the French context, where such services explicitly intended for caregivers' relief do not exist. There are general task-oriented services, as housework assistance or housekeeping services for instance, but there is a lack of a global management of such services focusing on relief. This need was formulated along with the disadvantages of the specialized institutions who look after patients on their own premises and above all, the caregivers complained about the cost of these services (Francis, 58 years old, said they cost about €80 per day). The caregivers have to take the patient to these institutions by car. They are sometimes far away and traveling with a patient is difficult.

Some other needs were less clearly expressed by caregivers, and these latent needs were brought to light by our analysis.

In the first place, the caregivers mentioned the fact that they had benefited from the "*tips*" and "*advice*" received at training sessions and support group meetings. The tips and advice were about problems such as what to do when the patient is wandering around at night, or why, at a certain stage in the disease, it is important to keep the main doors locked at home and sometimes to close the shutters. The support group constitutes an ideal place for caregivers to exchange *tips* and *advice* with each other. These exchanges of good practices were rarely explicitly mentioned by the caregivers, but were often referred to when discussing a specific topic or talking about the problems encountered since the previous support group meeting; the caregivers never said they needed tips and advice on an Internet platform, but consistently showed how much they appreciated those provided by the support group and the training courses they followed.

Another problem encountered by spouses who are caregivers is that of understanding the impact of the patient's medical treatment. At the support group meetings, they often questioned the RPM psychologist about the reason for each of the drugs prescribed and the possible side-effects. The neurologists and general practitioners in the group are the only persons authorised to prescribe treatments and doses, but caregivers are interested in discussing the treatment in order to be able to help their ailing spouse to support it.[3]

The last point worth mentioning is the need we identified among these family caregivers for help with administrative procedures, which are very hard to complete: hospital admissions, applying for a place in a specialised institution, applying

---

[3] It is worth noting that treatment for Alzheimer's disease only recently became available.

for monthly financial assistance, applying to benefit from the activities of a dedicated centre, and coping with death and the formalities involved, for example.

Contributions to Design

The above observations and interviews helped us to understand a typical group of
family caregivers, their daily life and expectations, and how they receive or provide
social support, especially during support group meetings. This information is of
vital importance when designing a support system for these persons.

This field study confirmed some of the findings we made upon analysing online
social support exchanges and brought to light some new findings:

First, experience sharing is also identified as a key point by the caregivers themselves. What links the members of the support group together is their experience of
Alzheimer's disease from the caregiver's point of view, especially as they feel no-
one else can understand what this experience is like unless they have been in a similar situation: "If you have not been through it yourself, you cannot understand what
it involves" was an expression which cropped up frequently in the interviews.

Secondly, the need for information was expressed very strongly. In fact, most of
the needs clearly expressed by the caregivers we met were related to information
seeking and information management. For instance, they were interested in *tips* and
advice, as mentioned in our account of the support group meetings, they would like
to learn about the side effects of the patients' medicine and how to improve the
patients' well-being, and they would like to be given some help with the paper-
work they have to deal with. This gave rise to the idea that the social support platform should include a section for exchanging documents and information. This
section could be structured in line with the categories of information listed above
(medicine, well-being, and paper-work).

Finally, reciprocity was again identified as a key factor in social support; the
caregivers clearly stated that they came to the support group to talk about themselves as well as with other people.

Implications for Design and Discussion

Presentation of the Mock-Up

As announced in Sections Contribution to Design and Contributions to Design, the
main findings which emerged from our analysis of computer mediated social support systems and our field studies were used to inspire the design of our social
support platform.

This does not mean that the results were translated directly one by one into
functionalities, as functionalities are complex combinations, and the models and
data on which they are based are often complex too. However, the results of our

analyses (the need for reciprocity, for instance) determined several design options. Some of our findings have not yet been introduced into our platform design and may be useful later on in the project (they may help to determine some of the details of the structure of social support messages).

The first stage in designing our platform consisted in producing a mock-up in order to collect feedback and comments from potential users (Fig. 1). In this mock-up, the project designers have taken into account some of the findings made in the above preliminary studies. For the moment, the platform consists of four main sections: (1) Users' personal pages (in line with the idea that self-fulfillment is a key to successful social support), (2) Document sharing, (3) Questions and Answers, mainly to provide informational support, (4) Personal stories and experience sharing. These four sections all contain a transversal communication functionality (*side discussions*).

Since we do not have room here to explain the inspiration of each functionality present in this mock-up, we will simply present here four examples showing how the findings obtained in the above studies were applied to the platform design and the choice of functionalities.

Reciprocity as a key to successful social support: As shown in previous studies on the use of greetings in computer mediated social support and as explained above, reciprocity is a key to successful social support (Fig. 2). This led the project designers to think about how to encourage reciprocity among the users of our platform. This cannot be achieved by simply using a single "reciprocity functionality", nor is it

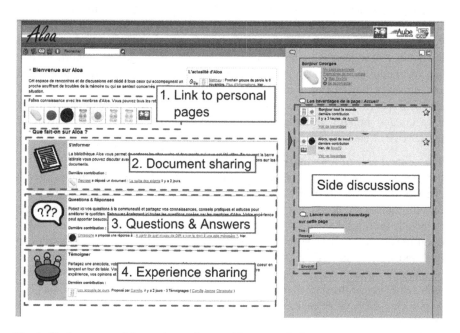

Fig. 1 The homepage of the mock-up of our social support platform

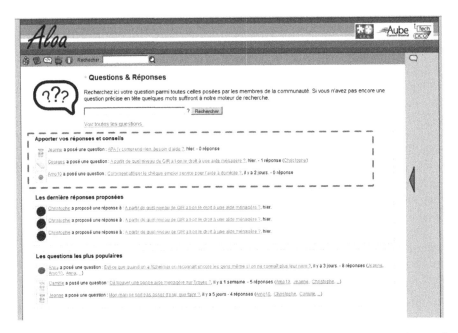

Fig. 2 Requests that have received few or no message of support are highlighted. This is one of the ways in which we implemented the fact that reciprocity is a key to successful social support

possible to compel users to act in a reciprocal way. The idea was to make people aware of each other's contributions (messages) in order to multiply the opportunities for reciprocity. By highlighting on the homepage and at the top of each section the number of requests that have received few or no messages of support, we can hope to encourage reciprocity. Providing users with "mail alert" features that signal any messages they receive is another functionality which may serve this purpose (it also helps people to stay in touch with the platform). Besides, the platform provides a weekly and monthly digest; a kind of newsletter helping members to be aware of the activity of the group.

The central role of informational support: What we learned by observing real-life support groups, such as the fact that caregivers come there to learn more about diseases and how to deal with patients' day to day care, and the fact that requests for information are prominent on social support websites led the project designers to include sections dedicated to exchanging information. The first section is dedicated to document sharing and to online discussion facilities (Fig. 3). Users can read and upload interesting file documents or websites links with the ability to organize documents around topics through keywords. The section is bootstrapped with some part of the domain literature like for instance, patients associations and respite care services websites, socio-demographic studies about family caregivers and document about memory disorders. The discussions sidebar, which has its proper instance for each document, enables users to comment, share their opinion

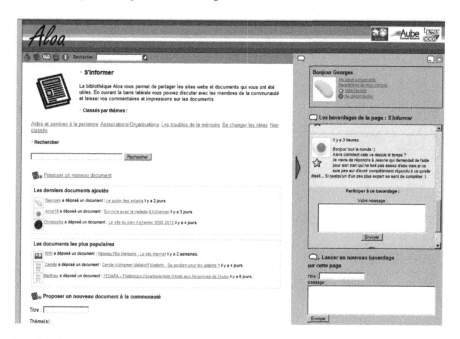

Fig. 3 Informational support – document sharing

and discuss the contents. The second section, which is dedicated to questions and responses (Q&A), is based on a metaphorical situation where users can ask other people questions via a one-line question text field followed by a larger text field for giving details. The rules and norms found to apply in situations involving the exchange of social support show how relevant this choice of metaphor and these technical features are, since our users are familiar with real-life situations of this kind, as compared with more abstract metaphors such as those on which forums and chat rooms are often based.

The central role of experience sharing: The importance of accounts on personal experience and stories in social support exchange has been emphasized both in the online social support analysis (i.e. description or narration of the problem, presentation of its negative consequences) and in the field analysis (i.e. caregivers come to the support group to talk with other people but also to talk about themselves). This led the project designers to create a "story and experience sharing" section where a user can post a new topic and share her/him story (Fig. 4). Other users are enabled to post their personal stories under the same topic. The "story sharing" form has also been designed keeping in mind the reciprocity factor, since it enables users to invite other people to share their experience on one topic through email alerts. Inside a topic, stories are sorted by authors, and each of them has a dedicated page to underline the personal dimension of such content. Discussions on the topic can be performed through the discussions sidebar.

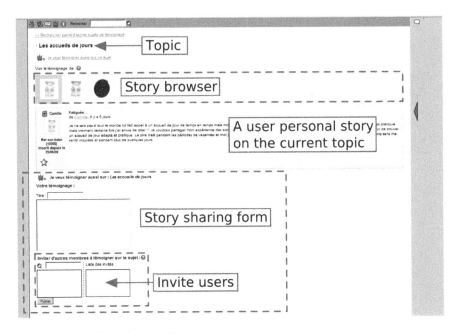

Fig. 4 Stories and experience sharing space

Tips and advice: Our interviews with caregivers and our field studies on support groups showed how important it is for caregivers to exchange tips and advice. The relevance of encouraging the exchange of good daily care giving practices based not only on the participants' own practices but also on more formal information such as the training documents provided by the healthcare network led the project designers to propose a functionality enabling users to mark the contents of the platform (documents, Q&A threads and members' stories) as "useful tips" in order help them browse easily among these precious contributions and retrieve them via a simple link.

Discussion

Although the present platform design was informed by interdisciplinary studies, it obviously has some limitations since designers have to make choices and thus impose some features on the users' practices. In our current mock-up, in line with the importance of caregivers' stories and experience sharing observed in social support practices, we decided to allocate a space to exchanging stories. However the researchers responsible for analyzing online social support exchanges drew our attention to an important aspect identified in their study, which should not be overlooked: sharing stories and personal experience (i.e., describing a problem and its negative consequences) is often used by participants to introduce their request.

This story often constitutes a preliminary phase before the act of asking a question occurs. Our Q&A functionality enables users to ask more detailed questions. However, since our story sharing functionality is in a separate space, it is disconnected from the opportunity of asking questions and does not let users easily go through this common sequence, even using the side-discussion. Further studies are required to address this point to restore the connection between questions and personal stories.

In the present case, the interdisciplinary studies on which the platform design was based cannot be regarded as a self evident corpus from which designers can directly extract data to be translated into functionalities. The initial review of design artifacts (mock-ups, prototypes) [25] carried out by the researchers involved in the various preliminary studies to determine how previous designers have translated their results brought to light many interesting ideas and opportunities for innovation, such as the question of connecting story sharing to Q&A.

The present mock-up based on our findings has been presented to the RPM coordinator, who authorized us to test it on some of the caregivers attending support group meetings. Their feedback, along with the comments of other stakeholders in the project, will help us to start an iterative process of development. Although the present group of end-users consisting of some of the family caregivers attending RPM support group meetings is relatively small, it is proposed to ultimately make this system available on the Web to caregivers who do not belong to this particular healthcare network.

Conclusion and Future Perspectives

Here we present a fine-grained analysis of face-to-face and online social support practices, including conversational analysis of online social support exchanges, field studies on meetings of a family caregivers' support group, and interviews with family caregivers. All the results of these different studies contribute to the design of a web-based platform for online social support.

This approach has several original aspects. First, its interdisciplinarity; In fact, from our point of view, designers of computer-based systems often seem to have directly applied the results of interviews with end-users and the descriptions of the corresponding face-to-face situations. In our project, the data and results coming from the analyses conducted by researchers in psychology, conversational analysis and sociology, were discussed with researchers in computer science, and not mechanically and simplistically translated into functionalities. Moreover, thanks to the conversational analysis of online social support exchanges, the medium into which social practices are being "translated" is taken into account. Finally, the data taken from the interviews go beyond the design of a platform. For instance, they question the role of health-related websites, which are providing information to patients and by then change their relationships with their practitioner. One can also mention the implementation of "respite care" services which is a matter for the public health policy. Our study in then included into a broader process of intervention research.

The next step in this study will consist in integrating the results of new interviews carried out by the sociologist in our team with caregivers outside the RPM who are regular users of discussion forums. These findings will be used to improve the present mock-up.

Secondly, the iterative process of development will involve assessing the platform. We plan to study the evolution of the RPM group of family caregivers on whom this tool has been tested. One of the topics on which it would be interesting to focus in the future is that of technological tools as catalysts for communities.

Acknowledgments This research was conducted with the support of Conseil Général de l'Aube in the framework of a UTT strategic research program.

References

1. IFOP 2008 Etude nationale « Connaître les aidants et leurs attentes », http://www. aveclesaidants.fr/index.php?rub=alaune&ssrub=enbref&lid=522#contenu
2. PIXEL Novartis 2000 Etude PIXEL - L'entourage familial des patients atteints de la maladie d'Alzheimer, http://www.mediathequenovartis.fr/novartis/spip.php?article107
3. Pillemer, K., Suitor, J.J.: Peer Support for Alzheimer's Caregivers: Is it Enough to Make a Difference? Research on Aging. 24(2), 171–192 (2002)
4. Salem, D.A., Bogat, G.A., Reid, C.: Mutual help goes online. Journal of Community Psychology. 25(2), 189–207 (1998)
5. Barnes, M.K., Duck, S.: Everyday communicative contexts for social support. In: Burleson, B., Albrecht, T., Sarason, I.G. (eds) Communication of social support: Messages, interactions, relationships and community, pp. 175–194, Sage, Thousand Oaks, CA (1994)
6. Caplan, S.E., Turner, J.S.: Bringing theory to research on computer-mediated comforting communication. Computers in Human Behavior. 23, 985–998 (2007)
7. Feng, J., Lazar, J., Preece, J.: Interpersonal Trust and Empathy Online: A Fragile Relationship. Behaviour and Information Technology. 23, 97–106 (2004)
8. Dunham, P.J., Hurshman, A., Litwin, E., Gusella, J., Ellsworth, C., Dodd, P.W.D.: Computer-Mediated Social Support: Single Young Mothers as a Model System. American Journal of Community Psychology. 26(2), 281–306 (1998)
9. Van Dama, H., Van Der Horsta, F.G., Knoopsb, L., Ryckmanc, R.M., Creboldera, H.: Social support in diabetes: A systematic review of controlled intervention studies. Patient Education and Counseling. 59, 1–12 (2005)
10. Gustafson, D.H., Hawkins, R.P., Boberg, E.W., McTavish, F., Owens, B., Wise, M., Berhe, H., Pingree, S.: CHESS: 10 years of research and development in consumer health informatics for broad populations. International Journal of Medical Informatics. 65, 169–177 (2002)
11. White, M., Dorman, S.M.: Receiving Social Support Online: implications for health education. Health Education Research -Theory & Practice. 16(6), 693–707 (2001)
12. Davison, K.P., Pennebaker, J.W., Dickerson, S.S.: Who talks? The social psychology of illness support groups. American Psychologist. 55, 205–217 (2000)
13. Coulson, N.S.: Receiving Social Support Online: An Analysis of a Computer-Mediated Support Group for Individuals Living with Irritable Bowel Syndrome. Cyberpsychology & Behavior. 8(6), 580–584 (2005)
14. Klaw, E., Dearmin-Huebsch, P., Humphreys, K.: Communication patterns in an on-line mutual help group for problem drinkers. Journal of Community Psychology. 28(5), 535–546 (2000)

15. Pfeil, U., Zaphiris, P.: Patterns of empathy in online communication. In: Proceedings of the SIGCHI Conference on Human Factors in Computing Systems, pp. 919–928. ACM Press, New York (2007)
16. Cheng, L., Stone, L., Farnham, S., Clark, A.M., Zaner, M.: HutchWorld: Lessons Learned A Collaborative Project: Fred Hutchsinson Cancer Research Center & Microsoft Research. In: Proceedings of Virtual Worlds, Second International Conference. LNCS, vol. 1834/2000, pp. 12–23. Springer, Berlin/Heidelberg (2000)
17. Leimeister J.M., Krcmar, H.: Acceptance and Utility of a Systematically Designed Virtual Community for Cancer Patients. In: Proceedings of the Second Communities and Technologies Conference, pp. 129–149. Springer, The Netherlands (2005)
18. Tixier, M., Lewkowicz, M.: Designing Social Support Online Services for Communities of Family Caregivers. In: W. Abramowicz and D. Flejter (eds.) BIS Workshop, LNBIP, vol. 37, pp. 336–347. Springer, Heidelberg (2009)
19. Gauducheau, N., Marcoccia, M.: Le soutien social dans les forums de discussion Internet: réalisations interactionnelles et contrats de communication, In: Castel, P., Lacassagne, M.-F., Salès-Wuillement, E. (eds.) Psychologie sociale de la communication. De Boeck Editions, Bruxelles (To be published)
20. Herring, S.C.: Computer-Mediated Discourse Analysis: An Approach to Researching Online Communities. In: Barab, S.A., Kling, R., Gray J.H. (eds.) Designing for Virtual Communities in the Service of Learning, pp. 338–376. Cambridge University Press, Cambridge (2004)
21. Goldsmith, D.: Communicating social support. Cambridge University Press, Cambridge (2004)
22. Knoll, L., Burkert, S., Schwarzer, R.: Reciprocal support provision: Personality as a moderator? European Journal of Personality. 20(3), 217–236 (2006)
23. Atifi, H., Gaglio, G.: L'entraide numérique en mots: le cas du forum « aide » des « Marocains d'ailleurs ». In: Actes du XVIII congrès de l'AISLF, pp. 344–351 (2008)
24. Tixier, M., Gaglio, G., Lewkowicz, M.: Translating social support practices into online services for family caregivers. In: Proceedings of the International ACM SIGGROUP Conference on Supporting Group Work, pp. 71–81. ACM Press, New York (2009)
25. Erickson, T.: Notes on Design Practice: Stories and Prototypes as Catalysts for Communication. In: J. Carroll (ed.) Scenario-Based Design: Envisioning Work and Technology in System Development, pp. 37–58. Wiley, New York (1995)

Creative Collective Efficacy in Scientific Communities

Jing Wang, Umer Farooq, and John M. Carroll

Abstract Studying collective creativity is critical for understanding how groups, organizations, and communities innovate and progress over time. However, analyzing creativity at the collective level remains an open and challenging issue. We adapt Bandura's construct of collective efficacy to understand beliefs about collective capacities for creativity among individual members part of scientific groups, organizations, and communities. We describe our preliminary studies on the development and refinement of a collective efficacy scale for creativity, the factor analyses of the scale items, and the validation of the scale in path models. Our collective efficacy scale for creativity can be adapted for use by researchers interested in investigating the creative capacity of other communities of practice.

Introduction

Investigating creativity is always challenging. Analyzing creativity in cooperative work is even more difficult [1, 2]. Recent research on creativity has been expanded from individual level to collective level, including groups, organizations and communities within which individuals collaborate with each other. One of the issues in studying collaborative creativity is to directly observe and assess collective creative outcomes. Collecting such data is very costly; combining and interpreting them is often ambiguous because of their diversity and complexity. The cost and ambiguity are particularly high when the groups are distributed or ad hoc, as commonly seen in Human Computer Interaction (HCI) and Computer Supported Cooperative Work (CSCW) [3].

J. Wang (✉) and J.M. Carroll
College of Information Sciences and Technology, The Pennsylvania State University, University Park, PA, USA
e-mail: jzw143@ist.psu.edu; jcarroll@ist.psu.edu

U. Farooq
Microsoft Corporation, One Microsoft Way, Redmond, WA 98052, USA
e-mail: umfarooq@microsoft.com

M. Lewkowicz et al. (eds.), *Proceedings of COOP 2010*,
DOI 10.1007/978-1-84996-211-7_18, © Springer-Verlag London Limited 2010

In this paper, we present an alternative way to investigate collective creativity in scientific communities. We develop the construct of creative collective efficacy by adapting Bandura's [4] construct of *collective efficacy*, a measure that can predict group or community performance by assessing members' beliefs in achieving goals in the face of possible challenges. Since it is a domain-specific construct, we investigate collective efficacy in the context of long-term scientific collaboration. In scientific communities, creativity is valued and pursued by scientists in their routine daily work. Our focus on scientific creativity is everyday creativity, such as writing a research paper. It is also known as which is also known as "little C" [5], which is more typical than revolutionary accomplishments or occasional incident.

The contributions of our study are as follows: First and most importantly, it develops the construct of creative collective efficacy, which perhaps is a key attribute to understand the social sources of collective creativity and can be adapted to other similar contexts of interest. Second, it offers indications for cooperative system design. Tools can be designed to enhance beliefs in certain domain-specific capacities in our efficacy scale. They may facilitate creative achievements in those aspects. Third, it provides an approach to investigate creativity in naturalistic settings rather than artificial ones with fabricated tasks. Moreover, it integrates contextual factors and processes of group creativity into an integral construct, delineating collective creativity more comprehensively. Finally, it amplifies the applications of collective efficacy, the use of which is still rare (e.g., [6]).

This paper is structured as follows. First, we describe how collective creativity is operationalized into collective efficacy in the domain of scientific collaboration. We then present our studies to develop, refine and validate the creative collective efficacy scale. Finally, we discuss future work.

Collective Efficacy

Collective efficacy is a psychometric construct that has not been adapted to investigate collective creativity. As defined in social cognitive theory, self-efficacy is perceived beliefs about one's capacity for specific achievements, given domain-specific obstacles [4]. We are analyzing the social construct of perceived collective efficacy, an extension of Bandura's concept that captures a member's beliefs about the collective capacities of a group, organization or community.

Efficacy is distinct from other general-purpose measures of self, such as self-concept, self-worth, and self-esteem. It is specific to a task or a domain [4, 7] and concerned with specific personal capabilities. Thus it is a more powerful predictor of individual behaviors than those self-worth conceptions [4, 8]. Another characteristic of efficacy judgments is that they are about what individuals believe they *can* do, rather than what they *typically* do, what they *have* done or what they *will* do. These beliefs influence the trajectory of action individuals choose to execute and the effort they spend on the execution [4, 7].

The scheme of efficacy items consists of two components: (1) a specified capacity in the domain of interest, and (2) a potential obstacle to achieving the goal. An example of regulating eating habits could be "I can maintain a healthy diet on a regular basis even when faced with appealing highfat foods in the supermarket" (adapted from [9]). In the example, the capacity is to "maintain a healthy diet on a regular basis" and the obstacle is "when faced with appealing highfat foods in the supermarket". In efficacy scales, belief in one's capacity is represented by Likert-scale ratings of agreement with the assertion of the capacity, given the assumption of the obstacle. The composite of efficacy items may appear to stretch traditional survey design principles because it has two parts; however, this is part of the specification and it sets up a concrete scenario of exercising efficacy for one's conjecture.

Collective efficacy extends self-efficacy to the beliefs about the collective power to produce desired joint outcomes [7]. Bandura [4] demonstrates that group members' beliefs about their shared capacities predict their performance as a group, similarly as self-efficacy. An illustration of collective efficacy from managing family could be "My family can celebrate family traditions even in difficult times" [9]. Another example from community managing conflict could be "Our community can enact fair laws, despite conflicts in the larger society" [6].

According to the properties of efficacy judgments, collective efficacy is promising and appealing for understanding collective creativity for at least three reasons. First, members' beliefs about their group's creative capacities for various attainments indicate the group's possible action towards those attainments. Creativity is a complex but important human capacity. Creativity as the capacity of groups, organizations, or communities is even more complicated. Collective efficacy provides an approach to understand collective creativity, particularly its social sources. Although self-efficacy has been applied to understand employees' creativity in firms [10] and analyze children's creative productivity [11, 12], collective efficacy have not been utilized for investigating either collective creativity or on creativity in the context of scientific communities. Second, collective efficacy is an indirect and relatively easy measure to assess, and has strong correlation with key aspects of behavior and performance. Measuring actual performance directly is difficult when interrogating complex capacities. The difficulty increases when evaluating performance of collective agencies. For instance, how can one predict when and where the interaction of most interest is going to happen [3]? Such difficulty is common in HCI and CSCW where computer-mediated behavior, often collaborative and distributed, is the focus. Finally, efficacy is task and domain specific. Thus it is appropriate for studying creativity, a construct that is highly contextualized.

Study Context and Scope

We are particularly interested in creativity within the context of scientific communities. The outcome of scientific creativity in our view is new knowledge production that is recognized as innovative by the relevant community [13].

This new knowledge can be produced by individuals (e.g. researchers), groups (e.g., one's research lab such as HCI), organizations (e.g., one's department such as computer science), and communities (e.g., one's network of peers such as the SIGHCI listserv).

This study mainly focuses on collective creativity at group level (i.e. research groups), which consists of individual intellects and interacts with its social environment—the context of the organizations and communities. Given this conceptualization, we integrate Csikszentmihalyi's systems model of creativity [13] and social psychological findings on group collaboration and creativity [14–16] to delineate the capacities and obstacles for creative collective efficacy. We expect that such theoretical foundation and integration can help construct comprehensive efficacy assessment to achieve good predication of creative performance.

The Creative Collective Efficacy Scale

As Bandura suggested [9], efficacy scales must be "tailored to activity domains and assess the multifaceted ways in which efficacy beliefs operate within the selected activity domain". Our domain, group creativity in scientific communities, is associated with various group characteristics and group process factors [17], and is affected by its social environment. Efficacy assessment for research groups can be linked to the factors affecting group processes and groups' interaction with their social environment because groups can exercise some control over these factors [9]. Therefore, we operationalize *creative collective efficacy* (CCE) scale on the basis of Csikszentmihalyi's systems model of creativity [9] as well as the studies on group creative processes [15] synthesized and contextualized by Farooq et al. [14, 16].

Part of our CCE scale is concerned with groups' interaction with their social environment. According to Csikszentmihalyi [9], creativity is situated in its social systems: The domain transmits rules and practices to the individual and the individual produces novel variation in the domain's content; this variation has to be evaluated and selected by the field for inclusion in the domain. Several societal conditions in this interaction affect the incidence of creativity. Without some form of social evaluation, it would be impossible to distinguish novel variations that are simply bizarre from those that are genuinely creative. A material surplus also gives a society the advantage of creativity occurrence. A wealthier community is able to make information more readily available. Such a community allows for a greater rate of specialization and experimentation, and provides more opportunities to reward and implement new ideas than subsistence societies. Moreover, in order to be accepted by their larger community, individuals' variation has to surpass social inertia and the protective boundaries around technical procedures, knowledge base, etc., which Csikszentmihalyi names "*the memes*" [13].

Different from individual creativity described in Csikszentmihalyi's systems model, group creativity is also characterized by its dynamic processes in which individuals cooperate with each other to approach joint creative outcomes. Therefore, the other part of our CCE scale depicts aspects that affect group creative processes.

Research on group creative processes suggests that divergent thinking and convergent thinking, social influences, information sharing, and reflexivity all influence group creativity [14–16]. Divergent thinking is the process of pooling different perspectives and generating alternative solutions, while convergent thinking allows groups to funnel down various alternatives and integrate them into one. Though one person can take multiple perspectives on a problem or task, a wider range of perspectives is more likely to emerge when several members approach an issue or problem from different angles or backgrounds [18]. Other than divergent thinking, groups also have to reach consensus for group creativity to occur. Nevertheless, available research results demonstrate that groups rarely achieve the level of the sum of the individuals [19]. Groups desire consensus without efforts on critical evaluation and integration. This suboptimal performance partially results from groupthink, which arises from situations like homogenous group members, strong and directed leadership, group isolation, and high cohesion [20]. Moreover, when the majority opinion holders achieve influence and exert social influence on the minority opinion holders, the minority would conform to the majority so as to attain uniformity [21]. Other than those ideation processes, group creativity also involves information sharing as well as metacognitive process. One necessary condition for creativity is that group members contribute their domain-specific knowledge and engage in sharing their unique information [22]. Typically, groups resort to common information pooling because members fear the criticism from other group members or because they are forced by other social influences such as normalization [23]. Group reflexivity include reflection, planning and action [24]. Knowing how well one is doing is essential for the one to work creatively [25]. Reflection generally consists of attention, awareness, monitoring, and evaluation of the object of reflection [24]. In particular, reflection requires evaluative and critical thinking, which is an important element in creative thinking [22]. Furthermore, selected ideas must be not only novel but practically feasible as well [18].

Procedure

We developed our CCE scale by reflecting on groups' creative scientific processes, their interaction with other groups, and their interaction with their scientific communities. Scale items were iteratively reviewed, critiqued, and revised during weekly research meetings over more than 1 year. To refine the CCE scale we administered two rounds of online surveys. Participants of both the surveys are researchers working in computer and information sciences related areas, and the second round recruited a larger number of participants. Having postulated on the results and feedback from the first round survey, we revised the problematic items and adapted the structure extracted from the first version of scale into our second version. The second round of survey confirmed the structure and validated our scale.

An Exploratory CCE Scale

As an exploratory stage, the first version of CCE scale consisted of 17 items. Ten of them are based on Farooq et al.'s [14, 16] framework of group creative processes in scientific collaboration. The other seven are based on Csikszentmihalyi's [13] systems perspective of creativity. Fifty-five respondents were researchers working in computer and information sciences related areas from three colleges at a large university. More than 70% of them were graduate students. Sixty percent of the participants were at the age between 21 and 30. They rated their agreement on a nine-point Likert scale, indicating their levels of agreement from strongly disagree to strongly agree. We chose nine points rather than fewer points in order to obtain a more elaborate distribution of responses, preventing variation being dismissed. After principal component analysis and principal axis factoring on the scale, five items were pruned and four factors were extracted. Table 1 shows the other 12 items on the scale and their corresponding factors in principal component analysis (We did not include the pattern matrix generated by principal axis factoring method in this paper because of the space limit).

We conducted exploratory factor analysis on the responses ($N = 55$) from the first round of survey by using principal axis factoring with direct oblimin rotation. Principal axis factoring is the most commonly used exploratory factor analysis method in social and behavioral research. We also applied principal component analysis to the efficacy ratings. The same structure of the scale as the one presented in Table 1 arose. We chose an oblique rotation method over orthogonal rotation methods because factors extracted should be correlated according to the previous creativity studies as described at the beginning of Section The Creative Collective Efficacy Scale. Table 2 shows the correlations between the factors we extracted. These intercorrelations are not approaching zero though we controlled them to be low. Thus oblique rotation is appropriate for our data.

Four factors emerged from our first version of CCE scale according to the rules of thumb for determining the number of factors (including both eigenvalue one as the cut-off value and the beginning point of eigenvalues levelling off as the cutting point). The four factors are interpreted as "*Extrinsic Evaluation*" (the field impacts on incidence of creativity and societal recognition and evaluation on group creativity), "*Idea Integration*" (group's convergent thinking and expertise integration), "*Reflexivity*" (group's reflection and evaluation on objectives and processes) and "*Diversity*" (group's divergent thinking and diverse member composite) in the order presented in Table 1. These factors are well supported by previous studies in creativity, representing our perspective from group dynamics (i.e. idea integration, reflexivity and diversity) and its social context (i.e. extrinsic evaluation). The contributions of each factor to explaining total variance are listed in Table 3.

Table 1 Structure matrix of rotated factors in Version 1 of CCE scale (Principal Axis Factoring; Oblimin with Kaiser Normalization, Delta = -0.5)

	Factor			
	1	2	3	4
Our research group is fully capable of acquiring external research funding even with the stiff competition from other researchers in our field.	**0.833**	-0.339	-0.234	0.355
Our research group can publish novel results in highly rated journals despite the rigorous review process.	**0.727**	-0.262	-0.556	0.464
Our research group can decide among multiple ideas even though the evaluation criteria are not clear.	**0.630**	-0.362	-0.411	0.322
Our work can become recognized as a contribution to the field despite the orthodox boundaries formed by long-standing and senior researchers in the field.	**0.585**	0.032	-0.337	0.384
Members in our research group are willing to share their unique ideas without fear of criticism from the group.	0.144	**-0.870**	-0.393	0.429
Our research group can take advantage of minority ideas even though they can be easily dismissed.	0.433	**-0.857**	-0.520	0.363
Our research group can converge on a single idea even though each member tends to see things through the lens of their own experience and expertise.	0.433	**-0.713**	-0.262	0.400
Our research group can effectively reflect on shared objectives, strategies, and processes even when we are against tight deadlines.	0.414	-0.407	**-0.816**	0.435
Our research group can critically evaluate and integrate multiple ideas into a single research opportunity without compromising overall novelty.	0.303	-0.285	**-0.750**	0.208
Our research group can generate different perspectives even though majority of the group members have similar backgrounds.	0.547	-0.410	-0.485	**0.809**
Our research group can put selected ideas into practice even though some of the required resources like equipment are currently not available.	0.295	-0.271	-0.099	**0.723**
Our research group is capable of pooling unique ideas from group members even though the group would like to converge toward common and shared ideas.	0.322	-0.337	-0.537	**0.711**

Table 2 Factor correlation matrix in Version 1 of CCE scale (Principal Axis Factoring; Oblimin with Kaiser Normalization, Delta = −0.5)

Factor	1	2	3	4
1	1.000	−0.225	−0.350	0.382
2	−0.225	1.000	0.288	−0.300
3	−0.350	0.288	1.000	−0.308
4	0.382	−0.300	−0.308	1.000

Table 3 Rotated extraction sums of squared loadings in Version 1 of CCE scale (Principal Axis Factoring; Oblimin with Kaiser Normalization, Delta = −0.5)

Factor	Eigenvalues	Percent of total variance explained	Cumulative variance
1	5.245	43.705	43.705
2	1.113	9.276	52.982
3	0.753	6.274	59.256
4	0.689	5.738	64.993

The reliability of our entire CCE scale and each factor are strong. The overall reliability of the 12 items has Cronbach's Alpha value of 0.892. The Cronbach's Alpha values for each factor, *"Extrinsic Evaluation"*, *"Idea Integration"*, *"Reflexivity"*, and *"Diversity"* respectively, are 0.785, 0.832, 0.744, and 0.812.

We followed up participants with open questions to examine whether any dimensions of group creativity were missing from our CCE scale. We asked participants to list three ways in which they and their research group are creative and three obstacles inhibiting creativity that their research group and themselves experience or may experience. Responses from total 11 participants illustrated similar scenarios in our scale items. Additionally, collaboration with other research entities and employing various methods to approach problems are also identified as creative capacities by respondents. Time constraint and distractions are the most emphasized obstacles that impede group creativity.

However, this scale is still problematic in several aspects. First, some factors do not have items cohesive enough: The second item with the high loading in factor *"Diversity"* (i.e. Our research group can put selected ideas into practice even though some of the required resources like equipment are currently not available.) depicts creativity in terms of its implementation and practice which should have stronger correlation with factor *"Reflexivity"*; the second item in factor *"Reflexivity"* (i.e. Our research group can critically evaluate and integrate multiple ideas into a single research opportunity without compromising overall novelty.) does not have strong contrast from factor *"Idea Integration"*. Second, some factors do not have enough items. Factor *"Reflexivity"* only has two items, which is not adequate for a proper factor size. Finally, the validity of the scale was not sufficiently verified by the data collected.

By reflecting on these problems and feedback from participants, we speculated that we might have described multiple aspects in one item and the goal and obstacle may not be matched appropriately. Also the items were framed too abstract for participants to assess. Therefore, we decided to decompose complicated items, match the goal and obstacle more consistently, phrase the items more specifically, and employ other methods for factor analysis with consideration of factor correlation.

A Refined CCE Scale

We refined and expanded our CCE scale on the basis of the structure identified in our preliminary survey. Five categories of 16 items in total were generated before analysis, four of which were adapted from the four factors extracted in our first survey (i.e. *diversity, idea integration, reflexivity and extrinsic evaluation*) and the other one "*Intergroup Information Exchange*" was an expansion to connect group dynamics to its social context. This classification is our attempt to analyze the complicated creative processes, although these different categories interact and co-occur in actual group activities. Except for items about "*Intergroup Information Exchange*", the majority of the items derived from the items working well in the old scale, while some of them were revised to be more concise and comprehensible. The other items integrated the specific capacities overlooked in the first round survey but raised by participants in follow-up questions, e.g. capacities to approach problems by various methods and converging on one method, and obstacles like time constraint as well as coordinative distractions. We also tried to balance the structure of the scale as three to four items per each category. A full list of items is presented in Table 4.

The first four factors maintained the dimensions distilled in the preliminary survey: "*Divergent Thinking*" delineates group's ability to generate and take advantage of a variety of ideas, options, alternatives and methods corresponding to research problems; "*Convergent Thinking*" involves narrowing the set of diverse opinions into one by reaching consensus on the best idea or integration; "*Reflexivity*" refers to members' collective reflection on the group's objectives, strategies, and processes as well as their wider organizations and environments, and adaptation and implementation; and "*Extrinsic Evaluation*" is the acceptance and recognition by the community that ensures scientific creativity.

The last factor "*Intergroup Information Exchange*" is new in the refined CCE scale. As one of the key components of communities, groups in their social environment do not operate in isolation but interact with each other. They should be open to communicate and exchange information and values across organizational boundaries [17, 26]. On the one hand, delivering ideas to other groups is one way for groups to be socially judged and acknowledged as well as to obtain support and other resources [27]. On the other hand, when connected with other groups, a group can benefit from others' creative ideas via knowledge transfer or learning from indirect experience [28, 29].

Participants of this refined scale were recruited from subscribers of ACM-SIGCHI (the Association for Computing Machinery Special Interest Group on Computer-Human Interaction) and AIS-SIGHCI (the Association for Information Systems Special Interest Group on Human-Computer Interaction) mailing lists.

Among total 129 respondents, 55.4% are male while 44.6% are female. 62.8% respondents were from ACM-SIGCHI while 37.2% were from AIS-SIGHCI. 99.2% of the respondents had completed 4-year college education or above, and

Table 4 Version 2 of CCE scale with five categories

Five categories of CCE items

Divergent thinking

1. Our research group can generate different perspectives even though majority of the group members have similar backgrounds.
2. Our research group can apply a variety of methods to problems despite the human tendency to use the same approach over and over.
3. Our research group can seriously consider "minority views" though it might be faster to reach consensus by focusing only on the majority view.
4. Members of our research group can share ideas without fear of criticism from the group.

Convergent thinking

5. Our research group can integrate the unique ideas of different members even though it could be easier to just pick one idea.
6. Our research group can agree on a single idea even though each person tends to see things through the lens of their own experience and interests.
7. Our research group can concur on a method for approaching a problem despite variation in individual preferences and familiarities.

Reflexivity

8. Our research group can take the time required to reflect on the big picture despite deadlines and other distractions.
9. Our research group can decide among ideas even when the evaluation criteria are not completely clear.
10. Our research group can put ideas into practice even when some of the required resources are not available.

Extrinsic evaluation

11. Our research group can publish novel results in highly rated journals and conferences even though their acceptance rate is low.
12. Our research group is fully capable of acquiring external research funding even with the stiff competition from other researchers in our field.
13. Our work can become recognized as a contribution to the field despite the community inertia towards radical changes.

Intergroup information exchange

14. Our research group can incorporate ideas from another group even though it can be challenging for us to understand those ideas' context.
15. Our research group can convey our opinions to another group although it can difficult to fully communicate our value.
16. Our research group can cooperate with other groups on a project though we may have different practices from those groups.

almost half of the respondents (49.6%) had received doctorate degree. Half of the participants (50.0%) were between 31 and 50 years old, while 25% of them were between 21 and 30 years old. Overall, participants in our second round of survey were more experienced and accomplished researchers with diverse backgrounds than those in our first round of survey.

Item 12 had the lowest mean (5.61 out of 9; 14 of 16 item means were greater than 6) with the largest standard deviation (2.400; 13 of 16 item standard deviations were less than 2). This might suggest that acquiring research funding involves many other opportunistic elements than creative capacities. Another feature of these items is that all the three items from the category *"Convergent Thinking"* had means larger than 7 (11 of 16 item means were less than 7) with standard deviations less than 1.5 (the other item standard deviations were all greater than 1.5). It may indicate that convergent thinking capacities we depicted are relatively easy to achieve so little variance of the collective efficacy in it was detected.

For confirmatory purposes, we conducted Confirmatory Factor Analysis (CFA) with maximum likelihood method provided by AMOS 16 to examine the structure of the refined CCE scale. Another advantage of CFA is to allow unconstrained correlation between factors, which is more appropriate for the structure we were investigating than the way we analyzed our preliminary CCE scale. The model we presumed did not achieve sufficient goodness of fit (χ^2 = 165.684, df = 94, CFI = 0.894, TLI = 0.847, RMSEA = 0.077[1]). To reach better goodness of fit, we tested other alternative models, keeping the latent-indicator relationships as unchanged as possible and deleting as few items as possible. The final model selected (Cronbach's alpha = 0.889) excluded item 4 and 5 with improved goodness of fit (χ^2 = 97.995, df = 67, CFI = 0.946, TLI = 0.915, RMSEA = 0.060). In this model item 16 was adjusted as an indicator for *"Extrinsic Evaluation"*.

Item 4 and 5 were dropped out from the scale because they were unique from the items. Item 4 is more about information sharing which is relatively distinct from the five underlying factors in the scale. Moreover, the way it was phrased – using "members of the group" as opposed to "our research group" – might have amplified its uniqueness. Item 5 might have the problem of including too many dimensions in the single item. Though it was generated to emphasize integration of ideas, the expressions, "unique ideas" and "different members", may have implications to respondents that individual differences would inhibit such integration, which was not stated explicitly as the obstacle in this item. Instead, its obstacle was about group-think. Table 5 shows the values of factor loadings (i.e. standardized regression weights)

Table 5 Reliability and factor loadings of refined CCE scale

Factor	Loadings
Divergent thinking (α = 0.681, CR = 0.703, AVE = 0.453)	
Item 1	0.441
Item 2	0.772
Item 3	0.755
Convergent thinking (α = 0.732, CR = 0.736, AVE = 0.540)	
Item 6	0.737
Item 7	0.788
Reflexivity (α = 0.651, CR = 0.669, AVE = 0.403)	
Item 8	0.582
Item 9	0.673
Item 10	0.648
Extrinsic evaluation (α = 0.723, CR = 0.734, AVE = 0.415)	
Item 11	0.521
Item 12	0.565
Item 13	0.758
Item 16	0.705
Intergroup information exchange (α = 0.613, CR = 0.618, AVE = 0.445)	
Item 14	0.666
Item 15	0.672

[1]CFI = Comparative Fit Index; TLI = Tucker-Lewis Index; RMSEA = root mean square error of approximation. Usually when RMSEA smaller than 0.06 and the other indices greater than 0.9 the model is considered as fits good.

Table 6 Correlation between refined CCE factors

	Correlation
Extrinsic evaluation ' Intergroup information exchange	0.839
Reflexivity <-> Divergent thinking	0.751
Intergroup information exchange <-> Divergent thinking	0.799
Extrinsic evaluation <-> Divergent thinking	0.838
Intergroup information exchange <-> Reflexivity	0.989
Extrinsic evaluation <-> Reflexivity	0.828
Convergent thinking <-> Divergent thinking	0.860
Convergent thinking <-> Reflexivity	0.826
Convergent thinking <-> Intergroup information exchange	0.839
Convergent thinking <-> Extrinsic evaluation	0.744

as well as metrics relevant to reliability and construct validity for each factor (i.e. α=Cronbach's alpha, CR=Composite Reliability and AVE=Average Variance Extracted). Table 6 presents the correlations between factors.

Our examination on reliability and validity of our refined CCE scale indicates that the scale is fairly reliable and valid. The reliability of each factor, particularly internal consistency, is fairly high with Cronbach's alpha and composite reliability greater than or at least close to 0.7. The construct validity of this scale was tested in terms of both convergent validity and discriminant validity. The convergent validity of each factor was well purported since the loading of each factor was significant in t-tests ($\alpha = 0.05$). The discriminant validity measures the extent to which the latent variables (i.e. factors in this case) are different. The simplest way to evaluate discriminant validity is to examine whether correlation is larger than 0.85. According to this criterion, in our refined CCE scale all the values of correlations between factors except the one between *"Intergroup Information Exchange"* and *"Reflexivity"* were smaller than or close to 0.85, which indicates the discriminant validity is acceptable. The results of our examination also suggest further improvements for our CCE scale. Specifically, factors *"Intergroup Information Exchange"* and *"Reflexivity"* were a bit inadequately reliable. The discriminant validity between *"Intergroup Information Exchange"* and *"Reflexivity"* was poor. We also employed another two methods to assess the discriminant validity of each CCE factor: comparing AVE with shared variance and comparing nested models in Structural Equation Modeling (SEM). Both of them showed that the five factors in our refined CCE scale were not distinct enough from each other.

Other than improving the reliability and validity of our scale, more items should be added to factors *"Intergroup Information Exchange"* and *"Reflexivity"* because these two factors only have two items for each after scale adjustment.

Validation of CCE

Validating collective efficacy scale not only encompasses verification of its construct validity as an integral construct and the construct validity of each factor within its internal structure, but more importantly involves hypothesis testing on its causal relationships with other variables [30]. The construct of collective efficacy in theory is interconnected with various factors. It can have "diverse effects on motivation, thought, affect and action, so there are many verifiable consequences that can be tested" [30]. Its causal relationship with actual outcomes and its ability of predicting conjoint creative performance are also appealing advantages for analyzing group creativity.

Given these requirements on efficacy scale validation, we examined the relationships between CCE and a variety of factors related to group creativity. We collected data about participants' research and collaboration behaviors, their personality characteristics and their group features. We are also interested in the role of information technology use in scientific creative collaboration. Its role may in the long term inform us of tool design for creativity support. Thus we asked participants about their Internet use in our survey as well.

We developed a series of path models to investigate the complex relationships between CCE and those factors we assessed. These models suggest that researchers with higher CCE are more engaged in group collaboration and produced more collective creative products. This adds evidence for the validity of the collective efficacy construct.

Path Models Using CCE as an Integral Construct

Other than CCE scale, our online survey collected indicators that may relate to CCE, including personality characteristics (e.g., 30-item Creative Personality Scale [14] derived from adjective checklist for creativity [31] and 18-item introversion scale [32]), the size of active collaboration circle (i.e. number of people the participant is recently cooperating on research), occupational status (e.g., full professor at a university, graduate student, and research associate/post doc), creative outcomes (e.g., number of individual publications, number of group publications in the last 3 years, and number of research projects individual involved in), co-authorship (i.e. percentage of coauthored publications in individual publications), effort (e.g., how much of working time is spent on research, how much of research time is spent on collaborating with colleagues), reading sources (e.g., frequency of professional reading, conference proceedings and academic journals), and Internet use (e.g., frequency of Internet use for interacting with research colleagues, and percentage of Internet use for group coordination, informal personal interaction, collaborative and individual work).

We conducted both conventional path analysis (every variable in the model is observed and directly measured) and Structural Equation Modeling (SEM) to develop our path models. In conventional path analysis, CCE is the mean score of the 14 items in our refined scale. Some of the variables, such as introversion and reading resources, were excluded in our path models because they were not correlated with CCE. Variables in the path models include (1) a set of exogenous variables, i.e. creative personalities, occupational status and number of recent research collaborators, (2) mediating variables, i.e. Internet interaction – frequency of

Internet use for interacting with research colleagues – and percentage of coauthored publications in individual publications, and (3) variables characterizing creative performance and researchers' behaviors to approach group creativity, i.e. creative outcomes and effort. The final path models are presented in Figs. 1 and 2.

Both models describe similar relationships between CCE and other variables. First, full professors report greater CCE than other researchers with lower occupational status. Full professors usually have more experience and have been more socially acknowledged in their field, so they are more confident in achieving those

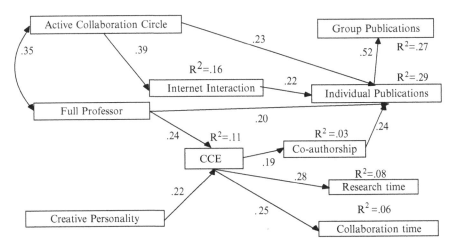

Fig. 1 Path model illustrating CCE involvement in creative activities using path analysis

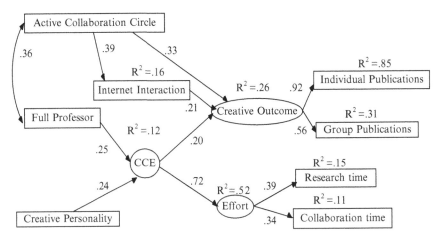

Fig. 2 Path model illustrating CCE involvement in creative activities using SEM (Ellipses denote latent variables and rectangles denote observed variables)

creative attainments. Most likely, they are also leaders in their research groups. They feel more responsible to facilitate group for creative accomplishments. They may have stronger intrinsic motivation and richer resources. Off the stress from tenure or status promotion, full professors probably devote themselves more to the research of their real interests. Second, people who have more creative personalities tend to believe more that the given attainments can be achieved. They may believe that their personal traits can facilitate group creative actions.

For the relationships between CCE and mediating variables, the path model using path analysis suggests that CCE is positively associated with the portion of coauthored publications in individual publications. Strong beliefs in group creative achievements may encourage researchers to contribute to their group creative activities by means of collaboratively producing publications with group members.

The two models also suggest that CCE has effects on the participants' research efforts and their actual creative outcomes. People who report greater CCE may be more encouraged to devote their work time to their research and their research time to collaborate with research colleagues. They may also commit themselves more to their group creative processes and activities. The commitment in turn is associated with both their individual and group creative productivity – number of publications. Although the number of publications can only partially represent creative outcomes, it served as a proxy measure for us to understand the relationship between CCE and scientific creativity. One interesting finding in our data set is that the self-report number of group publications was sometimes smaller than that of individual publications although the correlation between them was still positive throughout all the responses. It may be caused by several reasons: individuals might not count their publication that they attribute to their effort as publications of their group; individual might be involved in multiple research groups at the same time, from which they all produce papers but the number of group publications was only estimated for one of these groups; and individual researcher might have changed research group during the past 3 years and the group was referred to the current one. This in part reveals the difficulty of direct measurement on collective creativity.

As part of our interests, the role of information technology use in group creative activities was also illustrated by the two models. The larger the size of individuals' active collaboration circle, the more frequently they use Internet to interact with their colleagues. The direct effect of the circle size on creative outcomes may suggest that researchers with larger number of active collaborators may have more resources, or social capital, to produce more publications. Another side note for these models is the positive correlation between full professor occupation status and collaboration circle size, which may imply that full professors have more connections with other researchers.

Overall, the models provide encouraging demonstration with respect to CCE as a valid construct for collective creativity in scientific collaboration. They illustrate research group members' engagement in creative collaboration and in their self-report creative productivity.

Path Models Using CCE Factors

CCE's general role in the path models in Figs. 1 and 2 offers initial evidence that the construct is a useful variable in investigating collective creativity. To further articulate the scale's validity, we continued to examine the effects of each factor on group's creative performance by using path analysis and SEM.

With respect to the creative outcome variables we measured (i.e. publications), we found that they were only significantly correlated with the factor "*Extrinsic Evaluation*". The path model using conventional path analysis is shown in Fig. 3, which reached fair goodness of fit (χ^2 = 41.770, df = 32, CFI = 0.928, TLI = 0.877, RMSEA = 0.049). The path model tested by SEM is shown in Fig. 4. It fits a little weaker than the one in Fig. 3 (χ^2 = 72.280, df = 49, CFI = 0.900, TLI = 0.840, RMSEA = 0.061), and one of its paths from the latent variable "*Effort*" to "*Collaboration Time*" is not significant enough (p = 0.068).

The involvement of "*Extrinsic Evaluation*" with other variables is similar with that of the CCE construct: people with stronger beliefs in their abilities to win extrinsic evaluation indeed had more publications, of both their own and their group. One interesting difference is the direct effect of active collaboration circle size on the factor "*Extrinsic Evaluation*". This may indicate that researchers collaborating with more people recently are more confident to gain support and recognition from their groups' social environment.

The other four factors were not correlated with the creative outcome variables, but three of them were positively associated with effort variables at different degrees (here each factor is represented by the mean score of the items with it):

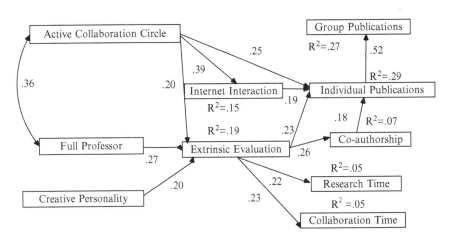

Fig. 3 Path model illustrating the involvement of extrinsic evaluation in creative activities using path analysis

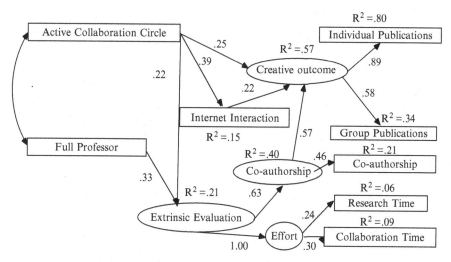

Fig. 4 Path model illustrating the involvement of *extrinsic evaluation* in creative activities using SEM

"Divergent Thinking" was correlated with both percentage of research time in work time ($r = 0.272$, $p = 0.003$) and percentage of collaboration time in research time ($r = 0.186$, $p = 0.048$); both *"Reflexivity"* ($r = 0.234$, $p = 0.012$) and *"Intergroup Information Exchange"* ($r = 0.205$, $p = 0.029$) were related to percentage of research time in work time. One possible reason for the difference of correlation with creative outcomes between these four factors and the *"Extrinsic Evaluation"* may be that *"Extrinsic Evaluation"* as beliefs in gaining societal recognition is more directly related to the final creative products – publications in our case. The goal in item 11 was even explicitly stated with respect to publications. Such difference suggests that CCE's structure still needs improvement (e.g., discriminant validity of each factor). The absence of association between *"Convergent Thinking"* and outcome or effort variables may manifest again that this factor is the easiest capacity among the five for groups to attain.

Though the validity of each CCE factor was not adequately purported by the variables we measured, the theoretical foundation for the substructure of this scale is still legitimate. Furthermore, the predicting power of CCE construct for collective creativity, as demonstrated in Section Path Models Using CCE as an Integral Construct, should not be dismissed. Our interpretation of the two sets of path models is necessarily provisional, but the findings about the relationships between CCE and its factors, personal characteristics, and creative performance and behaviors provide important and specific validation for the CCE scale. Further qualitative studies such as ethnography would improve our current interpretation of the results and enrich our understanding of creative scientific collaboration,

Discussion and Future Work

As one of the challenging issues emerged in creativity research, investigating collective creativity requires new methods and progress. Our studies present preliminary manifestation that *Creative Collective Efficacy* is a valid and useful construct for investigating collective creativity, particularly understanding its social sources. Our CCE scale was developed from theoretical frameworks and represents a comprehensive integration of collective creative capacities, though it did not include individual's inherent creative capacities which are less associated with social contexts. Although our study context was computer and information sciences, we anticipate that researchers interested in collective creativity can tailor our instrument to their specific study contexts. For example, our instrument can be used to study creative capacities in communities of practice [33]. A community of practice involves a set of socially defined ways of doing things in a specific domain: a set of common approaches and shared standards that create a basis for action, communication, problem solving, performance, and accountability. To adapt CCE scale to such a community, a software development community, we can keep the structure as well as most of the items in our current scale but only adjust terms for research into software production.

Our future directions to develop this scale include refining the multidimensional structure of CCE and improving its validation tests by introducing more variables that may relate to CCE and its factors. To refine our current CCE scale, we may have to enhance the discriminant validity of each factor, making the items in one factor more distinct from the ones in other factors. Some factors in our CCE scale do not have enough items. For instance, "*Convergent Thinking*" and "*Intergroup Information Exchange*" only have two items left respectively. Thus we need to create more items for them. Another concern is the little variation of items in "*Convergent Thinking*". Describing goals that are more difficult to achieve may increase the variation. We may also expand the variety of factors in the scale to augment its predictability of creative performance. For example, we did not create items with regard to developing shared objectives, which is also critical to group creativity [34, 35].

To enhance the validation of CCE and its usefulness in understanding creative collaboration, one option can be introducing more variables that may directly relate to CCE and also have established valid metrics. For example, as Bandura noted [30], efficacy can have effects on motivation and affect. One instrument available with respect to motivation and creativity is KEYS developed by Amabile et al. [36]. Another extension which might be more difficult is to appraise the performance of divergent thinking, convergent thinking and so on and test its relation with efficacy beliefs in those capacities. The set of exogenous variables can also be expanded by incorporating measures such as group composite. Group size as an indicator of group composite may contribute to both perceptions of collective efficacy and collective creative performance through their effects on coordination and cooperation [37, 38]. The mediating variables can also include other efficacy constructs to understand how they interact with CCE, for instance, creative self-efficacy.

An alternative design to test the validity of CCE construct is to compare groups with different CCE and examine whether they perform differently in terms of collective creative outcomes. A group's CCE can be assessed as either an aggregation of each group member's CCE or group members' consensus on it (tradeoffs of either way to measure collective efficacy are discussed in [7, 39]). The strength of this design is that groups' CCE is more directly associated with groups' attainments than individuals' CCE. Comparatively, greater CCE of an individual in our study cannot represent the whole group's level of CCE. Participants in this alternative design may also identify about which group they should report more easily. However, this approach also has its downsides, e.g., high cost of sampling a variety of groups with representative members.

Longitudinal studies would also be beneficial to examine the causal relationship between CCE and group creativity. The validity of CCE can be enhanced by considering temporal factors than measuring these variables at the same time, because collective efficacy is often augmented by mastery experience, e.g., previous creative performance may affect currently perceived CCE. Such studies will also enrich our understanding of how to enhance group creativity by tracking CCE evolvement.

In the long term, we also hope to develop cooperative systems that support creative collaboration within groups, communities and organizations by enhancing creative collective efficacy. Efficacy appears to purport their persistence level to cope with challenging circumstances that may impede their creative achievements [10].

Acknowledgment This research was supported by NSF SGER IIS-0749172. We thank Craig H. Ganoe and Shaoke Zhang for discussions about creative collective efficacy.

References

1. Mayer, R.E.: Fifty years of creativity research. In: Sternberg, R.J. (ed.): Handbook of creativity, Vol. 460. Cambridge University Press, New York (1999) 449–460
2. Mamykina, L., Candy, L., Edmonds, E.: Collaborative creativity. Communications of the ACM 45 (2002) 96–99
3. Neale, D.C., Carroll, J.M., Rosson, M.B.: Evaluating computer-supported cooperative work: models and frameworks. Proceedings of CSCW'04. ACM Press, Chicago, IL (Nov 2004) 368–377
4. Bandura, A.: Self-Efficacy: The Exercise of Control. W. H. Freeman, New York (1997)
5. Gardner, H.: Seven creators of the modern era. In: Brockman, J. (ed.): Creativity. Simon & Schuster, New York (1993) 28–47
6. Carroll, J.M., Rosson, M.B., Zhou, J.: Collective efficacy as a measure of community. Proceedings of CHI'05. ACM Press, Portland, OR (April 2005) 1–10
7. Goddard, R.D., Hoy, W.K., Hoy, A.W.: Collective Efficacy Beliefs: Theoretical Developments, Empirical Evidence, and Future Directions. Educational Researcher 33 (2004) 3–13
8. Pajares, F., Miller, M.D.: Role of Self-Efficacy and Self-Concept Beliefs in Mathematical Problem Solving: A Path Analysis. Journal of Educational Psychology 86 (1994) 193–203
9. Bandura, A.: Guide for constructing self-efficacy scales. In: Pajares, F., Urban, T. (eds.): Self-efficacy beliefs of adolescents, Vol. 5. Information Age Publishing, Greenwich, CT (2006) 307–337
10. Tierney, P., Farmer, S.M.: Creative self-efficacy: Its potential antecedents and relationship to creative performance. Academy of Management Journal 45 (2002) 1137–1148

11. Schack, G.D.: Self-Efficacy as a Mediator in the Creative Productivity of Gifted Children. Journal for the Education of the Gifted 12 (1989) 231–249
12. Beghetto, R.A.: Creative self-efficacy: Correlates in middle and secondary students. Creativity Research Journal 18 (2006) 447–457
13. Csikszentmihalyi, M.: Implications of a Systems Perspective for the Study of Creativity. In: Sternberg, R.J. (ed.): Handbook of Creativity. Cambridge University Press, New York (1999) 313–335
14. Farooq, U., Carroll, J.M., Ganoe, C.H.: Supporting creativity with awareness in distributed collaboration. Proceedings of GROUP'07. ACM Press, Sanibel Island, FL (2007) 31–40
15. Paulus, P.B., Nijstad, B.A.: Group Creativity: Innovation Through Collaboration. Oxford University Press, New York (2003)
16. Farooq, U., Carroll, J.M., Ganoe, C.H.: Supporting creativity in distributed scientific communities. Proceedings of GROUP'05. ACM Press, Sanibel Island, FL (2005) 217–226
17. Woodman, R.W., Sawyer, J.E., Griffin, R.W.: Toward a theory of organizational creativity. Academy of Management Review 18 (1993) 293–321
18. Milliken, F.J., Bartel, C.A., Kurtzberg, T.R.: Diversity and creativity in work groups: A dynamic perspective on the affective and cognitive processes that link diversity and performance. In: Paulus, P., Nijstad, B. (eds.): Group creativity: Innovation through collaboration. Oxford University Press, New York (2003) 32–62
19. McGrath, J.E.: Groups: Interaction and performance. Prentice-Hall, Englewood Cliffs, NJ (1984)
20. Janis, I.L.: Groupthink. Houghton Mifflin, Boston, MA (1982)
21. Ocker, R.J.: Influences on creativity in asynchronous virtual teams: a qualitative analysis of experimental teams. IEEE Transactions on Professional Communication 48 (2005) 22–39
22. Nickerson, R.S.: Enhancing creativity. In: Sternberg, R.J. (ed.): Handbook of creativity. Cambridge University Press, New York (1999) 392–430
23. Moscovici, S.: Social Influence I: Conformity and Social Control. In: Nemeth, C. (ed.): Social psychology: Classic and contemporary integrations. Rand McNally, Chicago, IL (1974)
24. West, M.A.: Reflexivity and work group effectiveness: A conceptual integration. In: West, M.A. (ed.): Handbook of work group psychology. Wiley, Chichester (1996) 555–579
25. Csikszentmihalyi, M.: Creativity: flow and the psychology of discovery and invention. HarperCollins, New York (1996)
26. Henry, J.: Creative Collaboration in Organisational Settings. Collaborative Creativity: Contemporary Perspectives (2004) 158–175
27. Hooker, C., Nakamura, J., Csikszentmihalyi, M.: The group as mentor: Social capital and the systems model of creativity. In: Paulus, P.B. and Nijstad, B.A. (eds.), Group Creativity: Innovation Through Collaboration. New York: Oxford University Press (2003)
28. Argote, L., Kane, A.: Learning from direct and indirect experience in organizations: The effects of experience content, timing, and distribution. In: Paulus, P.B. and Nijstad, B.A. (eds.) Group creativity: Innovation through collaboration. New York: Oxford University Press (2003) 277–303
29. Nijstad, B.A., Paulus, P.B.: Group creativity: Common themes and future directions. In: Paulus, P.B. and Nijstad, B.A. (eds.) Group creativity: Innovation through collaboration. New York: Oxford University Press (2003) 326–339
30. Bandura, A.: Guide for creating self-efficacy scales. In: Pajares, F., Urdan, T. (eds.): Self-efficacy beliefs of adolescents. Information Age Publishing, Greenwich, CT (2005)
31. Gough, H.G., Heilbrun, A.B.: Manual for the Adjective Check List. Palo Alto, CA: Consulting Psychologists Press (1965)
32. Eysenck, H.J.: Readings in extraversion-introversion. Staples Press, London (1970)
33. Wenger, E.: Communities of Practice: Learning, Meaning, and Identity. Cambridge University Press, Cambridge (1999)
34. Lawler, E.E., Hackman, J.R.: Impact of employee participation in the development of pay incentive plans: A field experiment. Journal of Applied Psychology 53 (1969) 467–471
35. West, M.A.: Innovation implementation in work teams. In: Paulus, P.B. and Nijstad, B.A. (eds.) Group Creativity: Innovation Through Collaboration. New York: Oxford University Press (2003) 245–276

36. Amabile, T.M., Conti, R., Coon, H., Lazenby, J., Herron, M.: Assessing the Work Environment for Creativity. The Academy of Management Journal 39 (1996) 1154–1184

37. Watson, C.B., Chemers, M.M., Preiser, N.: Collective efficacy: A multilevel analysis. Personality and Social Psychology Bulletin 27 (2001) 1057

38. Payne, R.: The effectiveness of research teams: A review. Manchester Business School, Manchester (1988)

39. Gibson, C.B., Randel, A.E., Earley, P.C.: Understanding group efficacy: An empirical test of multiple assessment methods. Group & Organization Management 25 (2000) 67